The Business Side of Learning Design and Technologies

The Business Side of Learning Design and Technologies provides a ready reference with actionable tools and techniques for recognizing the impact of learning design/technology decisions at the project, business unit, and organizational levels. Written for early- and mid-career learning designers and developers as well as students and researchers in instructional/learning design and technology programs, this volume focuses on the business issues underlying the selection, design, implementation, and evaluation of learning opportunities. Using scholarly and practitioner research, interviews with Learning and Development thought leaders, and the author's own experience, readers will learn how to speak the language of business to demonstrate the value of learning design and technologies.

Shahron Williams van Rooij is Associate Professor in the Learning Technologies Division of the College of Education and Human Development at George Mason University, USA.

The Business Side of Learning Design and Technologies

Shahron Williams van Rooij

Routledge
Taylor & Francis Group

NEW YORK AND LONDON

First published 2018
by Routledge
711 Third Avenue, New York, NY 10017

and by Routledge
2 Park Square, Milton Park, Abingdon, Oxon, OX14 4RN

Routledge is an imprint of the Taylor & Francis Group, an informa business

© 2018 Taylor & Francis

Library of Congress Cataloging in Publication Data
A catalog record for this book has been requested

ISBN: 978-1-138-69816-1 (hbk)
ISBN: 978-1-138-69818-5 (pbk)
ISBN: 978-1-315-51965-4 (ebk)

Typeset in Sabon
by diacriTech, Chennai

Contents

Figures

Tables

Preface and Acknowledgments

My involvement in the Learning and Development (L&D) field grew out of my more than 20 years of corporate experience that included management positions in learning technology solution development, software marketing, and market research in the financial and advertising industries. Learning was and is everywhere; but, the experience of learning has varied across time and context. My desire to learn more about learning motivated me to pursue a doctorate that combined the disciplines of instructional design and technology and software engineering, enabling me to study the field while working in the field, and observe the differences between theory and practice. I can attest firsthand to the gap between employer expectations and the business acumen of their employees charged with designing learning opportunities for internal and external clients. I have also watched organizations promote business school graduates to lead L&D teams, even if those graduates have had limited exposure to the various functional roles within L&D. All of those experiences drove me to sit down and write this book.

Writing a book as sole author is a hard slog, indeed. If it were not for my colleagues at George Mason University who encouraged me through a very long and sometimes painful process, as well as the encouraging words from my colleagues at the Association for Education and Communications Technology (AECT), this book would probably still be in "draft" mode. A heartfelt thank-you to everyone who offered comments, suggestions, and anything else that kept me focused while writing this book. Finally, a big thank-you to my students – past and present – who have found their feet in L&D roles in industry and government, and who have kept me posted as they build their careers. I share their lessons learned, as well as my own, to help the next generations of L&D professionals achieve their career dreams.

Introduction

> I do want my failures to make me stronger, of course, but I also want to become smarter, more talented, better networked, healthier and more energized. If I find a cow turd on my front steps, I'm not satisfied knowing that I'll be mentally prepared to find some future cow turd. I want to shovel that turd onto my garden and hope the cow returns every week so I never have to buy fertilizer again. Failure is a resource that can be managed.[1]

When Scott Adams, the man behind the comic strip Dilbert©, wrote these words in a 2013 issue of the *Wall Street Journal,* he was offering his own take on what it means to experience career success. Failures, office politics, and change (mis)management were and still are part of Dilbert's© world. Like Dilbert©, Learning and Development (L&D) professionals have also experienced ups and downs in their careers and in the field as a whole. For example, gone are the days when an instructional designer is called on to simply create classroom-based courses to comply with government regulations, or e-learning modules for others to train on their own time. Designers are now expected to be trusted learning advisors, able to engineer a variety of learning opportunities that contribute to organizational performance. Importantly, they are expected to be able to speak the language of business, to demonstrate the value of the L&D function by showing how L&D aligns with and supports the business. The focus of this book is on business issues underlying the selection, design, development, implementation, and evaluation of learning opportunities and uses selected Dilbert© strips as a humorous backdrop to the book's main themes.

Who Should Read This Book

The primary audience for this book consists of early- and mid-career practitioners in industry and government whose main role is to design learning opportunities and who seek to advance their careers beyond design. These professionals have a variety of titles (instructional designer, learning designer, learning design and technology specialist, training developer, etc.) that vary from organization to organization and from industry to industry. In order to advance their careers beyond design, practitioners need to strengthen their ability to "sell" the learning function to senior management by speaking the language of management and linking learning to organizational business goals. This book provides a ready reference with actionable tools and techniques for recognizing and anticipating the impact of learning design/technology decisions at the project, business unit/group, and organizational levels.

Learning designers come from a variety of backgrounds and educational experiences. Some have migrated into the role from other areas within their organizations, while others have undergone formal training and certification programs from professional associations and/or university-based degree programs. Learning theory, instructional/training design, learning technology selection, and learning intervention evaluation are the strengths of the university-based degree programs; missing (or appearing sporadically) is the impact of the environmental context – organizational culture, management philosophy, financial structures, competitive landscape, etc. – on the decisions that practitioners make in the workplace. Consequently, the secondary audiences for this book are students and faculty in university-based instructional/learning design and technology programs. The benefit for students will be (a) awareness and appreciation of the business context in which the instructional/learning design and technology professional operates; (b) acquisition of observable and measurable business skills to manage the learning design/technology function; and (c) identification and application of effective management of people, processes, physical infrastructures, and financial resources to achieve pre-determined goals that enable pre-determined business outcomes. The direct benefit for faculty will be a ready resource to support instructional strategies that simulate real-world workplace settings, reducing the gap between theory and practice.

Why You Should Read This Book

Closing the gap between the functional/occupational knowledge that practitioners acquire and the business acumen that is needed to advance in the L&D field is important because:

- The two professional associations that define the competency standards for L&D professionals – the International Board of Standards for Training, Performance and Instruction (IBSTPI) and the Association for Talent Development (ATD) – include business skill sets that map to an organization's goals/objectives among the professional competencies.

Moreover, the International Society for Performance Improvement (ISPI), a professional association of independent business consultants, deems business acumen to be fundamental to any practitioner focused on enhancing workplace performance.

- Job descriptions posted on electronic sites like Indeed.com and SimplyHired.com explicitly require business skills for L&D professionals of every specialty area. For example, a keyword search on "instructional designer" on Indeed.com yields requirements that include the expected occupational competencies, such as addressing the organization's learning needs and developing learning solutions, but the requirements also include business skill sets, such as building/maintaining client relationships, analyzing customer business needs, project management, and working/managing multidisciplinary teams.

- Research published in the scholarly and practitioner literature emphasizes the need for alignment between organizational business needs and learning opportunities, which requires learning professionals to know about business, not just about how to design, develop, and implement training.

What Differentiates This Book

Books aimed at early- and mid-career practitioners tend to be focused on the personal experiences and opinions of the authors. Consequently, the experiences chronicled in those books may be challenging for early- and mid-career practitioners to "translate" to their own organizations, which may operate in different industry sectors, have differences in corporate culture, or have other organizational characteristics. What differentiates this book is the use of scholarly and practitioner research, along with perspectives from L&D thought leaders, as the basis for concrete, actionable recommendations on what early- and mid-career practitioners need to do to advance their careers.

The book is grounded in the convergence of five professional disciplines that feed into the L&D field: Instructional Design, Human Performance Technology, Human Resource Development, Project Management, and Business Intelligence. The book's multi-disciplinary approach is evident in the following ways:

- The selection of chapter topics is grounded in the IBSTPI and ATD competency standards defining what practitioners must know and be able to do in the workplace.

- Each chapter includes a systematic review of the scholarly literature based on database searches, such as Business Source Complete/EBSCO, PsycINFO, Social Sciences Citation Index/Thompson Reuters, and JSTOR.

- Trends and issues associated with each of the book's topics are based on a synthesis of articles from practitioner publications, such as *Performance Improvement* from the International Society for Performance Improvement, *Talent Management Magazine* from Media Tec, *Human Resource Development International* from the Academy of Human Resource Development, and *HR Magazine* from the Society of Human Resource Management.
- Interviews with L&D thought leaders around each of the book's topics are included in each chapter in the section *E-Suite Views*. The interviews provide the decision-maker's perspective on what early- and mid-career professionals need to do to advance their careers.
- My own two-plus decades of experience in business provide some illustrative anecdotes to the book's research-based foundation.

How the Book Is Organized

Chapters that have a unifying theme are grouped together into parts, and each part opens with a Dilbert® strip that illustrates that part's theme/ focus. Readers who wish to enhance their skills in specific competency areas can focus on those chapter topics without having to move through the book in a linear fashion.

- *Part I: The Changing Practice of Learning Design and Technologies* consists of four chapters that provide the context and background for the book. Its focus is on the evolving scope of the field, so that readers can think of learning design and technologies as part of the larger context of supporting business goals.
  - Chapter 1 sets the stage by defining the various occupational roles and responsibilities within the L&D field, and how those roles may differ from expectations created in university-based degree programs. This chapter also introduces the professional association competencies that are the foundation of the book's topics.
  - Chapter 2 focuses on shifting the reader's mindset from solely designing formal instruction to designing solutions that will yield a change in behavior, specifically, improved work-related performance. Relevant principles and theories from the Change Management literature frame this chapter's contents.
  - Chapter 3 focuses on recognizing opportunities for a variety of solutions to performance problems, so that early- and mid-career practitioners can call on strategies other than formal instruction.
  - Chapter 4, the last chapter in Part One, focuses on the processes, tools, and techniques for identifying the cause(s) of performance problems, the desired changes in performance behavior(s), the extent to which learning can contribute to the desired changes in

performance, and solution alternatives for those changes that cannot be achieved with instruction.

- *Part II: The Workplace Environment* consists of three related chapters that focus on the challenges and opportunities associated with identifying and managing the expectations of internal and external stakeholders about the contribution of the learning design/technology function. A solid understanding of the workplace environment is essential to the diagnosis of performance problems and of the feasibility of solution alternatives.
  - Chapter 5 focuses on how to assess the internal landscape of an organization – the organizational culture – so that current and future organizational expectations drive the definition of desired performance. The chapter also addresses the impact of management perceptions of the role of L&D and the extent to which those perceptions support or challenge the practitioner's ability to identify and solve performance problems.
  - Identifying the relevant individuals impacted by a particular performance problem is the topic of Chapter 6. The chapter provides a process for identifying those with a direct or indirect stake in solving specific performance problems, as well as for assessing the degree of influence of the various stakeholders. The ability to recognize "friend vs. foe" is essential when diagnosing performance problems and implementing solutions that may (not) have instructional components.
  - Chapter 7, which is closely related to Chapter 6, focuses on interactions with internal and external stakeholders to achieve positive outcomes. This chapter addresses the various definitions of emotional intelligence and how organizations use emotional intelligence to identify star employees. The chapter concludes with some practical advice on how the practitioner can cultivate and capitalize on his/her own emotional intelligence to capture and secure buy-in to L&D initiatives.
- *Part III: Demonstrating the Value of Learning Design and Technologies* consists of four related chapters that focus on business cases, budgeting and cost management, project management, and evaluation, respectively. The emphasis is on successful workplace implementation of L&D interventions that align with the needs of the business.
  - Chapter 8 addresses the feasibility and sustainability of L&D interventions within the context of organizational goals for talent development. In addition to addressing the question of "What's in it for the business?" this chapter provides practical guidelines for writing persuasive business cases that generate decision-maker buy-in and promotes the value of the L&D function in the organization.
  - Chapter 9, which is closely related to Chapter 8, addresses the financial issues and expectations surrounding the selection of L&D

interventions. The chapter covers methods of calculating the costs of an intervention, along with various methods of identifying the financial and non-financial returns of L&D investments. Once a performance problem has been attributed to a knowledge or skill deficiency, the tools and techniques in this chapter enable the practitioner to demonstrate the cost-effectiveness of an L&D solution in simple, straightforward terms.

- Chapter 10 focuses on getting the work done that is necessary to implement an L&D intervention. The processes and structure for managing an L&D project are "married" with the people-factors discussed in Part Two of the book, enabling the practitioner to better meet the limitations and constraints associated with projects and develop strategies and behaviors that build and maintain a common vision of project success.

- Chapter 11 focuses on performance objectives and measurements before, during, and after intervention implementation. Emphasis is on the measurement of business impact vs. only measuring what is learned. The chapter explains how the practitioner can apply the same formative, summative, and confirmative evaluation methods learned in the context of the instructional/learning design process to evaluate a variety of learning interventions.

- *Part IV: Issues, Trends, and Opportunities* consists of four chapters that cover technology, ethics, self-reflection, and career futures and rounds out the discussion of professional development and advancement for L&D professionals.

  - Chapter 12 focuses on the various enterprise tools and technologies to support the L&D function. Emphasis is on the synergy between an organization's information technology systems, such as Human Resource Management systems and Customer Relationship Management systems, and systems that support learning, such as Learning Management systems. Much of the data the practitioner needs to diagnose performance problems can be found in an organization's existing databases/systems. Knowing what data is already available, where it is stored, who is responsible for that data, and how to apply analytics to data is essential to solving performance problems.

  - Chapter 13 addresses the ethical and cultural challenges associated with aligning interventions with business needs. The focus is on identifying what constitutes an ethical dilemma, then determining the appropriate approach(es) for your specific organization. The role of ethical codes of conduct from professional associations, such as the International Board of Standards for Training, Performance and Instruction (IBSTPI) and the Association for Talent Development (ATD), is also addressed.

- Chapter 14 is devoted to reflecting on current behaviors. The chapter provides helpful hints for recognizing behaviors that may adversely affect stakeholder confidence in the practitioner's ability to solve performance problems in a manner that is consistent with organizational goals and expectations and offers ways to establish, maintain, and recapture the confidence and trust necessary for success.
- Chapter 15, the final chapter, offers some suggestions for advancement in and beyond the design of learning opportunities. Trends that affect the L&D field, along with changes in the global economy, present the practitioner with multiple career paths, and discovering the right path can be just as complex as identifying the extent to which learning can (not) solve a performance problem.

Note

1 Adams, S. (October 12, 2013). Scott Adams' secret of success: Failure; what's the best way to climb to the top? Be a failure. *Wall Street Journal*. Retrieved from www.wsj.com/articles/scott-adams8217-secret-of-success-failure-1381639163.

Part I

The Changing Practice of Learning Design and Technologies

1 The Learning Design Profession

Your Job Is What?

Picture this. You are at a function, seated at a table with attendees from various organizations. Seated next to you is a colleague from your workplace who has just introduced himself to the woman on his right. You overhear the following conversation:

"So, what do you do?" the woman asks.

With confidence and pride, your colleague replies, "I'm an instructional designer."

The woman stares for a few moments then says, "Sorry but what?"

"I design learning opportunities for the employees at my company as well as for some of our clients," your colleague explains. "I develop online learning modules, job aids, things of that sort."

"So, you develop training courses," the woman concludes.

"Oh, it's much more than that," your colleague explains. "I develop a variety of solutions to learning problems."

"Uh-huh," the woman mutters, turning back to her salad. She takes a bite, and then begins chatting with someone else.

A Dilbert© moment? No, but certainly a moment that probably sounds familiar. Our profession is not as well known to the average person as is, for example, school teacher or corporate trainer. Part of it has to do with the way in which our profession has evolved over time and part of it has do with the variety of contexts in which we work, as well as what we have learned and continue to learn about how adults learn. Changes in the working environment have also impacted how, when and what employees must learn and, thus, the scope of the instructional designer's role. The biggest part, however, has to do with technology and how the dramatic developments in information and communication technology that have taken place since the 1990s have affected everything that we do.

The most common descriptor of our profession is *instructional design* or *instructional systems design*, with a rich body of literature focused on the theories, models, and processes that shape the development and delivery of instructional materials (Conrad & TrainingLinks,

2000; Morrison, Ross, Kalman, & Kemp, 2013; Smith & Ragan, 2004). Nevertheless, some scholars believe that the term *instructional design* is teacher-centric and grounded in the linear ADDIE model, preferring the term *learning design* as more learner-centered and focused on the innovative use of technology as part of the design of learning experiences (Koper, 2005; Sims, 2006). This book follows the research stream that deems the two terms to be interchangeable (Reigeluth, 1999), particularly since instructional design in theory and practice has capitalized on the affordances of technology to enable designers to create engaging, quality learning experiences in a variety of settings (Belland & Drake, 2013; Dabbagh & Kitsantas, 2012; Mao, 2014; Morrison & Anglin, 2012; Parchoma, 2014; Reigeluth, 1999). Consequently, you will see both sets of terms – *instructional design* and *learning design* – used throughout this book, with the former being used primarily in the context of discussions regarding research and theory, and the latter in the context of what employers and clients seeking designer services expect from the twenty-first-century designer.

To be able to clearly describe our field to others, we need to be clear about how the landscape of learning design and technologies has evolved, what factors have contributed to that evolution, and which functional titles/roles comprise the learning design and technologies profession. In this chapter, we will

- Examine how the workforce and learning for the workplace has changed since the mid-1990s;
- Review the various sources from which those in and outside of our profession get their information (and thus, their perceptions) about learning for the workplace;
- Identify the skills and competencies that designers need to possess in order to strengthen their employability in a rapidly changing environment; and
- Summarize some key take-aways for keeping the design function relevant in the modern workplace.

The Workplace Kaleidoscope

The Worker

Since the start of the twenty-first century, we have been noting the effects of the global economy, including the free movement of goods and services across borders, the expansion of transnational companies, the advances in technology shared across national boundaries, and labor migration. These same forces have also helped to alter the profile of the global workforce. Research conducted by the Society of Human Resource Management (SHRM) Foundation in collaboration with the Economist Intelligence Unit

(EIU) (Society of Human Resource Management, 2016) identified four factors characterizing the global workforce through 2030:

1 The workforce is older, more gender and ethnically diverse, with increased interconnectivity.
2 Country of origin and ethnicity no longer determine where a worker is employed, particularly with the so-called developing countries producing as many (if not more) skilled workers and managers as the developed countries.
3 Working from remote locations no longer prevents employees from communicating with colleagues, with digital technologies enabling teams to collaborate across national boundaries and time zones.
4 Increased global connectivity means that workers can move around more frequently and can move for both permanent and temporary jobs.

These trends are clearly visible in the United States. According to the Bureau of Labor Statistics (Toossi, 2016), by 2024, nearly half (46 percent) of the US labor force will consist of individuals born between 1979 and 2000, what has sometimes been called Generation Y or the Millennials, although there is no clear consensus as to what the exact cutoff dates are for the various "generations." Furthermore, nearly a quarter or 24.8 percent will be workers 55 years of age or older, of whom a good chunk consists of Baby Boomers. This means that although you do have Boomers retiring, that retirement is not going at the breakneck pace that was once predicted due to a variety of factors, such as financial considerations and improvements in health. The remainder of the workforce will consist of what has been called the Gen X'ers, those born in the 1960s and 1970s, and the first crop of Generation Z, those born after 2000. Mirroring global trends, age is not the only diversity factor. By 2024, Hispanics are projected to be nearly one-fifth of the labor force, while nearly half of all workers will be women. In short, the demographics of the workplace are changing and will continue to change.

Learning and the Workplace

What does this mean for Learning and Development (L&D) professionals? The obvious question is: How do we offer relevant learning opportunities that address the needs of such a varied and diverse work force, particularly since there are always many exceptions to the generalizations regarding the learning preferences of generational groups? Do all of these demographic segments place the same or similar value on L&D opportunities? There are data to support the importance of L&D to employee satisfaction and retention. Gallup (2016) reports that nearly six in ten Millennials stated that opportunities to learn and grow are extremely important to them when applying for a job; however, only one in three strongly agreed that their most recent learning opportunity at work was "well worth" their time. In a 2014 survey of more than 3,000 US full-time workers conducted by Harris for Career Builder (CareerBuilder.com, 2016), nearly one quarter stated that they were dissatisfied with training and learning opportunities in their organizations, with more than a third of those folks planning to change jobs. Importantly, that number did not differ significantly when the data was sliced by age, gender, and race. This is certainly a heads-up that L&D opportunities do play a role in employee satisfaction and retention. It also affirms the need to apply sound design principles to address the needs of the multigenerational workforce (Williams van Rooij, 2012).

This is not to say that organizations do not recognize the importance of employee learning. The issue is: what kind of learning, where, and when. The 70:20:10 Model is a commonly used formula to describe the optimal sources of learning. Developed back in the 1980s by three researchers at the Center for Creative Leadership in Greensboro, North Carolina (Center for Creative Leadership, 2016), the model holds that individuals obtain 70 percent of their knowledge from job-related experiences, 20 percent from interactions with others, and 10 percent from formal training and educational events. There has been some debate as to the exact percentages on the upper end, particularly when you get into the purpose of learning such as leadership development, which was the original inspiration for the model. Nevertheless, there is consensus that the smallest percentage for both immediate and long-term learning is the formal training event. And, how do organizations spend those training dollars? In a 2016 industry survey of more than 600 organizations in the private and public sectors (Training Industry, 2016b), instructor-led classroom training remained dominant (more than 40 percent of all training hours) among organizations with fewer than 10,000 employees. Only large organizations (>10,000 employees) had equal percentages of classroom and self-paced computer based training (33.8 percent and 36 percent, respectively). Given the costs associated with instructor-led classroom training, it is not surprising that employers tend to view training as a target for expense reduction when the going gets tough.

Another workplace trend with implications for L&D concerns the use of technology. Industry research firms, such as Gartner Group and International Data Corporation (IDC), see a growing trend in the use of mobile devices for work, whether resulting from BYOD (bring-your-own-device) mandates from employers or voluntarily for convenience. A 2014 survey (Gallup, 2015) of some 3,800 full-time US workers indicated that 96 percent use at least one type of mobile device on a daily basis. That usage is for work both during the regular business day and after business hours, as well as for personal use. Furthermore, eight in ten respondents liked the idea of being able to be plugged in 24/7, although only about a third reported working after hours on a regular basis. This probably reflects the idea of having the convenience afforded by mobile devices to meet family needs, attend school events, or make appointments during the day, knowing they can monitor email while out of the office or log on later to catch up with work, if needed. Yet, organizations have been slow in capitalizing on these everyday devices for delivering L&D opportunities, some citing security issues or control issues or oversight issues. The bottom line is that employees are using these devices as part of their work world anyway.

Summary

So, what does all this mean? We have a changing workforce that spans more flavors than commercial brands of ice cream. The workplace itself has gone beyond a physical place to a space where work and personal life overlap. Employees place value on L&D opportunities and that perceived value contributes to their stay-or-go decisions. Lastly, technology has enabled changes to the nature of work and the workforce. However, bridging the gap between commitment to employee L&D, and implementation remains challenging for many organizations, complicating the role of the designer and his/her ability to demonstrate the value of the L&D function.

Seeking the All-Knowing Source

There are a variety of voices when it comes to learning design and technologies in practice, with each voice focused on different audiences within the L&D domain.

Professional Organizations

Learning professionals are represented by a variety of organizations that tend to be segmented by audience focus. The two main audience segments are professionals in academic settings (K–12, postsecondary education) and professionals working in non-academic settings (government, industry). The professional associations to which learning professionals belong – and some are members of more than one association – are the following:

- The Association for Educational Communications & Technology (AECT) targets educators dedicated to improving instruction through technology. Learning designers employed in schools, post-secondary educational institutions, and non-profits with programs focused on education (e.g., museums and libraries) tend to view this association as their professional home. Although not an official accrediting body, AECT publishes a set of standards for educational programs at postsecondary institutions that prepare individuals to enter the field of learning/instructional design. In addition to its annual conference, AECT publishes the high-impact scholarly journal *Educational Technology*

Research & Development (*ETR&D*) and *TechTrends*, a peer-reviewed journal focused on research-based practices. The association's other peer-reviewed publications (e.g., *Internal Journal of Designs for Learning/IJDL, Journal of Computing in Higher Education/JCHE*, and *Journal of Applied Instructional Design/JAID*) are aimed at students, educators, and scholars interested in the practice of design. The association recognizes emerging scholars through a variety of awards and internship programs, as well as promotes the exchange of knowledge through research with its international affiliates. With roots going back to the 1920s, AECT is the oldest professional association focused on the use of technology to improve learning (Association for Educational Communications & Technology, 2016).

- The Academy of Human Resource Development (AHRD) focuses on scholar-practitioners, those who study all of human resource development (including learning) systematically and then apply their research findings to workplace contexts (Academy of Human Resource Development, 2016). AHRD publishes its Standards on Ethics and Integrity, a set of aspirational principles to help resolve conflicting needs between Human Resource Development (HRD) professionals and organizations. It also publishes the Standards for HRD Graduate Program Excellence aimed at providing a common set of expectations for existing and newly developing graduate programs. The association fosters dissemination of knowledge about HRD research through its two scholarly journals *HRD Quarterly/HRDQ* and *Human Resource Development Review/HRDR*, along with two research-based practitioner journals *Human Resource Development International/HRDI* and *Advances in Developing Human Resources/ADHR*. Other professional development opportunities include mentorship programs for burgeoning scholars and presentations at its annual meeting. Established in the 1990s, AHRD focuses on synergy between the field of Human Resource Development and other fields focused on improving human resources in organizations, including the field of Learning Design and Technologies (Academy of Human Resource Development, 2016).

- The Association for Talent Development (ATD), formerly known as the American Society for Training and Development (ASTD), focuses almost exclusively on practitioners, publishing books and case studies about what has (not) worked in individual organizations, and developing competency models based on what today's learning professional needs to know and do in order to be productive in the L&D field (Association for Talent Development, 2016a). The ATD Competency Model™ emphasizes a series of foundational competencies grounded in business acumen and interpersonal skills, with a series of specific areas of expertise as defined by occupational roles. Instructional design is one of those areas of expertise (ATD Certification Institute, 2014).

The association also offers its own credential (Certified Professional in Learning & Performance/CPLP®). The association's *TD Magazine* is published monthly and covers best practices in government and industry, along with emerging technologies and trends. ATD research is conducted primarily among its membership and focuses on the practices and activities of L&D professionals rather than on the relationship to a particular body of theory or scholarly research.

- As indicated by its name, the International Society for Performance Improvement (ISPI) targets performance improvement professionals who look at workplace performance improvement at the organizational, process and systems, and individual and team levels. Grounded in the field of Human Performance Improvement and Human Performance Technology (HPI/HPT), ISPI emphasizes the use of scholarly and practitioner research to effectively diagnose performance gaps and develop the appropriate solutions, which may or may not include L&D interventions. Learning/instructional design comes into play if, and only if, part or all of a performance problem can be solved through instruction. Established in the 1960s, ISPI offers certification (Certified Performance Technologist/CPT) and accreditation programs for performance improvement practitioners in industry and government worldwide. The association publishes the scholarly journal *Performance Improvement Quarterly/PIQ* and the practitioner-focused journal *Performance Improvement Journal/PIJ*, along with networking opportunities at its regional chapters and annual meetings (International Society for Performance Improvement, 2016).

- The International Board of Standards for Training, Performance and Instruction (IBSTPI) is a non-membership-based not-for-profit organization charged with developing and validating the standards for professionals in the field of training and performance. Composed of 15 Directors of the Board representing universities, government, business, and consultancies worldwide, IBSTPI fosters the research and development activities on which the standards, competencies, and performance statements are built and have been active since the mid-1970s. Focused on what practitioners need to be able to do in workplace settings, IBSTPI standards cover a variety of L&D-related occupations, such as instructional designers, evaluators, training managers, and performance improvement specialists. The structure of the IBSTPI competencies for instructional designers (Foundational, Advanced, Managerial) enables instructional design practitioners to benchmark their professional progress and career development in the L&D field (IBSTPI, 2014).

A summary of the various professional organizations is provided in Table 1.1. Professional standards and competencies are common themes

Table 1.1 Professional Organizations for Learning Design and Technologies

	AECT	AHRD	ATD	ISPI	IBSTPI
Target Audience	• Educators • Practitioners employed in educational settings	• Academics • Practitioners in all workplace settings	• Practitioners in non-academic settings	• Performance improvement practitioners in industry, government, private consulting, and academia	• Practitioners in L&D-related occupations
Focus	• Improving instruction through technology	• Applying HRD research to workplace contexts	• Sharing best practices among talent development professionals, including L&D professionals	• Applying HPI/HPT research and best practices to workplace contexts	• Developing, validating, publishing and disseminating standards, competencies, performance statements
Standards/ Competencies	• Educational programs at postsecondary institutions	• Graduate programs at postsecondary institutions	• ATD Competency Model™	• Certified Performance Technologies Standards	• IBSTPI Competency Sets®

Industry Certification	• N/A	• N/A	• CPLP©	• CPT©	• N/A
Scholarly/Academic Journals	• ETR&D • TechTrends • IJDL • JCHE • JAID	• HRDQ • HRDR	• N/A	• PIQ	• N/A
Non-Academic Practitioner Journals and Magazines	• N/A	• HRDI • ADHR	• TD	• PIJ	• N/A
Other Professional Opportunities	• Conferences • Internships • Awards • International affiliates	• Conferences • Mentorship	• Conferences • Regional chapters • International affiliates • Awards	• Conferences • Regional chapters • International affiliates • Awards	• N/A

Note: Cells marked N/A indicate that the corresponding characteristics are not applicable to that association or standards body.

among the organizations aimed at learning professionals working in non-academic settings. However, IBSTPI clearly states its competencies for instructional designers in observable, measurable performance statements (IBSTPI, 2014). Consequently, each of the chapters in this book will refer to the IBSTPI competencies as part of the rationale for designers to move beyond the design of formal instruction.

Other Information Sources

In addition to the professional organizations, there are a variety of other entities that address issues and practices in L&D. The eLearning Guild (eLearning Guild, 2016a) is a community of practice of professionals engaged in the hands-on of technology-based learning. The Guild is best known for its mLearn conferences that spotlight the latest and greatest learning products developed for mobile platforms, its Devlearn conferences that focus on the learning technologies themselves, and the Guild's annual salary survey that many learning professionals use during the job search process. The International Association of Continuing Education and Training (IACET) focuses on accreditation of continuing education programs. IACET has accredited continuing education programs from the Federal Deposit Insurance Corporation (FDIC), the US Army Defense Ammunition Center, and the Department of Energy's Federal Energy Management Program (International Association for Continuing Education and Training, 2016), to name just a few, while the National Council for Workforce Education (NCWE) focuses on skills/competencies in the technical and vocational occupations and serves as an advocate to policymakers (National Council for Workforce Education, 2016). The Society for Human Resource Management (SHRM) includes learning under its Organizational and Employee Development sector (Society for Human Resource Management, 2016), and the US Distance Learning Association (USDLA) focuses on distance learning research and practices in a variety of settings and sectors (United States Distance Learning Association, 2016).

Some general business publications occasionally conduct surveys and analyses on L&D. The *Harvard Business Review*, *Forbes Magazine*, *Fortune Magazine*, and *Bloomberg Business Week* have published L&D-related survey results, and those surveys tend to focus on challenges that measure business outcomes associated with learning, and employee dissatisfaction with L&D opportunities offered by their respective organizations (see, for example, Ferrazzi, July 31, 2015). They also publish analyses of organizations with exemplary L&D practices (e.g., Thottam, June 24, 2016), with "exemplary" usually defined as observable and measurable performance improvement outcomes of learning. These publications are on the reading lists of many a business decision-maker, helping to shape their perceptions of the value of L&D.

There are other commercial publications dedicated to issues and practices in L&D. *CLO Magazine* (CLOMedia, 2016), *eLearning Magazine* (B2B Media Company, 2016), and *Training Industry Magazine* (Training

Industry, 2016a) conduct surveys focused on what L&D decision-makers perceive as the issues and challenges, while *Learning Solutions Magazine* (eLearning Guild, 2016b) and *Training* magazine (Lakewood Media Group, 2016) focus on learning products and what practitioners are doing to create meaningful and engaging learning experiences in their respective organizations. In addition to publications, consulting companies, learning product development companies, learning management system (LMS) vendors, individual consultants, and bloggers regularly disseminate white papers and best-practice case studies, primarily based on what they see among their own clients. However, it is not always easy to know how similar or dissimilar their client organizations are from other organizations.

The Triple Lens

By now, it should be clear that there is no one central source that provides an aggregated view of L&D practices in an easily digestible form that is actionable. What all of the sources do provide is a view through three different lenses targeting three different audiences, as illustrated in Figure 1.1. The first audience is the business audience that looks at L&D through an organizational lens. This audience includes decision-makers in the

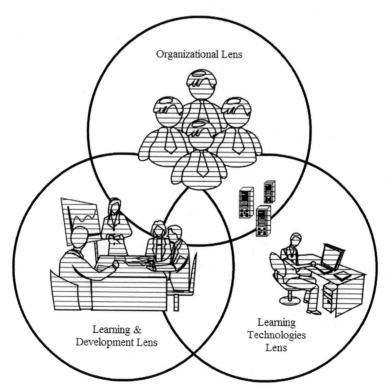

Figure 1.1 Trend-Tracking through Three Lenses.

various operational areas of an organization (e.g., sales, product/service development, finance, and technology), along with senior leadership – the C-suite consisting of the Chief Executive Officer (CEO), Chief Financial Officer (CFO), Chief Information Officer (CIO), etc. – who control the purse strings inside the organization. Looking at L&D through the organizational lens focuses on (a) strategy and how L&D strategies align with organizational goals; (b) the business impact of L&D programs, how they are measured and what metrics should be used; and (c) incorporating learning analytics into the overall business analytics that focuses on developing new insights and understanding of business performance based on data and statistical methods (Davenport & Harris, 2007). The organizational lens views learning as "an organizationally regulated collective learning process in which individual and group-based learning experiences concerning the improvement of organizational performance and/or goals are transferred into organizational routines, processes and structures, which in turn affect the future learning activities of the organization's members" (Schilling & Kluge, 2009, p. 338). Consequently, the organizational lens helps to shape the expectation that those in L&D functions demonstrate their value by way of performance outcomes rather than what is learned and how much is learned.

The second audience is the L&D professional, ranging from staff in the training department, to L&D managers, and up to the level of Chief Learning Officer. The view through the L&D lens shows the L&D professional as a L&D consultant, solving problems with a variety of approaches that extend beyond the traditional, structured learning events. Once a business problem has been deconstructed to its causes, the occupational specialties within L&D will then engage to build the necessary solutions. If a business problem is rooted in a lack of skills and abilities, then the learning design specialty can address the skills gap. If the root cause is associated with organizational issues, such as compensation and benefits, then the appropriate HR specialist can be selected.

The third audience is the learning technologies professional, the individuals who develop and support those technologies, those who can identify which learning technologies support which learning strategies. The view through the learning technologies lens focuses on a partnership between Information Technology (IT), L&D, and business stakeholders to flag opportunities for greater adoption of existing technology enablers of learning, as well as new and emerging technology enablers. The Venn layout of Figure 1.1 illustrates the fact that not only are these three lenses interconnected but also that there is often overlap. For example, the Chief Learning Officer uses both the organizational lens and the L&D lens as part of his/her job but also needs to evaluate the organization's technology infrastructure to support and encourage learning at the individual, group, and organizational levels.

The Learning Design and Technologies Professional

One Domain, Complementary Fields

So, where does the role of the traditional learning/instructional designer end and that of other types of L&D professionals begin? L&D is a domain, a sphere of activity that encompasses multiple occupations with a variety of functional roles. Think of Public Health, a domain that includes occupations ranging from clinicians (doctors, nurses, medical technicians, etc.) to public policy specialists and computer scientists. L&D also involves a wide variety of disciplines, of which learning/instructional design is only one. Consequently, it should come as no surprise that a search on any one of the major job sites on any given day yields nearly 2,000 hits with the keywords "learning and development." The job titles range from the obvious, such as "instructional designer," "trainer," "talent development specialist," and "learning content developer" to more imaginative titles, such as "people growth consultant," a position that includes design and delivery of training, coaching, and business management; "customer experience specialist," a position that includes identifying learning needs to enhance the performance of customer service staff; and "UX designer," a position focused on creating a positive overall learner experience. Although learning plays some role in all of these occupations and functional roles, the drive to demonstrate the business impact of the L&D function has contributed to the expansion of the designer's role to include skill sets from other fields in the L&D domain, particularly the domain of Human Performance Technology (HPT).

A spinoff from the educational technology and instructional technology fields, human performance technology (HPT) emerged in the 1960s in response to the failure of traditional instructional systems design to produce the desired improvements in organizational performance. The underlying assumptions of HPT are that (a) most workplace performance problems are rooted in the environment in which individuals perform rather than in the individuals themselves; (b) training can only improve individual knowledge, skills, and abilities but cannot remedy the environmental causes of performance problems; and (c) any intervention should be based on a clear identification of the root causes of performance problems to avoid the time and expense of addressing the symptoms or the consequences of a problem (Rothwell, Hohne, & King, 2007). Field practitioners of HPT have many titles but are generally referred to as Performance Improvement (PI) specialists. What the PI specialist and the learning designer have in common is identifying solutions to performance problems. Where the two professionals differ is in their respective starting points. The PI professional is solution-agnostic, with no predisposition to any particular type of solution until the causes of the problem have been thoroughly diagnosed. On identifying the problem, the PI specialist then designs and develops the solution(s) that best address the cause(s) of the performance problem. Should one or more causes be attributable to skill deficiencies, it is not uncommon for the PI specialist to engage the services of a learning designer. The starting point for the learning designer is a learning solution. Experienced learning designers tend to conduct some form of upfront analysis to verify that the performance problem can indeed be solved by instruction and, if not, to then hand off the issue to the appropriate functional area. Early-career designers tend to accept their charge as one that is solvable with instruction, usually because they have received a request for training.

Shifting Occupational Boundaries

One of the clearest representations of change in our profession is the job ad or job posting. Before the days of electronic job boards, newspaper classifieds were a mainstay in anyone's job search. Figure 1.2 shows an excerpt from a 1995 job ad in *The Washington Post* classifieds. Posted by a national association and aimed at early-career (less than 5 years of experience in the field) instructional designers, the ad specifies a set of occupation-specific skills and competencies, along with some basic "people" skills. The job description mirrors the then-current instructional design competencies published by the

INSTRUCTIONAL DEVELOPER

Qualifications: Required: Master's degree, preferably doctorate, in instructional design or the equivalent combination of education and direct experience required. A minimum of three years teaching experience, preferably in math or English at the community college with prior curriculum development experience. Ability to apply learning styles data and assessment of teaching strengths to the instructional development process. Ability to provide technical assistance in the selection or development of appropriate instructional materials and to assist with faculty development.

Desirable/Preferred: Experience in developmental studies, curriculum design, individualized instruction, open-entry courses, and computer-based instruction. Salary $45,000-$50,000.

Figure 1.2 1995 Instructional Design Job Ad.

(Source: *The Washington Post*, August 6, 1995, p. 154.)

International Board of Standards for Training and Performance (Foshay, Silber, & Westgaard, 1994), which was later renamed the International Board of Standards for Training, Performance and Instruction (IBSTPI).

Reading through this ad, several themes immediately become apparent:

- **Job title:** At first it appears as though the job title is misprinted and should read "instructional design specialist" instead of "instruction design specialist." However, a full reading of the ad makes it clear that the focus is on structured, event-based learning – training, workshops, meeting presentations, and the like – so that potential applicants are immediately aware of the bounded range of learning opportunities for which they will be designing.
- **ISD process:** The reference to Instructional Systems Design (ISD) rather than Instructional Design (ID) is a reflection of the then-prevalent thinking about design models. ISD models were deemed to be broad in scope and focused on the five phases of analysis, design, development, implementation, and evaluation or ADDIE model, but also reflected in the Dick & Carey model, with formative evaluation throughout all phases and summative evaluation after event completion (Banathy, 2013; Dick, Carey, & Carey, 2005; Kirby, Hoadley, & Carr-Chellman, 2005; Reigeluth, 1983; Schiffman, 1986; van Merrienboer, 1997). Instructional design models were viewed as focusing primarily on the analysis and design components, with models such as Gagné's nine events of instruction (Gagne, 1985) or Keller's ARCS model (Keller & Suzuki, 1988) often integrated into the ISD process. This ad explicitly states that potential applicants need to be versed in the entire ISD process.
- **Dual roles:** In addition to the occupational functions expected of the designer, the ad notes that the designer may also be called on to lead the design team. This serves as a heads-up to potential applicants that the organization sees the specialist as potentially serving as both designer and project manager.
- **Evaluation built-in:** Pilot testing of instructional materials is mentioned explicitly, making it clear to potential applicants that the organization is not only committed to evaluation but also expects evaluation to be an integral part of each project.
- **Credentials:** An advanced degree in the field, along with some experience doing end-to-end instructional design are the basic requirements for the position, as are basic business skills, such as writing and communication. The organization is making it clear that the so-called "soft skills" are just as important as the instructional design skills.

Fast-forward 20 years to the electronic job boards. Figure 1.3 contains an excerpt from an ad aimed at early-career designers and was posted by a professional association in the Washington, DC metro area. Aside from a job title of "instructional designer" rather than the "instruction design

INSTRUCTIONAL DESIGNER

The Instructional Designer is responsible for assessing, designing and developing curriculum for online training and professional development.Works collaboratively with organization and affiliates, associated departments and committees, Technical Education Consultants and Subject Matter Experts to clarify requirements, analyze tasks, and derive learning objectives, outcomes and metrics to improve business results; and trains staff on adult learning and educational design best practices.

KEY RESPONSIBILITIES:
•	Designs and develops training content and materials for organization utilizing Gagne's Theory of Instruction and the ADDIE model.
•	Works collaboratively with organization and its affiliates, associated departments, staff members, Subject Matter Experts and other volunteers.
•	Assists directors to develop and execute an annual curriculum development plan, assessing priorities and assigning resources through project management; contributes to development of annual budget requirements and managing related expenses according to budget and policy.
•	Examines scope and sequence of curriculum to identify learning gaps and creates a curriculum map
•	Conducts needs/audience analysis, develops training objectives and lesson plans, and collaborates on instructional treatment to develop high-quality participant course work.
•	Develops and modifies instructional material including participant guides, presentation materials and participant interactions.
•	Researches and organizes information and writes instructional materials (tutorials, job aids, references, audio and video scripts, story boards, navigational text, tests, etc.) that transform complex, industry-related information into professionally written, interactive multimedia instruction.
•	Applies best practices and knowledge of instructional design and adult learning theory to the strategy, design and delivery (online and/or on-ground) education courses and exams.
•	Ensures conversion of on-ground content to online environment and additional courseware as required.
•	Manages LMS structure of course content, course outline, learner evaluation and user experience; determines user instructional and navigational pathways based on course content and LMS.

QUALIFICATIONS:
•	Bachelor's degree (or equivalent experience) in Instructional Design; Masters in Instructional Design or Education highly desirable.
•	Minimum of 2 years of demonstrated experience in instructional design using current interactive multimedia technology.
•	Knowledge of emerging technologies and strong computer proficiency, particularly with course management/online learning platforms, multimedia authoring programs, Web 2.0 technologies, current and emerging social networking tools, and web development tools.
•	Experience training in an instructor-led and blended-learning environment. Demonstrated knowledge and practice of adult learning and education theory.
•	Strong project management skills and the ability to meet project quality expectations and scheduled commitments.
•	Microsoft Office Suite, Desktop publishing, and Articulate Storyline highly preferred.
•	Adobe Connect and Flash, with broad knowledge of web-based e-Learning and other new media applications.
•	Strong written and oral communication skills

Figure 1.3 2015 Instructional Designer Job Ad.

Source: SimplyHired.com, June 2015.

specialist" title of 1995, the 2015 job ad contains some noteworthy differences as shown below:

•	**Needs assessment.** Whereas the 1995 ad focused on design and development, the 2015 ad begins with assessment. This suggests that the organization may already have an inventory of learning interventions that need to be reviewed for currency and where necessary, updated and revised. Needs assessment, the process of identifying, prioritizing, and selecting gaps/needs to be filled (Altschuld & Kumar, 2010; Gupta, Sleezer, & Russ-Eft, 2007; Kaufman & Guerra-Lopez, 2013), speaks to the instructional designer's role as problem-solver, with an ability to determine whether or not instruction is all, part, or not part of the solution to a particular problem. The ad reinforces this message when it describes a range of learning opportunities for which the designer is responsible, such as training, professional development, and job aids.

- **Technology skills.** The 2015 ad clearly focuses on digital learning environments, with keywords such as "online," "interactive multimedia instruction," and "LMS" (learning management system), indicating the need to be proficient in the various learning technologies and courseware development applications. Advances in desktop and cloud-based courseware development tools have meant that programming skills are no longer required to create multimedia instruction. The contemporary designer has become the developer of what he/she has designed.

- **Commitment to a specific design model.** It is not uncommon for an organization to express preference for a particular design model or a specific brand of courseware development tool. The specific courseware development tools preferred are listed further down in the ad. This signals to the potential applicant that he/she must be prepared to make a strong case for an alternative if one or more organizational tools or model preferences is not appropriate for constructing the solution to a particular instructional problem.

- **Cross-functional collaboration.** The ability to work with a variety of functional areas is paramount to the organization posting this 2015 ad. In addition to the Subject Matter Experts (SMEs) that the designer expects, the ad lists the various stakeholders with whom the potential applicant must interact and also identifies the specific tasks and activities where cross-functional collaboration is expected to take place.

- **Alignment with business goals.** The 1995 ad talked about learning outcomes; the 2015 ad talks about outcomes and metrics that contribute to business results. The potential applicant needs to be able to demonstrate how his/her work impacts the organization's performance. This places learning/instructional design firmly in the context of the larger domain of L&D. L&D, sometimes called Training and Development, is part of the larger domain of Talent Management and is designed to align individual and group performance with the organization's vision and goals. The scope of L&D includes (a) identification of key employee skills and abilities and the methods for teaching and acquiring them; (b) training program design and delivery;

(c) leadership assessment and development programs; (d) internal and external executive coaching; and (e) metrics used to assess each of these programs (Society for Industrial and Organizational Psychology, 2016).

- **Financial acumen.** Budgeting and cost management skills are among the key responsibilities listed in the ad. The potential applicant needs to be able to identify the cost-benefit of his/her work and to monitor the budgeted expenses on a regular basis.

- **Designing the user experience.** The last but certainly not the least of the key responsibilities listed in the 2015 ad is management of the LMS-based user experience, largely through instructional and navigational pathways through course content on the organization's LMS. Grounded in the field of human-computer interaction (HCI), user experience (UX) focuses on the usability, emotional and motivational impact, and situational-temporal context in which a user interacts with technology (Hassenzahl & Tractinsky, 2006; Kramer & Noronha, 2014; Lin, 2011). The potential applicant must not only have technology skills but also be keenly aware of the affordances of technology in the design process.

- **Credentials.** Once the purview of for-profit and specialty colleges, undergraduate degrees in instructional design/technology are slowly becoming part of the offerings of traditional, not-for-profit institutions of higher education. The organization posting the 2015 ad appears open to undergraduate degrees although the traditional graduate degree is still preferred.

In sum, the 2015 ad includes skills in budget management, learning need identification, project management, alignment with organizational policy, collaboration, stakeholder relationships, and courseware development and delivery. All of these skills are included in the contemporaneous edition of the IBSTPI instructional design competencies (Koszalka, Russ-Eft, & Reiser, 2013).

Figure 1.4 contains an excerpt from an ad posted by a professional services firm in the New York City area. Aimed at the mid-career professional (5–10 years of experience), this ad goes above and beyond the skills and competencies expected of early-career designers in several ways:

- **L&D.** As indicated in the title and in the list of responsibilities, the emphasis is not so much on instructional design as it is on all types of learning and employee development. This indicates that the candidate must be able to identify a variety of non-instructional initiatives, such as coaching and mentoring, that would align with the organization's business goals.

LEARNING AND DEVELOPMENT MANAGER

Squarespace is seeking an experienced Learning and Development Manager for our Training and Development team, who will be responsible for helping evolve our company onboarding and leadership development programs.

You will provide guidance to various teams within the organization to help them meet their objectives, and establish a rhythm of continuous training that reinforces our core values. This position reports to the Director of Training and Development, and will be based in our New York office.

RESPONSIBILITIES
- Design Learning and Development initiatives by partnering with leaders across the organization to identify business and culture objectives
- Develop a training curriculum, and revise to reflect business need or organizational changes as necessary
- Recommend the best training solutions, which may include: e-learning, classroom training, 1:1 sessions, action learning, and a blended approach
- Draw on internal and external resources to ensure the design and delivery of the highest quality programs, materials, and other learning and development resources and activities, including e-learning, self-paced, ILT and other facilitated learning activities
- Act as a lead instructional designer to create cutting-edge training
- Regularly align with our recruitment and people teams to refine the talent hiring and onboarding experience
- Mentor training team members across all office locations to ensure consistent training globally
- Identify opportunities for improvement within the training team, and provide appropriate coaching or educational resources
- Proactively leverage technology, industry best practices, external networking, and alternative learning methods to continuously evolve Squarespace's learning and development activities
- Assess relevant training needs, including assessment methods and measurement systems
- Work with the team to optimize processes, incorporating automations where possible
- Monitor and report on team activities, costs, and the performance of training initiatives
- Evolve training assessment and evaluation methods to measure individual success and program effectiveness, continuously improving resource allocation
- Roughly 20% travel required

QUALIFICATIONS
- 7-12 years of on-the-job training facilitation and development experience
- Exceptional written and oral communication skills; confidence presenting to large audiences
- Self-motivation and the ability to inspire a team
- Impeccable organizational and project management skills
- Well-versed in adult learning theory, with a passion for translating your thoughts into engaging resources
- Technical writing experience and musings on how to transform those around you into knowledgeable communicators
- Experience utilizing e-learning software and solutions for training and continued education
- Experience working with third parties, including consultants and vendors
- A portfolio that demonstrates key aspects of your previous training experiences, including experience in management/leadership development
- An eye for design, with experience creating multimedia training materials
- Experience with the ADDIE Model, Thiagi's 4-door method, and Kirkpatrick's
- Participation in training organizations such as eLearning Guild, ATD or SHRM would be a bonus
- Degree, CIPD or CTP qualified, or equivalent

Figure 1.4 2015 Learning and Development Manager Job Ad.

Source: SimplyHired.com, June 2015.

- **Talent management.** Once the domain of Human Resources specialists, awareness of the significance of Talent Management and the relationship between L&D and the organization's pool of human resources is expected of management-level learning professionals.
- **Enterprise-wide technology affordances.** Beyond learning management systems, the mid-career learning professional is expected to capitalize on all of the organization's information systems and technologies to continuously improve the organization's learning and development capabilities.
- **Leadership skills.** The ability to motivate, inspire, and transform others are the signs of a burgeoning leader and go beyond the required managerial skills.
- **Evidence of the value of L&D.** The mid-career professional is expected to provide hard evidence of L&D's contribution at the individual initiative and program levels, along with the specific metrics and measures for ongoing and future contributions to the organization's success.
- **Non-academic certifications.** In addition to the academic degree, the employer in this ad will also consider candidates with non-academic, non-education certifications such as those offered by the Chartered Institute of Personnel and Development (CIPD), an international association dedicated to the professional development of Human Resources (HR) and L&D professionals (Chartered Institute of Personnel and Development, 2016), or the Certified Treasury Professional (CTP©) offered by the Association for Financial Professionals (Association for Financial Professionals, 2016).

The thought leaders in our field are keenly aware of this evolution in the scope of the learning design and technologies professional. In the first of our *E-Suite Views*, Patti Shank, President of Learning Peaks LLC and Research Director of the eLearning Guild, offers her take on the scope of learning design for the twenty-first century.

SvR: One of the questions I get from career changers but also from those who have just finished their undergraduate education …. They look at the job ads for instructional designers and see one of the requirements often called "business acumen" and they wonder what that is. What do you see as the specific business skills or acumen that instructional designers need to have?

PS: One of the skills is really a skill set and that is to understand the business that they work in; to me, that's been a skill set that an instructional designer needed to have all along. You cannot develop training materials without understanding the business you're in. To me, training, whether it's e-learning or classroom training or on-the-job training, was never going to be any good if you didn't understand the business you're in. I can give an example of that. I had a client that I worked with in healthcare. The first thing that you need to figure out, whether the client is internal or external, is what does the client need in order to solve that particular problem. The problem was with a patient calling in to customer service and asking about having a benefit or not, and not getting the right answer. I was asked to develop some training. Well, the first question is: Is it training that is needed? That's always the first question. A training person cannot assume that training is needed. Training is expensive. A lot of people will say, "Okay. I'll develop training for that." But the first question is: Is training needed and if so, what kind? You have to answer that question; you can't just decide that training is needed. So, you sit down with the person and you watch what they're doing. You have to understand the job, you have to understand the company, and you have to understand the context in which that job is being done. That led me to understand all kinds of outcomes and go back to service level agreements and various other things, and within three to four days, I understood it wasn't a training need. It was a complex business problem, and after looking at various things, including the systems that folks were using to do the job, I found out that it was a systems problem. It wasn't a training problem. So, no matter how many times you trained, they weren't going to be able to answer that patient's question. So, the business skills that were needed in that case were financial and IT-related and the reason they hired me was because I have a healthcare background but also a business background and a financial background and the ability to understand statistical models. So, I was able to go back and figure out what it was that was going wrong there, and I was able to help them figure out what was the real problem that we're solving – and it was about an $8 million problem; so, the answer was "yes" – so, the solution was about a $297,000 solution; so, it was certainly worth solving. So, the answer to the question is: You need to have financial skills and IT skills, and you need to understand the business. So, every single instructional designer or trainer has to be able to understand the business they're in.

SvR: So, it's not just the business but the industry, correct?

PS: Absolutely. When I was in healthcare training, every single person that the company hired had to spend time out in the business, the healthcare departments. They needed to understand what it is the business did, how is healthcare delivered, how they make money or lose money, and how training and

	education, which was our department, how we supported that and how we helped them support the business.
SvR:	One of the things I hear from folks who've been instructional designers for a long time is: "Well, that kind of thing is the job of the business analyst, *it's not my job*." What would you say to them?
PS:	It absolutely IS their job. It's every single person's job in the business. They support the business. Everybody supports the business; if they don't, they need to get out of there.

Staying Relevant in a Dilbert© World of Change

At the moment, you may be feeling the way Dilbert© felt when his boss asked him to work in the Accounting Department and Dilbert© retorted that he was an engineer, not an accountant. Fortunately, the move from traditional instructional design to learning design and technologies is not as big a leap as from engineering to accounting. The move does not require you to learn a new profession but rather to broaden your view of your profession and take stock of everything that you do beyond the creation of instructional events. Here are a few pointers to help you uncover the real value of everything that you do:

- **Successful learning outcomes are no guarantee of success.** Organizational decision-makers have little interest in learning outcomes; what does interest them is to determine how learning contributes to a rich employee talent pool that makes the organization more competitive in the marketplace. This requires the designer to be able to liaise and collaborate with other performance improvement professionals in the organization.
- **Solution-neutrality is a competency, not a knowledge deficiency.** Instruction is not always the solution to a performance problem. Other solutions could include compensation, clarity of roles/responsibilities, infrastructure, and reporting issues, to name a few. Consequently, the designer must be able to know how to identify non-instructional problems and how to hand those off to the appropriate specialists.
- **It's about doing, not just learning.** The 21st century designer is expected to demonstrate the value of the design function. When the designer's products or advice lead to visible improvements in relationships with clients, employees, external vendors – all of which contribute to the organization's bottom line – the learning design function is seen as integral to organizational learning and, thus, as a strategic asset.

Learning Design Profession Self-Check

The VP of L&D is working on the unit's strategic plan for the next three years. She is eager to emphasize the unit's performance improvement focus by clearly describing what happens when a performance problem cannot be solved with one or more learning interventions. To that end, she wants to include some handoff mechanism in her plan and asks your opinion about the approaches she has been considering. Which of the following handoff approaches do you feel would strengthen her plan?

a) Always offer a few learning-related solutions (e.g., coaching, mentoring), then hand off the issue to another part of the organization.
b) Detail specific procedures, with one or two examples, for handing off to other parts of the organization.
c) Partner with other solution providers specializing in a particular area early in the analysis phases.
d) Defer all non-learning issues to HR.

Considering that one-size-does-not-fit-all, option (b) is the strongest alternative among the choices given. This handoff approach allows the VP to clearly indicate through the examples how handoffs are carefully tracked to ensure that the ball does not get dropped and that the issue is addressed by the appropriate group. Option (c) has some merit in that it pulls in the partner early in the problem identification phase, so that the handoff appears seamless to the client. However, if identifying the partner requires searching for a solution provider outside of the organization, it is not immediately clear how this would impact costs and timing. Option (a) reinforces the role of the L&D unit as learning-focused rather than performance-focused and provides little evidence of coordination or follow-up with other units in the organization. Finally, unless your VP is seeking to end her career at your organization, option (d) is a non-starter.

Food for Thought

1 Using the electronic job board of your choice, search for mid-career (>5 years of experience) positions using the keywords "instructional design." Select any one of the job ads, then assess the extent to which you are a good fit for the position by rating yourself on each of the job requirements using a 5-point scale, where "5" means "highly qualified" and "1" means not at all qualified. When you finish, add up each of your ratings (total number of "5" ratings, total number of "4" ratings, etc.). Where are your greatest strengths (and why)? Where do you need to improve (and why)?

2 Repeat your search using the keywords "learning design" and follow the same self-assessment process. What similarities do you see vs. your first search? What are the differences?

3 Thinking about those areas in which you gave yourself the lowest ratings, how would you begin planning for self-improvement?

Up Next

In this chapter, we have (a) examined how the workforce and learning for the workplace has changed since the mid-1990s; (b) reviewed the various sources from which those in and outside of our profession get their information and perceptions regarding learning for the workplace; (c) identified the skills and competencies that designers need to possess in order to strengthen their employability in a rapidly changing environment; and (d) summarized some key take-aways for keeping the design function relevant in the modern workplace. The next chapter explores opportunities for addressing change, including ways in which the learning designer can become an agent for change.

References

Association for Educational Communications & Technology. (2016). *What Is AECT?* Retrieved from http://aect.site-ym.com/?page=about_landing.

Altschuld, J. W., & Kumar, D. D. (2010). *Needs Assessment: An Overview.* Thousand Oaks, CA: SAGE Publications.

Academy of Human Resource Development. (2016). *Who We Are.* Retrieved from www.ahrd.org/?who_we_are.

Association for Financial Professionals. (2016). *Certification.* Retrieved from www.afponline.org/certification/.

Association for Talent Development. (2016a). *About ATD.* Retrieved from www.td.org/About.

Association for Talent Development. (2016b). *Talent Development Magazine.* Retrieved from www.td.org/Publications/Magazines/TD.

ATD Certification Institute. (2014). *The ATD Competency Model™.* Retrieved from www.astd.org/Certification/Competency-Model.

B2B Media Company, LLC. (2016). *Elearning! Magazine.* Retrieved from www.2elearning.com/.

Banathy, B. H. (2013). Instructional systems design. In R. M. Gagne (Ed.), *Instructional Technology: Foundations* (2nd ed., pp. 85–112). Mahwah, NJ: Routledge.

Belland, B. R., & Drake, J. (2013). Toward a framework on how affordances and motives can drive different uses of scaffolds: theory, evidence, and design implications. *Educational Technology Research and Development, 61*(6), 903–25.

CareerBuilder.com. (2016). *Finding a New Job Among New Year's Resolutions at Work, According to CareerBuilder Survey – CareerBuilder.* Retrieved from www.careerbuilder.com/share/aboutus/pressreleasesdetail.aspx?sd=1%2F9%2F2015&id=pr862&ed=12%2F31%2F2015.

Center for Creative Leadership. (2016). *The 70-20-10 Rule – Center for Creative Leadership.* Retrieved from http://insights.ccl.org/articles/leading-effectively-articles/the-70-20-10-rule/.

Chartered Institute of Personnel and Development. (2016). *CIPD.* Retrieved from www.cipd.co.uk/.

CLOMedia, I. (2016). *Chief Learning Officer – Solutions for Enterprise Productivity.* Retrieved from www.clomedia.com/.

Conrad, K., & TrainingLinks. (2000). *Instructional Design for Web-Based Training.* Amherst, MA: HRD Press.

Dabbagh, N., & Kitsantas, A. (2012). Personal learning environments, social media, and self-regulated learning: a natural formula for connecting formal and informal learning. *The Internet and Higher Education, 15*(1), 3–8.

Davenport, T. H., & Harris, J. G. (2007). *Competing on Analytics: The New Science of Winning.* Boston, MA: Harvard Business School Press.

Dick, W., Carey, L., & Carey, J. (2005). *The Systematic Design of Instruction* (6th ed.). New York, NY: Prentice-Hall.

eLearning Guild. (2016a). *About the eLearning Guild.* Retrieved from www .elearningguild.com/.

eLearning Guild. (2016b). *Learning Solutions Magazine.* Retrieved from www .learningsolutionsmag.com/.

Ferrazzi, K. (2015 July 31). *7 Ways to Improve Employee Development Programs. Harvard Business Review.* Retrieved from https://hbr.org/2015/ 07/7-ways-to-improve-employee-development-programs.

Foshay, W., Silber, K., & Westgaard, O. (1994). *Instructional Design Competencies: The Standards* (2nd ed.). Charlotte, NC: Information Age Publishing.

Gagne, R. (1985). *The Conditions of Learning and the Theory of Instruction* (4th ed.). New York, NY: Holt, Rinehart, and Winston.

Gallup. (2015). *Most U.S. Workers See Upside to Staying Connected to Work.* Retrieved from www.gallup.com/poll/168794/workers-upside-staying-connected-work.aspx.

Gallup. (2016). *Millennials Want Jobs to Be Development Opportunities.* Retrieved from www.gallup.com/businessjournal/193274/millennials-jobs-development-opportunities.aspx.

Gupta, K., Sleezer, C. M., & Russ-Eft, D. F. (2007). *A Practical Guide to Needs Assessment.* San Francisco, CA: Pfeiffer.

Hassenzahl, M., & Tractinsky, N. (2006). User experience – a research agenda. *Behaviour and Information Technology, 25*(2), 91–7.

IBSTPI. (2014). *Instructional Designer Competencies.* Retrieved from http://ibstpi .org/instructional-design-competencies/.

International Association for Continuing Education and Training. (2016). *Who We Are.* Retrieved from http://iacet.org/about/who-we-are.

International Society for Performance Improvement. (2016). *Our Purpose.* Retrieved from www.ispi.org/ISPI/About/Our_Purpose/ISPI/About_ISPI/Our_ Purpose.aspx?hkey=1800e69e-3eee-4c00-a0c0-620d51efc5b0.

Kaufman, R., & Guerra-Lopez, I. (2013). *Needs Assessment for Organizational Success.* Alexandria, VA: ASTD Press.

Keller, J. M., & Suzuki, K. (1988). Use of the ARCS motivation model in courseware design. In D. H. Jonassen (Ed.), *Instructional Designs for Microcomputer Courseware* (pp. 401–34). Hillsdale, NJ: Lawrence Erlbaum.

Kirby, J. A., Hoadley, C. M., & Carr-Chellman, A. A. (2005). Instructional systems design and the learning sciences: a citation analysis. *Educational Technology Research and Development, 53*(1), 37–47.

Koper, R. (2005). An introduction to learning design. In R. Koper & C. Tattersall (Eds.), *Learning Design: A Handbook on Modelling and Delivering Networked Education and Training* (pp. 3–20). Berlin, Heidelberg: Springer-Verlag.

Koszalka, T. A., Russ-Eft, D. F., & Reiser, R. (2013). *Instructional Designer Competencies: The Standards* (4th ed.). Charlotte, NC: Information Age Publishing.

Kramer, J., & Noronha, S. (2014). Designing with the user in mind a cognitive category design based methodology. In A. Marcus (Ed.), *Design, User experience, and Usability: User Experience Design Practice* (pp. 152–63). Cham, Switzerland: Springer International Publishing.

Lakewood Media Group, L. (n.d.). *Lakewood Media Group*. Retrieved from https://lakewoodmediagroup.net/.

Lin, K. M. (2011). e-Learning continuance intention: moderating effects of user e-learning experience. *Computers & Education, 56*(2), 515–26.

Mao, J. (2014). Social media for learning: a mixed methods study on high school students' technology affordances and perspectives. *Computers in Human Behavior, 33*, 213–23.

Morrison, G. R., & Anglin, G. J. (2012). Instructional design for technology-based systems. In A. D. Olofsson & J. O. Lindberg (Eds.), *Informed Design of Educational Technologies in Higher Education: Enhanced Learning and Teaching* (pp. 38–56). Hershey, PA: IGI-Global.

Morrison, G. R., Ross, S. M., Kalman, H. K., & Kemp, J. E. (2013). *Designing Effective Instruction* (7th ed.). Hoboken, NJ: John Wiley & Sons, Inc.

National Council for Workforce Education. (2016). *NCWE Vision and Mission*. Retrieved from www.ncwe.org/?page=about.

Parchoma, G. (2014). The contested ontology of affordances: Implications for researching technological affordances for collaborative knowledge production. *Computers in Human Behavior, 37*(0), 360–8.

Reigeluth, C. M. (1983). *Instructional Design Theories and Models: An Overview of Their Current Status*. Hillsdale, NJ: Lawrence Erlbaum.

Reigeluth, C. M. (1999). *Instructional Design Theories and Models Volume II: A New Paradigm of Instructional Theory*. Hillsdale, NJ: Erlbaum.

Rothwell, W. J., Hohne, C. K., & King, S. B. (2007). *Human Performance Improvement: Building Practitioner Competence* (2nd ed.). Burlington, MA: Butterworth-Heinemann.

Schiffman, S. S. (1986). Instructional systems design: five views of the field. *Journal of Instructional Development, 9*(4), 14–21.

Schilling, J., & Kluge, A. (2009). Barriers to organizational learning: an integration of theory and practice. *International Journal of Management Reviews, 11*(3), 337–60.

Sims, R. (2006). Beyond instructional design: making learning a design reality. *Journal of Learning Design, 1*(2), 1–9.

Smith, P. L., & Ragan, T. J. (2004). *Instructional Design* (3rd ed.). Hoboken, NJ: John Wiley and Sons.

Society for Human Resource Management. (2016). *Organizational & Employee Development*. Retrieved from www.shrm.org/resourcesandtools/hr-topics/organizational-and-employee-development/pages/default.aspx.

Society of Human Resource Management Foundation, & Economist Intelligence Unit. (2016). *Profile of the Global Workforce: Present and Future – Future HR Trends*. Retrieved from http://futurehrtrends.eiu.com/report-2015/profile-of-the-global-workforce-present-and-future/.

Society for Industrial and Organizational Psychology. (2016). *Learning and Development*. Retrieved from www.siop.org/business/learning.aspx.

Thottam, I. (2016 June 24). 10 Companies with Awesome Training and Development Programs. *Fortune Magazine*. Retrieved from http://fortune.com/author/isabel-thottam/?id=sr-link4.

Toossi, M. (2016). *Labor Force Projections to 2024: The Labor Force Is Growing, but Slowly: Monthly Labor Review: U.S. Bureau of Labor Statistics*. Retrieved from www.bls.gov/opub/mlr/2015/article/labor-force-projections-to-2024.htm.

Training Industry, Inc. (2016a). *Training Industry Magazine*. Retrieved from www.trainingindustry.com/ezine.aspx.

Training Industry, Inc. (2016b). *2016 Training Industry Report*. Retrieved from https://trainingmag.com/sites/default/files/images/Training_Industry_Report_2016.pdf.

United States Distance Learning Association. (2016). *About.* Retrieved from www .usdla.org/about/.

van Merrienboer, J. J. G. (1997). *Training Complex Cognitive Skills: A Four-Component Instructional Design Model for Technical Training.* Englewood Cliffs, NJ: Educational Technology Publications.

Williams van Rooij, S. (2012). Training older workers: Lessons learned, unlearned, and relearned from the field of instructional design. *Human Resource Management, 51*(2), 281–98.

2 Designing to Improve Performance
It's All about Change

In the previous chapter, we examined the impact of changes in the nature of work, the workplace and, thus, in the role of the learning designer. These changes did not occur at a single point in time in response to some cataclysmic event, although to the individuals and organizations who do not keep abreast of what is going on around them, the changes may appear to be cataclysmic. Whether occurring globally, nationally, within an industry sector, inside an organization, or at the individual level, change is a process. Change can be major, minor, or something in between. For example, change is used to describe anything from a revision to an insurance application form to a bankruptcy filing. The challenge, however, is that when it comes to organizational changes that impact our roles and responsibilities as learning professionals, change can be continuous, evolving, and incremental, but it can also be episodic, discontinuous, and intermittent (Weick & Quinn, 1999).

If change is a process, the incidence and severity of which may not be predictable, then how do we manage the process of change? Or, like Dilbert©, do we just bob and weave and try to survive the winds of change whipped up by the decision-makers or other stakeholders who seek to initiate changes with or without our input? There is an entire field of study devoted to change management in organizations, as well as a robust field of change practitioners focused on best practices and approaches to change management. There is even a broad array of terms that falls under the umbrella of change management, including organizational change management (OCM), behavioral change management (BCM), business change management (also under the BCM acronym), people/employee change management, organizational readiness, change leadership, change implementation, organizational adoption, and transformation management, to name just a few (Jarocki, 2011). Nevertheless, an understanding of change management is essential for not only surviving organizational change but also for playing an active role in initiating and sustaining changes that advance the value of the Learning and Development (L&D) function to the organization. Therefore, in this chapter, we will:

- Review some of the key milestones in the development of the organizational change management literature;

- Explore opportunities for learning designers to serve as change agents; and
- Discuss what concrete changes the designer must make to his/her mindset in order to play an active role in the organization's change management process.

Organizational Change Management as a Field of Study

Change Management as Concept

A basic definition of organizational change is "a process in which a large company or organization changes its working methods or aims, for example in order to develop and deal with new situations or markets: sometimes deep organizational change is necessary in order to maintain a competitive edge" (Organizational Change, n.d.). This dictionary definition offers no insights about scope, duration, or impact of the process of change. Consequently, there is little to suggest that anyone experiencing organizational change needs to somehow manage the effects of change. One of the first indicators that organizational change is something that needs to be managed can be traced back to Coch and French's (1948) industrial experiment designed to determine why workers at a pajama factory in Virginia resisted job changes and what, if anything, could be done to overcome that resistance. The organization in their study had identified a need to change industrial operations in order to meet competitive conditions – aligning with the dictionary's definition and rationale for organizational change – and had introduced a variety of new measures, such as shift changes and revised production rates, to strengthen the company's market position. Their study results found that the organization's management could significantly reduce, if not eliminate, resistance to change by using occupational/ functional group meetings to clearly communicate the need for change and elicit group participation in planning the changes. In short, change resistance could be mitigated by enabling employees to "own" and manage the changes rather than communicating why changes had already been made.

The concept of change management has been approached from a variety of perspectives. For example, van de Ven and Poole (1995) defined change as an empirical observation of difference in form, quality, or state over time in an organizational entity, with an entity being a job function, a work group, an organizational strategy, a program, a product, or the organization as a whole. Other definitions include the deliberate introduction of new ways of thinking, acting, and operating within an organization to survive or accomplish organizational goals (Schalk, Campbell, & Freese, 1998); a means of adapting to the environment, of containing costs, consolidating management power and control without hierarchy (Leana & Barry, 2000); and a means of improving organizational performance (Boeker, 1997). Change management takes a proactive approach by monitoring the need for change, initiating change, and controlling change (Hiatt & Creasey, 2012), with the support of an organization's executives as essential to change management success. In addition, successful change initiatives tend to have not only one or more executive champions who provide the human and financial resources needed for the change-related intervention, but may also have a change agent – a person from inside or outside the organization who takes on the leadership of the change effort and has the responsibility of driving the change from initiation to implementation and evaluation.

The take-aways from these perspectives are two-fold: (1) that change should be planned, enabling those directly and indirectly affected by the change to arrive at a shared understanding of what is no longer working in the current state and why it no longer works, and (2) that there is a need to change. Once both management and employees recognize the need for change, the goals of the change can be defined in more concrete terms, such as a change in products/services, business processes, policies and procedures, tools and technologies, or organizational structures. Managing the process of change is particularly important since a change in one area can cause a cascade of changes – intended or otherwise – in some other area. For example, imagine if your organization determined that their current Learning Management System (LMS) was no longer meeting the organization's needs. The first step would not be to acquire a new system, then announce to all employees that a new system had just been acquired. Instead, a careful analysis would be conducted to identify where the current system falls short and why, what communications to employees need to be made about sharing their own experiences with the current system, what their ideal system would do, and what the implications (positive and challenging) of changing LMSs would mean for them as individuals. Armed with these data, the organization would then develop and implement a plan for changing the LMS, following up after implementation to ensure that the desired results were actually being achieved.

Figure 2.1 provides a graphic representation of the basic stages involved in planning for change. If those stages remind you of the stages and processes for designing a learning intervention, you are absolutely right. Learning designers also analyze the current state; they identify and diagnose the problems or opportunities that need to be addressed; they gather data and work with stakeholders to identify the best alternatives for addressing the need; and they plan for the design, development, implementation, and evaluation of the optimal solution. As such, the learning designer serves as a change agent for that particular initiative. Moreover, planning for change involves incorporating new information at each stage of the process, which may require returning to previous stages and making adjustments. Returning to our LMS example, the recognition of the need for change may not come until one of your colleagues in the L&D group has already gathered the data indicating that your current LMS is unable to support all but the most basic multimedia designs, while your most recent projects would have been

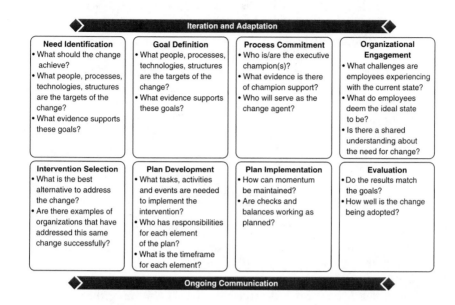

Figure 2.1 Planning for Change.

better served with simulations and gaming elements. This is similar to iteration and adaptation in the design process. Like everything else, however, the role of the learning designer as change agent is moving beyond leadership of formal instructional interventions to other types of interventions aimed at changing current skills and behaviors. Evidence of how and why change can and should be managed can be found in both the scholarly and practitioner literature on change management.

Change Management Research Highlights

The seminal work of Kurt Lewin (1947) marks the baseline of organizational change management theory. To analyze, understand, and initiate change at the group, organizational and societal levels, Lewin perceived change as an evolutionary process that was best managed through an integrated Planned Approach consisting of four concepts:

1   Field Theory, which postulates that individual behavior is a function of the group environment. Thus, any changes in behavior stem from changes in the forces within that environment or field. At the organizational level, examples of field forces would include competition, government regulatory requirements, organizational leadership, and so forth. By identifying, plotting, and establishing the strength of these forces, it would be possible to understand why individuals, groups, and organizations behave the way they do, but also it would

be possible to determine which forces would need to be strengthened or weakened to produce change.

2 Group Dynamics, which posits that group behavior rather than individual behavior should be the main focus of change because the individual in isolation is constrained by group pressures to conform. Consequently, when managing change, the focus should be on factors such as group norms, roles, interactions, and socialization processes.

3 Action Research, which emphasizes that change requires action and is directed at achieving action, but also it recognizes that successful action is based on a correct analysis of the situation, identifying all possible alternative solutions and choosing the solution most appropriate to the situation. Success, however, requires a "felt need" or an individual's inner realization that change is necessary. Action Research is an iterative process whereby research leads to action and action leads to evaluation and further research. That process draws on Field Theory to identify the forces that affect the group to which the individual belongs, and on Group Dynamics to understand why group members respond to those forces in the way they do.

4 The 3-Step Model, often deemed the most significant of the four components (see, for example, Bamford & Forrester, 2003; Buchanan et al., 2005; Cummings & Huse, 1989; Schein, 1988), involves the following: Step 1, Unfreezing, whereby the current equilibrium must be destabilized (unfrozen) before old behaviors can be discarded (unlearned) and new behaviors adopted successfully; Step 2, Moving, whereby the iterative approach of research, action, and more research enables groups and individuals to move from a less acceptable set of behaviors to more acceptable behaviors; and Step 3, Refreezing, whereby the new behaviors are made permanent and the group is stabilized to a new equilibrium to ensure that regression does not occur.

Although the totality of Lewin's scholarly work focused on resolving social conflict through behavioral change, his work on organizational change fostered the Organization Development (OD) stream of research that was prominent in the management literature through the early years of the twenty-first century. Among the notable refinements to the Lewin model were the inclusion of organizational culture and the role of leadership in culture change actions (Schein, 1988), the elaboration of the role of the change agent (e.g., cheerleader, facilitator, and expert) up to the point at which change becomes part of the organizational culture (Lippitt, Watson, & Westley, 1958), and lessons learned from Fortune 500 companies that have been successful in institutionalizing change management (Mento, Jones, & Dirndorfer, 2002). Nevertheless, dramatic changes in the global economy spurred by the oil crises of the 1970s, the rise of the Japanese corporation as the model organizational form, and economic challenges in the American and European economies spurred theorists to challenge the notion of organizational change as evolutionary, group-based, and consensual (see, for example, Buchanan & Storey, 1997; Dawson, 1994; Hatch, 1997; Kanter, Stein, & Jick, 1992). Other critics cited the lack of empirical evidence about what does (not) constitute successful change management processes (Todnem By, 2005). Conversely, some theorists have found Lewin's work as relevant today as it was then and attribute much of the criticism of Lewin to overly narrow interpretations of the Planned Approach (Burnes, 2004b), noting that it serves as the starting point for organizational theory approaches, such as theories of motivation and leadership (Miner, 2002) and complexity theories (Burnes, 2004a).

Lewin's conceptualization of change as a process and his 3-Step Model served as the basis of four well-known models that recommended a series of stages or phases for change agents to follow in implementing change. The Judson model (1991) postulated five phases of change implementation, namely: analysis and planning, communication, acceptance, changing to a desired state, and consolidation and institutionalization of the new state. The model included recommendations for overcoming resistance to change, such as alternative media, reward programs, bargaining, and persuasion. Kotter (1995) proposed an eight-step model for transformational change: (a) establish a sense of urgency by relating environmental conditions to challenges and threats to the organization; (b) form a powerful guiding coalition of individuals who firmly believe in the need for change and can inspire others to support change efforts; (c) create a vision of the desired end-state; (d) communicate the vision through multiple channels, (e) empower others to act by changing policies, procedures, systems, and structures in ways that will facilitate the implementation of change; (f) plan and create short-term wins by publicizing successes to build momentum; (g) build on the change and consolidate improvements; and (h) anchor the changes in corporate culture to sustain the new state. Unlike the Judson or Lewin models, the Kotter model focused on high-level executives seeking to lead transformational change and, as such, is not a good fit for change projects that are not transformative.

A third model in the Lewin tradition is Galpin's (1996) nine-wedge wheel model comprised of (a) establishing the need to change; (b) developing and disseminating a vision of planned change; (c) diagnosing and analyzing the current state; (d) generating recommendations; (e) detailing the recommendations; (f) pilot testing the recommendations; (g) preparing the rollout of the recommendations; (h) rolling out the recommendations; and (i) measuring, reinforcing, and refining the change. Central to Galpin's model is an understanding of organizational culture as evident in rules and policies, norms, events, rewards, and recognition. Armenakis, Harris, and Fields (1999) focused on change messaging as a mechanism for facilitating change readiness and minimizing resistance to change, on the one hand, and facilitating adoption and institutionalization of the desired change, on the other hand. The change message should include the need for change, affirmation of the capability to change, the benefits of change, identification of those driving the change, and evidence that the change is right for the organization.

In addition to the stream of research focusing on change management as process, there is a research stream focused on identifying the factors that comprise the targets of organizational change efforts and how those factors relate to organizational effectiveness. A milestone in this stream is Burke and Littwin's (1992) content model of organizational performance and change. The model centered on 12 organizational dimensions, how those dimensions link to each other, and how the external environment may interact with the dimensions within an organization. Another research stream focuses on the impact of internal and external factors, such as organizational characteristics (size, years in business, etc.) on the organization's effectiveness in responding to environmental changes (Armenakis & Bedeian, 1999), while other studies focus on the interface between the external dynamics of the environment and the internal tensions generated by organizational change initiatives (Biedenbach & Söderholm, 2008). Other areas of focus in the change management literature originated in the research centers and think tanks of multinational firms and include the ADKAR (awareness, desire, knowledge, ability, reinforcement) model, which emphasizes individual change as a necessary precursor to organizational change (Hiatt, 2006); the interplay between personal change, emotional intelligence, and organizational change detailed in Stephen Covey's book, *The 7 Habits of Highly Effective People* (Covey, 2004), and the role of coordination and interdependence of people, structures, and systems to effective change management in the McKinsey 7-S framework (Peters & Waterman, 1982).

Summary

Figure 2.2 contains a graphic illustration of some of the key milestones in the development of organizational change management as a field of study.

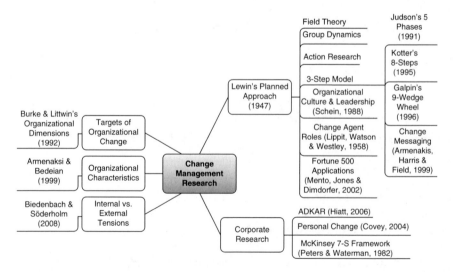

Figure 2.2 Change Management Research Streams.

A theme that cuts across the various streams of change management research is the desire to identify the factors associated with organizational change and how those factors are interrelated and interdependent. Many of these change management models and concepts have served as the framework for consultancy firms offering change management services and for organizations seeking to integrate change management processes into the fabric of their organizations. Change management models offer the promise of an opportunity to (a) forecast the direction of change, so that expectations can be set in advance of visible results; (b) measure the rate at which the change is being adopted and reflected in observable behavioral, process, financial or productivity improvements; (c) empower all employees to own and, thus, be accountable for their own transitions; (d) strengthen employee self-efficacy by sharing change experiences within a common framework that the model provides; (e) reduce resistance to change by identifying potential challenges in advance and implementing strategies to mitigate resistance throughout the duration of the change lifecycle; (f) monitor and control investments in human and material resources throughout the change lifecycle; and (g) engage various occupational and functional areas of the organizations in a shared understanding of the benefits to them on personal and professional levels. Although no one model is "best" for all types of change, they do provide a roadmap from which organizations can select what is valuable in a particular context at a particular time.

Despite the richness of the change management literature, the conventional wisdom is that most organizational change initiatives are unsuccessful, with failure rates purported to be as high as 70 percent. This failure rate has been seriously challenged as rhetoric informed by a lack of grounded empirical research, with suggestions that the concept of organizational change failure or success rates is a non-starter due to (a) the ambiguities of organizational change; (b) the highly context-dependent nature of organizational change; (c) different perspectives on time and organizational change outcomes; and (d) the measurability of organizational change outcomes. It has also been suggested that the practitioner literature has deliberately focused on the change management failure rate as a means of justifying fixed internal change agency structures or the hiring of external change management expertise:

> Promoting the existence of a 70 per cent change failure rate provides a rationale for further academic theorising and research, a rationale for consultancy services through emphasising the problematic nature of change, and legitimizes the work of those managers managing change. (Hughes, 2011, p. 460)

Whether or not the notion that change management initiatives tend to suffer high rates of failure is fact, fiction, or fantasy, it is unlikely that the true rate of failure or success can ever be known, particularly because organizations are reluctant to share failures (or even successes) so as not to risk losing some perceived competitive advantage.

Becoming an Agent of Change

Change Agency Revisited

The change literature discussed in the previous sections tended to be management-focused, stressing what organizational leadership should (not) do to affect change, particularly if the change is intended to be transformational. This suggests that all other employees of the organization are change recipients, those affected either positively or negatively by the outcomes of the change but who may or may not have played an active role in the change process. Recently, however, the processes for planning change are being viewed through the lens of the change recipient, with an emphasis on understanding recipient motivations to support organizational changes (Figure 2.1). That way, the change agent (i.e., manager, leader) can have insights into how best to lead change with the right choice of strategies and techniques for mitigating recipient resistance (see, for example, the work of Armenakis & Harris, 2009; Lunenburg, 2010; Westover, 2010).

The changes in the environment in which organizations conduct business and the nature of work and of the workplace that we discussed in the previous chapter have led most organizational leaders to realize that planning, implementing, and sustaining change is no longer an evolutionary process, but rather an ongoing incorporation of new capabilities and ways of operating. The interconnectivity of regional, national, and local economies, whereby changes in one tend to ripple through the others, means that planning change is no longer moving from a current steady state to a desired new steady state, but now involves forecasting the outcomes of a variety of what-if scenarios. In this new environment, the traditional manager-as-change agent is being replaced by the empowered-employee-as-change agent. This shift is also reflected in the stream of change management research focused on non-traditional change management roles. For example, Sims and Sims (2002) emphasized the importance of empowering the frontline employee in the process of successful change, while Dirks, Cummings, and Pierce (1996) stressed the need for employees to develop psychological ownership of change to facilitate a successful change initiative. To encourage employees to become actively involved in change initiatives and processes, Smith and Mouier (1999) suggested that organizations create rewards and recognition programs that favor those who actively support change initiatives, while more recent studies have focused on the relationship between non-manager employee change agency and career development (Gerwing, 2015; Lysova, Richardson, Khapova, & Jansen, 2015). Moreover, the change agent need no longer be a single individual but can be a team of people whose combined skills and abilities connect people throughout the organization to identify what needs to change and to help make change happen. For example, in their case study of a major change initiative at a large healthcare services organization in the Pacific Northwest of the US, Worley and Mohrman (2014) noted that the effort was led by a "design team" composed of managers and non-managers from across the organization who were able to teach and diffuse knowledge of design and change to the organization, approach change incrementally, build on small successes to gain momentum, engage a large number of employees in planning and implementing change, and institutionalize change capability.

The downside of the empowered-employee-as-change agent, however, is the potential risk of selecting change agents solely on the excellence of their functional, occupational skills rather than for their abilities to diagnose and make sense of change contexts. Unfortunately, there is no standard set of change agent competencies, resulting in a tendency to rely on subjective levels of current occupational competence and expertise (Doyle, 2002). Nevertheless, organizations continue to seek employees at all levels who are willing to serve as change agents, in many instances as a means of strengthening employee engagement and retention.

The Learning Designer as Change Agent

In recent years, our profession has come to realize that when learning interventions are implemented successfully, the learning designer who has played an active role in the implementation of the intervention, particularly if the intervention is an innovative one, is effectively serving as an agent of change. Building on Donald Ely's (1990, 1999) work on the conditions that facilitate the implementation of instructional innovations, Ensminger, Surry, Porter, and Wright (2004) stressed that designers need to have an understanding of change theory to facilitate implementation of their instructional products, and they identified a set of individual and organizational factors that designers must address before and during implementation to be effective change agents. Although the sample used to construct those factors consisted primarily of designers in educational settings, some factor components (e.g., rewards, resources) are consistent with change agent requirements identified in the business change management literature. Similarly, in a three-year study of a small group of designers in Canadian universities, Campbell, Schwier, and Kenny (2009) postulated that the designer's role as change agent is multidimensional, covering interpersonal, professional, institutional, and societal roles. Given the highly contextual nature of change and change management, however, we cannot assume that designers in corporate and government work settings, where organizational cultures, structures, and ways of doing business differ dramatically, can play the same roles as found in the education-based research studies.

In non-academic settings, where learning designers are expected to link their initiatives to the organization's strategic goals, designer-as-change-agent is a logical consequence of that business focus. Whether developing instructional or non-instructional interventions, change management activities, such as engaging and retaining strong stakeholder relationships and clear communication of change benefits to those to be impacted by change, improve the chances of successful intervention implementation (Molenda & Pershing, 2004). However, the role of designer-as-change-agent is in itself an idea that requires change, namely, a change in thinking on the part of the organization as well as of the designer. In *E-Suite Views*, Gerry Lang, VP, Learning Services Marketing at Conduent, offers his take on change and how the designer can facilitate change:

SvR: Let's start with a general question. How has the instructional design profession evolved/changed over the past 10 years or so?

GL: I don't know that it's as respected. And what I mean by that is even some very well thought of and respected people in the learning industry, especially around the year 2000 when e-learning tools were becoming more prominent in terms of ease of use, had this idea that anybody could build training, anybody could do instructional design because they have all of these tools. I think it hurt some of the really good instructional design that was going on. But I do think there's a resurgence and it's becoming more respected again. But it did hurt because there's some really bad e-learning out there, some really bad training and I think that's because of that idea that anybody could build training.

SvR: To what do you attribute that change?

GL: I think it was because of the tools. The tools have gotten so easy to use. The old computer-based training that you saw in the 1990s and early 2000s was much more difficult to work with and was built on instructional design theory and you had to really have been educated in instructional design in order to understand the tools. Now, things like Captivate are fairly easy. So, there is the idea now that anybody can develop training. What's missing is the design and people aren't paying for the design, although they are beginning to, again. There are a lot of companies who feel that it all can be done so easily, that the respect for rigorous design of good learning is missing.

SvR: What do you think is needed to change that perception or to help organizations be more realistic about what is involved in good training design?

GL: I'm one who has already pushed for good learning evaluation and making sure that learning is really making an impact. I think the real need is for the training to be aligned with business needs. Not just teaching skills so that someone can do his/her job better but teaching the skills needed to really move the business. If you look at the businesses that lead in training, like pharmaceuticals or the military, instructional design is respected because they can show the business impact of the training and how the business is doing better because of the training. Every business is trying to do one of two things: cut costs or make more money and maybe customer satisfaction is the third one. But you should be able to look at those three things and be able to say somewhere along the way that performance is impacting those things. And as companies understand that more and more, then I think instructional design will regain the respect it once had and understand that good instructional design is really needed.

SvR: Let's dive a little deeper into the idea of business acumen and the instructional designer. How does the instructional designer demonstrate the relationship between the work that he/she does and the impact on the business?

GL: I believe that the instructional designers who work for a vendor, a learning company, probably do that better than instructional designers who work internally for an organization. And I say this from both personal experience and from knowing designers out there working in the field. When I was at Microsoft, for instance, we had a great group of instructional designers internally and we were developing training for how to install back office Microsoft products. I don't know that we ever thought about the impact of what we were doing. Whether it was to get people to buy more Microsoft products or customer satisfaction, I don't think we thought about that at the time. I think that's really hard to do internally unless you've got a group that's really aligned with business goals. So, if you're working internally, it's really important for the instructional designers to understand what the company is trying to do from a business standpoint. And that takes really good managers and leaders to help them understand that. It's not just a job; you're not just developing training. There's a reason for it and if you understand what the company is trying to do and can draw a line back to what it is you're trying to do, that really helps you understand the focus of what you're doing. When I talk about the vendors, they move from one client to another client, business to business, where you might be doing something for aeronautics one day, UPS the next day, and then you might be doing something for retail. You can't be a really good learning vendor if you don't understand the client's business, you have to understand their business and what they're trying to do in order to develop good training and I think that's what separates the good vendors from the poor vendors. There's a lot of lip service when you're selling – "we develop training to impact your business" – but the folks who really do that are the ones who stand out. When you're looking at an RFP [sic], if you can put a line item in for evaluation, if you can say we're going to measure these things to show that the training is really impacting your business, the client always wants that. But when it comes down to paying for evaluation, then the clients really don't want it. And that's the first thing that always seems to get cut and that's too bad because that really will show people the impact that the training is having on the business. That's the business skill that instructional designers really need to understand. I know I didn't learn that at school; we talked more about designing good training; we didn't talk about aligning that to business results. And I think that's key.

SvR: Any final thoughts or comments about the learning profession in general that you'd like to make?

GL: I think that there's a lot of new thinking out there. It's not just training anymore; there are lots of new things companies can be doing for knowledge transfer besides training. Millennials don't want to sit in a classroom; they want it when they need it. If you can get instructional designers to think about knowledge transfer beyond training, that's more in line with the new thinking I'm seeing out there.

Change Management as the Un-Dilbert© Mindset

The key take-away from Gerry Lang is that designer-as-change-agent is rooted in a new way of thinking, a change management mindset that takes the designer beyond formal learning opportunities to learning that aligns with business needs. But, what if you are unsure as to whether or not your organization would be open to you, the designer, as change agent? Here are some tips for getting out of that Dilbert©-like perception of your role as merely a cog in the organization's wheel and into a change management mindset:

- **Persistence dulls resistance.** The very idea of change stirs up a variety of feelings all along the spectrum of human emotion. Although some people are more vocal than others when it comes to articulating their feelings about change, there is always some resistance behind the curtain. As a change agent, you need to develop a strong stomach and push on against overt and covert resistance. A good way to fuel your persistence in the face of opposition is to seek out colleagues who are as ambitious and enthusiastic as you are and who see the change initiative as an opportunity to not only help them do their jobs better but also see the change initiative as a career development opportunity to help them advance within the organization. There is nothing like a strong network of committed individuals to build and sustain momentum for success.

- **Know thine own organization.** You cannot be an effective change agent without knowing how your organization works. This includes the nature of the business but also the politics and human dynamics involved. Just as you research, analyze, and document the characteristics of your target learners and their environment to design instruction, you also need to have a clear picture of how your organization really works, how it has addressed change in the past, and which change initiatives have (not) worked and why.

- **Ask the tough questions.** Questions are not only a means of gaining information; they are a mechanism to help other people think. When you were a student, you were asked to reflect on what you were learning by asking yourself questions. Questions for reflection help people develop an emotional connection to your change initiative, so that the initiative becomes theirs, not just yours. Questions like, "How can we show that by changing this process we are really contributing to the company's success?" helps people come up with ideas based on their own experiences and gain ownership in the change initiative while providing you, the change agent, with multiple perspectives on how others in the organization really think about change.

- **Share your own past successes.** Think back to your most successful projects and what kind of changes those projects created. Were they changes in employee performance? Customer satisfaction? Employee satisfaction? Large projects or small, they all contributed to some type of change. Sharing those success stories is a good way of demonstrating your ability to be an effective agent of change, strengthening your credibility for current and future change agency efforts.

- **Max out those people skills.** You probably chose to work in the learning professions because you like to work with and help people. That includes people above your pay grade as well as peers and those in the lower ranks of the organization. Applying your people skills up and down the organization, as well as with those outside who can facilitate your change initiative, will keep you focused and reinforce that network of relationships that is so constructive in strengthening your change management mindset.

Designing for Change Self-Check

During a team meeting, your supervisor mentions that senior management is looking for new ways to improve employee productivity without increasing the time or money spent on training events. One executive suggested that the L&D group undertake a change management initiative to restructure the way it produces training. Your supervisor asks the team for ideas. What would you recommend as the first step in undertaking this change management initiative?

a)   Hire an external change management consultant;
b)   Conduct an analysis of how the group produces training;
c)   Conduct a needs assessment; and
d)   Volunteer to be the change agent.

Of these four options, (c) is the best choice. Just because an executive suggests a solution does not mean it is the correct solution, particularly since that executive offered no evidence as to why he/she felt restructuring the L&D group would improve productivity throughout the organization. The starting point would be to determine where levels of productivity are not at the desired rate and why, which requires a needs assessment. Option (a) would achieve the same result as option (c) – assuming the external consultant was reputable and experienced in this area – but at a cost that might exceed any potential savings through increased productivity. Moreover, an external consultant requires time to learn your business, and you may not have the luxury of time, given the cut-the-budget mindset of the executives. Option (b) assumes that the executive in this scenario knows that the structure of the L&D group is the cause of unsatisfactory employee productivity, but again, no evidence has been presented to support that assumption. Finally, you may indeed see change agency as an opportunity to advance your career (option d), but that would not answer your supervisor's question.

Food for Thought

1   What organizational change initiatives has your company undertaken in the last three years? Did any of these initiatives involve L&D? Why (not)?
2   There are a variety of self-assessment tools on the web that purport to help you to identify whether or not you have what it takes to be an effective change agent. Conduct a search using the keywords "change agent self-assessment." Select one of the tools and take the self-assessment. What strengths/weaknesses/opportunities for improvement did you uncover?
3   There are 28 groups on LinkedIn.com that are dedicated to change management and learning. What are the similarities/differences between these groups?

Up Next

In this chapter, we have (a) reviewed the highlights of the change management literature; (b) explored the role of the change agent and proposed how the learning designer can serve as change agent; and (c) discussed some concrete ideas for developing a change management mindset. Next, we turn our attention to an aspect of change that is particularly challenging to early-career learning designers or to mid-career designers who have spent the majority of their careers working exclusively on training interventions. That challenge involves a shift in mindset away from instruction as the starting point for addressing performance problems.

References

Armenakis, A., & Bedeian, A. G. (1999). Organizational change: A review of theory and research in the 1990s. *Journal of Management, 25*(3), 293–315.

Armenakis, A. A., & Harris, S. G. (2009). Reflections: Our journey in organizational change research and practice. *Journal of Change Management, 9*(2), 127–42.

Armenakis, A. A., Harris, S. G., & Fields, H. S. (1999). Making change permanent: A model for institutionalizing change interventions. *Research in Organizational Change and Development, 12*, 97–128.

Bamford, D. R., & Forrester, P. L. (2003). Managing planned and emergent change within an operations management environment. *International Journal of Operations & Production Management, 23*(5), 546–64.

Biedenbach, T., & Söderholm, A. (2008). The challenge of organizing change in hypercompetitive industries: A literature review. *Journal of Change Management, 8*(2), 123–45.

Boeker, W. (1997). Strategic change: The influence of managerial characteristics and organizational growth. *Academy of Management Journal, 40*(1), 152–70.

Buchanan, D., Fitzgerald, L., Ketley, D., Gollop, R., Jones, Saint Lamont, S., & Whitby, E. (2005). No going back: A review of the literature on sustaining organizational change. *International Journal of Management Reviews, 7*(3), 189–205.

Buchanan, D. A., & Storey, J. (1997). Role-taking and role-switching in organizational change: The four pluralities. In I. McLoughlin & M. Harris (Eds.), *Innovation, organizational change and technology* (pp. 127–45). London, UK: International Thomson Business.

Burke, W., & Litwin, G. (1992). A causal model of organizational performance and change. *Journal of Management, 18*(3), 523–45.

Burnes, B. (2004a). Kurt Lewin and complexity theories: Back to the future? *Journal of Change Management, 4*(4), 309–25.

Burnes, B. (2004b). Kurt Lewin and the planned approach to change: A re-appraisal. *Journal of Management Studies, 41*(6), 977–1002.

Campbell, K., Schwier, R. A., & Kenny, R. F. (2009). The critical, relational practice of instructional design in higher education: An emerging model of change agency. *Educational Technology Research & Development, 57*(5), 645–63.

Coch, L., & French Jr., J. P. (1948). Overcoming resistance to change. *Human Relations, 1*(4), 512–32.

Covey, S. R. (2004). *The 7 habits of highly effective people* (2nd ed.). New York, NY: Free Press.

Cummings, T. G., & Huse, E. F. (1989). *Organization Development and Change* (4th ed.). St. Paul, MN: West Publishing.

Dawson, P. (1994). *Organizational Change*. London, UK: Sage Publications Ltd.

Dirks, K. T., Cummings, L. L., & Pierce, J. L. (1996). Psychological ownership in organizations: Conditions under which individuals promote and resist change. In R. W. Woodman & W. A. Pasmore (Eds.), *Research in Organizational Change and Development* (Vol. 9, pp. 1–23). Greenwich, CT: JAI Press, Inc.

Doyle, M. (2002). Selecting managers for transformational change. *Human Resource Management Journal, 12*(1), 3–15.

Ely, D. P. (1990). Conditions that facilitate the implementation of educational technology innovations. *Journal on Research on Computing in Education, 23*(2), 298–305.

Ely, D. P. (1999). Conditions that facilitate the implementation of educational technology innovations. *Educational Technology, 39*, 23–7.

Ensminger, D. C., Surry, D. W., Porter, B. E., & Wright, D. (2004). Factors contributing to the successful implementation of technology innovations. *Educational Technology & Society, 7*(3), 61–72.

Galpin, T. (1996). *The Human Side of Change: A Practical Guide to Organization Redesign.* San Francisco, CA: Jossey-Bass.

Gerwing, C. (2015). Meaning of change agents within organizational change. *Journal of Applied Leadership and Management, 4*, 21–38.

Hatch, M. J. (1997). *Organization Theory: Modern, Symbolic and Postmodern Perspectives.* Oxford, UK: Oxford University Press.

Hiatt, J. M. (2006). *ADKAR: A Model for Change in Business, Government and Our Community: How to Implement Successful Change in Our Personal Lives and Professional Careers.* Loveland, CO: Prosci Research.

Hiatt, J. M., & Creasey, T. J. (2012). *Change Management: The People Side of Change.* Loveland, CO: Prosci Research.

Hughes, M. (2011). Do 70 percent of all organizational change initiatives really fail? *Journal of Change Management, 11*(4), 451–64.

Jarocki, T. L. (2011). *The Next Evolution: Enhancing and Unifying Project and Change Management.* Princeton, NJ: Brown & Williams Publishing, LLC.

Judson, A. (1991). *Changing Behavior in Organizations: Minimizing Resistance to Change.* Cambridge, MA: Basil Blackwell.

Kanter, R. M., Stein, B. A., & Jick, T. D. (1992). *The Challenge of Organizational Change.* New York, NY: The Free Press.

Kotter, J. (1995). Leading Change: Why Transformation Efforts Fail. *Harvard Business Review, 73*(2), 59–67.

Leana, C. R., & Barry, B. (2000). Stability and change as simultaneous experiences in organizational life. *Academy of Management Review, 25*(4), 753–9.

Lewin, K. (1947). *Change Management Model.* New York, NY: McGraw Hill.

Lippit, R., Watson, J., & Westley, B. (1958). *The Dynamics of Planned Change.* New York, NY: Harcourt, Brace and World.

Lunenburg, F. C. (2010). Managing change: The role of the change agent. *International Journal of Management, Business and Administration, 13*(1), 1–6.

Lysova, E. I., Richardson, J., Khapova, S. N., & Jansen, P. G. W. (2015). Change-supportive employee behavior: A career identity explanation. *Career Development International, 20*(1), 38–62.

Mento, A., Jones, R., & Dirndorfer, W. (2002). A change management process: Grounded in both theory and practice. *Journal of Change Management, 3*(1), 45–59.

Miner, J. B. (2002). *Organizational Behavior: Foundations, Theories, and Analyses.* Oxford, UK: Oxford University Press.

Molenda, M., & Pershing, J. A. (2004). The strategic impact model: An integrative approach to performance improvement and instructional systems design. *TechTrends, 48*(2), 26–32.

Organizational Change [Def. 1]. (n.d.). *Cambridge Business English Dictionary.* Retrieved from http://dictionary.cambridge.org/us/dictionary/english/organizational-change.

Peters, T. J., & Waterman, R. H. (1982). *In Search of Excellence: Lessons from America's Best-Run Companies.* New York, NY: Harper & Row.

Schalk, R., Campbell, J. W., & Freese, C. (1998). Change and employee behaviour. *Leadership & Organization Development Journal, 19*(3), 157–63.

Schein, E. H. (1988). *Organizational Psychology* (3rd ed.). London, UK: Prentice Hall.

Sims, S. J., & Sims, R. R. (2002). Employee involvement is still the key to successfully managing change. In R. R. Sims (Ed.), *Changing the Way We Manage Change* (pp. 33–54). Westport, CT: Quorum Books.

Smith, M. E., & Mourier, P. (1999). Implementation: Key to organizational change. *Strategy & Leadership, 27*(6), 37–41.

Todnem By, R. (2005). Organisational change management: A critical review. *Journal of Change Management, 5*(4), 369–80.

van de Ven, A. H., & Poole, M. S. (1995). Explaining development and change in organizations. *Academy of Management Review, 20*(3), 510–40.

Weick, K. E., & Quinn, R. E. (1999). Organizational change and development. *Annual Review of Psychology, 50*(1), 361–86.

Westover, J. H. (2010). Managing organizational change: Change agent strategies and techniques to successfully managing the dynamics of stability and change in organizations. *International Journal of Management and Innovation, 2*(1), 45–50.

Worley, C. G., & Mohrman, S. A. (2014). Is change management obsolete? *Organizational Dynamics, 43*(3), 214–24.

3 Instructional vs. Non-Instructional Interventions

What's the Difference?

Think outside the box.
Step out of your comfort zone.
Push the envelope.
That's right in our wheelhouse.

These four catchphrases are among the favorites of Dilbert's© boss, but they have also been favorites among business professionals for years. To the delight of some and the chagrin of others, these phrases are still in fashion among those seeking a more attention-getting way of calling for people to change, be it a change in behavior, attitudes, or both. In Dilbert's© case, however, the boss is paying lip service to new ways but really wants his employees to keep thinking *inside* the box or, in some cases, not think at all. Hopefully, your boss is not like Dilbert's© boss and he/she truly wants employees to embrace change and reflect on what it is that you do and potentially can do.

The change management mindset discussed in the previous chapter involves re-focusing your thoughts about the scope of your role as a learning design and technologies professional and what is (not) in your wheelhouse, as the expression goes. If you have spent the majority of your Learning and Development (L&D) career creating training interventions or other forms of formal instruction, you may not think of other types of performance improvement interventions as falling under your purview. Oftentimes, this may be a function of how learning is viewed inside your organization. If, for example, learning resides in a unit labeled "Training Department," it seems logical that everyone in the organization associates learning with training. In addition, the evolution of the learning design profession, with its roots in traditional face-to-face training interventions, has contributed to the comingling of *learning* and *training*. However, changing perceptions does take time. As L&D professionals, we can contribute to that change by demonstrating that learning and training are not synonymous. In fact, one of the advanced competencies for designers set down by the International Board of Standards for Training, Performance, and Instruction (IBSTPI) is the ability to identify and recommend potential instructional and non-instructional solutions to a performance problem (IBSTPI, 2014). Consequently, competency in and comfort with training solutions alone is no longer an assurance of ongoing employability, let alone career advancement.

"But I'm an instructional designer, so all of my solutions should include instruction," you say. Label alert! You may have fallen into the terminology soup that is sometimes stirred in the scholarly literature (Aziz, 2013, p. 32). The variety of terms, such as training, course, instruction, professional development, and class, to name a few, only thickens the soup. The concoction becomes almost inedible when practitioners with no background in design or adult learning jump in with their own list of terms and *how to's*. Which ones are learning interventions? Non-learning interventions? Instructional interventions? Non-instructional interventions?

Throughout this book, the term "intervention" is defined as "a set of sequenced and planned actions or events intended to help the organization increase its effectiveness. Interventions purposely disrupt the status quo" (Cummings & Worley, 2015, p. 173). Consequently, a performance intervention is a set of planned actions designed to help an individual, a team, a business unit, or the entire organization to improve one or more aspects of performance. The solution to a performance problem may include one or more interventions, particularly if the performance problem is complex and pervasive across the organization.

Performance can be measured in terms of revenues, productivity, savings, and a host of other observable indicators of how an individual, group, or the organization is doing vs. objectives and overarching goals. As learning designers, our performance interventions normally target individuals and groups, although improvements in individual and group performance (hopefully) bubble up to organizational performance improvement. The question is: How do we as designers facilitate the learning process so that the learner can apply what is learned and improve his/her performance? In other words, what methods, tools, and techniques do we have at our disposal to facilitate learning? Instruction is just one method that we can use to improve knowledge and skills. It is when performance problems are due to factors other than knowledge and skills that instruction is most likely NOT the appropriate type of intervention, but it is the solution to which our mindsets naturally gravitate as the starting point. As performance improvement guru Allison Rossett noted, learning professionals need to "turn from their habitually favored interventions, like training, to solutions that match the customer and situation, even if it is not what was originally requested" (Rossett, 2009, p. 19).

Knowing how to select a particular intervention requires in-depth analysis of the scope, depth, and causes of the performance problem, which is the subject of Chapter 4. Right now, we need to be clear about what the suite of potential interventions includes. This requires an understanding of what is meant by learning, what the scope of learning-related interventions includes, and how instruction fits into the mix of interventions. So, in this chapter, we will:

- Review the key constructs related to learning, instruction, and performance interventions that are addressed in the scholarly literature;
- Describe the performance interventions that learning designers are expected to be able to create and implement; and
- Identify which performance interventions to hand off to other functional occupations.

Learning, Instruction, and Performance Interventions

Learning and Instruction

To begin, *learning* is a construct, a complex set of models and theories we use to describe what may be going on inside the human mind in our ongoing exposure to and interaction with the world around us:

> Learning is a multidimensional process that results in a relatively enduring change in a person or persons, and consequently how that person or persons will perceive the world and reciprocally respond to its affordances physically, psychologically, and socially. The process of learning has, as its foundation, the systemic, dynamic, and interactive relation between the nature of the learner and the object of the learning ecologically situated in a given time and place as well as over time. (Alexander, Schallert, & Reynolds, 2009, p. 186)

As a construct, we can neither observe nor measure learning, relying instead on a variety of indicators to determine whether or not cognitive, behavioral, and/or attitudinal changes have taken place as a result of some action designed to enhance learning. Instruction, the intentional arrangement of experiences and conditions designed to facilitate the attainment of explicit, identified learning goals, is one such action. Instruction is observable and its outcomes are measurable.

The Education literature has long drawn a distinction between learning and instruction based on the locus of the activity, with instruction occurring outside the learner and driven by the instructor/facilitator, and learning as something only the learner can do (Bereiter & Scardamalia, 1989; Fleming & Levie, 1978; Jonassen & Grabowski, 2011). In their discussion on the various theories of learning and instruction, Min, Kommers, Vos, and van Dijkum (2000) categorized instruction as the *supply side* of education because it characterizes what is offered to the learner, while learning is the demand side because that describes the knowledge that the learner seeks to acquire. This supply vs. demand paradigm is also a fairly well-developed stream in the Human Resource Development (HRD) literature

(Argyris, Putnam, & McLain Smith, 1985; Martin, McKay, & Hawkins, 2010; Rik, 2003). Similar differentiations between learning and instruction define learning as a change in human performance or performance potential resulting from experience and practice, whereas instruction refers to what is done to help individuals to learn (Newby, Stepich, Lehman, & Russell, 1996; Uden & Beaumont, 2006).

The Learning Sciences field views instruction as one of two approaches to helping people learn. Instruction is deemed to be a collection of methods that focus on how content is presented to learners in a way that prepares our cognitive processes for selecting, organizing, and integrating new knowledge. This is essentially how most instructional design textbooks define instruction, which is then executed through one or more instructional strategies. An instructional strategy is a combination of methods, media, and techniques to elicit specific and defined outcomes. Direct instruction, which is an example of an instructional strategy, uses activities such as lectures, drill and practice, and demonstrations. The other approach to helping people learn is through learning strategies, a series of activities in which the learner engages in order to activate appropriate cognitive processing during learning (Fiorella & Mayer, 2015; Mayer, 2003). Learning strategies do not teach content; they provide mechanisms for learners to draw on what they know to approach and make meaning with new content. Examples of learning strategies include concept mapping, which supports the cognitive process of organizing information within a coherent structure, and think aloud techniques, such as self-explanation that support the cognitive process of integration by enabling learners to integrate new knowledge with prior knowledge. Research on specific applications of learning strategies for work-related learning is expanding into areas such as executive education (Wuestewald, 2016), workplace training (Westover, 2009), and occupational health and safety training (Galbraith & Fouch, 2007). Table 3.1 summarizes the various themes around the relationship between learning and instruction.

In sum, learning is a construct that describes the cognitive and behavioral changes to improve learner performance. Instruction is one approach to supporting the learning process, but it is also the most documented approach because it is observable, measurable, and grounded in robust bodies of literature that include theory and practice in both educational and workplace settings. However, the growing interest in performance in the workplace has drawn attention to other opportunities beyond instruction to support learning.

Forms of Work-Related Learning

Research on learning for workplace performance is largely concentrated in the Human Resources Development (HRD) and Human Performance Technology (HPT) literature. HRD focuses on cultivating and deploying human expertise for the purpose of improving performance at the

Table 3.1 Learning and Instruction in the Literature

Themes	Authors	Main Points

Supply vs. Demand	Argyris, Putnam, & McLain Smith (1985)
	Bereiter & Scardamalia (1989)
	Fleming & Levie (1978)
	Jonassen & Grabowski (2011)
	Martin, McKay, & Hawkins (2010)
	Min, Kommers, Vos, & Dijkum (2000)
	Newby, Stepich, Lehman, & Russell (1996)
	Rik (2003)
	Uden & Beaumont (2006)
		• Instruction:
		  • Supply side
		  • Offered to the learner
		  • Occurs outside the learner
		  • Instructor-/facilitator-driven
		  • What is done to help individuals learn
		• Learning:
		  • Demand side
		  • What learner seeks to acquire
		  • Change in human performance/performance potential
		  • Results from experience and practice

Supporting Learning	Fiorella & Mayer (2015)
	Galbraith & Fouch (2007)
	Mayer (2003)
	Westover (2009)
	Wuestewald (2016)
		• Instruction:
		  • Focuses on content presentation
		  • Prepares cognitive processes for selecting, organizing, integrating new knowledge
		  • Executed through one or more instructional strategies
		• Learning Strategies:
		  • Series of activities performed by the learner
		  • Activates appropriate cognitive processing
		  • Provides mechanisms to make meaning with new content

individual, work group, and organizational levels. Consequently, interventions that enable and facilitate learning are key components of the HRD process and, thus, the HRD literature. Similar to the Education literature and the Learning Sciences literature, the HRD literature defines learning as a permanent or quasi-permanent change in capability – and by extension, behavior – resulting from the learner's experience and interaction with his/her environment (De Houwer, Barnes-Holmes, & Moors, 2013; Driscoll, 2000). The theoretical and empirical studies of learning in HRD contexts focus on a set of constructs addressing the forms of learning. For example, the constructs of formal and informal learning have been well researched. Watkins and Marsick (1992) categorized the forms of learning as being formal, informal, and incidental. Generally, formal learning refers to planned, intentional, and structured learning with prescribed and specific outcomes that are institutionally sponsored or endorsed (Jacobs & Park, 2009; McGuire & Gubbins, 2010). Training events are examples of formal learning opportunities in that training tends to involve systematic instruction and task-oriented actitivies focused on a specific job-related area, offered on the job or at an external venue or provider, with outcomes targeted to improved job performance (Jacobs, 2003). Training is generally a part of an employee's professional development that includes a broader set of actitivies that have both learning and career advancement goals (Noe, 2008).

Informal learning is generally deemed to be learner-directed, self-guided and occuring in non-institutional settings in which the learner learns through everyday practices and activities (Eraut, 2000; Garrick, 1998; Marsick & Volpe, 1999; Tannenbaum, Beard, McNall, & Salas, 2010). Informal learning activities include participation in communities of practice, networking via social media such as LinkedIn, or sharing resources, such as books and articles with co-workers. Incidental learning occurs as an unintended consequence of some other activity, such as trial-and-error use of a new software package or networking at an event. The purpose of the activity is to complete a particular task, but other skills, abilities, or knowledge may be acquired in the process, even though the individual undertaking the activity may not be aware of it.

In Chapter 1, we noted that the 70:20:10 model is a commonly used formula within the training profession to describe the optimal sources of learning. The general consensus among HRD scholars appears to be that approximately 80 percent of employee learning occurs through informal and incidental means and only 20 percent occurs through formal means (Berg & Chyung, 2008; Cross, 2007; Watkins & Marsick, 1992). Thus, it is not surprising that researchers are interested in the impact of informal learning on individual and organizational performance. For example, a survey of 188 managers in a Fortune 500 company in New England showed that core managerial skills as defined by the company tend to be acquired through informal learning activities, such as interacting with others and day-to-day job experience, rather than through formal activities, such as training (Enos, Kehrhahn, & Bell, 2003). Other empirical studies have explored the contextual factors that promote or inhibit informal learning (Choi & Jacobs, 2011; Ellinger, 2005; Lohman, 2005), identifying an organization's leadership, culture, infrastructure, and access to colleagues as the organizational contextual factors that, together with the personal characteristics of the learners themselves (initiative, love of learning, commitment to professional development, etc.), influence employees' informal learning.

However, there has been considerable research challenging the formal vs. informal dichotomy. A variety of studies noted that work-related learning is the cumulative result of a blend of formal and informal elements, with characteristics of formal learning to be found in informal learning situations and characteristics of informal learning found in formal situations (Gherardi, 2006; Goldstein & Ford, 2002; Malcom, Hodkinson, & Colley, 2003; Rowden, 2007; Shipton, Dawson, West, & Patterson, 2002). Moreover, informal social interactions among employees are often unplanned – think of one employee asking another in the next cubicle how to do something. As such, when and how often learning occurs cannot be systematically observed or measured with any certainty (Cseh & Manikoth, 2011; Marsick, 2003). Figure 3.1 illustrates the blend of elements contributing to work-related learning described in the HRD literature.

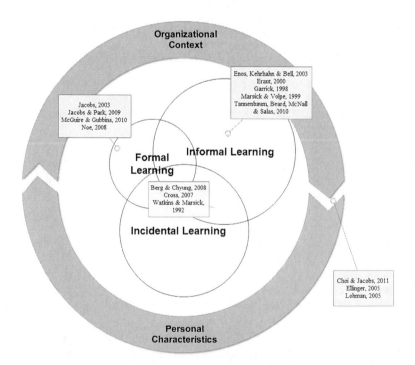

Figure 3.1 Elements Contributing to Work-Related Learning.

Classification of Interventions

In addition to the forms of learning, studies on learning have emphasized its position within the domain of individual performance improvement. For example, Holton (1999a, b) saw the optimization of learning and expertise as one of the drivers or leading indicators of future outcomes of individual performance. Learning can be optimized through interventions that help individuals to increase knowledge, skills, and abilities or through interventions that change the circumstances in which individuals work, so that the desired performance can be achieved. In the Human Performance Technology (HPT) literature, the classification of performance interventions falls into two research streams: the stream that categorizes interventions as instructional or non-instructional, and the stream that compares learning and non-learning interventions.

Instructional vs. Non-Instructional Interventions

This stream of research gained currency in the 1980s and 1990s as the traditional field of instructional design began to expand to include needs assessment as a core component of the design process, shifting the focus to performance as well as instruction (Gilbert, 1978; Harless, 1995; Rodriguez, 1988; Rosenberg, 1996; Rossett, 1987; Stolovich & Keeps, 1999). *Instruction* was deemed to be a very broad category encompassing the entire spectrum of formal learning (Molenda & Russell, 2006), from training events to institution-based education programs, all of which are purposive, controlled, and intended to achieve one or more learning goals.

Van Tiem, Moseley, and Dessinger (2000) as well as various chapters in the performance technology handbook edited by Stolovich and Keeps (1999) summarized the instructional interventions cited most often in the HPT literature:

- **Classroom instruction:** This refers to the traditional face-to-face, one-to-many method of delivering instruction that is still prevalent in many workplace settings.
- **Structured team activities:** A form of group learning involving peer-to-peer as well as instructor-to-learner interaction, this type of intervention is designed to achieve specific, measurable outcomes.
- **Mentoring:** Structured and formal, this is a process whereby two people with different skills and experiences are deliberately paired in order to transfer the skills and experiences from the one who has them to the one who needs them.
- **Multimedia/e-Learning:** HPT deems this to be the integration of multimedia tools and technologies to deliver instruction.
- **On-the-job-training (OJT):** This is a planned process of developing specific task-levels of expertise by having an experienced employee train a novice employee in or near the actual work setting.

- **Distance education and distributed learning:** HPT differentiates these two in terms of the locus of control, with the latter focusing on the needs of individuals seeking immediate access to learning opportunities, tools, and content.
- **Self-directed learning:** This is deemed synonymous with self-paced, on demand learning.
- **Knowledge management:** This refers to the process of acquiring, storing, and managing access to knowledge resources that are relevant to job performance.

"But this looks more like a list of instructional strategies and delivery methods," you say. When viewed through the theoretical lens that draws on the Instructional Design body of knowledge, you are absolutely right. The designer is not likely to think of a team activity as an intervention but rather as an instructional method to support a larger strategy within an instructional intervention, such as a course or a workshop. Nevertheless, the list clearly reflects the basic definition of an intervention, as well as the historic emergence of HPT from classic instructional design theory and practice. Furthermore, HPT practitioners use the same models and methods to create instructional interventions as those used by designers, so that a considerable body of research informs the practices associated with the instructional interventions that HPT practitioners create.

Non-instructional interventions were defined as those that seek to change the contextual circumstances in which people work and, thus, reduce barriers to performance. Barriers to performance can range from individual and personal conditions, such as motivation, engagement, and self-efficacy, to organizational conditions, such as workspace design, technology infrastructure, and compensation. Consequently, it would be nearly impossible to generate an exhaustive list of specific non-instructional interventions. Instead, the performance technology handbook edited by Stolovich and Keeps (1999) groups non-instructional interventions by their targets for improvement, namely: interventions that seek improvements in organizational and job structures (e.g., job descriptions and specifications, quality measures, compensation packages, organizational policies, and practices) and interventions to improve communication and documentation (e.g., performance support tools, enterprise-wide information technology systems, and human resource selection and development).

Learning vs. Non-Learning Interventions

As the field of HPT matured, HPT scholar-practitioners re-classified performance interventions into learning interventions and non-learning interventions. Learning interventions were defined as the range of actions or events that someone initiates to help people acquire new knowledge and skills needed to survive and thrive in the workplace (Stolovich & Keeps, 2007).

Specific learning interventions were placed on a continuum ranging from natural experience and experiential learning on one end of the continuum, to classroom training and self-study on the other end of the continuum. Non-learning interventions were defined as any action or event that either removes an obstacle or adds a facilitative element to performance. Non-learning interventions were classified as (a) performance aids, such as job aids and performance support tools and systems, all providing information and procedures to be called on as needed; (b) environmental interventions, which are adjustments to the work environment such as workspace design or matching the right employees to the right jobs through competency mapping; and (c) emotional interventions, which focus on removing barriers to employee motivation through actions such as incentives, compensation, and benefits. As with the instructional vs. non-instructional classification, this new classification tended to mix strategies and activities.

By the close of the first decade of the twenty-first century, the International Society of Performance Improvement (ISPI) adopted a three-part classification of performance interventions into learning interventions, performance support interventions, and non-learning interventions (Van Tiem, Moseley, & Dessinger, 2012). Learning interventions were deemed to be those that are largely information and learning-based. With this definition, the list of learning interventions expanded to include things such as learning management systems (LMS), social learning, games and simulations, and blended learning. Performance support interventions were defined as those supporting the performer on the job and just in time to either enhance or replace learning. Examples of performance support interventions are job aids, electronic performance support systems (EPSS), documentation and standards, and expert systems grounded in artificial intellegience. The remaining interventions that had previously been classified as non-instructional or as sub-categories of non-learning interventions were refined to target the sources of barriers to performance and focused on development or growth at the individual, departmental or organizational level. For example, development interventions at the individual level would include communities of practice, cultural intellgence, feedback, and coaching and mentoring, with the latter having previously been classified as an instructional intervention. Interventions at the departmental and organizational levels would focus on things like talent management, social media, and strategic planning. This re-classification reflects what Lauer (2006, p. 567) called the "big tent nature" of HPT, whereby the performance improvement specialist focuses on actions that can be taken on an ongoing basis to improve organizational performance, a requirement for business survival.

Given the scope of the HPT practitioner's role, this learning-performance support-all other performance improvement interventions perspective makes sense. The performance improvement specialist is charged with addressing all types of business problems, not just those related to gaps in knowledge, skills,

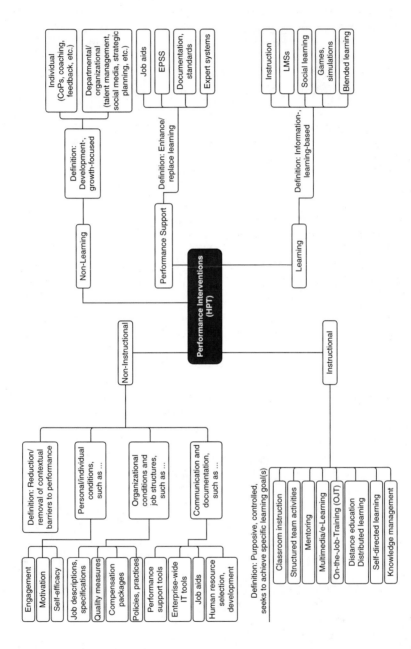

Figure 3.2 Classifications of Performance Interventions in the HPT Literature.

and abilities. As such, the suite of performance improvement interventions in the HPT practitioner's toolbox is larger than the suite of interventions in the learning designer's toolbox. Figure 3.2 provides a graphical representation of the instructional vs. non-instructional and the learning vs. non-learning paradigms in the HPT literature.

Summary

Performance interventions have been framed in slightly different ways in the HRD literature versus the HPT literature. Although both bodies of knowledge make the connection between learning and job performance, HPT tends to cast a wider net that enables the HPT practitioner to utilize a variety of performance improvement solutions that extend beyond individual learning and address performance issues systemically, with some solutions covering an extended period of time so that the solution becomes an integrated component of the organization's method of working. Learning designers traditionally engage in event-based interventions, although some learning opportunities may consist of multiple events over a period of time. Consequently, it is not surprising that the two professions define interventions differently. Nevertheless, the HPT paradigms illustrated in Figure 3.2 are problematic for the learning design professional. Specifically, the differentiation between instructional vs. non-instructional or learning vs. performance support vs. non-learning is not as discrete as it may appear. An intervention may fit the definition of an instructional intervention in that it is purposive and controlled but that same intervention may focus on providing cognitive support rather than the acquisition and retention of knowledge (Rossett & Gautier-Downes, 1991). The Help function in your office productivity software packages, digital user guides for software product end users and other job aids are examples of non-instructional interventions that provide just-in-time assistance without having a specific learning goal. Formal mentoring is another example of a non-instructional intervention that can possess the characteristics of an instructional intervention. Mentoring may target growth and development of an individual employee but may also provide that employee with new knowledge and methods of work to apply and retain that knowledge. Similarly, interventions designed to foster changes to the environmental context do not have learning as a goal but are deemed to be necessary precursors to learning (Ellstrom, 2001; Matthews, 1999). Furthermore, an intervention that focuses, for example, on development at the individual level to strengthen employee cultural intelligence – a non-learning intervention under the HPT paradigm – but consists of a three-day workshop with specific learning goals and online resouces for knowledge reinforcement, then that intervention also fits the definition of a learning intervention. This throws us right back into the terminology soup from which we have been trying to extricate ourselves. We can simplify our lives and save our sanity by taking a slightly different tack by focusing on **who** needs to improve and **what** specifically needs improvement.

The Learning Designer's Wheelhouse

Remember the story in Chapter 1 in which your colleague described his role as the "creator of learning opportunities"? Any intervention that you create in which an individual or group is a direct participant can contribute to learning and, thus, be considered a learning opportunity, regardless of the subject matter of that intervention. For example, if you are designing an intranet portal through which all employees can access company policies and procedures, you are in fact creating a learning opportunity in that employees need to be aware of and, thus, have knowledge about those policies and procedures. Consequently, trying to strictly categorize interventions as learning vs. non-learning or instructional vs. non-instructional may not be the most productive way of organizing the almost infinite number of performance interventions.

A more productive starting point for identifying which performance improvement interventions fall within the learning designer's purview and which do not would be to examine the results of your upfront analysis conducted when a performance problem or challenge is first brought to your attention. That upfront analysis includes a gap/root cause analysis describing

Figure 3.3 Root Causes of Perfomance Gaps: Examples.

differences between the desired performance and the actual performance, along with identification of the reasons for the performance gap (Swanson, 2007). Figure 3.3 provides a sampling of causes labeled A through I:

A   Lack of individual employee knowledge/skills: To support the acquisition or strengthening of skills necessary to perform a specific role/function, interventions to consider include formal training (classroom-based, online, workshops, and seminars), on-the-job-training provided by managers or supervisors, coaching, mentoring, or work shadowing where the employee acquiring the skills/knowledge follows another employee through the workday. Knowledge management is another intervention that addresses lack of skills/knowledge and involves creating, retrieving, and distributing organizational knowledge through computerized databases, while a community of practice (CoP) would enable employees to share their learning with others on an ongoing basis.

B   Lack of resources to perform the job: The nature of the resource gap determines what intervention options to consider. Provision of the lacking resources would be an appropriate intervention, although a business case may have to be made to show that the benefits outweigh the costs of the resources. Resources may range from desktop software tools to additional office equipment to greater access to technical support.

C   Problem(s) with workflow structure/process: It is not uncommon for there to be a disconnect between the way a job has been described and what the employee must actually do to achieve desired performance levels. A redesign of the job description may be the most basic intervention to address this gap. Computerization – i.e., supplementing human performance with hardware and software – may also be considered if employees are required to process large amounts of information rapidly, reliably, and with consistent results.

D   Lack of information at point of need: For work that requires readily accessible information, procedures, or examples, then electronic performance support systems (EPSS), an online resource similar to printed job aids, should be considered. The EPSS would contain digital versions of job aids, such as printed checklists, decision tables, worksheets, glossaries, and flowcharts that are available to guide and facilitate a specfic role or function.

E   Lack of leadership/change in leadership: This requires an enterprise-wide intervention and may incorporate leadership programs to clarify vision, mission, strategies, as well as involvement of employees at different levels of the organization.

F   Lack of accountability/consequences for poor performance: If employees are not meaningfully rewarded or do not perceive the reward system as being fair, interventions, such as incentives/consequences and compensation systems, are among the possible interventions to be considered.

G Unclear expectations: For new hires, onboarding programs that include complete and consistent information about the organization, its vision, functions, policies, and procedures set the tone for employee confidence and trust. At the individual and work group levels, performance appraisal as an ongoing process that includes defining and setting performance goals, measurement, and feedback reduces the likelihood of disconnects between employees and management around performance expectations.

H Inadequate feedback: Feedback systems that provide timely information about an employee's performance and its impact on the department/business unit/organization should be considered. Ideally, this would be part of a whole-system intervention that addresses accountability and expectations.

I Problems with recruitment/selection/promotion policies and/or practices: This calls for a variety of Human Resource interventions associated with misalignment of a performer with the required performance throughout the employee's tenure and involves gathering and analyzing past behaviors and experiences in a way as to predict outcomes of future performance.

Causes A, B, C, and D relate to employee knowledge, skills, abilities, or tools to do their jobs and are the purview of the Learning Design and Technologies professional, while Causes E, F, G, H, and I relate to organizational issues that affect employee attitudes and willingness to perform, the domain of the HPT professional. In *E-Suite Views*, Dr. Claudia Barnett, Performance Improvement Consultant and CEO of CGB Associates, offers her take on the suite of interventions that learning professionals and performance improvement professionals need to have at their disposal.

SvR: New professionals, or those with only four or five years of experience under their belt, are trying to differentiate between learning interventions, non-learning interventions, and so forth. What would you tell them about getting to the heart of that? I mean, training is never the answer to everything. But how do you tease that out, particularly for someone who doesn't know what's going on at the client side?

CB: Well, the first thing I would draw their attention to is that they really have to do a gap analysis. It's all been done on several levels and a lot of people want to take the shortcut and say, "Well, you know I can help you, I can design this, I can do that" without doing that major step. What I would suggest to the individuals is that they really make an investment in finding out what the needs are. "What do you want? You know, what's your end result? What does it look like to you?" Because the thing about it is, if we're not speaking the same language, we're not going to have the same result. And I think sometimes what happens is that we're so gung ho, you know, into problem solving, we don't know what that really looks like on their end. We are making the assumption that it should look a certain way and it may not.

SvR: Sure. Sure and I think that maybe the challenge for those who haven't been in the profession that long, they're kind of scared to ask the questions.

CB: Sure. Sure. Because if they don't ask proper questions, it will seem as if they're not prepared or ignorant.

SvR: So, how did they go over that?

CB: Be confident in what you do know, that I'll say. Because I think that you're really comfortable in what you know. You want to make sure the things that you are really sure of, you could speak to those things intelligently.

SvR: Right.

CB: There are going to be times where you are going to be totally ignorant. And you know what? That's okay. But there should be certain areas in which you should be very proficient and maybe, take one area and master that one area. Don't try to be all things to all people. Let me give you an example. I have been a performance improvement person for a number of years and the last, how would I say, eight years, I've reinvented myself. And what I did was, I tackled an area which I did not have really any knowledge base about and that was healthcare. I decided to go into healthcare and what I did was, I became a trainer in the area of electronic medical records. And once I did that, I focused on optimization and I started working with one organization that wanted to go with a particular brand of software. What they charged for upgrades, I thought of showing them the difference in terms of, "This is what you would need for optimization." So, I say all that to say, now, I'm proficient in that area. Now, of course, over the years, I have been training for a long time. And I have mastered the area of training, but I wanted to do something different and that's why I said I had to reinvent myself because times are changing and you have to be willing to change with those times. The question is: What are you doing for yourself to reinvent yourself when there is a need?

SvR: Absolutely. Absolutely. One question I often hear from students of instructional design, those who are just getting into the field, is: "Where does the instructional designer's role end and the human performance improvement specialist's role begin? Do they overlap?"

CB: They do overlap because the thing about it is: To design something, you're going to have to be very proficient in asking pointed questions so that you're giving a good product at the end. So,

	you're working to improve the performance. Sometimes, you are going to ask the same question as a person who is doing performance improvement only.
SvR:	Right.
CB:	Now, the question is: Is your instructional design a proficient and performance improvement strategy?
SvR:	And vice versa?
CB:	*And vice versa and vice versa.*

Making a Smooth Handoff

Dilbert's© boss often accuses his employees of passing the buck when they say that some task is not part of their job. Part of the problem there is that the boss does not know – and Dilbert© would probably add, *care* – what the various roles and responsibilities are of his employees. Fortunately, most bosses are committed to a clear definition of roles and responsibilities in their organizations, to ensure that all functional areas are working toward achieving the organization's goals. Doing other people's jobs is not only time-consuming but counterproductive.

That said, the learning designer whose analyses indicate that an issue requires an intervention that is outside the scope of his/her professional area of expertise needs a way to identify and hand off the issue to the appropriate person(s) smoothly and with evidence that a handoff is indeed necessary. Here are some concrete actions you can take to ensure that there is not even a hint of buck-passing:

- **Trust but verify.** You may have heard that expression used in the context of political discussions. Here, it refers to validating the results of the upfront analysis with your stakeholders. In fact, validation should apply to almost any data collection and analysis. Whether you conducted the upfront analysis yourself or you are working with an analysis that someone else conducted, you need to be sure that key decision-makers, subject matter experts, and representatives of the group(s) targeted for the intervention have a shared understanding of the scope, severity, and business impact of the gap between the current and the desired performance. Even if you work for a small organization and bear sole responsibility for L&D, colleagues in other areas of the organization can help you to (a) affirm your interpretation of the findings; (b) identify which gaps have the highest priority based on business needs; and (c) uncover barriers to implementing performance interventions, such as a history of previous interventions that have failed, pre-established cost-effectiveness thresholds, or a culture that deems one type of intervention, such as training, to be the most acceptable solution to any performance gap. The desired outcome of the validation process is a list of criteria for determining which interventions have the highest priority.

- **Mark out your wheelhouse.** Using the selection criteria created in the validation process, identify which interventions fall within your purview and which do not. Here is your opportunity to demonstrate your abilities as a trusted advisor by indicating who and/or where the most appropriate resources can be found to design interventions that are outside your areas of expertise. For example, if a high-priority gap identified in the validation process concerned inadequate feedback about employee performance, you might recommend that HR put together a small team to work on optimization of the performance review process. Conversely, if lack of awareness of organizational policies on career development and advancement opportunities was deemed to be a high-priority gap, you would claim this as part of your area of expertise because it speaks to employee knowledge and you would offer intervention alternatives that would fill that knowledge gap.

- **Get it in writing.** Your goal here is to share what was discussed and agreed during the first two steps with other decision-makers and obtain authorization for assigning the agreed-upon performance interventions to the respective functional areas for further development. This makes it clear who is responsible and accountable for which interventions as well as why each performance intervention lives in its respective occupational/functional area.

Intervention Selection Self-Check

You are the senior designer in the L&D group of your organization. Your supervisor has just emailed you a two-page document titled *In-house Customer Service Call Center Performance Analysis* report. Prepared by a work group outside of L&D, the report notes an increase in the last six months in the number of complaints about how long it takes for customer service issues to be resolved. Two particularly troubling issues are: (a) call times have increased for call center representatives at all levels of experience; and (b) lack of proficiency with call system software despite completion of training in the last 12 months. Your supervisor asks you to prepare a plan for solving the performance problem and have that plan ready in one week. What would be the first step in coming up with a plan?

a) Contact the person(s) who prepared the analysis and ask for more information;

b) Review the report to see if there are specific statements about desired performance levels vs. current performance levels, along with reasons for gaps;

c) Put together a group of key stakeholders to fill in information missing from the report; and

d)   Create a list of potential interventions on your own, then validate them with your supervisor.

Of these four options, (b) is the best choice. You cannot fill in missing information (option c) or create a list of potential interventions (option d) or even ask the report writer for more information (option a) without confirming whether or not the report you received clearly describes the current state vs. the desired state in observable, measurable terms, and what the impact is on the business (e.g., lost customers and, thus, revenue). Once you have established what is (not) detailed in the report, you can contact the report writer to see if he/she collected data that was not included in the report. You would then move to option (c) to fill in the blanks and validate the gaps/root causes, as well as brainstorm potential interventions.

Food for Thought

1   What types of performance improvement interventions has your organization implemented in the last three years? Which ones involved an intervention other than training (and why)?
2   What is the process for selecting performance improvement interventions in your organization? What are the strengths and weaknesses of that process?
3   Have you ever been involved in the selection of a performance improvement intervention? How does that experience compare with what you have learned in this chapter about intervention selection?

Up Next

In this chapter, we have (a) reviewed the key constructs related to learning, instruction, and performance interventions that are addressed in the scholarly literature; (b) described the performance interventions that learning designers are expected to be able to create and implement; and (c) identified which performance interventions to hand off to other functional occupations. Next, we will take a closer look at the processes, tools, and techniques for identifying the causes of performance problems, the desired changes in performance behavior(s), and how this informs the intervention selection process.

References

Alexander, P. A., Schallert, D. L., & Reynolds, R. E. (2009). What is learning anyway? A topographical perspective considered. *Educational Psychologist*, 44(3), 176–92.
Argyris, C., Putnam, R., & McLain Smith, D. (1985). *Action Science*. San Francisco, CA: Jossey-Bass.

Aziz, D. M. (2013). What's in a name? A comparison of instructional systems design, organization development, and human performance technology/improvement and their contributions to performance improvements. *Performance Improvement, 52*(6), 28–35.

Bereiter, C., & Scardamalia, M. (1989). Intentional learning as a goal of instruction. In L. B. Resnick (Ed.), *Knowing, Learning, and Instruction: Essays in Honor of Robert Glaser* (pp. 361–92). Hillsdale, NJ: Lawrence Erlbaum Associates.

Berg, S., & Chyung, S. (2008). Factors that influence informal learning in the workplace. *Journal of Workplace Learning, 20*(4), 229–44.

Choi, W., & Jacobs, R. (2011). Influences of formal learning, personal learning orientation, and supportive learning environment on informal learning. *Human Resource Development Quarterly, 22*(3), 239–57.

Cross, J. (2007). *Informal Learning: Rediscovering the Natural Pathways That Inspire Innovation and Performance.* San Francisco, CA: John Wiley & Sons.

Cseh, M., & Manikoth, N. (2011). Invited reaction: Influences of formal learning, personal learning orientation, and supportive learning environment on informal learning. *Human Resource Development Quarterly, 22*(3), 259–63.

Cummings, T. G., & Worley, C. G. (2015). *Organization Development & Change* (10th ed.). Stamford, CT: Cengage Learning.

De Houwer, J., Barnes-Holmes, D., & Moors, A. (2013). What is learning? On the nature and merits of a functional definition of learning. *Psychonomic Bulletin & Review, 20*(4), 631–42.

Driscoll, M. P. (2000). *Psychology of Learning for Instruction.* Boston, MA: Allyn & Bacon.

Ellinger, A. (2005). Contextual factors influencing informal learning in a workplace setting: the case of "reinventing itself company." *Human Resource Development Quarterly, 16*(3), 389–415.

Ellstrom, P. E. (2001). Integrating learning and work: Problems and prospects. *Human Resource Development Quarterly, 12*(4), 421–35.

Enos, M. D., Kehrhahn, M. T., & Bell, A. (2003). Informal learning and the transfer of learning: How managers develop proficiency. *Human Resource Development Quarterly, 14*(4), 369–87.

Eraut, M. (2000). Non-formal learning and tacit knowledge in professional work. *British Journal of Educational Psychology, 70,* 9–22.

Fiorella, L., & Mayer, R. E. (2015). *Learning as a Generative Activity: Eight Learning Strategies that Promote Understanding.* New York, NY: Cambridge University Press.

Fleming, M., & Levie, H. (1978). *Instructional Message Design: Principles from the Behavioral Sciences.* Englewood Cliffs, NJ: Educational Technology Publications.

Galbraith, D. D., & Fouch, S. E. (2007). Principles of adult learning: Application to safety training. *Professional Safety, 52*(9), 35–40.

Garrick, J. (1998). *Informal Learning in the Workplace.* London, UK: Routledge.

Gherardi, S. (2006). *Organizational Knowledge: The Texture of Workplace Learning.* Malden, MA: Blackwell Publishing.

Gilbert, T. (1978). The behavior engineering model. In T. Gilbert (Ed.), *Human Competence: Engineering Worth Performance* (pp. 73–105). New York, NY: McGraw-Hill.

Goldstein, I., & Ford, J. (2002). *Training in Organizations: Needs Assessment, Development, and Evaluation* (4th ed.). Belmont, CA: Wadsworth.

Harless, J. (1995). Performance technology skills in business: Implications for preparation. *Performance Improvement Quarterly, 8*(4), 75–88.

Holton, E. F. (1999a). An integrated model of performance domains: Bounding the theory and practice. *Performance Improvement Quarterly, 12*(3), 95–118.

Holton, E. F. (1999b). Performance domains and their boundaries. *Advances in Developing Human Resources, 1*(1), 26–46.

IBSTPI. (2014). Instructional Designer Competencies – Welcome to ibstpi. Retrieved from http://ibstpi.org/instructional-design-competencies/.

Jacobs, R. (2003). *Structured On-the-Job Training: Unleashing Employee Expertise in the Workplace.* San Francisco, CA: Berrett-Koehler.

Jacobs, R., & Park, Y. (2009). A proposed conceptual framework of workplace learning: Implications for theory development and research in human resource development. *Human Resource Development Review, 8*(2), 133–50.

Jonassen, D. H., & Grabowski, B. L. (2011). *Handbook of Individual Differences, Learning and Instruction.* New York, NY: Routledge.

Lauer, M. J. (2006). Interventions at the workplace and organizational levels. In J. A. Pershing (Ed.), *Handbook of Human Performance Technology* (3rd ed., pp. 567–9). San Francisco, CA: Pfeiffer.

Lohman, M. (2005). A survey of factors influencing the engagement of two professional groups in informal workplace learning activities. *Human Resource Development Quarterly, 16*(4), 501–27.

Malcom, J., Hodkinson, P., & Colley, H. (2003). The interrelationships between informal and formal learning. *Journal of Workplace Learning, 15*(7/8), 313–18.

Marsick, V. (2003). Invited reaction: Informal learning and the transfer of learning: How managers develop proficiency. *Human Resource Development Quarterly, 14*(4), 389–95.

Marsick, V., & Volpe, M. (1999). The nature and need for informal learning. *Advances in Developing Human Resources, 1*(3), 1–9.

Martin, J., McKay, E., & Hawkins, L. (2010). Educating a multidisciplinary human services workforce: Using a blended approach. In J. Martin & L. Hawkins (Eds.), *Information Communication Technologies for Human Services Education and Delivery: Concepts and Cases* (pp. 1–14). Hershey, PA: IGI Global.

Matthews, P. (1999). Workplace learning: Developing a holistic model. *The Learning Organization, 6*(1), 18–29.

Mayer, R. E. (2003). The promise of multimedia learning: Using the same instructional design methods across different media. *Learning and Instruction, 13*(2), 125–39.

McGuire, D., & Gubbins, C. (2010). The slow death of formal learning: A polemic. *Human Resource Development Review, 9*(3), 249–65.

Min, R., Kommers, P., Voss, H., & van Dijkum, C. (2000). A concept model for learning. *Journal of Interactive Learning Research, 11*(3/4), 485–506.

Molenda, M., & Russell, J. D. (2006). Instruction as an intervention. In J. A. Pershing (Ed.), *Handbook of Human Performance Technology* (3rd ed., pp. 335–69). San Francisco, CA: Pfeiffer.

Newby, T. J., Stepich, D. A., Lehman, J. D., & Russell, J. D. (1996). *Instructional Technology for Teaching and Learning: Designing Instruction, Integrating Computers, and Using Media.* Englewood Cliffs, NJ: Prentice-Hall.

Noe, R. (2008). *Employee Training and Development.* New York, NY: McGraw-Hill.

Rik, M. I. N. (2003). Simulation and discovery learning in an age of zapping and searching: Learning models. *Turkish Online Journal of Distance Education, 4*(2), 1–19.

Rodriguez, S. R. (1988). Needs assessment and analysis: Tools for change. *Journal of Instructional Development, 11*(1), 23–8.

Rosenberg, M. (1996). Human performance technology. In R. Craig (Ed.), *The ASTD Training & Development Handbook* (4th ed., pp. 370–93). New York, NY: McGraw-Hill.

Rossett, A. (1987). *Training Needs Assessment.* Englewood Cliffs, NJ: Educational Technology Publications.

Rossett, A. (2009). *First Things Fast: A Handbook for Performance Analysis* (2nd ed.). San Francisco, CA: Pfeiffer.

Rossett, A., & Gautier-Downes, J. (1991). *A Handbook of Job Aids*. San Diego, CA: Pfeiffer.

Rowden, R. (2007). *Workplace Learning: Principles and Practice*. Malabar, FL: Krieger Publishing.

Shipton, H., Dawson, J., West, M., & Patterson, M. (2002). Learning in manufacturing organizations: What factors predict effectiveness? *Human Resources Development International*, 5(1), 55–72.

Stolovich, H. D., & Keeps, E. J. (1999). What is human performance technology? In H. D. Stolovich & E. J. Keeps (Eds.), *Handbook of Human Performance Technology* (2nd ed., pp. 3–23). San Francisco, CA: Pfeiffer.

Stolovich, H. D., & Keeps, E. J. (2007). Performance improvement interventions. *HSA e-Xpress*, 6(1). Available online at www.hsa-lps.com/E_News/ENews_Jan07/HSA_e-Xpress_Jan07.htm.

Swanson, R. (2007). *Analysis for Improving Performance: Tools for Diagnosing Organizations and Documenting Workplace Expertise*. Oakland, CA: Berrett-Koehler Publishers.

Tannenbaum, S., Beard, R., McNall, L., & Salas, E. (2010). Informal learning and development in organizations. In S. Kozlowski & E. Salas (Eds.), *Learning, Training and Development in Organizations* (pp. 303–32). New York, NY: Routledge.

Uden, L., & Beaumont, C. (2006). *Technology and Problem-Based Learning*. Hershey, PA: Information Science Publishing.

Van Tiem, D. M., Moseley, J. L., & Dessinger, J. C. (2000). *The Fundamentals of Performance Technology: A Guide to Improving People, Process and Performance*. Washington, DC: International Society for Performance Improvement.

Van Tiem, D. M., Moseley, J. L., & Dessinger, J. C. (2012). *Fundamentals of Performance Improvement* (3rd ed.). San Francisco, CA: Pfeiffer.

Watkins, K., & Marsick, V. (1992). Towards a theory of informal and incidental learning in organizations. *International Journal of Lifelong Education*, 11(4), 287–300.

Westover, J. H. (2009). Lifelong learning: Effective adult learning strategies and implementation for working professionals. *International Journal of Learning*, 16(1), 435–43.

Wuestewald, T. (2016). Adult learning in executive development programs. *Adult Learning*, 27(2), 68–75.

4 Needs Assessment and Analysis
Is Instruction the Solution?

In the previous chapter, we focused on a variety of performance improvement interventions in the scholarly literature. We also described the interventions that learning designers are usually expected to be able to create and implement versus interventions that are handed off to other functional occupations. Prior to selecting potential intervention alternatives, however, the designer should have determined in advance what performance gaps need to be filled, what the causes of those gaps are, and what types of interventions can address each of those gaps. In other words, designers need to do some research to ensure that they have a firm grasp of the issues to be addressed, why the issues need to be addressed, and why the issues are affecting performance.

> *Research takes too long; let's put together some resources for people to use.*
> *We don't need research, we know what we need.*
> *Analysis-paralysis; just put some training slides online with maybe a quiz or two.*

If you have gotten similar reactions when you asked about conducting some research before developing an instructional intervention, you are not alone. Despite the rise of data-driven decision-making and a growing number of research studies showing the correlation between data-driven decision-making, profitability and productivity, when it comes to improving performance, there is often some reluctance to gather and analyze data. The preference for the tried-but-not-necessarily-true solutions, such as training, remains. This reluctance is due, in large part, to (a) not knowing where to start; (b) lack of clarity about the human and financial resources required to collect and analyze data systematically; and (c) misconceptions about the turnaround time required for data collection and analysis. Nevertheless, decision-makers are regularly asking Learning and Development (L&D) professionals to provide an evidence-based rationale for funding L&D interventions.

The value of using data to guide the selection of performance improvement interventions can be traced back to the beginning of the twentieth century, when Frederick Taylor posited that by analyzing work and breaking a job down to its component parts through data gathering, the best way of performing that work would be found and employees could then be taught to perform based on the joining of individual skills and work methods (Taylor, 1913). Taylor's work provided a foundation for conducting assessments to identify individual and organizational needs and for using the needs assessments to inform performance improvement interventions. Employed in a variety of fields, such as healthcare, transportation, education, and disaster recovery planning, needs assessments produce quantitative as well as qualitative data that help an organization's management to identify and prioritize areas where strategies and resources can be applied most effectively. In workforce planning, needs assessments are used to uncover performance deficiencies and select areas for which an intervention strategy can be developed and applied to correct that deficiency. Needs assessments can be conducted at the organizational level to investigate problems and/or opportunities in operations, systems, processes, and policies, as well as in the organization's external environment (competition, suppliers, industry regulators, etc.). At the individual level, needs assessments focus on an individual employee's contributions to improving performance, the knowledge, skills and abilities employees used to accomplish tasks, and the organizational environment in which employees must accomplish those tasks. Often, a needs assessment will uncover factors or conditions that do not directly contribute to filling a knowledge or skills gap but contribute indirectly to performance by increasing motivation or engagement. These conditions are generally considered to be "wants" rather than needs:

> Needs are defined as a gap between current and desired skill or knowledge levels, while wants are defined as those things that would be nice to have but that may not necessarily contribute to furthering individual and organizational performance. Wants, however, should not be entirely dismissed as being noncontributory to further the goals of the organization. Many times wants and needs represent the same things to different groups. If viewed objectively, both individual as well as organizational needs and wants can be met simultaneously. (McLelland, 1995, p. 14)

In practice, there is no common understanding of what constitutes a needs assessment. In the Instructional Design literature, needs assessment is sometimes deemed to be synonymous with needs analysis (see, for example, Andrews & Goodson, 1980; Cooperstein & Kocevar-Weidinger, 2004; Panke, 2016) and the starting point for designing a training intervention. Examples of the conflation of assessment and analysis can also be found in the Human Resources Development (HRD) literature (van Eerde, Simon Tang, & Talbot, 2008). The Human Performance Technology (HPT) literature deems needs analysis to be a component of the needs assessment process (Christensen, 2015; Moseley & Heaney, 1994), along with performance analysis to identify and prioritize gaps in individual, group, or organizational performance. Kaufman and Watkins (2000) argued that this lack of consistency in definitions and terminology "seems almost to encourage a number of confusions that 'allow' for lack of precision and consequences" (p. 24), making it challenging for professionals in our field to prove the value of what it is that we do.

This book takes a holistic view of needs assessment as a process that begins with the identification of the organization's strategic business goals, which, in turn, determine the needs for employee on-the-job performance. The needs assessment process includes the identification of factors that may impact on-the-job performance (e.g., employee motivation, knowledge/skills, supervisor involvement, benefits, and compensation). Once performance gaps have been identified and prioritized against the business goals, a detailed analysis of each of those gaps is conducted and used to make recommendations to management about what corrective actions should (not) be taken. Furthermore, the ability to conduct a needs assessment is one of IBSTPI's advanced instructional designer competencies and, thus, is critical to career advancement.

In this chapter, we will:

- Review the development of needs assessment definitions and models in the various scholarly bodies of knowledge;
- Examine the various ways that practitioners have translated theories and models of needs assessment into practice;
- Describe the opportunities for learning designers to capitalize on their existing knowledge of data collection tools and techniques to conduct needs assessments; and
- Summarize some lessons learned about needs assessment.

Needs Assessment: What the Scholars Say

Definitions

Scholars have long wrestled with the concept and definition of needs assessment and where needs assessment fits within the various instructional design models or within the context of human performance improvement. McGehee and Thayer (1961) focused on training needs assessment, stating that it consists of three levels of analysis: (a) organization analysis; (b) operations analysis (now called task or work analysis); and (c) man analysis (now called individual or person analysis), with the most effective needs assessments addressing all three levels of analysis. Burton and Merrill (1977) defined needs assessment as "a systematic process for determining goals, identifying discrepancies between goals and the status quo, and establishing priorities for action" (p, 21). However, their focus was exclusively on educational settings, with the assumption that goals are either course goals or program goals and center on what instructional materials should be included in the course or program. Kaufman and Gavora (1993) sought to extend McGehee and Thayer's levels of analysis to include societal outcomes of organizational activities, particularly for public sector organizations. Guerra (2003) suggested expanding the traditional ADDIE to AADDIE (Assessment, Analysis, etc.) to call out gaps in performance results before starting the instructional design process. Underlying all of these definitions is the assumption that needs assessment results will be used to create instruction.

As the literature expanded to include research and scholarship around performance improvement, needs assessment began to be defined without the built-in assumption that the results would be used to create instruction. Rossett (1992) described needs assessment as a means of providing information about optimal performance, actual performance, how key sources feel, what's causing the problem, and solutions to close gaps between optimal and actual performance. The solutions may or may not include instruction. Scholars also began to differentiate between needs assessment and needs analysis. Kaufman, Rojas, and Mayer (1993) defined needs assessment as a process that serves to identify gaps between current results and desired ones, to prioritize gaps, and to select the most important ones to be addressed, whereas needs analysis is the process used to analyze the causes of the gaps. To ensure that individual performance improvement remained grounded in the results of the needs assessment process, Herbert and Doverspike (1990) sought to integrate performance appraisals into the needs assessment process.

In a review of the literature published from 1970 to 1988, Benjamin (1989) concluded that the literature defines needs assessment as a process that determines and prioritizes gaps between current and required outcomes, with the most important gaps selected for resolution prior to a detailed analysis of needs. The needs analysis breaks down the already prioritized need(s) into their component parts to flesh out causes and identify potential solutions. However, Benjamin argued that the two need to be viewed not as separate processes but rather as part of a holistic effort to identify problems, causes of those problems, and potential directions for resolution of those problems. When integrated into an organization's strategic planning process, needs assessment can provide data about the costs of ignoring gaps in results versus the costs of closing those gaps, preparing for the process of selecting appropriate solutions while building shared commitment to the organization's future direction (Leigh, 2006).

Watkins, Leigh, Platt, and Kaufman (1998) also differentiated needs assessment from needs analysis, stating a needs assessment identifies gaps in results, while needs analysis identifies gaps in resources, training, or other deficiencies. The discussion on needs assessment vs. needs analysis also included a differentiation between *needs* and *wants*. Holton, Bates, and Naquin (2000) noted that in assessing training needs in large organizations, there is a reliance on "felt-needs" methodologies that ask employees to simply list or rank desired training courses, with the outcome usually being a list of wants, not needs. Similarly, Kaufman, Oakely-Brown, Watkins, and Leigh (2003) posited that at the organizational level, needs assessments are generally wants assessments, resulting in outcomes that may or may not contribute to the organization's strategic goals.

Needs Assessment Models

In parallel with the development of needs assessment definitions, models for conducting a needs assessment appear in both the Instructional Design literature and in the literature focused on performance improvement. One of the earliest models was developed by Mager and Pipe (1970) to identify performance problems. Designed like a flowchart with decision points to guide you through the analysis, the model begins with the discovery of a problem. The problem needs to be measurable and observable to expose a performance gap. Furthermore, the problem/gap needs to be clearly described so that a proper solution can be implemented. The first and perhaps most important question is whether the performance problem is worth solving. If so, you can then proceed to answer further questions on the flowchart, such as whether there are clear expectations, adequate resources, and whether poor performance is rewarded. Interestingly, the last step in the flowchart is to implement training. Mager and Pipe believed that training should be one of the last interventions the practitioner should consider because training is usually the most expensive intervention. Cheaper alternatives, such as clarifying expectations or simplifying a task, could often achieve the desired correction. Due to its simplicity, the Mager and Pipe model is an extremely easy model to use when attempting to address performance problems. However, this same simplicity may lead to a failure to expose the hidden causes of a performance problem, resulting in limited or no improvement after what the model indicated was the optimal solution was adopted.

Harless's (1973) Front-end Analysis model offers the practitioner a bit more guidance in troubleshooting performance problems and identifying potential solutions. The goals of front-end analysis include (a) isolating performance problems that have potentially high "worth" or value for individual, business unit, or organizational performance; (b) isolating the precise performance deficiencies within the problem area that account for the greatest loss in performance; (c) increasing the probability that the solution to a given problem is effective by matching the cause of the problem to the appropriate type of remedy; (d) increasing the probability that the type of solution selected is the most cost effective; (e) isolating the root cause of the performance problem rather than the symptoms or effects of the problem; and (f) increasing the probability that there is a match between the precise performance deficiency and the individuals who have the deficiency. Harless then constructed 13 questions, shown in Table 4.1, that the practitioner should ask him-/herself before making a decision on an intervention. Harless's model is often described as the first step in

Table 4.1 Front-End Analysis Questions

Questions	*Drill-Down Questions/Indicators*
1. Do we have a problem?	What is the evidence that indicates there is a problem?
2. Do we have a performance problem?	A performance problem is: • Someone is not doing something he/she is expected to do. • Someone is doing something he/she should not be doing. • A prediction of what should or should not be done in the future.
3. How will we know when the problem is solved?	When indicators from the first question are the exception.
4. What is the performance problem?	
5. Should we allocate resources to solve it?	Do the benefits of solving the problem outweigh the costs?
6. What are the possible causes of the problem?	Lack of data, tools, incentives, knowledge, capacity, and motives
7. What evidence bears on each possibility?	
8. What is the probable cause?	Based on questions 6 and 7, what is the probable cause?
9. What general solution type is indicated?	
10. What are the alternate subclasses of solution?	What else could be done to solve the problem?
11. What are the costs, effects, and development times of each solution?	Research the costs of each solution.
12. What are the constraints?	Research the constraints of each solution.
13. What are the overall goals?	What goals would management like to adopt?

Source: Adapted from "An Analysis of Front-End Analysis," by J. Harless, 1973, *Improving Human Performance: A Research Quarterly*, 4, p. 332. Copyright 1973 by the National Society for Performance & Instruction.

the instructional design process to determine whether or not instruction is all part of the solution to the problem (Dick, Carey, & Carey, 2005; Danielson, Lockee, & Burton, 2000). Nevertheless, it is unclear as to how much attention is given to helping practitioners apply the model before creating an intervention.

Gilbert's seminal work on human competence (1978) introduced the Behavior Engineering Model (BEM), which separated performance problems into the individual or person level and the environmental level. At the individual level, the model looked at performance-supporting factors related to information (knowledge, skills), instrumentation (capacity), and motivation (motives). Performance-supporting factors at the environmental level centered on data and feedback, tools and resources, and consequences, rewards, and incentives. Although performance improvement practitioners deem BEM to be the gold standard of cause analysis, i.e., the means of determining *why* a performance gap exists, the model has been criticized for not including all performance-support factors in the environment, nor does it help the practitioner to flesh out exactly where in the environment the cause of the performance gap lies (see, for example, the critique by Marker, 2007).

In the third edition of their book, Mager and Pipe (1997) fleshed out their original flowchart to address both training and non-training interventions as part of the set of solutions to apply following needs assessment. For each step in their flowchart, a series of questions can help guide one through each decision point. The model started with describing the performance deficiency (Step 1), followed by the question of whether the problem is worth fixing (Step 2). Evaluating whether the problem is worth fixing usually included a cost effectiveness analysis of the potential procedures, which is helpful in solving performance problems. Steps 3 and 4 determined whether non-training solutions exist for solving the performance problem, particularly for performance barriers, such as unclear expectations, unclear performance measures, inadequate resources, and rewards/consequences not directly linked to the desired performance. The non-training solutions are consistent with Gilbert's (1978) environmental factors in the Behavior Engineering Model (BEM). Mager and Pipe called these non-training solutions a "fast fix" to the performance problem. Step 5 determined whether there are training needs, emphasizing that only a lack of skills and knowledge warrants training. Steps 6 and 7 reflected the evaluation of the solution. In sum, Mager and Pipe's model emphasized cost-effectiveness in solving performance problems, such as determining whether the performance problem is worth fixing at all, choosing cheaper non-training solutions over training solutions, and identifying simpler solutions.

In 1998, Watkins, Leigh, Platt and Kaufman conducted a review of needs assessments models documented in 14 books and 16 peer-reviewed journal articles published between 1978 and 1997, noting that each model was geared to a different target audience (education, corporate, and government), had a different focus (e.g., organizational results, acquisition of skills, and application of skills), described different functional processes (continuous improvement, evaluation, guidelines for prioritization, etc.), and utilized different criteria (tools and methods, goals/objectives, and data sources). The authors saw the challenge with these models as being the almost exclusive focus on training interventions rather than on the results to be achieved through performance improvement. They concluded their literature review by offering a series of five if-then questions (shown in Figure 4.1) to help organizations determine which assessment model(s) is (are) a good fit for their respective organizations. Each of the five if-questions refers to the target audience of the needs assessments, followed by the then-statements that identify what types of results can be addressed

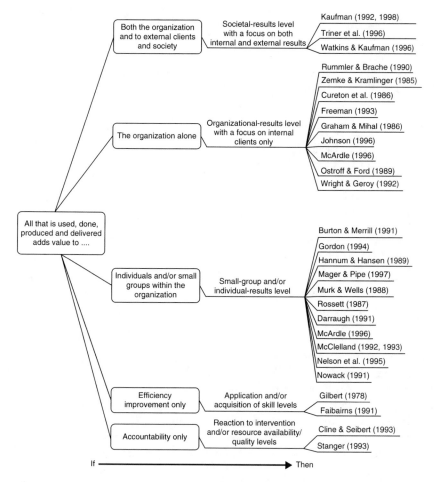

Figure 4.1 Needs Assessment Models in the Literature: 1978–1997.

(Adapted from "Needs Assessment – A Digest, Review, and Comparison of Needs Assessment Literature" by R. Watkins, D. Leigh, W. Platt, and R. Kaufman, 1998, *Performance Improvement*, 37(7), 40–52. Copyright 1998 by John Wiley & Sons, Inc.)

by an given needs assessment model and the scholarly publications that best represent those models. For example, if an organization wants to ensure that all of its activities add value to both the organization and to its external clients and society as a whole, then it would implement a needs assessment model that focuses on results at the societal level. The three needs assessment models that focus on societal results are Kaufman's Mega Planning model (1992, 1998), Triner, Greenberry, and Watkins's Training Needs Assessment (TNA) model (1996), and Watkins and Kaufman's update on needs assessment model selection (1996). In a later publication, the authors affirmed the results of their 1998 literature review and added the following:

> The model you and your organization select as a basis for needs assessment initiatives should emphasize the difference between ends and means, focusing on the what before selecting the how. It should be applied in the service of internal as well as external clients and beneficiaries of the organizational actions. The model should also be malleable in order to facilitate revisions to processes informed by data rather than solely by preferences. (Leigh, Watkins, Platt, & Kaufman, 2000, p. 92)

Summary

With the variety of needs assessment models discussed in the literature, it is no wonder that practitioners grapple with identifying the optimal way to apply the models – either in their entirety or specific elements – to their workplace contexts. Like everything else in the learning professions, there is no one size that fits all.

Conducting a Needs Assessment: What the Practitioners Do

Just as individuals vary in their workplace performance, organizations vary in their commitment to and adoption of needs assessment as a means of enhancing organizational development and improving individual and group performance. Some organizations use needs assessments proactively to identify opportunities to improve performance; others use needs assessments in response to the consequences of below-target results, while others use them continuously as part of a continuous improvement program. Practitioners agree that needs assessment is essential to talent development and workforce planning (see, for example, Ketter, 2016; Society of Human Resource Management, 2015). However, practitioners often find it challenging to implement needs assessment as a regular component of their organization's planning processes:

> In addition to lacking the influence (and likely the culture in the business setting) required for conducting a comprehensive needs assessment, practitioners are saddled with two other challenges. First,

to be valued, a needs assessment must link the data that were gathered and analyzed to the drivers (i.e., priorities) of the organization's business model. For example, a high-tech company that has "innovation" as a priority may be less interested in improving efficiency and more interested in building knowledge assets (acquiring patents, expanding R&D). In this case, a needs assessment focusing on efficient operations is not likely to play well in a company driven by innovation. The second challenge facing practitioners is that many of the performance improvement models are overly complex, lack a systemic perspective, and/or are too mechanistic to be of value. (Wedman, 2014, p. 49)

There are a few published case studies in which organizations describe their needs assessment processes, along with what works and what does not work when conducting needs assessments. For example, Barker Steege, Marra, and Jones (2012) described an application of Wedman's Performance Pyramid approach to needs assessment in the U.S. Army. The Performance Pyramid consists of a model accompanied by a set of data gathering tools grounded in the belief that in order to accomplish something of significance, vision, resources, and a support system must be in place and aligned with each other (Wedman, 2016). Although Barker Steege et al. praised the Performance Pyramid for its ease of use and holistic structure, they noted the model's inability to assist in taking a deep dive into the performance issues that are identified. Lundberg, Elderman, Ferrell, and Harper (2010) described the application of a needs assessment process that combined elements from Harless's (1973) front-end analysis and Gilbert's (1978) BEM to assess performance needs at a retailer. The key lessons learned by the retailer focused on the importance of using a variety of data analysis tools to ensure full comprehension of the situation and focus on the right issues for solution development. There are also industry-specific guides created by professional associations to help organizations in that industry sector customize the needs assessment process. For example, the Aspen Institute published a practitioner's needs assessment guide for companies in the manufacturing sector (Yatie, Shapira, & Roessner, 1995), while the Federal Government provides multiple professional development opportunities around needs assessment for its L&D professionals (Office of Personnel Management, n.d.).

Organizations are still wrestling with what constitutes a needs assessment, a performance analysis, or a needs analysis, as well as when and how to conduct them. In the fourth of our series of *E-Suite Views*, here is what Russ Powell, Principal and Training and Development Consultant at Peregrine Performance Group, has to say about needs assessment, performance analysis, and needs analysis:

SvR: One of the key competencies for learning designers is the ability to conduct a needs assessment to identify appropriate design solution strategies, but more and more employers expect the designer to be able to create learning and performance improvement solutions, and to do this requires the knowledge of how to do a performance analysis. Thinking like a designer for a moment and thinking back over the years when you were first getting into this field, how does the performance analysis differ from what the entry-level designer knows as needs analysis?

RP: I think we have different definitions on those kinds of things, depending on who you talk to. I think of the needs analysis as almost like when you go in to see the doctor and there is somebody up front who kind of does a quick workup to get the basics done: "What is the problem?" "Where does it hurt?" That kind of thing, and then they pass it over to the doctor. The needs analysis is kind of like that. The performance analysis is when you are really getting into the nitty-gritty of the diagnosis. They are actually trying to figure out what is the problem, the behavior that is not happening that should be happening.

SvR: Right.

RP: To me, it is so many different skills. The needs analysis needs to follow that kind of interviewing and kind of getting the lay of the land. The performance analysis is where you're really paying attention to the tasks somebody performs. I honed my skills in the Coast Guard. We had a lot of time, and money, to spend with the performers and analyze how they did what they did, and walk them back saying, "You know, I am not getting all this. Can you walk me back and tell me how this works?" and those kinds of things. So, you need a lot of attention to details, skills to understand the performance and how it works. Flowcharts are often common for the performance analysis. Is that something that answers it?

SvR: Yes, it does, because when students are first learning how to become designers, needs analysis or needs assessment already assumes that instruction is part of the solution; and so, the needs analysis tends to concentrate on what kind of instruction, who, etc.

RP: Right, and the tasks that need to be performed, how those work, that is a big part of it, to me. I may be jumping the gun a little bit, you know, because in performance analysis, you may just be discovering the tasks and then you get into task analysis when you really dig into how the task is performed.

SvR: So, bottom line: The performance analysis is much more holistic in terms of the relationship to what is going on in that department or unit or organization as opposed to, "Okay, let us see what the learning needs are."

RP: Yeah, that is well said.

SvR: Can you share a story about how actually doing a performance analysis either helped or hindered you with a client and what your key take-aways were?

RP: Well, I think I could spend about an hour on that question. What I think about first is: I run my own business and just diving into what we need to do, the performance analysis often gets in the way. If the client wants something tomorrow and, you know, as a seasoned professional, I know I can give that to you but it is not going to work, I really need to go back and do a performance analysis. So, just the fact that I am raising a flag, it will take another whatever it is, you know, a week, two weeks, or a month, or whatever, but to really understand this problem and come back with some specific diagnosis, and I don't have a specific time. But people don't want that. So, it is a simple problem but people just don't want to do it.

SvR: Can you say more about *why* they are reluctant to do so?

RP: Because it takes a certain amount of time before they can clearly identify that it is a training problem. So, we were working with a cellular company, and we were fixed on sales at this point, and what they were trying to do was get ... you have probably seen in Home Depot, where somebody approaches you about whether you have a cellular phone and if you have utility bills, and it's a cellular company that is trying to sell you a phone card system.

SvR: Right.

RP: So, we were working with a cellular company and we were hired to train people to do that. As part of our performance analysis, we learned that people could do this, they could engage with customers.

SvR: Sure.

RP: So, the main thing for me was the guy on the floor who is trying to engage you, find out if you're interested, take you to the kiosk, and enter your information. So, we found out that these people were really skilled at that but they weren't selling. They weren't getting the numbers that they needed and so once we studied this, what we found was that they got you to the kiosk but the link that they needed was so buried in the system that it sometimes took up to three minutes for them to get to the link. If it's a Saturday morning and you are in a rush, you know, three minutes is too long. So, this was a tools and resource issue. It wasn't a training issue and if it wasn't for the performance analysis, we would have focused entirely on training when what really needed to happen was to get that link to the top level, so that the next time you walk up to the kiosk, you can enter the person's name.

SvR: That is a great story.

RP: That made the point of not wanting a quick fix. There is another example of that. A drilling company that hired us to build training for them and the first thing that we did was to see if performance analysis worked. The insurance company came to them and said, "We would like to look at your procedures and how you train your people." So, they hired us to build training for them and we said the same thing. We said, "Let us take a look at your procedures" and they didn't have anything. So, we had to go back and, you know, ask questions about how you do what you do. They had nothing, so we had to then go and do task analyses to look at the drillers and what kind of drilling they did, what they did. All that came about from performance analysis.

SvR: Great.

RP: We documented their procedures as a result of the performance analysis and two things happened. One was, we were able to build training for them based on those procedures but the guy who hired us was able to pick out flowcharts from the task analysis at this point and show the people, and they got more business from two places. They got more business from people who hired them for drilling purposes, but they also got more interest from, I don't know what to call them, drillers, because they could see that here was a company that was interested in their safety. Just by showing the work that we had done … you don't even have to understand it, but being able to show it convinces the clients to hire you again and again, and convinced the workers that it is really a best place to work. So, that kind of started off with the performance analysis.

SvR: That is very, very helpful. Thank you so much. I love that. Those were great stories.

Russ Powell's stories of clients who started out thinking training was the solution illustrate how, by asking probing questions, you can identify whether the cause of the performance gap is really due to knowledge, skills, and abilities or has other causes. At the outset of his interview, he noted how definitions of performance analysis, needs analysis, and needs assessment vary but the definitional issue does not necessarily serve as a barrier to getting to the causes of performance problems nor to the learning professional's ability to persuade a client that training is (not) the solution. Russ also talked about using the Task Analysis – a component of the design process – to help a client identify hidden sources of opportunity. In short, many of the processes, procedures, and tools that learning designers use to create instructional events can also serve to identify and diagnose problems and opportunities long before the design of a solution begins.

Doing More with What You Already Know

Dogbert©, the talking dog in the Dilbert© comic strips, often serves as Dilbert's© advisor, reminding him to make the most of what he already knows before looking for new tools and resources. As learning professionals, we are regularly striving to keep pace with the latest and greatest, sometimes forgetting that what we currently have in our toolbox will suit a particular project very well. This applies to needs assessment just as much as to the creation of individual learning opportunities.

Current State

To start, we need to be aware of what our organization is already doing to identify and prioritize performance gaps. In consultation with your supervisor and others in your L&D group, ask these five quick questions to help you determine the process your organization currently uses to identify performance gaps:

1 When a request for training is received, how do we confirm that training is really what is needed?
2 Do we routinely seek to identify the underlying causes of a performance problem, and if not, when do we?
3 Who are the people involved in identifying performance problems?
4 Do our processes vary based on who is making the request for our services (i.e., internal client, external client)?
5 Do we have a way of determining whether or not the requests that come to us align with the organization's strategic business goals?

Asking these questions will help you to determine not only your organization's current approach to identifying gaps but also what terminology is used for each element of that approach. If your L&D group is unable to answer these questions, you have just raised awareness of a core component that is missing from the group's processes that can impact not only the value of the learning products you create but also how the rest of your organization perceives the value of the L&D function.

The Needs Assessment Express

Like any study, the length of time to conduct a needs assessment depends on the study's scope. The needs assessment for a community revitalization project will take far longer than the needs assessment for a new learning management system. On the one hand, you want to be sure that you have enough information to identify deep-seated performance deficits; on the other hand, you need to be able to design and deliver targeted, high-impact solutions at hyper-speed. Whether or not your organization conducts needs assessments on a regular basis, you can conduct a quick needs assessment that ensures that you are delivering an appropriate solution to the real problem rather than simply satisfying "wants" on an ad hoc basis. Figure 4.2 illustrates this Needs Assessment Express process using the example of a request for customer service training:

- **Initial Diagnosis:** More often than not, training requests are stated in broad terms rather than in terms of business needs. Comments such as, "The reps take too long to answer customer questions" or "We need to increase the scores on our post-call surveys" require the designer to be able to translate these generally stated goals into solutions that deliver the results expected by the individual requesting the solution. By asking probing questions like the ones shown in Figure 4.2, the designer can uncover the real business need rather than simply responding to the symptoms. For example, the answers to the questions might indicate that the real need is call center workflow process checks, such as customer identity verification, question clarification, or call routing.
- **Needs vs. Wants Check:** Every organization has an internal resource who is well versed in organizational culture, history, and competing interests. That individual is a good source for helping the designer sift through any potential biases or major barriers that push toward

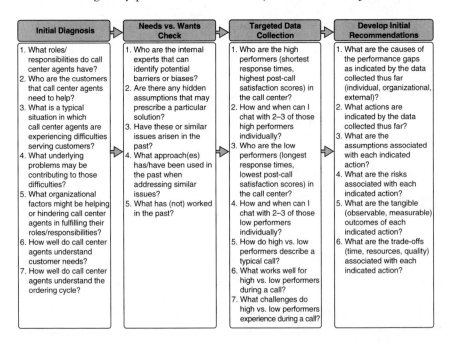

Figure 4.2 Needs Assessment Express: A Customer Service Example.

a foregone conclusion or prevent consideration of more efficient and effective solution alternatives. In our customer service example, suppose that the request for training comes from the call center manager who has worked in the call center her entire career. When she came on board 15 years ago, she received 10 days of classroom-based training; so, she proposes that you prepare a 7-day classroom-based training for the current call center agents, all of whom have at least three years of experience. The internal resource can provide background and context for call center training as it existed 15 years ago vs. current new agent training. You can then explain to the manager why the 7-day classroom based training is (not) the optimal solution, particularly since it exacerbates the very problem that the manager is seeking to solve by increasing issue resolution time due to a shortage of available agents.

- **Targeted Data Collection:** At this stage, research methodology issues, such as reliability, validity, statistical significance, and triangulation, do not come into play. Instead, you want to get a few key data points as quickly as possible. Informal interviews, questions asked at the end of a meeting, or casual but focused conversations can provide you with enough data to get you started when there is no time for surveys, focus groups, or other more systematic methods of data collection. Continuing with our customer service example, let's say your conversations with the high-performing call center agents (those with the shortest response times and the highest post-call satisfaction scores) reveal that they consistently conclude their calls by alerting customers to the online post-call survey, adding that they hoped to have provided excellent service on this particular call. The low-performing call center agents (those with the longest response times and lowest post-call satisfaction scores) simply finish with a thank-you-for-calling-and-have-a-nice-day type of ending. When viewed in conjunction with other feedback from these sources, you may get a good indication that formal training may not be needed but rather more opening and closing statements need to be added to agent call scripts.

- **Develop Initial Recommendations:** If the results of your initial diagnosis, needs vs. wants check, and targeted data collection indicate that training is not the solution, you not only need to say that but you also need to offer some solution alternatives. Finishing up with our customer service example, if your data indicates that high performers tend to work the 8AM to 4 PM shift when call volume is lowest, and low performers tend to work the 4 PM to midnight shift, when call volume is highest, then one alternative you might recommend is for HR to examine staffing patterns and the various internal and external factors associated with shift work. The point is that you are providing the manager with some evidence of what will (not) get to the actual business need.

This Needs Assessment Express process can be documented with simple office productivity tools, such as spreadsheets and Word documents, if your organization has no templates or forms with which to record the data. Working with your L&D group, you may also adapt one or more of the numerous needs assessment templates that are freely available in the public domain.

Data Collection Tools and Techniques

When conducting a more robust needs assessment, the data collection process involves more formalized tools and techniques than with the Express approach. Many of the same tools you currently use to collect data for the design and development of instructional events are also useful for gathering and recording needs assessment data. The usual starting point is searching for any secondary data in- and outside of the organization that may provide insights into the issues or opportunities that have triggered consideration of a needs assessment. The next step is the collection of primary data. The following provides a quick refresher on the most commonly used data collection tools:

- **Observation:** Observation is an inexpensive way of gathering evidence about actual behaviors rather than reported behaviors. You can create simple observation templates that enable you to capture the data in a variety of formats – textual descriptions, drawings, photos – and make notes about your impressions of what you see. However, observation is not always possible nor can you be sure that those you are observing are behaving "normally" while knowing they are being observed.
- **One-on-one interviews:** You begin your interview with a list of questions or themes to structure the conversation. This ensures consistency between interviews and allows more than one person to conduct the interviews. Obtain written permission to audio/video record the interview in advance – depending on the organizational context, that permission can be a legal Release Form or a simple email consent form – so that you can focus on interviewer-interviewee interaction. If you are unable to record the interview, take notes and organize them in a more structured, permanent form immediately after the interview. This highly flexible method can be adapted on-the-fly because it allows you to ask probing questions triggered by interviewee comments and responses, yielding rich insights into individual perspectives and attitudes. The length of the interview can be adjusted to accommodate busy schedules, and interviews can be conducted virtually. However, the strengths of the one-on-one interview can also have limitations to their use. Specifically, they are time intensive because

of their one-on-one nature and do not include large numbers of people. Consequently, the findings may not be representative of the entire group or population.

- **Focus groups:** These are group interviews intended to bring together a group of participants to discuss their opinions and insights about a set of issues. They offer an opportunity to obtain detailed feedback through group dialogue as well as opportunities for probing questions from the interviewer. Focus groups require a skilled moderator who can build rapport with the participants, encourage them to speak, and keep the discussion moving in a positive manner. They also require one or two additional staff to take detailed notes during sessions (for body language, visual cues, etc.) and monitor the audio/video-recording of the session. Unlike one-on-one interviews, focus groups require a great deal of advance planning (recruiting and scheduling eight to ten participants per session) as well as resources to conduct the groups and analyze the focus group data.

- **Surveys:** Structured survey questionnaires enable you to capture large quantities of data fairly quickly and efficiently given the many digital survey tools currently available. Surveys can provide information about preferences, behaviors, attitudes, as well as capture limited qualitative information through the inclusion of open-ended questions. However, if you have ever taken a survey, you can appreciate how challenging it can be to write clear, unbiased survey questions. Moreover, people have become almost numb to surveys, with low response rates endemic in just about every industry, even when target respondents are offered incentives for participation.

Just as you framed your Needs Assessment Express with a series of questions, your framing questions help you to define what kind of data you need to collect and how you are going to collect it. Table 4.2 provides an example data collection plan for formal needs assessments at the business unit level. For each of your questions, you can identify which data collection sources and tools would be most appropriate to document and analyze the answers.

As a learning designer, you may not (as yet) have had the opportunity to conduct a needs assessment at the business unit level. However, the answers to the framing questions at the business unit level inform your assessment of needs at the individual performance level. At a minimum, the questions related to strategy and goals will help you to determine which performance issues have the highest priority. Liaise with your supervisor or internal expert to determine the best source(s) for this information. Table 4.3 provides an example of a data collection plan for a formal needs assessment at the individual performance level.

Table 4.2 Business Unit Needs Assessment Data Collection Plan

Framing Questions	Secondary Data Sources	One-on-One Interviews	Focus Groups	Surveys
1. What are the current needs and strategies that this unit needs to support?				
2. What challenges or opportunities do you have or do you anticipate having in meeting those needs or supporting those strategies?				
3. What have you observed that indicates that there is or may be a challenge or opportunity?				
4. Where do you believe that challenge/opportunity occurs?				
5. When or how frequently do you observe it?				
6. What other sources have you seen or heard that provides information about these challenges or opportunities?				
7. What types of measures or indicators would tell you that you are successful?				
8. What's happening in the business unit that should not be happening?				
9. What is happening in your business unit that should be happening?				
10. What activities or initiatives must be done to accomplish your unit's goals?				
11. If all of these activities were done, what is the probability of success? Is that good? If not, what else would need to be accomplished?				

Table 4.3 Performance Needs Assessment Data Collection Plan

Framing Questions	Secondary Data Sources	One-on-One Interviews	Focus Groups	Surveys
1. What does excellent performance look like?				
2. What specific behaviors determine excellence in performance?				
3. What does current performance look like?				
4. What specific behaviors are occurring that should not be occurring?				
5. Which job roles/positions are involved?				
6. What knowledge, skills and behaviors are required to perform excellently in those roles/positions?				
7. How important are each of those knowledge areas, skills, and behaviors that you just mentioned?				
8. Do the individuals in these job roles/positions have a clear understanding of what is expected (e.g., work requirements, procedures)?				
9. Is there a process in place for providing those individuals with feedback about how they are doing against those expectations?				
10. How do you know if they are doing well (e.g., what performance metrics and measures are captured)?				
11. Are there positive and negative consequences associated with expected performance?				

(continued)

Table 4.3 Performance Needs Assessment Data Collection Plan (*continued*)

Framing Questions	Secondary Data Sources	One-on-One Interviews	Focus Groups	Surveys
12. Do organizational structures (teams, collaborative workgroups, management structures, etc.) support excellent performance?				
13. Does the organization's technology infrastructure support excellent performance?				
14. Do individuals have ready access to the information they need to perform their jobs?				
15. Does the work environment support physical and mental well-being?				

Some Lessons Learned

If you have ever read a Dilbert© strip focused on one of his company's meetings, the tangle of terminology in those meetings might remind you of how scholars and practitioners talk about needs assessment. Here are some lessons learned to help you stay focused on promoting the needs assessment process rather than on clarifying definitions:

- **Watch your language.** *Just a few quick questions to help me create solutions that support your business goals* will resonate with your client much more than *I need to do a needs assessment/performance analysis/needs analysis.* When professionals in other fields start talking to us using their jargon, we generally don't hesitate to ask for a "translation" (think of conversations you may have had with doctors, lawyers, accountants, etc.). As learning professionals, we want to be sure that those we support won't require a "translation" and perhaps stop listening before we've had a chance to get our points across.
- **Training? Says who?** If we are to really be learning advisors – and be perceived by others as such – we should not take training requests as commands or the reasons why training is being requested at face value. Asking questions and probing for underlying issues does not mean that you are being belligerent or challenging someone else's authority.

It does mean that you are seeking to support the organization by providing evidence for decisions about how best to address issues with or opportunities to improve performance.

- **A bad solution is worse than no solution at all.** The consequences of not doing your homework to flesh out the is-should-because questions and default to the quick fix of training will come back to haunt you and your colleagues and potentially affect your career.
- **Ambiguity is good.** Getting to the root of performance issues and comparing and contrasting options to accomplish desirable and sustainable results requires the patience and (sometimes) courage to ask probing questions of individuals up and down the hierarchy who may not clearly or consistently articulate what it is they are trying to accomplish. Ambiguity affords you the opportunity to summarize frequently and repeatedly, until you and your client are on the same page about what it is that needs to be done and how you will know it's been done successfully.

Needs Assessment Self-Check

A new manager has just taken over your L&D group and he is very enthusiastic about needs assessment following a consultant's presentation at a corporate university symposium. To show that his group is proactive about needs assessment, he asks you to design a survey to send to all employees, asking them what kinds of learning opportunities they would like the L&D group to provide. Your initial response to this request should be:

a) How fast do you want this?
b) Great, but I'd like to first get some performance information from various perspectives, so I can give employees some context for the survey.
c) We can send them a list of our current offerings and ask them which ones they find the most valuable.
d) Seriously?

In this scenario, option (b) is the strongest choice. Although individual perspectives on what learning opportunities people would like to have is important when making decisions, they are not in and of themselves of great help to informed decision-making. Moreover, you risk setting the expectation that the resulting list of *wants* will actually be offered, resulting in disappointment if the *wants* are not fulfilled, which would reflect badly on L&D and, thus, on the new manager. Option (c) has value once you have received performance information from various perspectives and seek to determine whether or not your current inventory of offerings addresses any of the identified performance gaps. Options (a) and (d) are both career-limiting for reasons that should be self-evident.

Food for Thought

1   As part of a regular group meeting or as a stand-alone session, schedule about 15 minutes with your colleagues to discuss the group's experiences with needs assessment. When has it been used? Why (not)? What were the outcomes when used? Was there a particular time when they wished it had been used?

2   Visit the site http://needsassessment.org/ and explore some of the resources. What are some of the tools and templates that would be helpful to your organization? Why?

3   Visit one or more of your professional networks (e.g., LinkedIn) and search for conversations related to needs assessment. What are some of the main themes discussed? Are there common challenges and lessons learned?

Up Next

In this chapter, we have (a) reviewed the development of needs assessment definitions and models in the scholarly literature; (b) examined how practitioners have translated needs assessment theories and models into practice; (c) described how learning designers can capitalize on their existing knowledge of data collection tools and techniques to conduct needs assessments; and (d) summarized some lessons learned about needs assessment. Now that we have placed learning design and technologies in the larger context of supporting business goals through solving human performance problems, we turn our attention to the workplace environment.

References

Andrews, D. H., & Goodson, L. A. (1980). A comparative analysis of models of instructional design. *Journal of Instructional Development*, 3(4), 2–16.

Barker Steege, L. M., Marra, R. M., & Jones, K. (2012). Meeting needs assessment challenges: Applying the performance pyramid in the U.S. Army. *Performance Improvement*, 51(10), 32–41.

Benjamin, S. (1989). A closer look at needs analysis and needs assessment: Whatever happened to the systems approach? *Performance & Instruction*, 28(9), 12–16.

Burton, J. K., & Merrill, P. F. (1977). Needs assessment goals, needs, and priorities. In L. J. Briggs (Ed.), *Instructional Design Principles and Application* (pp. 21–45). Englewood Cliffs, NJ: Educational Technology Publications.

Christensen, B. (2015). *Needs assessment vs. needs analysis:* What's the diff? Retrieved from www.ispi.org/PerformanceXpress/PX/Articles/Editors__Pick/Needs_Assessment_vs_Needs_Analysis__What_s_the_Diff_.aspx.

Cline, F., & Seibert, P. (1993). Help for the first-time needs assessors, *Training & Development Journal*, 47(5), 99–102.

Cooperstein, S. E., & Kocevar-Weidinger, E. (2004). Beyond active learning: A constructivist approach to learning. *Reference Services Review*, 32(2), 141–8.

Cureton, J., Newton, A., & Teslowski, D. (1986). Finding out what managers need. *Training & Development Journal*, 40(5), 106–107.

Danielson, J., Lockee, B., & Burton, J. (2000). ID and HCI: A marriage of necessity. In B. Abbey (Ed.), *Instructional and Cognitive Impacts of Web-based Education* (pp. 118–28). Hershey, PA: Idea Group Publishing.

Darraugh, B. (1991). It takes six (six-step model for needs assessment). *Training & Development Journal*, *45*(3), 21–24.

Dick, W., Carey, L., & Carey, J. (2005). *The Systematic Design of Instruction* (6th ed.). New York, NY: Prentice-Hall.

Fairbairns, J. (1991). Plugging the gap in training needs analysis. *Personnel Management*, February, 43-45.

Freeman, J. (1993). Human resources planning: Training needs analysis. *Management Quarterly*, *34*(3), 32–33.

Gilbert, T. (1978). *Human Competence: Engineering Worthy Performance*. New York, NY: McGraw-Hill.

Gordon, S. (1994). *Systematic Training Program Design: Maximizing Effectiveness and Minimizing Liability*. Englewood Cliffs, NJ: Prentice Hall.

Graham, K., & Mihal, W. (1986). Can your management development needs surveys be trusted? *Training & Development Journal*, *40*(3), 38–43.

Guerra, I. (2003). Key competencies required of performance improvement professionals. *Performance Improvement Quarterly*, *16*(1), 55–72.

Hannum, W., & Hansen, C. (1989). *Instructional Systems Development in Large Organizations*. Englewood Cliffs, NJ: Educational Technology Publications.

Harless, J. (1973). An analysis of front-end analysis. *Improving Human Performance: A Research Quarterly*, *4*, 229–44.

Herbert, G. R., & Doverspike, D. (1990). Performance appraisal in the training needs analysis process: A review and critique. *Public Personnel Management*, *19*(3), 253–70.

Holton, E. F., Bates, R. A., & Naquin, S. (2000). Large-scale performance-driven training needs assessment: A case study. *Public Personnel Management*, *29*(2), 249–68.

Kaufman, R. (1992). *Strategic Planning Plus: An Organizational Guide*. Newbury Park, CA: Sage (Revised).

Kaufman, R. (1998). *Strategic Thinking: A Guide to Identifying and Solving Problems*. Arlington, VA and Washington, DC: The American Society for Training & Development and the International Society for Performance Improvement.

Kaufman, R., & Gavora, M. J. (1993). Needs assessment and problem solving: A critical appraisal of a critical reappraisal. *Performance Improvement Quarterly*, *6*(2), 87–98.

Kaufman, R., Oakley-Browne, H., Watkins, R., & Leigh, D. (2003). *Strategic Planning for Success: Aligning People, Performance and Payoffs*. San Francisco, CA: Jossey-Bass/Pfeiffer.

Kaufman, R., & Watkins, R. (2000). Getting serious about results and payoffs: We are what we say, do, and deliver. *Performance Improvement*, *39*(4), 23–32.

Kaufman, R. A., Rojas, A. M., & Mayer, H. (1993). *Needs Assessment: A User's Guide*. Englewood Cliffs, NJ: Educational Technology Publications.

Ketter, P. (2016). The core components of talent development. *TD Magazine*. Retrieved from www.td.org/Publications/Magazines/TD/TD-Archive/2016/02/Editors-Note-the-Core-Components-of-Talent-Development.

Leigh, D. (2006). SWOT analysis. In J. A. Pershing (Ed.), *Handbook of Human Performance Technology* (3rd ed., pp. 1089–106). San Francisco, CA: Pfeiffer.

Leigh, D., Watkins, R., Platt, W. A., & Kaufman, R. (2000). Alternate models of needs assessment: selecting the right one for your organization. *Human Resource Development Quarterly*, *11*(1), 87–93.

Lundberg, C., Elderman, J. L., Ferrell, P., & Harper, L. (2010). Data gathering and analysis for needs assessment: a case study. *Performance Improvement*, *49*(8), 27–34.

Mager, R., & Pipe, P. (1970). *Analyzing Performance Problems* (2nd ed.). Belmont, CA: Pitman Learning.

Mager, R., & Pipe, P. (1997). *Analyzing Performance Problems or You Really Oughta Wanna* (3rd ed.). Atlanta, GA: The Center for Effective Performance, Inc.

Marker, A. (2007). Synchronized analysis model: linking Gilbert's behavior engineering model with environmental analysis models. *Performance Improvement*, 46(1), 26–32.

McArdle, G. E. H. (1996). Conducting a needs assessment for your work group. *Supervisory Management*, 41(3), 6–7.

McClelland, S. (1992). A systems approach to needs assessment. *Training & Development Journal*, 46(8), 51–64.

McClelland, S. B. (1993). Training needs assessment: An "open-systems" application. *Journal of European Industrial Training*, 17(1), 12–18.

McClelland, S. B. (1995). *Organizational Needs Assessment: Design, Facilitation, and Analysis*. Westport, CT: Quorum Books.

McGehee, W., & Thayer, P. W. (1961). *Training in Business and Industry*. Oxford, UK: Wiley.

Moseley, J. L., & Heaney, M. J. (1994). Needs assessment across disciplines. *Performance Improvement Quarterly*, 7(1), 60–79.

Nelson, R. R., Whitener, E. M., & Philcox, H. H. (1995). The assessment of end-user training needs. *Communications of the ACM*, 38(7), 27–40.

Nowack, N. M. (1991). A true training needs analysis. *Training & Development Journal*, 45(4), 69–73.

Office of Personnel Management (OPM). (n.d.). *Training needs assessment*. Retrieved from www.opm.gov/policy-data-oversight/training-and-development/planning-evaluating/.

Ostroff, C., & Ford, J. K. (1989). Assessing training needs: Critical levels of analysis. In I. Goldstein (Ed.), *Training and Development in Organizations: Frontiers of Industrial and Organizational Psychology* (pp. 25–62). San Francisco, CA: Jossey-Bass.

Panke, S. (2016). *Creative needs assessment in instructional design: selected examples*. Paper presented at EdMedia: World Conference on Educational Media and Technology, Vancouver, BC.

Rossett, A. (1992). Analysis of human performance problems. In H. D. Stolovitch & E. J. Keeps (Eds.), *Handbook of Human Performance Technology* (pp. 97–113). San Francisco, CA: Jossey-Bass.

Rummler, G. A., & Brache, A. P. (1990). *Improving Performance: How to Manage the White Space on the Organization Chart*. San Francisco, CA: Jossey-Bass.

Society of Human Resource Management (SHRM). (2015). *Practicing the discipline of workforce planning*. Retrieved from www.shrm.org/resourcesandtools/tools-and-samples/toolkits/pages/practicingworkforceplanning.aspx.

Stranger, J. (1993). How to do a work/family needs assessment. *Employment Relations Today*, 20(2), 197–206.

Taylor, F. W. (1913). *The Principles of Scientific Management*. New York, NY and London, UK: Harper & Brothers.

Triner, D., Greenberry, A., & Watkins, R. (1996). Training needs assessment: A contradiction in terms? *Educational Technology*, 36(6), 51–5.

van Eerde, W., Simon Tang, K., & Talbot, G. (2008). The mediating role of training utility in the relationship between training needs assessment and organizational effectiveness. *The International Journal of Human Resource Management*, 19(1), 63–73.

Watkins, R., & Kaufman, R. (1996). An update on relating needs assessment and needs analysis. *Performance Improvement*, 35(10), 10–13.

Watkins, R., Leigh, D., Platt, W., & Kaufman, R. (1998). Needs assessment – A digest, review, and comparison of needs assessment literature. *Performance Improvement, 37*(7), 40–52.

Wedman, J. (2014). Needs assessment in the private sector. *New Directions for Evaluation, 144,* 47–60.

Wedman, J. (2016). *Needs assessment basics: exploring the performance pyramid.* Retrieved http://needsassessment.missouri.edu/.

Wright, P., & Geroy, G. (1992). Needs analysis theory and the effectiveness of large-scale government sponsored training programmes: A case study. *Journal of Management Development, 11*(5), 16-27.

Yatie, J., Shapira, P., & Roessner, J. D. (1995). *Manufacturing Assistance Program Needs Assessment Guide: Firm-level Needs Assessment Approaches* (Vol. 2). Washington, DC: The Aspen Institute.

Zemke, R., & Kramlinger, T. (1985). Figuring Things Out: *A Trainer's Guide to Needs and Task Analysis.* Reading, MA: Addison-Wesley.

Part II

The Workplace Environment

5 The Impact of Organizational Culture
Walking the Walk

In Part I, we explored the evolving scope of learning design and technologies as an occupational field. Now, we turn our attention to the challenges and opportunities associated with identifying and managing the expectations of internal and external stakeholders. For the learning designer, a solid understanding of the workplace environment is essential to successfully diagnosing performance problems of internal and/or external clients, and crafting feasible solution alternatives. Part of that understanding is derived from a firm grasp of the organizational culture, sub-cultures, and their influence on the role of learning in the organization. Organizational culture reflects management perceptions of the world and, thus, impacts the extent which those perceptions support or challenge the designer's ability to identify and solve performance problems. Understanding the organization's culture ensures that the designer takes current and future organizational expectations into account when addressing performance issues.

So, what does organizational culture mean and how can you recognize it? When you were last interviewed for a job, you were probably asked questions, such as, *Why do you want to work here?* or *What's your ideal workplace?* These are typical interview questions intended to assess your cultural fit with that organization. Cultural fit, the likelihood that a job candidate will be able to adapt to and/or adopt the core beliefs, attitudes, and behaviors that make up the organization (O'Reilly III, Chatman, & Caldwell, 1991) has long been an important criterion for screening job candidates (Bouton, 2015). Several studies have explored the relationship between cultural fit and job satisfaction, staff turnover, and employee retention (Allen, 2008; Gosh, Satyawadi, Joshi, & Mohd, 2013; Kristof-Brown, Zimmerman, & Johnson, 2005; Sheridan, 1992; Testa, Mueller, & Thomas, 2003; Verquer, Beehr, & Wagner, 2003). However, applying cultural fit in practice has not always led to positive results. Some practitioners report that the phrase "cultural fit" is being used as a filter to discriminate based on demographic factors or to assess a candidate's likeability, sometimes to the detriment of competency and job qualifications (Anderson, 2015; Calhoun, 2015; Dunn, 2015; Hill, 2013). If you have ever encountered that go-along-to-get-along colleague who contributes little to the project at hand, then you may have experienced the challenges associated with employees who "fit" the organizational culture. But the deliberate use of cultural fit for discriminatory purposes is difficult to prove and is often unintentional.

Using cultural fit for hiring, promotion, and retention is challenging for the simple reason that there is generally a lack of consensus about what constitutes an organization's culture. Conventional wisdom states that it is the senior leadership who defines and models organizational culture through its behavior and decisions (Schein, 2004) and, thus, sets the tone for its dissemination throughout the organization. However, a 2016 market research study indicated that while the leadership believed it defines organizational culture, employees believed that they are the ones who define culture or that culture is not well defined (Workforce Institute at Kronos, 2015). Moreover, employees had a different view of the attributes of culture, of how leaders nurture culture, and of the major obstacles to maintaining a positive workplace culture. Consequently, how culture is articulated within organizations or even across organizations in the same industry sector may vary greatly.

But I'm happy where I work, so why do I need to consider the culture? If you are happy at work, chances are that at least one of the reasons is related to the culture of your organization. Think about some of the projects you have had since you started at your organization. What performance problems did those projects aim to solve? Did those projects address skill gaps for current job functions or preparation for future job functions? Did the individuals who used the learning product you created participate voluntarily or were they compelled to do so as a result of a performance problem or a regulatory mandate? Organizational culture serves as a filter for decisions about who can take advantage of learning opportunities to keep skills current and who should advance to the next level in the organization. Importantly, the culture helps to define the parameters within which the designer can expand and grow beyond the creation of training interventions to the creation of solutions to performance problems that may not be limited to training. It also determines the extent to which the designer who prefers to work only on training interventions is deemed to be valuable to the organization, especially when his/her interventions have been successful. In short, the designer has a vested interest in understanding the culture of the organization in which he/she is employed. When you design learning solutions, your analysis of the learner and of the context in which the learner performs have been key inputs to your choice of solution alternatives. Similarly, an analysis of your own workplace context and culture will be a key input into determining your alternatives for career advancement and development. In this chapter, we will

- Review the various definitions, analytical methods, and measures of organizational culture and sub-cultures in the scholarly literature;
- Examine the characteristics of organizational cultures that are supportive of learning; and
- Identify some concrete actions that designers can take to be successful within (or work around) their workplace culture and sub-cultures.

The Nature of Organizational Culture and Sub-Cultures

Understanding the nature of organizational culture and sub-cultures requires an understanding of the meaning of the world "culture" as well as the approaches to the study of culture. However, the scope of the scholarly literature dealing with some aspect of culture and its relationship to organizations is broad, covering decades of conceptual and empirical studies across a variety of academic disciplines and domains. Consequently, it would be impossible to cover all of the research streams in a single chapter. We will instead focus on a few key studies that provide some insights into the evolution of the topic, contributing to our understanding of why organizational culture continues to be a factor in how organizations and their internal and external stakeholders interact.

The Meaning of Culture

It has been suggested that the concept of "culture" began in the fifteenth century as a translation of the Latin reference to soil cultivation; then, it evolved into a reference to individuals with taste and manners in the nineteenth century (Tharp, 2009). However, the scholarly study of culture has its roots in the social sciences as researchers sought to describe the rituals, myths, values, and beliefs observed in exotic regions of the world. For example, British anthropologist Edward Tylor (1871) defined culture as "that complex whole which includes knowledge, beliefs, arts, morals, law, custom, and any other capabilities and habits acquired by man as a member of society" (p. 1). At the beginning of the twentieth century, some definitions of culture emphasized the pragmatic aspects of human actions and interactions in social groups and contexts (Boas, 1911; Mead, 1937), while culture as a value concept that guides human reality (Weber, 1949) offered another approach to defining culture. As researchers sought to build on these definitions to guide further studies, attempts to catalog the characteristics of culture emerged. In reviewing the literature on culture, sociologist Albert Blumenthal identified 20 different definitions of culture (Blumenthal, 1936), but expressed a preference for those definitions that focused on the human consciousness and perceptions of culture over time. Another attempt to catalog the various definitions of culture produced 79 divisions of culture and 637 subdivisions (Murdock, Ford, & Hudson, 1938). For instance, one major division was called "food quest" and its three subdivisions were "collecting," "hunting," and "fishing."

Efforts to identify the most useful elements of culture continued throughout the twentieth century and persist in the twenty-first century. In a seminal work on the state of inquiry in the field, Kluckhohn, Untereiner, and Kroeber (1952) identified 164 definitions of culture with different areas of focus, such as the symbolic (arbitrarily assigned meanings shared by a society), the normative (ideals, values), and the behavioral (shared, learned human behavior). Parsons, Shils, and Olds (1965) focused on the learning and diffusion of culture, as well as on how actors within a culture orient themselves to the complex patterns in culture. Expanding on the symbolic focus, Geertz (1973) defined culture as "a system of inherited conceptions expressed in symbolic forms by means of which men communicate, perpetuate, and develop their knowledge about and attitudes toward life" (p. 89). In contrast, Moore (1952) called for the abandonment of the effort to create a definition in lieu of a focus on characteristics or forms of culture. Bodley (1994) sought to emphasize some of the common themes across the various definitions in the anthropology literature by defining culture as having three components: what people think, what people do, and the material products that people produce. Arguments have also been made for defining culture in terms of the relevant identifiers of the individuals under study (Straub, Loch, Evaristo, Karahenna, & Srite, 2002), while others have offered an updated listing of over 300 definitions of culture and a roadmap for social science researchers seeking to integrate culture into their work (Baldwin, Faulkner, Hecht, & Lindsley, 2006). Echoing earlier arguments about culture as a system was the focus on the synergy between culture and the context and environment in which the individual lives (Kuper, 2009).

Figure 5.1 illustrates the various definitions, foci, and elements of culture that have emerged from the social sciences. Common to all of these is the recognition that culture consists of a complex set of tangible and intangible elements as defined and perceived by the members of that culture. Although there has yet to be consensus about how best to categorize or define the relationships among the various elements of culture, what is clear is that culture is not a static concept but rather evolves with context, time, and analytical focus.

Organizational Culture and Sub-Cultures

The multiple approaches to defining and analyzing culture that existed and still persist in the social sciences spilled over into the field of organizational behavior, particularly into management science, with the publication of the results of the Hawthorne studies conducted at the Western Electric Company in the 1920s. Using a combination of qualitative and quantitative methods, the Hawthorne studies examined the effects of social relations, motivation, and employee satisfaction on factory productivity and showed

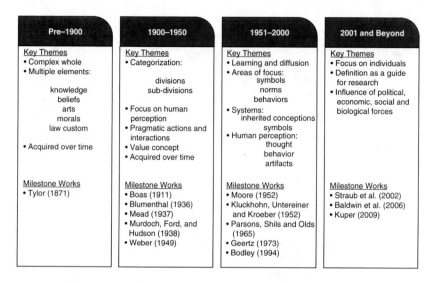

Pre–1900	1900–1950	1951–2000	2001 and Beyond
Key Themes • Complex whole • Multiple elements: knowledge beliefs arts morals law custom • Acquired over time	Key Themes • Categorization: divisions sub-divisions • Focus on human perception • Pragmatic actions and interactions • Value concept • Acquired over time	Key Themes • Learning and diffusion • Areas of focus: symbols norms behaviors • Systems: inherited conceptions symbols • Human perception: thought behavior artifacts	Key Themes • Focus on individuals • Definition as a guide for research • Influence of political, economic, social and biological forces
Milestone Works • Tylor (1871)	Milestone Works • Boas (1911) • Blumenthal (1936) • Mead (1937) • Murdoch, Ford, and Hudson (1938) • Weber (1949)	Milestone Works • Moore (1952) • Kluckhohn, Untereiner and Kroeber (1952) • Parsons, Shils and Olds (1965) • Geertz (1973) • Bodley (1994)	Milestone Works • Straub et al. (2002) • Baldwin et al. (2006) • Kuper (2009)

Figure 5.1 Culture Definitions and Classifications in the Social Sciences.

the importance of workplace groups and the psychosocial factors associated with group membership and participation in affecting the behavior of individuals at work. Specifically, the studies found that employees were not merely motivated by financial gain, and productivity was not simply a byproduct of incentives and optimized working spaces. People were motivated by inclusion, constructive feedback, interest, autonomy, and a wide variety of other intangible, non-monetary factors (Roethlisberger & Dickson, 1939). The Hawthorne studies have been acknowledged as the first systematic attempt to use a concept of culture to understand the work environment and explore ideas concerning motivational influences, job satisfaction, resistance to change, group norms, worker participation, and effective leadership as elements of an organization's culture that are critical to business success (Gillespie, 1991; Sonnenfeld, 1985).

Although the Hawthorne studies marked the start of the application of social science concepts of culture to the study of corporations, this research stream really gained traction in the 1970s with the focus on organizations as systems and the Japanese corporation as the model of system efficiencies (Pettigrew, 1979). In a review of the cultural anthropology literature, Allaire and Firsirotu (1984) deemed ludicrous the notion that organizations can have cultural properties; generate meanings, values, and beliefs; develop and promote rituals, stories, legends; and other properties common to societal cultures due to the lack of consensus among anthropologists about the definition of culture. To illustrate this, they identified eight different schools of thought about what constitutes organizational culture, each school with its own theorists and research traditions. However, this did not prevent Allaire and Firsirotu from offering their own conceptual model of organizational culture as a system of symbols that shaped the society in which the organization conducts its operations, as well as the organization's history, leadership, and accumulated shared experiences. Although acknowledging the contributions of anthropology, another literature review covering the mid-1950s through the early 1980s deemed the study of organizational culture to be an extension of organizational sociology, with a focus on the norms and shared understandings that regulate social life in organizations (Ouchi & Wilkins, 1985). This research stream continued through the 1980s with a focus on sustaining competitive advantages (Barney, 1986).

Another stream of organizational culture research centered on economic and industry context as the primary determinant of what constitutes an organization's culture. The popularity of organizational culture as a scholarly field of study and as a topic in the practitioner literature was attributed, for example, to the emergence of globalization, with modern businesses becoming increasingly international in nature, fostering frequent interactions with customers, suppliers, and partners from different cultures (Alvesson, 1990). The demand for new ideas on effective management, the flattening of traditional organizational hierarchies, as well as societal changes, such as changed work morality and increased need for involvement and expressivity, were also identified as drivers of interest in organizational culture. Gordon (1991) contended that organizations are founded on industry-based assumptions about customer requirements, the competitive environment, and societal expectations, with all three of these – which he described as the industry environment – forming the basis of company culture or values about how to conduct business. These assumptions and values informed the strategies, structures, and processes developed by management to achieve desired performance goals and ensure the survival of the business. Culture could change if either the organization's top management or a large enough group within the organization decided that the current way of doing business was no longer working, then created a new vision, and began to act on and promote that new vision (Kotter, 2012). In time, new norms would form and new shared values would grow. Still, the industry-focused stream of research emphasizing the strong, positive effect of culture on competitive effectiveness and performance began to lose its appeal when the companies that were deemed to exemplify this focus (IBM, Hewlett-Packard, Japanese corporations, among others) began to experience problems in the late 1980s (Alvesson, 2002). This indicated that the direct correlation between culture and performance was tenuous at best and that other variables in- and outside the organization needed to be considered when assessing business performance.

Other researchers have focused on organizational sub-cultures as the key to understanding organizational culture. Sub-cultures have generally been defined as a group or subset of an organization's members who self-identify as a distinct group whose members interact with each other on a regular basis and solve shared problems based on collective understandings unique to the group (Bolon & Bolon, 1994; Gelder, 2007; Gregory, 1983; Trice & Beyer, 1993). Looking at the dynamics of organizational culture at the individual level, Harris (1994) postulated that support for the importance of sub-cultures is found in the operation of organization-specific schemas that individuals use to make sense of organizational culture. Schemas were the cognitive structures in which an individual's knowledge was acquired organized, processed, and retained, enabling him or her to differentiate his/her own subgroup perspectives from those of other subgroups. International studies of the impact of occupational cultures on individual and organizational performance in specific industries, such as healthcare (Johansson, Åström, Kauffeldt, Helldin, & Carlström, 2014; Willis et al., 2016), manufacturing (Shearman, 2013), finance (Gerdhe, 2012), banking (Van Maanen & Barley, 1984), and telecommunications (Singh, 2013) are also part of this research stream.

Among the newer, evolving research streams is the stream that examines organizational culture from the perspective of human resource management and development. The management of organizational culture is deemed to be achieved through human resource management practices, particularly employee recruitment, development and rewards, and employee retention, all of which require new employees to be sensitized to the values and norms of the organization in order to be effective performers (Aryee, 1991; Evans, 1986). Empirical studies appear to affirm these links, with the organizational culture-employee retention link particularly strong (Sheridan, 1992). In their review of conference proceedings of the Academy of Human Resource Development (AHRD) from 1994 to 2009, Plakhotnik and Rocco (2011) identified two themes in their analysis of the various definitions of organizational culture: an enterprise-wide culture and sub-cultures within the enterprise-wide culture. Although both themes focused on shared values, beliefs, and behaviors, enterprise-wide cultures mirrored the definitions prevalent in the social sciences literature (Denison & Mishra, 1995; Pettigrew, 1979; Schein, 2004), while sub-cultures were grounded in shared occupational values, beliefs, and behaviors as defined in the sub-culture research stream of organizational culture theory (Bolon & Bolon, 1994; Trice & Beyer, 1993). Furthermore, Plakhotnik and Rocco noted that AHRD research tended to focus on the managerial perspective for employee performance improvement, which was too narrow a focus and excluded the perspectives of other disciplines and fields.

Central to understanding the many streams of research on organizational culture is the work of Edgar Schein. Schein posited that if we want to truly understand organizational culture, we have to look beyond the visible manifestations and dig into the underlying assumptions that are the core of an organization's culture. As a starting point, he offered the following definition of organizational culture:

> Organizational culture is the pattern of basic assumptions that a given group has invented, discovered, or developed in learning to cope with its problems of external adaptation and internal integration, and that have worked well enough to be considered valid, and therefore, to be taught to new members as the correct way to perceive, think, and feel in relation to those problems. (Schein, 1984, p. 3)

For Schein, this definition offered a tool for discovering how organizational culture works, is learned, passed on, and changed over time. To get to the basic assumptions underlying an organization's culture required slicing through three levels of culture. The first level consisted of the organization's visible artifacts, such as processes, structures, dress code, and other visible representations of the organization. These artifacts described the "what" but not the "why" associated with an organization's behavior. At the second level were the espoused beliefs and values, the organizational goals, aspirations, and rationalizations that are articulated in mission statements, marketing materials, and other venues for promoting a particular image of the organization. However, these espoused values may or may not be congruent with actual behavior. Level three contained the basic underlying assumptions, the unconscious, taken-for-granted beliefs, and values that determine behavior, perception, thought, and feeling. Schein concluded by offering some approaches to uncovering those underlying assumptions, with all of the approaches requiring access to an organizational insider to facilitate interpretation and analysis of what was visible at levels one and two.

Hatch (1993) built on Schein's approach to organizational culture by including symbols alongside assumptions, values, and artifacts and showing linkages among them to represent culture as a dynamic model. Schein later refined his approach to organizational culture by defining four categories of culture: (a) macro-cultures, or nations, ethnic and religious groups, and occupations that exist globally (e.g., doctors, nurses); (b) organizational cultures, found in private, public, nonprofit, and government organizations; (c) sub-cultures, occupational groups within organizations; and (d) micro-cultures, or small groups within sub-cultures (Schein, 2004). For example, learning designers could be a micro-culture within the L&D departmental sub-culture of an organization. Schein noted that an organization's survival depends on how it handles problems of internal integration or problems that deal with the group's ability to function as a group, and problems of external adaptation or problems that deal with the group's basic survival or the primary task of the group. The way these two types of problems were resolved was what marked organizations with their individuality and, thus, differing cultures. Thus, organizational culture was a complex set of assumptions or core beliefs about reality and human nature, of values and social principles, philosophies, goals and standards that are deemed to have intrinsic worth, and artifacts or the visible, tangible, and audible results of activity anchored in values and assumptions. Culture defined the way in which an organization does business.

The study of organizational culture has been characterized as reflecting the tensions between academics about which social science paradigm (cognitive psychology, functional anthropology, phenomenology, etc.) is the most appropriate for understanding organizational culture, and what methods of study (e.g., field observation, multivariate statistical analyses) are appropriate (Marcoulides & Heck, 1993). The challenges associated with applying the concepts borrowed from one discipline to another were well described in Meek's (1988) review of the literature:

> There is nothing wrong with one discipline borrowing concepts from another discipline; this process has resulted in important theoretical innovations. However, there is a danger that, when one area of study borrows key concepts from other disciplines, the concepts become either stereotyped or distorted in the transfer. Also, when concepts are borrowed from other disciplines, they may not be transferred "in toto": that is, rather than accepting an entire "package" – which may include the historical debates surrounding the "proper" uses of the concepts – people only select aspects of the concepts that suit their interests and thinking at a particular time. This may result either in a slanted and biased application of the concepts or a dilution of their original analytical power. (p. 454)

Meek argued that culture was a defining characteristic (what the organization "is") rather than a variable (what the organization "has") that can be controlled and manipulated by management. For Meek, culture was an abstraction at best, having use only in relation to the interpretation of observed concrete behavior.

Other criticisms have challenged the notion of shared values as a central element of organizational culture. One such study sought to measure the extent to which employee perceptions of their organization's culture varied by their (a) hierarchy within the organization; (b) demographic characteristics (age, tenure with the organization, ethnicity, and gender); (c) organizational sub-unit within the organization; and (d) function area (Helms & Stern, 2001). Using Ott's (1989) 42-item questionnaire designed to assess the behavioral norms in an organization (e.g., "If one of my coworkers criticized the organization and the people in it, most other employees would join in or silently agree"), Helms and Stern found significant variation in employee perceptions across age, gender, and ethnicity, and organizational sub-unit, suggesting that personal background and experiences more strongly influenced employee perceptions of organizational culture than did work experiences. Furthermore, the results suggested that organizational sub-cultures fostered greater identification than did the larger organizational culture, all of which may lead to conflicts and miscommunications. In another study conducted among 300 practitioners (Watkins, 2013), shared values were identified as only one of many factors that drive culture, particularly when looking at the level of sub-cultures. Cultures were dynamic and shifted in response to internal and external changes.

Another challenge to the shared values idea, particularly in terms of organizational performance, critiqued the nature of the various instruments used to measure culture as being too sweeping to be useful in practice (Ginevicius & Vaitkunaite, 2006). Similarly, in their review of 70 qualitative and quantitative instruments for measuring organizational culture that were published across the social sciences, Jung et al. (2009) noted dimensional approaches, typological approaches, and various combinations thereof. They concluded that *there is no ideal instrument for cultural exploration and that the appropriateness of any measure depends on the particular reason for which it is to be used and the context within which it is to be applied.*

Nevertheless, shared values remain a dominant theme in the study of organizational culture. For instance, Van Tiem, Moseley, and Dessinger (2012) defined organizational culture as "a shared system of values, beliefs, and behaviors that characterizes a group or organization" (p. 386). Egan (2008) defined organizational culture in a similar way, stating that it is "characterized as the attitudes, beliefs, experiences, and values of a given organization" (p. 301). A third definition defined organizational culture as the behavioral norms and expectations that direct the way in which employees work (Glisson, 2015), while a much-quoted definition attributed to Herb Kelleher, former CEO of Southwest Airlines (Hanselman, 2013), described organizational culture as "what we do when we think no one is looking."

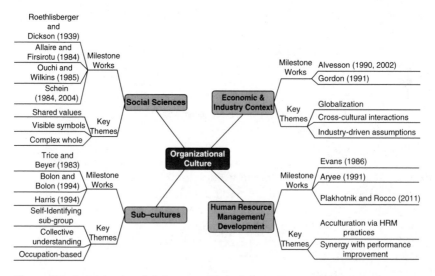

Figure 5.2 Organizational Culture and Sub-Culture Research Streams.

Figure 5.2 illustrates the various research streams in the literature on organizational culture, including key themes and milestone conceptual studies. Importantly, current conceptions of organizational culture remain grounded in the shared values notion, which, in turn, informs the streams of research focused on the relationship between organizational culture and learning (Galperin & Lituchy, 2013).

Supporting a Culture of Learning

If an organization's culture serves as a guide for action within the organization and with the external environment, how can we know the extent to which the organizational culture is supportive of learning? If the organizational culture supports innovation, continuous improvement, and receptiveness to change, then it seems reasonable to assume that the culture would also support learning opportunities to increase the knowledge, skills, and performance improvement efforts of its employees and, thus, contribute to overall business performance. This may not be as simple as it seems, however. Like culture and organizational culture, learning culture is a construct for which scholars and practitioners offer no single agreed-upon definition. Depending on which discipline you consult, you may come across the terms "organizational learning" or the "learning organization" or "organizational learning culture" or "organizational knowledge," each with its own nuances.

Key Constructs

Cook and Yanow (1993) described organizational learning as a category of activity that can only be done in the aggregate and as one that does not necessarily imply observable change. They equated organizational learning with preserving cultural identity, which, in turn, affects the mindset and, ultimately, the practices of an organization. Another definition of organizational learning describes it as "a process of improving organizational actions through better knowledge and understanding" (Edmondson, 2002, p. 128). For Edmondson, organizational learning involves actions and interactions that take place between people who are typically situated within smaller groups or teams, and that through these sub-units making appropriate changes in how they do their work (driven by both team-specific and organizational objectives), an organization maintains its effectiveness in a changing world. Organizational learning includes learning at both the individual and collective levels of analysis, with mechanisms in place to capture and share that learning across the organization (Anderson & Lewis, 2014; Argote & Miron-Spektor, 2011; Carswell, 2012; Schilling & Kluge, 2009).

A learning organization is generally one that facilitates opportunities for its members to learn. and in so doing, transforms itself continuously

(Jamali, 2006). Peter Senge (2006) popularized the concept of the learning organization and proposed a typology of five characteristics associated with learning organizations:

1   Systems thinking, in which the various functions and components of the organization are immediately apparent and interdependent and must work together.
2   Personal mastery, or an individual commitment to identifying the important things that workers need to do and learning how to do them as well as they can.
3   Mental models, the assumptions that individuals and organizations hold, must be unlearned and adapted to existing values in order to develop shared values.
4   Shared vision, a deep understanding of the organization's mission and values.
5   Team learning, accumulating team understanding and knowledge that is stored and made available to everyone.

Nonetheless, learning organization and organizational learning are often used interchangeably. The most visible case in point is the scholarly journal *The Learning Organization*, which describes itself as "an international journal of critical studies in organization learning" (Editorial objectives, n.d.).

In contrast, learning culture goes beyond the facilitation of learning for organizational adaptation and transformation. A strong learning culture recognizes that employees have a right to receive time for training, for reflecting on their professional development needs, and for seeking out opportunities to meet those needs (Hoyle, 2015). Hoyle noted that three things need to be in place to enable the development of a learning culture: (a) standards that are clear and easily understandable and that the employees can use to review their own performance, identify where they need new skills, new knowledge, or more experience; (b) structures that encourage people to try out things on the job and be supported while the new work practices are still evolving; and (c) groups that work together are given more than just the common experience of being enrolled in the same program, but are given the resources and direction to learn. A strong learning culture is one in which the management voluntarily institutes personal development plans and in which learning is "commonplace, natural, and not 'other'" (Hoyle, 2015, p. 34).

In the first edition of his book *Organizational Culture and Leadership*, Schein (1992) posited that employees must participate in decision-making activities and exert some control over their own careers and development. He described a learning-supportive organizational culture as possessing ten characteristics, such as environment, involvement in decision-making, and openness to change among others, and that these characteristics can be presented as a continuum. He predicted that a learning culture would fall at certain points on the continuum. Few attempts have been made to subject the original Schein model to empirical testing (Kluge & Schilling, 2003; Thompson & Kahnweiler, 2002). Nevertheless, Schein went on to refine his characterization of learning culture and tied it to the characteristics of a learning leader. In the third edition of his book (Schein, 2004), he described the ten characteristics of a learning culture as consisting of:

1 Proactivity, whereby a learning culture assumes that the appropriate way for humans to behave in their relationship to the environment is to be proactive problem-solvers and learners.
2 Commitment to learning to learn, whereby all in the organization agree that learning is a sound investment in time and resources and that learning to learn through reflection and experimentation should be encouraged.
3 Positive assumptions about human nature or Theory Y (McGregor, 1960) on human motivation, in which a participative style of management that is decentralized will strengthen employee self-motivation to learn when given the resources and the necessary psychological safety.
4 Belief that the environment can be changed.
5 Commitment to truth through pragmatism and inquiry, whereby the inquiry process itself is flexible, and it is not assumed that wisdom and truth reside in any one source or method.
6 Positive orientation toward the future, to be able to assess the systematic consequences of different courses of action while also being able to assess whether or not current solutions are working.
7 Commitment to open and task-relevant communication.
8 Commitment to cultural diversity.
9 Commitment to systemic thinking.
10 Belief that cultural analysis is a valid lens through which we can understand and improve the world.

In 2003, an entire issue of the journal *Advances in Developing Human Resources* was devoted to diagnosing learning culture and to testing a research-based instrument – called the Dimensions of Learning Organization Questionnaire (DLOQ) – designed to measure learning culture in a variety of organizational and national contexts. The basis for the DLOQ lies in the premise that only a strong learning culture and climate can support employee learning, and that climate and culture are built by leaders and influencers who learn from their experience, influence the learning of others, and create an environment of expectations that determines desired results that, when achieved, are measured and rewarded (Marsick & Watkins, 2003). That environment is characterized by the creation and promotion of (a) continuous learning opportunities, where learning is designed into the work and opportunities are offered for ongoing education and development; (b) inquiry and dialogue, whereby people gain the capacity to express their views, listen to the views of others; (c) collaboration and team learning, which the culture values and rewards; (d) technology systems to capture and share learning across the enterprise; (e) empowering people toward a collective vision, motivating people to learn what they are held accountable to do; (f) connecting the organization to its environment, so that people can see the impact of their work on the business; (g) strategic leadership for learning, whereby leaders use learning strategically for business results; (h) financial performance, or the state of financial health and resources available for growth; and (i) knowledge performance, where learning and knowledge capacity enhance the organization's products or services. The DLOQ has been used to identify relationships between learning culture and financial and knowledge performance (Ellinger, Ellinger, Yang, & Howton, 2003; Yang, 2003), to compare employee vs. management perceptions of the learning culture (Dymock & McCarthy, 2006), as well as a tool for including learning culture into the strategic planning process (Milton, 2003). Nevertheless, the empirical studies employing the DLOQ instrument have not been consistent in declaring whether they were assessing learning culture or learning organization. Moreover, the use of survey instruments for measuring learning culture has been criticized for variations in the dimensions used to operationalize learning culture (Egan, 2008) and the inability of surveys to capture all the dimensions of culture without being burdensomely long, making question selection a challenge (Schein, 2004).

In a spirit of Dilbert©-like cynicism, Marquardt (2011) postulated that the culture of most organizations is one of non-learning, or even anti-learning, with risk taking, innovation, and information sharing discouraged and not rocking the boat being rewarded. He proposed a list of ten values that characterize a corporate learning culture:

1 A facilitative climate that encourages and prizes learning – learners as heroes – through performance appraisals, public recognition in award ceremonies, and pay and incentive plans that compensate employees for acquiring new knowledge;
2 Learning how to learn, which is as important (if not more important) as the learning content, so that the focus should be on continuous learning and on defining learning needs.
3 Shared responsibility for learning, where employees are responsible for their own learning and the learning of others, where they understand the relationship between their responsibilities and the goals of the organization as a whole;
4 Trust and autonomy, where the culture encourages feedback and disclosure;

5 Incentives for development;

6 Financial commitment to training and development;

7 Collaborative creativity, variety, and diversity;

8 Commitment to continuous product and service improvements, with an eye to achieving world class standards in quality and service;

9 Responsiveness to change and chaos; and

10 Quality of work life, commitment to the development of the full range of human potential in an environment that invites participation and enjoyment.

Writing for *HR Magazine*, a professor of management studies at Marist College defined learning culture as "a community of workers instilled with a 'growth mindset.' People not only want to learn and apply what they've learned to help their organization, they also feel compelled to share their knowledge with others" (Grossman, May 2015, p. 36). Missing from that definition, however, is any linkage to the culture of the organization in which people are learning and sharing their knowledge with others. Table 5.1 summarizes the highlights of the literature related to supporting a culture of learning.

In this chapter and throughout the remainder of this book, we will use Schein's definition of organizational culture as the basis for defining an organization's learning culture. Thus, learning culture encompasses the artifacts, espoused values and beliefs, and basic underlying assumptions that encourage continuous, shared learning to increase knowledge, competence, and performance of individuals, business units, and the organization as a whole. A learning culture encourages people to take charge of their own learning and development (L&D) and facilitates opportunities to make them better performers in their current jobs and prepares them to advance in their careers, should they desire to do so.

Learning Culture in Practice

There is no shortage of advice in the practitioner literature on how to create a learning culture. For instance, a nine-point self-assessment aimed at talent management professionals (Lucas, 2006) includes a series of statements covering the extent to which the professional is aware of how he/she is currently doing in areas such as celebrating successes and empowering individuals, advancing coherent arguments for plans, engaging managers, engaging individuals, being willing to experiment with different methods, measuring the impact of learning through the use of hard indicators (e.g., reduced attrition rate) and soft measures, and being flexible. Consultancy firms offer their own proprietary instruments for creating and sustaining a learning culture, while a YouTube search using the keywords "building a learning culture" yields more than 10,000 hits from practitioners across the full spectrum of knowledge, experience, and credibility. Common to

Table 5.1 Supporting a Culture of Learning: Key Constructs

Key Construct	Main Ideas	Selected Authors
Organizational Learning	• A group-based, organizational culture perspective • Consists of of learning processes within multiple teams, some of which help an organization explore and develop new capabilities while others help to execute and improve existing capabilities • Individual and group-based learning experiences concerning the improvement of organizational performance and goals are transferred into organizational routines, processes and structures, which in turn affect the future learning activities of the organization's members	• Anderson and Lewis (2014) • Argote and Miron-Spektor (2011) • Cook and Yanow (1993) • Edmondson (2002) • Carswell (2012) • Schilling and Kluge (2009)
Learning Organization	• Facilitates opportunities for learning, enabling continuous organizational transformation • Organizational functions and components apparent, interdependent • Individual commitment to learning need identification, followed by mastery of that need • Shift from individual to shared values • Shared vision • Commitment to team learning	• Jamali (2006) • Senge (2006)
Learning Culture	• Structures that encourage experimentation with and support of new work practices • Continuous learning opportunities • Open inquiry and dialogue • Collaboration and team learning • Technology systems to capture and share learning enterprise-wide • Collective vision of learning • Connect the organization to the environment • Commitment to learning to learn	• Dymock and McCarthy (2006) • Ellinger, Ellinger, Yang, & Howton (2003) • Hoyle (2015) • Marquardt (2011) • Marsick and Watkins (2003) • Milton (2003) • Schein (1992, 2004) • Yang (2003)

nearly all of these practitioner sources is the focus on those in a position to create or at least influence an organization to build and sustain a learning culture, i.e., managers.

That said, learning professionals who are not in management positions still have a stake in the learning culture of their organizations. Harold Cypress, Human Resources Training and Development Manager at Planned Systems International, offers his take on organizational culture and learning in *E-Suite Views*.

SvR: You mentioned the importance of understanding your organization's business model. Is understanding the business model the same as understanding organizational culture or is organizational culture something different altogether?

HC: It's not different but the business model is made up of choices, right? So, the executive team, the leader, the owner, whoever makes fundamental choices. What do we want to be? What position do we want in the market and all? The culture is also a choice but you have fewer degrees of freedom because culture builds up over a long period of time. It's brought by people. It's enabled or enhanced or debilitated or ruined by people's actions, and employees will perceive culture change very, very quickly. So, any kind of perturbation, an outside influence, a stimulus, a change or something like that can affect the culture. You don't have as much control over it as you do over the other choices that you make for the business model. Culture is something that you can assess where you're at, you can identify what you would like to be better but your ability to make a change is much more difficult, slower, or sometimes constrained.

SvR: Isn't it the leadership that makes the culture?

HC: I wouldn't say that leadership makes the culture. I would say that leadership needs to understand what it is that helps people do a good job, using the culture as a lever. But there are some cultural aspects that one can find out about or observe. For example, in some businesses, they might see turnover and they might look into it a little bit further, interview people both before they quit and after they quit and you might learn something like, "I left because I really couldn't see a path forward to either grow and develop or make more money" or whatever, or someone might say, "I just don't like the way the managers hide things," et cetera, et cetera. So, if you can find out about those things and you can do things to change them, all the better, and you may impact the culture. But the culture is made up of, first of all, shared beliefs. That's one thing. But there are other elements of the culture: how people

	make decisions and how information is shared and then, some practical things. How much money does this company invest in making it a nice place to work? Or responding to your suggestions? If you start asking employees about things, they'll tell you 150,000 things.
SvR:	Right.
HC:	It can range from the trivial to the monumental, but even the trivial will bother somebody. The trivial is like, "The vending machines don't work all the time."
SvR:	Right.
HC:	Nobody at the Harvard Business School is doing a case study on the problematic vending machine, but it can have an impact. So, all those things contribute to cultural artifacts and all. Now, one thing that's worth noting is that learning professionals, including instructional designers, have realized over the years what the impact of cultural manifestations can be on the workplace environment and they've taken that into account in understanding what kind of solutions work best to help people do a better job. And by the way, that's my way of concisely saying, "Why? Why do we ask people to learn or become more aware of information or use their strengths or develop their strengths or whatever? Why? Why is it?" There's only one reason; help people to do a better job.

Harold Cypress's comments make it clear that organizational culture can impact how learning designers perform their work, interact with others, contribute to the decision-making process, and view their own role within the organization. Taking the time to recognize and understand your own organization's culture and sub-cultures will help you to estimate how receptive the organization may be to new and different ways of thinking about learning and the contribution of learning design and technology to individual and organizational performance.

In a 2015 interview with *Forbes* magazine (Higginbottom, 2015), Vlatka Hlupic, Professor of Business and Management at Westminster University, noted how poor managers reflect badly on organizational culture and contribute to employee attrition, even though the job itself may be viewed favorably. Another manifestation of a negative organizational culture is what has been termed the "toxic employee" (Fielkow, 2013), the employee whose words and actions adversely influence colleagues and, ultimately, the organization. When management does not step in – whether reactively or proactively – to eliminate toxic behaviors, this is in all likelihood a clear sign of a negative organizational culture. If you feel that your manager or a colleague illustrates a negative culture but you are not (yet) in a position to change positions or employers, you will need to find ways to either work around that culture or, preferably, contribute to a slow but sure cultural change.

Navigating Your Organization's Cultural Waters with Dilbert© at the Helm

You cannot change or manage an organization's culture on your own but you can manage how you respond to the culture. Although most organizational cultures are not totally toxic, most will have dysfunctional processes and people that will make work less than ideal. After all, Dilbert© continues to navigate the choppy waters of his organization's culture. So, here are some cultural cues he might recommend that you observe:

- **My space, your space, our space, no space.** One of the oldest and most recognized indicators of organizational culture is the physical space in which employees work. In the traditional top down cultures of yesteryear, executives and senior managers were in closed offices, sometimes on a different floor than the rest of the organization, with the size of one's office, desk, or cubicle correlated with one's function level and value as defined by the organization. Although such cultures still exist, they have become less prevalent as organizations began to focus on team work, collaboration, and transparency. If your organization's leaders say they value team work and collaboration but either offer no physical or virtual spaces in which to collaborate or offer no recognition and reward for collaboration, chances are there is a disconnect. Look around and observe your working space and those of others in various functions and departments. What do the spaces tell you about your organization's culture?
- **Use the middy advantage.** Like midshipmen who have just joined the fleet, employees who are new to the organization and/or the profession are expected to ask questions, with more senior employees eager to answer and show what they know about the business. Based on conversations with recruitment and career planning professionals, Casserly (2012) identified five topics that new employees should ask about their first day on the job: (a) review and evaluations, to make sure that the new employee and his/her supervisor and team members are all on the same page when it comes to performance expectations; (b) reputation of the work group within the context of the larger organization, to gain insights into the various sub-cultures and micro-cultures; (c) procedure and process, to go beyond what was shared at the new employee orientation; (d) availability and flexibility, in terms of hours and personal time; and (e) the person who previously held the position, to gauge career trajectory and job "life expectancy."
- **Seek the old salts.** Company policies and procedures for advancement, promotion, and L&D are generally documented and available for all

employees. However, there may be unwritten rules that you need to know in order to be successful in your organization, rules that are not accessible to all employees but are communicated through informal networks. Find the most seasoned colleagues in your workgroup. They are good starting points for learning about those unwritten rules. How and what types of learning opportunities for advancement are offered? What factors make it more likely that someone will get the opportunities desired? Must employees only go through their immediate supervisors to learn about L&D opportunities, or can they explore opportunities through others?

- **Keep a weather eye on those culture cues.** Educate yourself about differences in verbal and non-verbal messages across functions, departments, and groups that work together on a regular basis. This will give insights into the various sub-cultures and how they navigate the waters of the larger organizational culture.
- **Mutiny has its risks.** If you have been on the job for some time and believe you have hit that organizational culture wall, find a group of like-minded colleagues and brainstorm some workarounds. This can be a bit risky, though, particularly in smaller organizations where managers and non-managers are more likely to know employees outside of their direct reporting line. Some managers may see mutiny around every corner.
- **Keep calm; your health plan may not cover treatment for high blood pressure.** It is not always easy to keep our emotions in check (more on that in Chapter 7) and not respond to negativity with more negativity or by just bottling up our feelings inside to avoid unpleasant confrontations. As humans, fight-or-flight is one of our many response mechanisms, both of which not only boost the adrenaline but can also wreak havoc on the blood pressure. When faced with negative behaviors, be they from colleagues or managers, draw on the various healthy coping mechanisms that you may have used in the past (e.g., deep breaths, counting to ten) to give yourself some time to take a step back and ask if the negative behaviors you are encountering are just a one-off – anyone can have a bad day and behave badly – or a regular occurrence that is tolerated and encouraged inside your organization. Remaining calm may not change these behaviors but it will help you to avoid internalizing those behaviors, to the detriment of your health and sanity.

Organizational Culture Self-Check

One of your organization's stated core values is the commitment to continuous learning for all employees. To demonstrate this commitment, the executive team announced a clear and transparent process for obtaining support for L&D opportunities, such as types of learning opportunities supported, amount of financial support for various opportunities, and policies on time off to participate in such opportunities. Although you have submitted three requests for L&D in the last 12 months, none of the requests have been approved, even though you have followed the approval process and your requests fall within the various documented categories approved for support. Your supervisor agrees that you have followed the process correctly, but does not think the opportunities you requested are really essential for doing your job. What do you do?

a) Prepare a one-page, outcomes-driven rationale as to why your preferred opportunity is essential for your job; then, schedule a one-on-one meeting with your supervisor to share your document.
b) Ask other members of your team if they have obtained L&D approvals in the last 12 months; then, meet with your supervisor to discuss why your team members were approved and not you.
c) Go over or around your supervisor to obtain support for your request.
d) Take advantage of your preferred learning opportunity at your own expense; then, demonstrate how you have applied what you learned as an argument for future request approvals.

Of the four options, (a) is the optimal choice. You are not only showing initiative, you are showing your ability to align your personal learning goals with your performance outcomes and with the company's stated core values. Your manager's response will then indicate the extent to which that expressed commitment to employee learning is "real" and speak volumes about the organization's support of a learning culture. Options (b) and (c) run the risk of pulling you into the minefield of office politics and can damage your reputation as a team player and good cultural fit, even though the quality of your work may be excellent. Option (d) is certainly acceptable but shows your commitment to your own L&D somewhat after the fact, rather than proactively.

Food for Thought

1 Your organization has just been acquired by a larger organization in a different but related industry sector. Rumor has it that the acquiring organization has a more competitive culture than your current organization. In addition, your L&D department will no longer be a stand-alone area serving the entire organization but will be integrated into the Human Resources function area of the acquiring organization, serving only select but as yet unknown areas of the new, larger entity. Your manager has assured you that your own job is not in jeopardy but is unable to say whether or not your specific responsibilities will change. How would you go about identifying the culture of the new, larger organization? When would you start?
2 Find and complete an organizational culture quiz on the Internet. Are the resulting scores in line with what you expected?

Up Next

In this chapter, we have (a) reviewed the various definitions, analytical methods, and measures of organizational culture and sub-cultures in the scholarly literature; (b) examined the characteristics of organizational cultures that are supportive of learning; and (c) identified some concrete actions that we can take to be successful within our workplace culture and sub-cultures. The next chapter takes a deep dive into those individuals – some visible, some hidden – who are sometimes the bane of Dilbert's© existence but, nevertheless, contribute to successes and failures, namely, organizational stakeholders.

References

Allaire, Y., & Firsirotu, M. E. (1984). Theories of organizational culture. *Organization Studies, 5*(3), 193–226.

Allen, D. G. (2008). *Retaining talent: A guide to analyzing and managing employee turnover*. Retrieved from www.shrm.org/about/foundation/research/Documents/Retaining%20Talent-%20Final.pdf.

Alvesson, M. (1990). On the popularity of organizational culture. *Acta Sociologica, 33*(1), 31–49.

Alvesson, M. (2002). *Understanding Organizational Culture*. Thousand Oaks, CA: Sage Publications.

Anderson, E. (2015, March). Is "cultural fit" just a new way to discriminate? *Forbes*. Retrieved from www.forbes.com/sites/erikaandersen/2015/03/17/is-cultural-fit-just-a-new-way-to-discriminate/#71b2ccbf73b9.

Anderson, E., & Lewis, K. (2014). A dynamic model of individual and collective learning. *Organization Science, 25*(2), 356–76.

Argote, L., & Miron-Spektor, E. (2011). Organizational learning: From experience to knowledge. *Organization Science, 22*(5), 1123–37.

Aryee, S. (1991). Creating a committed workforce: Linking socialization practices to business strategy. *Asia Pacific Journal of Human Resources, 29*(1), 102–12.

Baldwin, J. R., Faulkner, S. L., Hecht, M. L., & Lindsley, S. L. (Eds.). (2006). *Redefining Culture: Perspectives across the Disciplines*. Mahwah, NJ: Lawrence Erlbaum Associates, Inc.

Barney, J. B. (1986). Organizational culture: Can it be a source of sustained competitive advantage? *Academy of Management Review, 11*(3), 656–65.

Blumenthal, A. (1936). The nature of culture. *American Sociological Review, 1*(6), 875–93.

Boas, F. (1911). *The Mind of Primitive Man*. New York, NY: The Macmillan Company.

Bodley, J. H. (1994). *Cultural Anthropology: Tribes, States, and the Global System*. Mountain View, CA: Mayfield Pub. Co.

Bolon, D. S., & Bolon, D. S. (1994). A reconceptualization and analysis of organizational culture: the influence of groups and their idiocultures. *Journal of Managerial Psychology, 9*(5), 22–7.

Bouton, K. (2015, July). Recruiting for cultural fit. *Harvard Business Review*. Retrieved from https://hbr.org/2015/07/recruiting-for-cultural-fit.

Calhoun, L. (2015). 5 big reasons not to hire for culture fit. *Inc.com*. Retrieved from www.inc.com/lisa-calhoun/5-big-reasons-not-to-hire-for-culture-fit.html.

Carswell, P. (2012). Strategies for organizational learning in healthcare. *Organization Development Journal*, 30(4), 25–31.

Casserly, M. (2012). The five questions every new employee should ask on their first day. *Forbes*. Retrieved from www.forbes.com/sites/meghancasserly/2012/10/16/five-questions-new-employee-should-ask-first-day/#6736fdc516a3.

Cook, S., & Yanow, D. (1993). Culture and organizational learning. *Journal of Management Inquiry*, 2(4), 373–90.

Denison, D. R., & Mishra, A. K. (1995). Toward a theory of organizational culture and effectiveness. *Organization Science*, 6(2), 204–23.

Dunn, K. (2015). The big lie of hiring for cultural fit. *Workforce*. Retrieved from www.workforce.com/2015/12/20/the-big-lie-of-hiring-for-cultural-fit/.

Dymock, D., & McCarthy, C. (2006). Towards a learning organization? Employee perceptions. *The Learning Organization*, 13(5), 525–37.

Editorial objectives. (n.d.). *The Learning Organization*. Retrieved from http://emeraldgrouppublishing.com/products/journals/journals.htm?id=tlo.

Edmondson, A. (2002). The local and variegated nature of learning in organizations: A group-level perspective. *Organization Science*, 13(2), 128–46.

Egan, T. M. (2008). The relevance of organization subculture for motivation to transfer learning. *Human Resource Development Quarterly*, 19(4), 299–322.

Ellinger, A. D., Ellinger, A. E., Yang, B., & Howton, S. W. (2003). Making the business case for the learning organization concept. *Advances in Developing Human Resources*, 5(2), 163–72.

Evans, P. (1986). The context of strategic human resource management policy in complex firms. *Management Forum*, 6, 309–18.

Fielkow, B. L. (2013). *Driving to Perfection: Achieving Business Excellence by Creating a Vibrant Culture*. Minneapolis, MN: Two Harbors Press.

Galperin, B. L., & Lituchy, T. R. (2013). Human resource development in service firms across cultures. *Human Resource Development Review*, 13(3), 336–68.

Geertz, C. (1973). *The Interpretation of Culture: Selected Essays*. New York, NY: Basic Books.

Gelder, K. (2007). *Subcultures: Cultural Histories and Social Practice*. New York, NY: Routledge.

Gerdhe, S. (2012). The policies that affect the extent of the sub-cultures' alignment in organization. *Journal of Knowledge Management, Economics, and Information Technology*, 2(1), 191.

Gillespie, R. (1991). *Manufacturing Knowledge: A History of the Hawthorne Experiments*. Cambridge, MA: Cambridge University Press.

Ginevicius, R., & Vaitkunaite, V. (2006). Analysis of organizational culture dimensions impacting performance. *Journal of Business Economics and Management*, 7(4), 201–11.

Glisson, C. (2015). The role of organizational culture and climate in innovation and effectiveness. *Human Service Organizations: Management, Leadership & Governance*, 39(4), 245–50.

Gordon, G. C. (1991). Industry determinants of organizational culture. *Academy of Management Review*, 16(2), 396–415.

Gosh, P., Satyawadi, R., Joshi, J. P., & Mohd, S. (2013). Who stays with you? Factors predicting employee intention to stay. *International Journal of Organizational Analysis*, 21(3), 288–312.

Gregory, K. L. (1983). Native-view paradigms: Multiple cultures and culture conflicts in organizations. *Administrative Science Quarterly*, 28, 359–76.

Grossman, R. J. (2015, May). A learning culture. *HR Magazine*, 60(4), 36–42.

Hanselman, A. (2013, July). What's culture – and what's yours? *Management. Issues*. Retrieved from www.management-issues.com/opinion/6719/whats-culture-and-whats-yours/.

Harris, S. G. (1994). Organizational culture and individual sensemaking: A schema-based perspective. *Organization Science*, 5(3), 309–21.

Hatch, M. J. (1993). The dynamics of organizational culture. *Academy of Management Review*, 18(4), 657–93.

Helms, M. M., & Stern, R. (2001). Exploring the factors that influence employees' perceptions of their organization's culture. *Journal of Management in Medicine*, 15(6), 415–29.

Higginbottom, K. (2015, September). Bad bosses at the heart of employee turnover. *Forbes*. Retrieved from www.forbes.com/sites/karenhigginbottom/2015/09/08/bad-bosses-at-the-heart-of-employee-turnover/#4712d1fd4075.

Hill, L. (2013, January). Job applicants' cultural fit can trump qualifications. *BloombergBusiness*. Retrieved from www.bloomberg.com/news/articles/2013-01-03/job-applicants-cultural-fit-can-trump-qualifications.

Hoyle, R. (2015). *Informal Learning in Organizations: How to Create a Continuous Learning Culture*. London, UK: Kogan Page Limited.

Jamali, D. (2006). Insights into triple bottom line integration from a learning organization perspective. *Business Process Management Journal*, 12(6), 809–21.

Johansson, C., Åström, S., Kauffeldt, A., Helldin, L., & Carlström, E. (2014). Culture as a predictor of resistance to change: A study of competing values in a psychiatric nursing context. *Health Policy*, 114(2), 156–62.

Jung, T., Scott, T., Davies, H. T. O., Bower, P., Whalley, D., McNally, R. et al. (2009). Instruments for exploring organizational culture: A review of the literature. *Public Administration Review*, 69(6), 1087–96.

Kluckhohn, C., Untereiner, W., & Kroeber, A. L. (1952). *Culture: A Critical Review of Concepts and Definitions*. New York, NY: Vintage Books.

Kluge, A., & Schilling, J. (2003). Organizational learning and learning organizations: Theory and empirical findings. *The Psychologist-Manager Journal*, 6(1), 31–50.

Kotter, J. (2012). The key to changing organizational culture. *Forbes*. Retrieved from www.forbes.com/sites/johnkotter/2012/09/27/the-key-to-changing-organizational-culture/#7eeb8f8d7238.

Kristof-Brown, A. L., Zimmerman, R. D., & Johnson, E. C. (2005). Consequences of individuals' fit at work: A meta-analysis of person-job, person-organization, person-group, and person-supervisor fit. *Personnel Psychology*, 58, 281–342.

Kuper, A. (2009). *Culture: The Anthropologists' Account*. Cambridge, MA: Harvard University Press.

Lucas, B. (2006). How to … create a learning culture. *People Management*, 12(18), 46–7.

Marcoulides, G. A., & Heck, R. H. (1993). Organizational culture and performance: Preparing and testing a model. *Organization Science*, 4(2), 209–25.

Marquardt, M. J. (2011). *Building the Learning Organization: Achieving Strategic Advantage through a Commitment to Learning* (3rd ed.). Boston, MA: Nicholas Brealey Publishing.

Marsick, V. J., & Watkins, K. E. (2003). Demonstrating the value of an organization's learning culture: The dimensions of the learning organization questionnaire. *Advances in Developing Human Resources*, 5(2), 132–51.

McGregor, D. (1960). *The Human Side of Enterprise*. New York, NY: McGraw-Hill.

Mead, M. (1937). The Arapesh of New Guinea. In *Cooperation and Competition among Primitive Peoples* (pp. 20–50). New York, NY: McGraw-Hill Book Company.

Meek, V. L. (1988). Organizational culture: Origins and weaknesses. *Organization Studies*, 9(4), 453–73.

Milton, J. (2003). Professional associations as learning systems: Learning + strategy + action = strategic learning. *Advances in Human Resource Development*, 5(2), 173–81.

Moore, O. K. (1952). Nominal definitions of 'culture.' *Philosophy of Science*, 19(4), 245–56.

Murdock, G. P., Ford, C. S., & Hudson, A. E. (1938). *Outline of Cultural Materials*. New Haven, CT: Cross-Cultural Survey, Institute of Human Relations, Yale University.

O'Reilly III, C. A., Chatman, J., & Caldwell, D. F. (1991). People and organizational culture: A profile comparison approach to assessing person-organization fit. *Academy of Management Journal*, 34(3), 487–516.

Ott, J. (1989). *The Organizational Culture Perspective*. Chicago, IL: Richard D. Irwin.

Ouchi, W. G., & Wilkins, A. L. (1985). Organizational culture. *Annual Review of Sociology*, 11, 457–83.

Parsons, T., Shils, E. A., & Olds, J. (1965). Systems of value orientation. In T. Parsons, E. A. Shils, & N. J. Smelser (Eds.), *Toward a General Theory of Action: Theoretical Foundations for the Social Sciences*. Saint John, New Brunswick, Canada: Transaction Publishers.

Pettigrew, A. M. (1979). On studying organizational cultures. *Administrative Science Quarterly*, 24(4), 570–81.

Plakhotnik, M. S., & Rocco, T. S. (2011). What do we know, how much, and why it matters: Organizational culture and AHRD research. *Human Resource Development Review*, 10(1), 74–100.

Roethlisberger, F. J., & Dickson, W. J. (1939). *Management and the Worker: An Account of a Research Program Conducted by the Western Electric Company, Hawthorne Works, Chicago*. Cambridge, MA: Harvard University Press.

Schein, E. H. (1984). Coming to a new awareness of organizational culture. *Sloan Management Review*, 25(2), 3–16.

Schein, E. H. (1992). *Organizational Culture and Leadership* (1st ed.). San Francisco, CA: Jossey-Bass.

Schein, E. H. (2004). *Organizational Culture and Leadership* (3rd ed.). San Francisco, CA: Jossey-Bass.

Schilling, J., & Kluge, A. (2009). Barriers to organizational learning: An integration of theory and practice. *International Journal of Management Reviews*, 11(3), 337–60.

Senge, P. M. (2006). *The Fifth Discipline: The Art & Practice of the Learning Organization* (2nd ed.). New York, NY: Random House Business Books.

Shearman, M. S. (2013). American workers' organizational identification with a Japanese multinational manufacturer. *The International Journal of Human Resource Management*, 24(10), 1968–84.

Sheridan, J. E. (1992). Organizational culture and employee retention. *Academy of Management Journal*, 35(5), 1036–56.

Singh, L. (2013). Study of organizational culture of a telecom company. *International Journal of Management Prudence*, 52(2), 39–46.

Sonnenfeld, J. A. (1985). Shedding light on the Hawthorne studies. *Journal of Occupational Behavior*, 6(2), 111–30.

Straub, D., Loch, K., Evaristo, R., Karahenna, E., & Srite, M. (2002). Toward a theory-based measurement of culture. In E. J. Szewczak & C. R. Snodgrass (Eds.), *Human Factors in Information Systems* (pp. 61–83). Hershey, PA: IRM Press.

Testa, M. R., Mueller, S. L., & Thomas, A. S. (2003). Cultural fit and job satisfaction in a global service environment. *MIR: Management International Review*, *43*(2), 129–48.

Tharp, B. M. (2009). *Defining "culture" and "organizational culture": From anthropology to the office*. Company White Paper. Haworth The RCF Group. Holland, MI. Retrieved from www.thercfgroup.com/files/resources/Defining-Culture-and-Organizationa-Culture_5.pdf.

Thompson, M. A., & Kahnweiler, W. M. (2002). An exploratory investigation of learning culture theory and employee participation in decision making. *Human Resource Development Quarterly*, *13*(3), 271–88.

Trice, H., & Beyer, J. (1993). *The Cultures of Work Organizations*. Upper Saddle River, NJ: Prentice Hall.

Tylor, E. B. (1871). *Primitive Culture: Researches into the Development of Mythology, Philosophy, Religion, Art and Custom* (Vol. 1). London, UK: John Murray.

Van Maanen, J., & Barley, S. R. (1984). Occupational communities: vulture and control in organizations. In B. Staw & L. L. Cummings (Eds.), *Research in Organizational Behavior* (pp. 287–365). Greenwich, CT: JAI Press.

Van Tiem, D. M., Moseley, J. L., & Dessinger, J. C. (2012). *Fundamentals of Performance Improvement* (3rd ed.). San Francisco, CA: Pfeiffer.

Verquer, M. L., Beehr, T. A., & Wagner, S. H. (2003). A meta-analysis of relations between person-organization fit and work attitudes. *Journal of Vocational Behavior*, *63*(3), 473–89.

Watkins, M. (2013, May). What is organizational culture? And why should we care? *Harvard Business Review*. Retrieved from https://hbr.org/2013/05/what-is-organizational-culture.

Weber, M. (1949). *The Methodology of the Social Sciences*. New York, NY: The Free Press.

Willis, C. D., Saul, J., Bevan, H., Scheirer, M. A., Best, A., Greenhaigh, T. et al. (2016). Sustaining organizational culture change in health systems. *Journal of Health Organization and Management*, *30*(1), 2–30.

Workforce Institute at Kronos. (2015). *The Workforce Institute at Kronos and Workplace Trends Employee Engagement Lifecycle Series: Who's the boss of workplace culture?* Chelmsford, MA. Retrieved from www.kronos.com/about-us/newsroom/whos-boss-workplace-culture-hr-managers-and-employees-disagree-says-new-workforce.

Yang, B. (2003). Identifying valid and reliable measures for dimensions of a learning culture. *Advances in Developing Human Resources*, *5*(2), 152–62.

6 Stakeholder Analysis
Who's on First?

In the previous chapter, we looked at organizational culture and sub-cultures and discussed how those cultures can affect your work as a learning designer. We also explored the ways in which to identify the people who could provide you with insights about the culture and sub-cultures of an organization. Depending on who those individuals are and what role they serve in any given context, we might consider them to be organizational stakeholders. But then again, we might not.

It would appear that stakeholders are everywhere. In our day-to-day work, we focus on engaging stakeholders, getting stakeholder buy-in to our ideas, managing stakeholder expectations, communicating with stakeholders, not to mention keeping track of stakeholders whose identities may change as our projects or circumstances change. Like Dilbert©, we may feel that stakeholders are more concepts than corporal beings. Well, to some extent, they are. Here are three definitions of the word "stakeholder":

- One who is involved in or affected by a course of action (Stakeholder [Def. 3], n.d.).
- A person, group, or organization that has interest or concern in an organization. Stakeholders can affect or be affected by the organization's actions, objectives, and policies. Some examples of key stakeholders are creditors, directors, employees, government (and its agencies), owners (shareholders), suppliers, unions, and the community from which the business draws its resources (Stakeholder, n.d.a).
- A person, such as an employee, customer, or citizen who is involved with an organization, society, etc., and therefore has responsibilities toward it and an interest in its success (Stakeholder, n.d.b).

The first definition is generic in nature, unrelated to any particular situation or context. If we were to take this definition literally, we would be involved in or affected by an infinite number of known and unknown courses of action that would be humanly impossible to identify, let alone manage. The second definition offers the organization – public and private sector – as the situating context and provides examples of stakeholders in- and outside of the organization in question. We are better able to move from stakeholder-as-concept to stakeholder-as-individual with this definition, although we are still pressed to differentiate between stakeholders who are "key" and those who are not, and what the specific roles of the various stakeholder groups would be in any given situation. The third definition introduces the idea of responsibilities toward the organization, which may include not only functional responsibilities but ethical and moral ones as well.

At this point, you may be thinking, *Why can't I just focus on those who are going to help me do my job?* The short answer is: yes, please do. Among the competencies expected of designers seeking to advance their careers and move to the management of design teams (IBSTPI, 2014) is the ability to manage relationships, including relationships with stakeholders in a variety of work-related contexts. However, because your job is complex, probably project-driven, with multiple touchpoints within your department, as well as across and outside of your organization, there are multiple stakeholders whose interests and support are critical to your job. The identity of stakeholders may change depending on what you are doing and when. Their roles may change, and their interests in the outcomes of your work may also be subject to change. Consequently, stakeholders are an evolving, almost amorphous group of individuals whom you must continuously evaluate and engage in order to do your job successfully. Some stakeholders may also be instrumental for ensuring that you receive recognition for doing your job well and for supporting your career advancement efforts. For that reason, you should view stakeholder relationships as a process whereby you are frequently identifying, engaging with, and managing stakeholder expectations at multiple levels and situations. In this chapter, we will

- Review the various definitions of and theories about stakeholders in an organizational context;
- Examine the most common approaches to identifying, analyzing, and managing stakeholders; and
- Identify some easy-to-use techniques for setting and managing expectations of multiple stakeholders in various situational contexts.

Stakeholder Theory and the Organization

R. Edward Freeman is generally acknowledged as the first scholar to offer a comprehensive theory about stakeholders in an organizational context. In his seminal book *Strategic Management: A Stakeholder Approach* (Freeman, 1984), Freeman began with a relatively broad definition of a stakeholder in an organization as "any group or individual who can affect or is affected by the achievement of the organization's objectives" (p. 46). Drawing on various disciplines, concepts, and literature, including systems theory, corporate planning, and corporate social responsibility, Freeman's book identified and modeled the individuals and groups who are stakeholders of a corporation and whose interests must be addressed as part of management's decision-making process. In addition to those with financial ownership (i.e., shareholders), Freeman identified other entities with interests in the organization, including employees, customers, suppliers, communities, competitors, governmental entities, professional associations, and trade unions. To better understand stakeholder interests and predict their behaviors, Freeman recommended that managers use market segmentation techniques, such as geographic segmentation, demographic segmentation, psychographic or values and beliefs segmentation, and behavioral segmentation, to categorize stakeholders into subsets, with each subset having similar or related needs, interests, and priorities. Management could then develop different communication strategies, products, and services to meet the needs of the various subgroups.

Several scholars have built on Freeman's foundational stakeholder theory. For instance, Donaldson and Preston (1995) focused on how the theory is to be used, and they identified three distinctive but mutually supportive approaches. The first approach, the descriptive approach, is used in research to describe the characteristics and behaviors of organizations, focusing on how senior management makes decisions, how it identifies and accommodates its constituents, what it deems the role of management to be, and the nature of the organization itself (industry sector, size, structure, etc.). In this approach, the emphasis is on what you do with the stakeholders once they are identified. The second approach is the instrumental approach. This approach uses empirical data to identify connections between stakeholder management efforts and organizational profitability and efficiency. The instrumental approach implicitly links means and ends, with organizations that successfully manage their stakeholders having a competitive advantage over organizations that do not (Jawahar & McLaughlin, 2001). Here, the emphasis is on the impact of stakeholders on an organization's ability to function in a competitive environment. The third approach, or the normative approach, explores the function of the organization and identifies the moral and philosophical principles that guide the organization's operations and management. The normative approach focuses on that slice of organizational culture that reflects the shared values and vision and demonstrates how those values and vision contribute to stakeholder interests in the organization. In short, Donaldson and Preston expanded the stakeholder theory into a theory of organizational management that includes moral and ethical values.

Mitchell, Agle, and Wood (1997) differentiated between the stakeholder theory and what they termed the "stakeholder approach." For them, the stakeholder theory seeks to clearly and systematically identify which groups are stakeholders deserving of or requiring management attention and who are not. This is what we would consider to be identification of key stakeholders, because it involves a ranking or rating of various potential stakeholders in order of importance to and/or their impact on the project or organization. By way of contrast, the stakeholder approach examines the organization in the context of its environment and seeks to broaden the management's vision of stakeholder roles and responsibilities beyond the profit maximization function. This would include those who may not be directly impacted by an organizational decision but who nevertheless have some interest in that decision. Although this would appear to be similar to Freeman's view of stakeholders as including both shareholders and non-shareholders, Mitchell et al. wrestled with how best to define what it means to be a stakeholder, citing more than 27 definitions used in the literature from 1963 to 1995, and observing the following:

> There is not much disagreement on "what kind of entity" can be a stakeholder. Person, groups, neighborhoods, organizations, institutions, societies, and even the natural environment are generally thought to qualify as actual or potential stakeholders. We find that it is the view taken about the existence and nature of the 'stake' that 'what counts' is ultimately decided. (pp. 855–6)

Based on their review of the literature, they concluded by arguing that stakeholders must possess a combination of three attributes: (a) power, or the extent that an individual or group has the means to impose its will on the relationship; (b) legitimacy, or socially accepted and expected structures or behaviors; and (c) urgency of a claim, the time sensitivity, or criticality of the stakeholder's claims. Power and legitimacy are interrelated and the three attributes can overlap. These three attributes are the filters through which an organization's managers give priority to competing stakeholder claims, what Mitchell et al. defined as stakeholder "salience," with the highest priority given to those possessing all three attributes. By constructing pairs of these attributes, Mitchell et al. identified eight types of stakeholders along with the implications of each stakeholder pair for the organization and displayed them in a Venn diagram (Figure 6.1):

1 Dormant stakeholders: This type of stakeholder has the power to impose his/her will but lacks both a legitimate relationship and an urgent claim, so that his/her power remains unused. In a design context, an example of a dormant stakeholder would be a former team member who has moved on to a different organization but has the ability to share positive or negative views on social media regarding his/her design team experiences. Unless the dormant stakeholder actually exercises that power, management has no need to actively engage with that stakeholder.

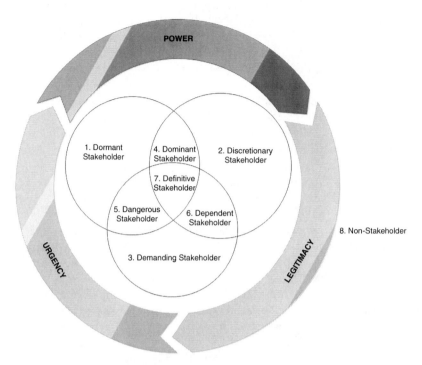

Figure 6.1 Stakeholder Salience Model.

(Adapted from Toward a Theory of Stakeholder Identification and Salience: Defining the Principle of Who and What Really Counts. R. K. Mitchell, B. R. Agle, and D. J. Wood, 1997, *Academy of Management Review*, 22, p. 873. Copyright 1997 by the Academy of Management.)

2 Discretionary stakeholders: This type of stakeholder possesses legitimacy but not power or urgency and, thus, does not require management engagement. An example of a discretionary stakeholder would be the beneficiaries of the work of a charitable organization. In a design context, the clients of your clients could be considered discretionary stakeholders in that your management is not required to engage directly with your clients' clients.

3 Demanding stakeholders: This type possesses urgent claims but neither power nor legitimacy. An example would be the lone team member whose relatively brusque manner during meetings is annoying but has no effect on either team performance or project progress.

4 Dominant stakeholders: Often considered to be among the "key" stakeholders, this type possesses both power and legitimacy. In the private sector, examples of this type include shareholders and boards of directors; in the K–12 sector, Parent Teacher Associations and local school boards would fall into this category. This type of stakeholder receives considerable attention from an organization's management team.

5　Dangerous stakeholders: Possessing both power and urgency but lacking legitimacy, Mitchell et al. deemed this type of stakeholder to be "dangerous" in that he/she tends to use coercive tactics to foster claims that may not be legitimate. An example of this type of stakeholder would be the disgruntled team member who sabotages a project prior to leaving the organization.

6　Dependent stakeholders: This type possesses legitimacy and urgency but must rely on other stakeholders for the power to address his/her claims. In K–12 education, students are dependent stakeholders who rely on teachers, parents, and others in the education sector to satisfy his/her claim to an education.

7　Definitive stakeholders: This type of stakeholder possesses two of the three attributes and then gains the relevant missing attribute. Often, dominant stakeholders with an urgent issue, or dependent groups with powerful legal support become definitive stakeholders. The 2001 ouster of Hewlett-Packard's CEO by the company's board of directors is an example of dominant stakeholders, with the urgent issue of the tumbling share price, who seize power to change the organization's leadership. Such shifts rarely occur within learning and development (Learning and Development) units but the units may be affected when those shifts are accompanied by restructuring, mergers, or acquisitions.

8　Non- or potential stakeholders: While not possessing any of the three attributes at a particular moment, this type may acquire one or more of the required attributes, should circumstances change.

Mitchell et al.'s model of stakeholder salience is a dynamic model because the extent to which a stakeholder is deemed to possess the required attributes is based on management perception and, as such, may change under any given circumstance. Moreover, the stakeholders may not be aware of how the managers are categorizing them and, as such, may not behave in ways that those managers expected. The model has been tested empirically and appears to be sound (Magness, 2008; Weber & Marley, 2012).

Based on a review of the literature published in the decade since Freeman laid the foundation of the stakeholder theory, Jones and Wicks (1999) noted that the stakeholder theory has gained the most traction in two streams of research, namely, the business and society stream, and the business ethics stream, with a divergence of perspectives between the streams. They defined the business and society stream as viewing the stakeholder theory as a potential foundation for the growth of social science-based research, while the business ethics stream views the stakeholder theory as an umbrella term describing a class of narrative accounts, each based on its own moral principles. Referring to the Donaldson and Preston (1995) discussion of descriptive, instrumental, and normative approaches, Jones and Wicks called for a convergent stakeholder theory that combines normative and instrumental elements and demonstrates how managers can create ways of doing business that are both moral and workable. Consequently, the basic premises of the stakeholder theory would include the following:

- The corporation has relationships with many constituent groups (stakeholders) that affect and are affected by its decisions. This was Freeman's (1984) original use of the term "stakeholder."
- The stakeholder theory is concerned with the nature of these relationships in terms of both processes and outcomes for the organization and its stakeholders. The relationships and outcomes are implicit in the stakeholder salience model developed by Mitchell et al. (1997).
- The interests of all "legitimate" stakeholders have intrinsic value and no set of interests is assumed to dominate the others. Stakeholder legitimacy arises from the principle of stakeholder fairness (Phillips, 1997), whereby stakeholder obligations and, thus, stakeholder status are created when the organization voluntarily accepts the contributions of a group or individual.
- The stakeholder theory focuses on management decision-making.

Other scholars have emphasized roles rather than individuals as central to stakeholder identification and management. Referencing the software development industry, Sharp, Finkelstein, and Galai (1999) advocated contextualizing stakeholder identification in terms of specific projects. Using requirements engineering as an example, they identified what they called a baseline of stakeholders consisting of users, developers, legislators, and decision-makers. A web of stakeholders surrounds each of the baseline groups. To flesh out that web, you must identify all specific roles within the baseline group, followed by supplier stakeholders for each baseline role, client stakeholders for each baseline role, and satellite stakeholders for each baseline group. Similar step-by-step processes for project-based stakeholder identification have been applied in the construction industry (Olander, 2007), in hospitality and tourism (Currie, Seaton, & Wesley, 2009), and in environmental studies (Reed et al., 2009).

Other role-focused models of stakeholder theory seek to explain why different stakeholders influence organizations in different ways. One such model (Friedman & Miles, 2002) suggested four structural configurations of stakeholders. The structures are defined by the extent to which the goals, needs, and desires of a particular stakeholder group are compatible with those of the organization (e.g., shareholders, top management, companies connected through common trade associations and initiatives) or incompatible (e.g., trade unions, low-level employees, customers, and lenders), rendering them necessary stakeholders or contingent stakeholders. A similar role-focused model examined stakeholders as actors who have an interest in the issues at hand and are affected by the issues and who could influence issue outcomes, and included empirical testing of that model in a case study of a New Zealand supermarket with declining market share

(Elias & Cavana, 2001). The study results supported the value of applying stakeholder analysis to the retooling of organizational objectives that take into account multiple stakeholder perspectives. The role-based focus has also extended to a body of knowledge in the fields of business ethics (DeGeorge, 2009; Shafritz & Madsen, 1990; Velasquez, 2014), economics (Jones, 1995; Kaufman & Englander, 2011; Tse, 2011), and human resource management (Ferrary, 2009; Greenwood & Anderson, 2009; Greenwood & Freeman, 2011). However, it is in the field of business, specifically organizational management, where stakeholder theory has generated the most robust body of knowledge.

The application of market segmentation techniques that Freeman (1984) advocated has also gained some adherents. In a systematic review of the management literature from 1990 to 1999, Wolfe and Putler (2002) argued against what they called the "role primacy approach" to the stakeholder theory because there are situations in which self-interest does not constitute the primary motivator of an individual's attitudes and priorities. In such cases, individuals or sub-groups, each within different role-based stakeholder groups, have more similar priorities with respect to a particular issue than they have with others within their own role-based stakeholder groups. In other words, the nature of a stakeholder's interest is a central determinant of the homogeneity or heterogeneity of the group's priorities. As a result, Wolfe and Putler advocated using benefit segmentation – classifying groups by benefits they seek from a particular product/service – then, following that up with segment profiling or determining whether there is a common set of demographics or other characteristics that the members of the segment hold in common and which distinguishes them from members of other segments. Integrating elements from the stakeholder salience model (Mitchell, Agle, & Wood, 1997), Wolfe and Putler offered the following process steps for analyzing stakeholders:

1　Identify stakeholder roles (employees, customers, etc.);
2　Determine which stakeholders are salient (i.e., those who are powerful and have legitimate and urgent claims);
3　Assess the priorities of individuals within the salient stakeholder groups;
4　Develop priority-based clusters by placing individuals into groups with relatively homogeneous priorities;
5　Cross-classify priority-based and role-based stakeholder groups; and
6　In cases in which cross-classification indicates that the role-based stakeholders are diffused broadly across priority-based clusters, profile the latter to determine a set of demographic or other characteristics that members have in common. Together with step five, this step is needed to determine the priorities that should be addressed when communicating with salient stakeholders and to determine what media vehicles should be used to accomplish this communication.

Some 20 years after setting down his theory on stakeholders in an organizational context, Freeman revisited stakeholder theory in collaboration with two other scholars (Freeman, Wicks, & Parmar, 2004) and noted that stakeholder theory asks two core questions: (a) What is the purpose of the firm, aimed at encouraging managers to articulate the shared sense of value they create, and specify what brings its core stakeholders together? and (b) What responsibility does management have to the stakeholders? These questions infer that stakeholder theory begins with the assumption that values are necessarily and explicitly part of doing business. These questions also seem to align with Jones and Wicks's (1999) call for the convergence of normative, descriptive, and instrumental elements into stakeholder theory.

Freeman's work remains the principal starting point for scholars seeking to describe and explain the evolution and impact of stakeholder theory in an organizational context. In a review of articles published from 1984 to 2007 that directly addressed Freeman's work, Laplume, Sonpar, and Litz (2008) identified five themes associated with the stakeholder theory, namely: (a) stakeholder definition and salience; (b) stakeholder actions and responses; (c) firm actions and responses; (d) firm performance; and (d) theory debates. Laplume et al. observed these themes in multiple research fields, beginning with the field of strategic management from 1984 to 1991, which they term the period of Incubation. The period of Incremental Growth (1991–1998) saw the spread of stakeholder theory into organization theory and business ethics, marked by the seminal work of Donaldson and Preston (1995) and by the special issue of the *Academy of Management Review* dedicated exclusively to articles on stakeholder theory. Large academic conferences focused on stakeholder theory, as well as popular references to stakeholders in interviews and speeches by public figures, such as the U.K.'s Tony Blair also sprang up in this period. The third period, the period of Maturity (1999–present) has seen increased attention to social issues and attacks from advocates of shareholder primacy. Laplume et al. further noted that despite this apparent growth in the breadth and depth of stakeholder theory research, the majority of scholarly research tended to focus on large, publicly traded corporations.

Figure 6.2 illustrates in organizational contexts the various definitions and theoretical approaches to stakeholder theory. While it is clear that the seeds planted by Freeman (1984) have branched out into a variety of research streams and foci, what is common to nearly all of the post-Freeman research is the application and enrichment of stakeholder theory as a tool for management decision-making. The emphasis on management has led some scholars to criticize stakeholder theory as being too corporation-centric (Jensen, 2002; Marcoux, 2000; Sternberg, 2000) and focused on management opportunism. Others have criticized stakeholder theory for being a moral doctrine with socialist overtones (Barnett, 1997; Orts & Strudler, 2002). However, Freeman and others have refuted these

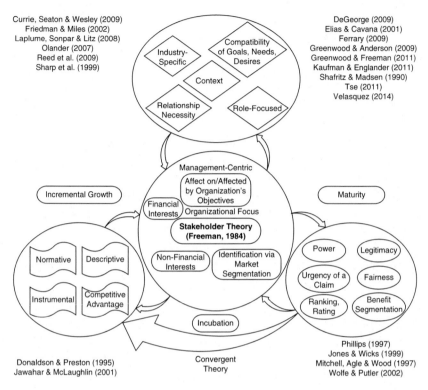

Figure 6.2 Overview of Stakeholder Theory in Organizational Contexts.

criticisms as either "friendly misinterpretations" or outright distortions (Phillips, Freeman, & Wicks, 2003). Nevertheless, if theory is to inform practice, then stakeholder theory should be usable to more organizations than just publicly traded corporations. Furthermore, it is the "how" of stakeholder theory that is valuable to the learning professional.

Stakeholder Theory in Practice

Applying stakeholder theory to the actual implementation of a stakeholder analysis requires a systematic, orderly approach. One of the challenges for practitioners seeking to apply stakeholder theory is a lack of clear direction in the literature about methods and tools to identify all stakeholders and their interests, including tips and techniques for addressing the emergent nature of relationships based on individual situations and contexts (Missonier & Loufrani-Fedida, 2014). However, there are signs that this gap is beginning to be addressed. For instance, Aaltonen (2011) described stakeholder analysis as an interpretive process that could produce varying understandings of the stakeholder environment.

Using project management as an example of a field where stakeholder analysis is central, Aaltonen defined the interpretation process as including (a) scanning, which involves data collection that serves as the input for the actual project stakeholder identification and characterization; (b) interpretation, in which data is given meaning and involves the actual project stakeholder identification, characterization, and classification; and (c) strategy formulation and decision-making, in which the formulation of project stakeholder management strategy occurs. Using four different projects as case studies, Aaltonen found considerable variation in the way project teams interpreted the data collected during the identification phase, with some project management teams actively reaching out to stakeholders and continuously engaging in stakeholder analysis activities, while other project management teams were more passive with regard to stakeholder analysis activities and reacted to external stakeholders only when crises occurred. Aaltonen offered several hypotheses about the reason for the various approaches to stakeholder analysis, including project manager experiences, project complexity and impact, as well as project team skills/abilities. Aaltonen emphasized the point that openness, dialogue, and active engagement of stakeholders, particularly in the front-end phases of a project, reduce the potential for conflict in the execution phase, where time and resources are at a premium.

Bryson (2004) sought to fill the gap in the literature about how to systematically identify and analyze stakeholders by focusing on the public sector. Bryson reasoned that public sector managers need stakeholder analysis to either directly help their organizations perform better or help create an environment that would indirectly improve organizational performance through efforts, such as changing the organization's decision-making protocols, accountability mechanisms, or externally imposed mandates. He noted the adverse consequences (e.g., budget cuts) of not satisfying key stakeholders, with the choice of which stakeholders are "key" characterized as "inherently political, has ethical consequences, and involves judgment." (p. 26). Bryson then presented fifteen stakeholder identification and analysis techniques that could be used in group brainstorming sessions with standard facilitation materials, such as flip charts, colored sticky notes, and marking pens. Although acknowledging that applying the techniques is both time- and labor-intensive, Bryson argued that the effort is modest compared with the consequences of failing to address key stakeholders, their interests, and their input.

Complex projects often involve strategic decisions, conflicting or unclear requirements and expectations, and other hidden factors that make stakeholders central to project success. Trentim (2013) posited that stakeholders should be treated as clients rather than as partners. Drawing on Donaldson & Preston's (1995) normative, instrumental, and descriptive approaches to the application of stakeholder theory, Trentim set down a four-step process for conducting stakeholder analysis at the project level, a process to be repeated at regular intervals throughout the project life cycle:

1   Identify and understand: The goal here is to discover who your stakeholders are at the beginning of your project and gather insights into their values and expectations. To obtain information about the stakeholders, ask questions of fellow team members, supervisors, and those who have worked on similar projects in the past to provide the names of individuals they believe to be stakeholders of the current project. The project sponsor, usually a manager with the authority to provide resources for the project, is also a source of potential stakeholders' names. Recommendations from known stakeholders, as well as from outside suppliers, can provide their thoughts on who the stakeholders of the current project could be.
2   Focus and build: The goal is to define what it is you want from your stakeholder and to build a relationship with that individual in order to assess the nature of his/her interests in your project and his/her influence to affect the progress of your project. You can document and track your stakeholders in a simple spreadsheet with column headings, such as stakeholder name, category (e.g., supplier, supervisor), expectations (theirs, not yours), and influence (friend, foe, and neutral).
3   Influence and persuade: The goal is to emphasize the value and benefits of your project and the need for support from all stakeholders. This is the *WIFM* (what's in it for me) for the stakeholder, the main messages that you communicate to your stakeholders to draw them in. It is also a way of uncovering those hidden stakeholders who may not have yet revealed themselves.
4   Get commitment: The goal is to keep stakeholders abreast of project progress and keep them engaged as the project evolves. This is where your ability to communicate clearly in written and oral form, a foundational competency of instructional designers (IBSTPI, 2014), comes into play.

The not-for-profit sector appears to have done a solid job of providing concrete guidelines for conducting stakeholder analysis within the context of a specific organizational mission, goals, and objectives. For example, the World Bank (World Bank, n.d.) and the World Health Organization (Schmeer, 1999) offer toolkits and guidelines for conducting stakeholder analysis in various countries and contexts. Tools4dev, a website that provides free tools, templates and how-to guides to international development professionals, offers a Stakeholder Analysis Matrix template (Bullen, 2014) to support new program design.

In the L&D field, however, stakeholder analysis tends to be treated as a component of the needs and/or context analysis of the instructional design process, with both scholars and practitioners stressing the importance of stakeholder analysis for designing and testing instructional interventions (Ertmer, Parisio, & Warduk, 2013; Konings, Seidel, & van Merrienboer, 2014; Piskurich, 2006; Rothwell, Benscoter, King, & King, 2015). L&D practitioners view stakeholder analysis as particularly important at the project level. Barbara Wilson-Tarver, Director of Training and Outreach at the U.S. Department of Defense, offers her take on stakeholder analysis in this segment of *E-Suite Views*.

SvR: One of the key competencies for instructional designers is the ability to identify and manage stakeholders. How would you recommend they go about doing that?

BWT: I have learned that the communications director knows who all the stakeholders are – both internal and external. When working on a specific project, the instructional designer should set up a meeting to discuss the project with the head of the department. If this is not the person or manager who will make the decisions about the training project, ask who that person is and set up a meeting with that person. A best practice is to conduct a needs analysis with specific questions about stakeholders and ask the manager to complete it. This is actually one of the most important steps to take before the design begins. You have to know who the stakeholders are or the design may miss the mark. Ask for the contact information of known stakeholders and set up a meeting with them to assess their training needs; they will probably know more than the manager does.

SvR: Can you share a story about how the stakeholders helped or hindered you in your work as a learning professional and what your key take-aways were?

BWT: To be quite honest, stakeholders are a pain sometimes because they often don't understand how instructional design works. Recently, my team designed a training module for a program that one of the directors in my office is responsible for overseeing. The director wanted the design to be very text heavy without any learner engagement or interaction. He believed that we were trying to make the training entertaining as opposed to just providing the information about the program. We tried everything to convince him, but every demo resulted in him wanting us to lose the interaction and add more text.

One day I walked down to his office and started a discussion on how he felt when we'd both recently attended a mandatory training class and the instructor lectured on and on from many PowerPoint slides. He agreed that it was boring and all he wanted to do was get it over with until next year. I used that experience to describe how his stakeholders would feel when they took the course we were designing for his program. I went on to explain that the best way to design an eLearning course is from the learner's perspective. Using his own learning experience helped him understand how important it is to ensure the course was engaging and interactive with just the right amount of text.

Dr. Wilson-Tarver's anecdote about the text-focused director is an excellent example of Trentim's (2013) Influence and Persuade step in the stakeholder analysis process. By recalling the director's own experience with the non-interactive training he was advocating, Dr. Wilson-Tarver was able to tap into the director's *WIFM* to show the value and benefits of interactivity to the learning experience.

Who's on First? Dilbert's© Guide to Stakeholder Analysis

"Who's on First?" is a classic English-language theatrical sketch made famous in the 1930s by the American comedy team of William "Bud" Abbott and Lou Costello. In the sketch, Abbott is identifying to Costello the players on a baseball team, but the names of the players are pronouns like "who," "what," and "why" or conjunctions and phrases used in nonsensical context (Baseball Almanac, Inc., 2016). The resulting confusion between the comedy duo would probably resonate with Dilbert© as he struggles to connect with his own project stakeholders. Process steps, templates, and toolkits intended to facilitate the stakeholder analysis are not particularly helpful without a clear understanding of the end goal. This means thinking about the "why" before selecting the various tools and techniques to facilitate the "how."

Triggers and Time-Boxes: "Why" and "When"

To begin, there is a set of interrelated questions that you should ask yourself before you undertake a stakeholder analysis. First, why do you need to conduct a stakeholder analysis? What were the triggers that made you think that a stakeholder analysis should be conducted? What role do you want the stakeholder to play? What are the time frames and available resources associated with those triggers? For example, let's say the trigger is an instructional design project that you've been given or to which you've been assigned as a project team member, or you've been asked to create training (and have confirmed that training is all/part of the solution) to address a performance problem in a business unit or function group. A stakeholder analysis should be used to inform the design, preparation, and implementation of your instructional product and as part of an evaluation during and after project completion. If your project calls for new and creative ways to address the problem or the client for whom you are constructing a solution has a firm, pre-conceived notion of what the solution should look like, you may want to include stakeholders who are willing and able to serve as counterbalances to that client's perspective.

Pre-established delivery dates will define not only the duration of the entire project but also the time-box available to perform stakeholder analysis. For large, complex projects, such as the development of an entire program or curriculum with a year-long time frame, an in-depth analysis with a detailed assessment of stakeholder interests, identities, positions of authority, and relative influence can take several weeks. Conversely, for a small, simple project, such as updates to an instructional module or job aids that need to be completed in a couple of weeks, a quick phone or online interview with a few stakeholders and one or two well-defined questions would be sufficient for immediate decision-making. The answers to these "why" and "how much time" questions can be part of the front-end analysis that you conduct to determine whether all or part of the problem you've been asked to solve can be solved with instruction (Branch & Kopcha, 2014; Spector & Muraida, 2013).

Overall, a stakeholder analysis provides the following benefits:

- Reveals the interests of stakeholders in relation to your project's objectives. Stakeholders who will be directly affected by or who could directly affect project outcomes are more likely to require your attention than those who are only indirectly affected.
- Identifies actual and potential conflicts of interest, enabling you to better plan for how to engage with a stakeholder who has priorities other than your project.
- Detects attitudinal and emotional issues that may affect project outcomes.
- Discovers the relationships between different stakeholders that help to identify a potential coalition of the willing to promote project success.

Culture and Context: "Where" and "Whether"

In the previous chapter, we explored the impact of organizational culture and sub-cultures on the Learning and Development function. Similarly, organizational culture and context impact our decisions regarding how to analyze and interact with stakeholders. Ideally, you'd like to call on a range of information sources to help minimize individual biases and use different ways of capturing and interpreting information about stakeholder interests and positions. Your analysis can take place at one or more levels, which affects how you go about collecting data and who you identify as a stakeholder. For instance, managerial "insiders" often have strong views about who should be considered a stakeholder and what that stakeholder's interests are. Those views may not align with non-managers or even with managers from other function areas. If your organizational context includes remote employees as well as co-located employees, the geographic location is another source of input that can inform your analysis.

Analysts: The "Who"

The stakeholder analysis is not a solitary process to be undertaken from the comfort of your office. Much of the data you will be collecting is qualitative in nature, requiring interpretation and judgment. A team approach to data collection and analysis reduces the risks of individual biases and assumptions, facilitating a more balanced analysis. A single analyst can ensure a more uniform approach to data collection, increasing data validity and reliability. A supervisor or support group can be used as a sounding board for preliminary findings and proposed next steps in the stakeholder analysis process. However, time and resource constraints will determine whether you are a one-person data collection and analysis operation or whether to have a team of analysts at your disposal.

Identifying Stakeholders: The "Which Ones"

You have answered your preparatory questions and defined the time and resource boundaries. Now you can define the individuals who have an interest in or who, by virtue of their position, can influence the problem you are seeking to solve. Gaining access to potential stakeholders depends on how you approach them and how well you can articulate the benefit to them of providing you with the information you need. At this point, you can dip into your designer's toolkit and pull out some tried and true methods that you have probably already used in the design process. One way of generating an initial list of stakeholders is to "snowball" or "chain sample" your preliminary list of stakeholders. A widely used method of sampling in qualitative research, snowballing involves contacting a group of participants, asking them for the names of others who may be interested in participating, then repeating the process until the desired sample is reached. Snowballing is particularly helpful for accessing hard-to-reach and hidden stakeholders (Atkinson & Flint, 2001; Noy, 2008). The trigger questions that you asked yourself in preparing for the analysis can also be used to help each contact person identify other potential stakeholders with similar interests in the issue you are addressing. Furthermore, a referral increases the likelihood of gaining access to a potential stakeholder than would a cold call via email or phone.

Data Collection: The "How"

Beginning with the end in mind, you want to be sure that your data collection instruments enable you to answer the following questions:

- Who does the problem you are seeking to solve affect most?
- Within that problem-affected group, who is most likely to be able to change?

- Who is most likely to be resistant to change or difficult to engage?
- Who is in a position to help bring about change to address the problem?
- Who has a vested interest in maintaining the status quo (no change, no action)?
- Who is not directly affected by the problem but, nevertheless, wants to see the problem addressed?
- Are there any third parties who should be involved or engaged to make the solution a success?

In a perfect world, you would collect data from your potential stakeholders through a two-way means of communication, such as one-on-one interviews conducted face-to-face, via telephone, via web conferencing, or through focus groups. These "live" venues enable you to ask probing questions, follow up on responses that may point in different directions than originally intended, and provide a wealth of explanatory data to provide a detailed portrait of your stakeholders' interests, influence, and willingness to engage. However, there may be situations in which all the important stakeholders are believed to be known and the goal of your analysis is to build consensus around a specific direction, such as the "must have" requirements for an instructional product. In such cases, the Delphi method is an excellent way of getting the data you need fairly quickly. The Delphi method involves the systematic solicitation and collation of judgments on a particular topic obtained from a set of carefully designed and sequential questionnaires interspersed with summarized information and feedback of opinions derived from earlier responses (Delbecq, Van de Ven, & Gustafson, 1986; Grisham, 2009). Free, easy-to-use web-based collaboration tools make the Delphi method even more efficient than in the past. Delphi also enables you to have participants rank and rate the stakeholders' level of importance and influence. To ensure confidentiality and avoid ruffled feathers, it is best to conduct the Delphi in such a way that the panel members who are doing the rankings/ratings remain anonymous. Using generic salutations, such as "Dear Panelists," or phrases, such as "some experts have said that the following individuals have a strong interest in our topic. Using the 5-point scale below, please rate what you think is the level of interest of each person," help support a level of trust and comfort in the objectivity of the process.

Organizing and Analyzing: The "What"

As you collect your data, a best practice is to analyze-as-you-go to gradually build a picture of your stakeholders and what they can bring to the table that would help or hinder the purpose for which you intended the stakeholder analysis. Tabular displays (see the sample display in Table 6.1) are a simple but effective way of capturing the highlights of the data

Table 6.1 Sample Stakeholder Analysis Data Collection Summary

Stakeholder Name	Business Unit/ Organizational Context	Level of Interest in Project	Level of Influence on Project	Role in Project	Project Expectations	Facts of Interest	Optimal Ways to Manage Relationship
Elizabeth Anderson	Internal, VP of Sales	Very high (requested the project)	Very high, support essential	Project sponsor	Improved sales in quarter following project implementation	Outspoken, likes quick results, clashed with L&D in the past about time-to-development	Keep informed, highlights only, refer to SOW regularly
Harold Smith	Internal, Tech Support Manager	Low to medium (only directly involved after project implementation)	Low to medium	None	No impact on tech support until well down stream	Quiet, limited previous contact with L&D, appears open to new ideas as long as they do not increase his workload	General company communication about project is sufficient; no special efforts needed

collection process. It is also an easy way to share your highlights with supervisors or managerial insiders to gain feedback or identify potential inaccuracies.

Using the Findings: The "So What"

The results of your stakeholder analysis should enable you to determine how much and what kind of attention to pay to your stakeholders. Specifically, you will use the findings to determine:

- What must be communicated to each stakeholder. The individual stakeholder's level of interest, influence, or desired involvement determine how much detail and interactivity are required;
- How often communication must take place. Some stakeholders require attention on a daily basis while others only need updates every month or so. Digital communication tools make it easy for you to meet these varying needs; and
- Where the stakeholders will receive their communication. Again, the digital worlds makes it easy to employ multiple channels to satisfy the stakeholders' communication preferences.

Summary

Figure 6.3 illustrates a high-level view of the thought processes and tasks involved in conducting stakeholder analysis. The results of stakeholder

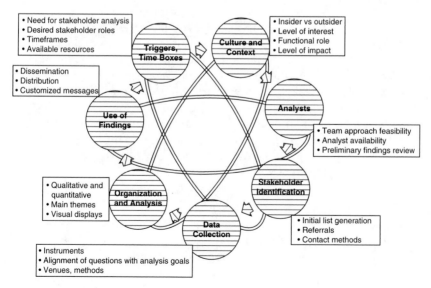

Figure 6.3 Stakeholder Analysis Process.

analysis will not only help you to remove potential obstacles but will also enable you to use stakeholder time, expertise, and influence to achieve your end goals. Furthermore, the results of the analysis helps you to manage stakeholder expectations and ensure that the stakeholders view your goals in a positive light, even though there may be hits and misses along the way.

Stakeholder Analysis Self-Check

You work for a company that develops learning solutions for various Federal Government agencies. Your company has just been awarded a contract to convert an agency's 4-day New Employee Orientation program to a series of online training modules, and you have been assigned to the design team that will be working on those modules. Your supervisor has provided the design team with copies of the agency's Statement of Work (SOW) describing the agency's needs and requirements. At what point should you begin conducting a stakeholder analysis?

a) Concurrently with the Learner and Context Analysis;
b) When designing and developing the online modules;
c) Immediately after reviewing the SOW; or
d) Not at all; it's a government contract so stakeholder analysis is unnecessary.

Of the four options, (c) is the optimal choice. The SOW is the design project trigger containing key information about target learners, timeframes, required deliverables, and budgetary parameters. What is not normally included in an SOW is information about what problem the program conversion was seeking to solve and why converting the entire program to a totally online delivery method was the best solution. Also, not included is information about who other than the target learners would be affected by the change and who could be affected by or have an interest in the change. You want to identify stakeholders who are willing and able to confirm that the root cause of the problem described in the SOW is solvable by a change to another single mode of delivery and what are the best ways to involve and engage with stakeholders throughout the duration of the project. The other three options carry the risk of overlooking key stakeholders and insufficient time to conduct your stakeholder analysis.

Food for Thought

1 Your organization has traditionally taken a minimalist approach to analysis when it comes to designing learning opportunities. What can you as the designer do to help demonstrate the benefits of conducting stakeholder analyses for Learning and Development projects?

2   Within any given organization, individual business units or departments may perceive the importance of stakeholder analysis differently. Thinking about your own organization, which business unit(s) or department(s) regularly conduct stakeholder analyses and why?

3   What advantages (if any) do the business units/departments in your organization that conduct stakeholder analyses have over those that do not?

Up Next

In this chapter, we have (a) reviewed the various definitions of and theories about stakeholders in an organizational context; (b) described the most common approaches to identifying, analyzing, and managing stakeholders; and (c) identified some easy-to-use techniques for setting and managing expectations of multiple stakeholders that even Dilbert© would love. Both stakeholder analysis and the analysis of organizational culture and sub-cultures require us to draw on the best of our "people skills" to persuade people to reveal all of the things we want to know. That ability to persuade is part of our emotional intelligence, the subject of the next chapter.

References

Aaltonen, K. (2011). Project stakeholder analysis as an environmental interpretation process. *International Journal of Project Management, 29*(2), 165–83.

Atkinson, R., & Flint, J. (2001). Accessing hidden and hard-to-reach populations: Snowball research strategies. *Social Research Update, 33*(3), 1–4.

Barnett, A. (1997). Towards a stakeholder democracy. In G. Kelly, D. Kelly, & A. Gamble (Eds.), *Stakeholder Capitalism* (pp. 82–98). London, UK: MacMillan Press.

Baseball Almanac, Inc. (2016). *Who's on First? By Abbott and Costello.* Retrieved from www.baseball-almanac.com/humor4.shtml.

Branch, R. B., & Kopcha, T. J. (2014). Instructional design models. In J. M. Spector, M. D. Merrill, J. Elan, & M. J. Bishop (Eds.), *Handbook of Research on Educational Communications and Technology* (pp. 77–87). New York, NY: Springer.

Bryson, J. M. (2004). What to do when stakeholders matter. *Public Management Review, 6*(1), 21–53.

Bullen, P. B. (2014). *Stakeholder Analysis Matrix.* Retrieved from www.tools4dev.org/resources/stakeholder-analysis-matrix-template/.

Currie, R. R., Seaton, S., & Wesley, F. (2009). Determining stakeholders for feasibility analysis. *Annals of Tourism Research, 36*(1), 41–63.

DeGeorge, R. T. (2009). *Business Ethics* (7th ed.). New York, NY: Pearson.

Delbecq, A., Van de Ven, A., & Gustafson, D. (1986). *Group Techniques for Program Planning: A Guide to Nominal Group and Delphi Processes.* Middleton, WI: Green Briar Press.

Donaldson, T., & Preston, L. (1995). The stakeholder theory of the corporation: Concepts, evidence, implications. *Academy of Management Review, 20*(1), 65–91.

Elias, A. A., & Cavana, R. Y. (2001). *Stakeholder Analysis for Systems Thinking and Modeling*. Paper presented at the System Dynamics Society Annual Conference, Atlanta, GA. Retrieved from www.systemdynamics.org/conferences/2001/papers/Elias_1.pdf.

Ertmer, P., Parisio, M. L., & Warduk, D. (2013). The practice of educational/instructional design. In R. Luckin, S. Puntombekar, P. Goodyear, B. Grabowski, J. Underwood, & N. Winters (Eds.), *Handbook of Design in Educational Technology*. New York, NY: Routledge.

Ferrary, M. (2009). A stakeholder's perspective on human resource management. *Journal of Business Ethics, 87*(1), 31–43.

Freeman, R. E. (1984). *Strategic Management: A Stakeholder Approach*. Boston, MA: Pitman.

Freeman, R. E., Wicks, A. C., & Parmar, B. (2004). Stakeholder theory and "the corporate objective revisited." *Organization Science, 15*(3), 364–9.

Friedman, A. L., & Miles, S. (2002). Developing stakeholder theory. *Journal of Management Studies, 39*(1), 1–21.

Greenwood, M., & Anderson, E. (2009). "I used to be an employee but now I am a stakeholder": Implications of labeling employees as stakeholders. *Asia Pacific Journal of Human Resources, 47*(2), 186–200.

Greenwood, M., & Freeman, R. E. (2011). Ethics and HRM: The contribution of stakeholder theory. *Business & Professional Ethics Journal, 30*(3–4). Retrieved from www.pdcnet.org/8525737F0058014C/file/B07EA9A851DF0198525792D005014DC/$FILE/bpej_0030_0003_0097_0120.pdf.

Grisham, T. (2009). The Delphi technique: A method for testing complex and multifaceted topics. *International Journal of Managing Projects in Business, 2*(1), 112–30.

IBSTPI. (2014). *Instructional Designer Competencies – Welcome to ibstpi*. Retrieved from http://ibstpi.org/instructional-design-competencies/.

Jawahar, I. M., & McLaughlin, G. L. (2001). Toward a descriptive stakeholder theory: An organizational life cycle approach. *Academy of Management Review, 26*(3), 397–414.

Jensen, M. C. (2002). Value maximization, stakeholder theory, and the corporate objective function. *Business Ethics Quarterly, 12*(2), 235–56.

Jones, T. M. (1995). Instrumental stakeholder theory: A synthesis of ethics and economics. *Academy of Management Review, 20*(2), 404–37.

Jones, T. M., & Wicks, A. C. (1999). Convergent stakeholder theory. *Academy of Management Review, 24*(2), 206–21.

Kaufman, A., & Englander, E. (2011). Behavioral economics, federalism, and the triumph of stakeholder theory. *Journal of Business Ethics, 102*(3), 421–38.

Konings, K. D., Seidel, T., & van Merrienboer, J. J. G. (2014). Participatory design of learning environments: Integrating perspectives of students, teachers, and designers. *Instructional Science, 42*(1), 1–9.

Laplume, A., Sonpar, K., & Litz, R. (2008). Stakeholder theory: Reviewing a theory that moves us. *Journal of Management, 34*(6), 1152.

Magness, V. (2008). Who are the stakeholders now? An empirical examination of the Mitchell, Agle and Wood theory of stakeholder salience. *Journal of Business Ethics, 83*(2), 177–92.

Marcoux, A. M. (2000). Balancing act. In J. R. DesJardins & J. J. McCall (Eds.), *Contemporary Issues in Business Ethics* (4th ed., pp. 92–100). Belmont, CA: Wadsworth/Thompson Learning.

Missonier, S., & Loufrani-Fedida, S. (2014). Stakeholder analysis and engagement in projects: From stakeholder relational perspective to stakeholder relational ontology. *International Journal of Project Management, 32*, 1108–22.

Mitchell, R. K., Agle, B. R., & Wood, D. J. (1997). Toward a theory of stakeholder identification and salience: Defining the principle of who and what really counts. *Academy of Management Review*, 22(1), 853–86.

Noy, C. (2008). Sampling knowledge: The hermeneutics of snowball sampling in qualitative research. *International Journal of Social Research Methodology*, 11(4), 327–44.

Olander, S. (2007). Stakeholder impact analysis in construction project management. *Construction Management and Economics*, 25(3), 277–87.

Orts, E., & Strudler, A. (2002). The ethical and environmental limits of stakeholder theory. *Business Ethics Quarterly*, 12(2), 215–34.

Phillips, R. A. (1997). Stakeholder theory and a principle of fairness. *Business Ethics Quarterly*, 7, 51–66.

Phillips, R., Freeman, R. E., & Wicks, A. C. (2003). What stakeholder theory is not. *Business Ethics Quarterly*, 13(4), 479–502.

Piskurich, G. M. (2006). *Rapid Instructional Design: Learning ID Fast and Right*. San Francisco, CA: Pfeiffer.

Reed, M. S., Graves, A., Dandy, N., Posthumus, H., Hubacek, K., Morris, J. et al. (2009). Who's in and why? A typology of stakeholder analysis methods for natural resource management. *Journal of Environmental Management*, 90, 1933–49.

Rothwell, W., Benscoter, B., King, M., & King, S. B. (2015). *Mastering the Instructional Design Process: A Systematic Approach*. Hoboken, NJ: John Wiley & Sons.

Schmeer, K. (1999). Section 2: Stakeholder analysis guidelines. *Stakeholder Analysis Policy Toolkit for Strengthening Health Sector Reform*. Retrieved from www .who.int/workforcealliance/knowledge/toolkit/33.pdf.

Shafritz, J. M., & Madsen, P. (Eds.). (1990). *Essentials of Business Ethics*. New York, NY: Plume.

Sharp, H., Finkelstein, A., & Galai, G. (1999). *Stakeholder Identification in the Requirements Engineering Process*. Paper presented at the Tenth International Workshop on Database and Expert Systems Applications, Florence, Italy.

Spector, J. M., & Muraida, D. J. (2013). Automating instructional design. In S. Dijkstra, N. Seel, F. Schott, & R. D. Tennyson (Eds.), *Instructional Design: International Perspectives* (2nd ed., Vol. 2, pp. 59–81). New York, NY: Routledge.

Stakeholder. (n.d. a). *BusinessDictionary.com*. Retrieved from www.businessdictionary .com/definition/stakeholder.html.

Stakeholder. (n.d. b). *Cambridge Dictionaries Online*. Retrieved from http:// dictionary.cambridge.org/dictionary/english/stakeholder.

Stakeholder [Def. 3]. (n.d.). *Merriam-Webster Online*. Retrieved from www .merriam-webster.com/dictionary/stakeholder.

Sternberg, E. (2000). *Just Business*. New York, NY: Oxford University Press.

Trentim, M. H. (2013). *Managing Stakeholders as Clients*. Newtown Square, PA: Project Management Institute, Inc.

Tse, T. (2011). Shareholder and stakeholder theory after the financial crisis. *Qualitative Research in Financial Markets*, 3(1), 51–63.

Velasquez, M. G. (2014). *Business Ethics: Concepts and Cases*. Essex, UK: Pearson Education, Ltd.

Weber, J., & Marley, K. A. (2012). In search of stakeholder salience: exploring corporate social and sustainability reports. *Business and Society*, 51(4), 626–49.

Wolfe, R. A., & Putler, D. S. (2002). How tight are the ties that bind stakeholder groups? *Organization Science*, 13(1), 64–80.

World Bank. (n.d.). *What is Stakeholder Analysis?* Retrieved from www1 .worldbank.org/publicsector/anticorrupt/PoliticalEconomy/PDFVersion.pdf.

7 Emotional Intelligence
Catchphrase or Competency?

Like Dilbert©, you may find it challenging to keep up with the latest catchphrases to hit the workplace. Readers of *Forbes* magazine are probably familiar with that publication's list of annoying business catchphrases (Nelson, 2013), while learning designers employed in the private or government sectors have been told that there are 12 e-learning catchphrases that are "must-knows" (Wroten, 2014). The challenge becomes particularly trying when these catchphrases or concepts are bandied about or worse, are applied to contexts for which they may not have originally been intended or for which there is little evidence to support the way in which they are being defined.

When Salovey and Mayer (1989–1990) coined the term "emotional intelligence," (EI) they probably did not foresee the popularization to which their concept would be subjected. For instance, a typical Google Scholar search on the keywords "emotional intelligence" yields nearly 750,000 hits since the year 2000; some 2.5 million hits appear in a standard search with the phrase "emotional intelligence in the workplace." Instruments and methodologies that purport to measure EI abound, as do consulting companies offering the "best methodology" for using EI for recruiting, retaining, and advancing the best talent for an organization. Many companies are working to raise the EI of their employees to increase sales, improve customer service, and ensure that international managers are performing successfully in global assignments. Moreover, networking groups for learning professionals interested in EI can be found on social media sites, such as LinkedIn.com, along with self-assessment instruments that anyone can take online to check his/her own EI. However, there is little consensus as to what EI really means and whether it is a construct that is distinct from other constructs, such as personality, empathy, and a host of other constructs and conceptualizations that fill the scholarly and practitioner literatures.

But I'm an instructional designer, so why should I care? Well, if you work or are considering working in the private or public sectors, you will be subject to the same promotion criteria and processes as other professionals that the organization hires. In other words, to get past junior designer and advance in your career, you will need to demonstrate your EI in a way that the organization's decision-makers deem consistent with star employees worth targeting for promotion. Although not all organizations explicitly tout EI as a criterion for advancement, there are some components of EI that all organizations deem to be important employee characteristics that can give the organization a competitive edge. Bottom line: You can't stand like the proverbial deer in the headlights when the words "emotional intelligence" crop up in job ads, job interviews, or in the workplace itself. Instead, you will need to know how to use what an organization **perceives** as a high level of EI to support efficient and effective job performance and enhance your chances of career advancement.

To achieve this requires getting a grip on the concept of EI, understanding what EI means, determining how organizations view and use it, and knowing how you can make it one of your strengths. In this chapter, we will:

- Review the various definitions, models, and measures of EI in the scholarly literature;
- Explore the translation of EI from theory to practice in workplace settings; and
- Summarize some EI lessons learned.

Definitions, Models, and Measures: What the Scholars Say

Human emotion has been the subject of research in a variety of disciplines, including psychology, sociology, biology, and management. No wonder the EI body of knowledge is huge, with thousands of books, articles, reports, conference papers, and other peer-reviewed documents generated over the last three decades alone. As such, it is beyond the scope of this chapter to cover the full spectrum of that body of knowledge. We will just hit the highlights and provide an overview of the various EI perspectives in the scholarly literature.

Roots of EI

The term "emotional intelligence" first appeared in the psychology literature with the publication of Salovey and Mayer's article titled "Emotional Intelligence" (Salovey & Mayer, 1989–1990). Salovey and Mayer defined EI as the ability to monitor and discriminate among one's own emotions as well as those of others, along with the ability to use the information as a guide for thinking and acting. In contrast with previous conceptualizations of emotion and intelligence as being diametrically opposed and emotion as being a barrier to rational decision-making, Salovey and Mayer suggested that emotions make cognitive processes adaptive and individuals can think rationally about emotions.

In one of the more robust reviews of the EI scholarly literature (Dulewicz & Higgs, 2000), the impetus for the development of the concept of EI was traced back to the inability of traditional cognitive measures, such as IQ tests, SAT scores, and standardized tests in education, to predict who will succeed in either an educational or organizational context. However, research seeking to look beyond IQ goes back as far as the 1920s with the development of theories of social intelligence, multiple intelligences, and group intelligence, all as constructs that are distinctly different from IQ.

Similarly, Brackett, Rivers, and Salovey (2011) saw the impetus for interest in EI as an outgrowth of two areas of psychological research that emerged nearly half a century ago: the area of cognition and affect that focused on how cognitive and emotional processes interact to enhance thinking, and the evolution in models of intelligence that began considering intelligence as a broad array of mental abilities. Cartwright and Pappas (2008) hypothesized that the appeal and influence of EI in the U.S. may be related to the social context in which the theory was presented and popularized, namely, the resurgence of the discussion about the link between race, IQ, and social mobility following the 1994 publication of Hernstein and Murray's *The Bell Curve*. Cartwright and Pappas posited that the publication of *The New York Times* social science journalist Daniel Goleman's book on EI in 1995 presented a positive counterpart to the message of *The Bell Curve* by arguing that success was more dependent on the way in which individuals handle emotions and the emotions of others, rather than on their cognitive intelligence.

Yet, another take on the roots of EI's appeal stated that interest in the topic has been fueled by a combination of anecdotal evidence suggesting that mental ability by itself is not enough for success in life and clinical research that shows how people can do well on traditional IQ tests but do poorly in areas such as self-regulation and social relations (Cherniss, 2010). Clinical research on conditions such as Asperger's syndrome was offered as a case in point. Studies of child development and the importance of children's feelings conducted in the U.S. and internationally, along with studies of the relationships between emotions and culture, gender and neurobiology – for example, Pert's (1999) work on the effects of emotions on the body's electrochemical signals – all contributed to the explosion of research on EI.

Definitions

Not surprisingly, there are as many definitions of EI as there are researchers. For example, Dulewicz and Higgs's (2000) literature review identified a variety of terms – emotional literacy (Goleman, 1995), emotional quotient (Bar-On, 1996a,b), personal intelligence (Bar-On & Parker, 2000), and early terminology, such as social intelligence, interpersonal intelligence – that have been equated with EI. However, they deemed Goleman's definition of EI to be useful in helping researchers wrap their arms around the construct. Basically, Goleman defined EI as being able to motivate oneself to get jobs done, be creative, and perform at one's peak; to sense what others are feeling; and to handle relationships effectively. Based on a content analysis of the literature, Dulewicz and Higgs identified seven component elements of EI:

1 Self-awareness: The ability to know one's own feelings, emotions; to be in touch with feelings, self-knowledge; to use feelings to make decisions with confidence.
2 Emotional management: Expressing one's own emotions productively; the ability to form an accurate and truthful model of oneself and use the model to work effectively; to focus on results/what needs to be done.
3 Self-motivation: Delaying gratification; marshaling emotions in search of a goal; working effectively under pressure; not giving up in the face of setbacks.
4 Empathy: Sensing what others are feeling; ability to understand others, learn what motivates them, and understand how they work; recognizing emotions in others; talent for settling disputes, negotiating, deal-making; naturally taking the lead in organizing groups.
5 Relationships: Working cooperatively; building trust; striving toward effective team work; turning divergent views into creative energy; building rapport.
6 Communication: Listening to others; expressing one's own emotions productively; speaking one's mind.
7 Personal style: Balancing "hard/soft" in decisions; having accountability; engaging in stress management; accepting personal responsibility.

For Dulewicz and Higgs, popular interest in EI was a result of Goleman's book, the publicity for which led to more books and articles examining EI's application and development at the individual and corporate levels. Corporate interest was related to the continuing search for a way of securing sustainable competitive advantage that could be developed through attention to "people issues." However, Dulewicz and Higgs concluded that little research has been done in an organizational context and that existing EI research has been largely drawn from physiological research developments, educational-based research, and developments in the therapy field.

Zeidner, Matthews, and Roberts (2004) also contended that there is disparate terminology in the literature. Instead, they looked at the EI literature in terms of two facets that define the competencies associated with EI, namely, ability or awareness vs. management of emotion, and target whether competence relates to self vs. others. The product of these two facets yields four components: (a) awareness of emotions in self; (b) awareness of emotions in others; (c) management of emotions in self;

and (d) management of emotions in others. However, the authors argued that this analysis fails to identify a unifying common element to the different components, nor does it differentiate EI from other distinct abilities and personality traits that may influence how we recognize and regulate our emotions.

While acknowledging definitional confusion in the literature, Ashkanasy and Daus (2005) ascribed much of the confusion to the failure of some scholars to differentiate between scientifically grounded research, namely, the research of Mayer and Salovey, and populist versions of EI, such as that of Goleman and Bar-On, respectively. Ashkanasy and Daus offered a four-point summary of views of EI based on the scholarly literature:

1   EI is distinct from, but positively related to, other intelligences.
2   EI is an individual difference, where some people are more endowed, and others are less so.
3   EI develops over a person's life span and can be enhanced through training.
4   EI involves, at least in part, a person's abilities to effectively identify and perceive emotion (in self and others), as well as possession of the skills to understand and manage those emotions successfully.

Efforts to define EI are ongoing. For example, Fontaine (2016) placed EI within the context of the componential emotion approach, which defines emotions as multi-componential processes elicited by goal-relevant situations. Fontaine deconstructs EI into three components:

1   Emotion understanding or understanding the likely appraisals, action tendencies, bodily reactions, expressions, and feelings in response to goal-relevant situations.
2   Emotion identification, which is the ability to identify an ongoing emotion process by using one or more emotion components.
3   Emotion regulation knowledge or the ability to know how an ongoing emotion process can be regulated by intervening in the flow of one or more emotion components or by changing the antecedent situation that causes the emotion.

Fontaine contended that this reconceptualization of EI based on the componential emotion approach provides a point of reference to evaluate the representativeness of existing EI instruments and to develop new instruments in the future.

Figure 7.1 illustrates the various definitions, synonyms, characteristics, and components of emotion intelligence described in the scholarly literature. Conceptually, recognizing and managing emotions in oneself and in others represent common themes across the various definitions, characteristics, and components. What is not clear is the extent to which emotion is distinct

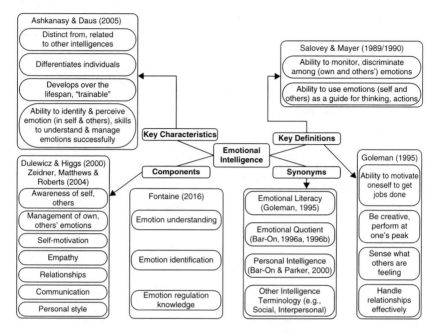

Figure 7.1 EI Definitions, Synonyms, Components, and Key Characteristics.

from or embedded in other human "soft skills," such as communication or the ability to build/maintain relationships. Perhaps, in seeking a formal definition of EI, we should recall the words of U.S. Supreme Court Justice Potter Stewart when describing his threshold test for obscenity (*Jacobellis vs. Ohio*: The Oyez Project at IIT Chicago-Kent College of Law, 1964):

> I shall not today attempt further to define the kinds of material I understand to be embraced within that shorthand description ["hardcore pornography"]; and perhaps I could never succeed in intelligibly doing so. But I know it when I see it, and the motion picture involved in this case is not that.

In other words, we cannot define EI, but we know it when we see it.

Models and Measures

Some scholars have examined the EI literature not in terms of definitional approaches but in terms of models of EI as a construct. Ashkanasy and Daus (2005) identified three streams of research on EI models, with each stream associated with its own measurement instruments. The first stream is based on Mayer and Salovey's (1997) four-branch abilities model: the ability to perceive emotions; the ability to use emotions to facilitate thought;

the ability to understand emotions; and the ability to manage emotions. The model's associated Mayer-Salovey-Caruso EI Test (MSCEIT) is an ability test designed to measure EI by evaluating actual performance on a variety of tasks. For example, the ability to perceive emotions is measured, in part, by having the test taker rate the emotional expressions on a number of faces.

The second research stream on EI models identified in Ashkanasy and Daus's literature review includes self- and peer-report measures based on the Mayer and Salovey model, while the third stream encompasses all other models and associated measurement instruments (e.g., Bar-On's EQ-i). Not unlike Ashkanasy and Daus, O'Boyle, Humphrey, Pollack, Hawver, and Story (2011) classified EI studies into three streams: ability-based models that use objective test items; self-report or peer report measures based on Mayer and Salovey's four-branch model of EI; and mixed models of emotional competencies. The analysis by O'Boyle et al. showed that the three streams have correlations of 0.24–0.30 with job performance and correlate differently with cognitive ability, neuroticism, extraversion, openness, agreeableness, and conscientiousness. In determining which stream researchers should select as the framework for further studies, O'Boyle et al. recommended the ability-based models for establishing that there is an underlying ability called EI that meets the traditional criteria for intelligence measures. They noted that for practitioners, ability-based models are a good choice for selection and hiring because their associated tests may make them less susceptible to social desirability and faking effects. For those most interested in predicting job performance without concern for overlaps with other variables, O'Boyle et al. recommended the mixed models since their analysis showed that the mixed model measures have the greatest incremental predictive value and encompass broad definitions of emotional competencies.

Cherniss (2010) expanded upon the three-stream identification in previous literature reviews and identified four models that dominate the EI research field. The first is Bar-On's model (Bar-on, 1996a,b) of emotional and social intelligence and its associated emotional quotient inventory (EQ-i). The Bar-On model suggests that the traits and skills people need to adapt to the social and emotional demands of life include (a) the ability to be aware of, understand, and express oneself; (b) the ability to deal with strong emotions and control one's impulses; and (c) the ability to adapt to change and solve problems of a personal or social nature. The five main components of the Bar-On model are intrapersonal skills, interpersonal skills, adaptability, stress management, and general mood.

Cherniss next addressed the Mayer and Salovey mental ability model or information processing model and the associated MSCEIT test (Mayer, Salovey, & Caruso, 2004), with measures that tend to correlate more highly with cognitive ability tests than with personality tests. The four components of the model are the ability to perceive emotions, the ability to use emotions to facilitate thought, the ability to understand emotions, and the ability to manage emotions. Cherniss noted that several studies based on the MSCEIT published from 2002 and 2009 had found a relationship between EI and performance, although similar results have been obtained with self-report and multi-rater measures across an equal number of studies. Cherniss concluded that EI will play an important role in jobs involving social interaction and influence, such as sales, politics, teaching, and for team performance vs. individual performance.

The Boyatzis–Goleman model (Boyatzis, Goleman, & Rhee, 2000) is the third model and was designed to encompass the social and emotional competencies that are linked to outstanding workplace performance. This model consists of a number of specific competencies organized into four clusters, namely, self-awareness, self-management, social awareness, and relationship management. The model's primary measures are the emotional competence inventory (ECIT) and the emotional and social competence inventory (ESCI), both of which are multi-rater instruments.

The fourth and last model discussed in Cherniss's review is the Trait EI model that is based on a content analysis of early measures of EI and is meant to include all personality facets that are specifically related to affect. The four components of the model are well-being (including self-confidence, happiness, and optimism), sociability (social competence, assertiveness, and emotion management of others), self-control (stress management, emotion regulation, and low impulsiveness), and emotionality (emotional perception of self and others, emotion expression, and empathy) (Petrides, Pita, & Kokkinaki, 2007). The model is measured using a self-report instrument known as the Trait EI Questionnaire or TEIQue (Mikolajczak, Luminet, Leroy, & Roy, 2007).

As with the definitions, updates to EI models are ongoing. For example, Mayer, Caruso, and Salovey (2016) stated that sometimes it makes sense to consider emotional, personal, and social intelligences as a set and be sensitive to their distinctions and overlap. In their introduction to the special issue of Emotion Research focused on EI, Barchard, Brackett, and Mestre (2016) posited that there are currently two main streams of research on EI: ability EI, consisting of discrete emotional skills measured with performance assessments, and trait EI, consisting of dispositions around emotions and emotional self-efficacy measured with self-report instruments.

Figure 7.2 illustrates the models and measures of EI that dominate the scholarly literature. With the exception of the mental abilities model, all of the models contain a blend of characteristics and inter- and intra-personal skills that reflect the definitional turbulence discussed earlier. The mixed models also rely on subjective self- and/or peer-rating instruments to determine the test takers' EI level. There is certainly enough evidence of the relationship between our image of ourselves and how we behave; there is, however, little consensus as to whether or not our self-assessments are too high, too low, or on target. Consequently, the choice of EI models and measures is as challenging as the choice of definitions.

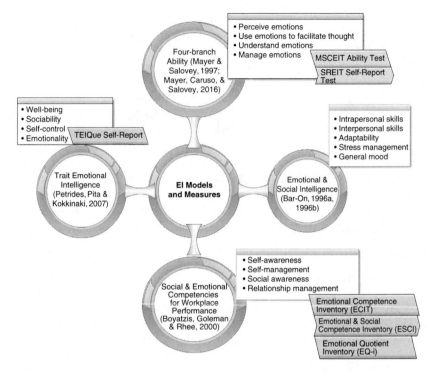

Figure 7.2 EI Models and Measures.

Studies of EI in the Workplace

In exploring the scholarly literature that focuses on the role of EI in the workplace, two themes emerge across a variety of industries and workplace settings: EI and leadership ability, and EI and team effectiveness. The relationship between EI and leadership has been well explored. There are conceptual studies and literature reviews of the contribution of EI, particularly in terms of the ability to regulate one's own emotions, to essential elements of effective leadership. The leadership elements associated with EI include the development of collective goals and objectives; instilling in others an appreciation of the importance of work activities; generating and maintaining enthusiasm, confidence, optimism, cooperation, and trust; encouraging flexibility in decision-making and change; and establishing and maintaining a meaningful identity for the organization (George, 2000; Haver, Akerjordet, & Furunes, 2013). Other studies have noted the relationship between emotionally intelligent leadership and business profitability (Ryan, Spencer, & Bernhard, 2012) as well as the relationship between emotionally intelligent leadership and employee task performance and corporate citizenship in international settings (Yuan, Hsu, Shieh, & Li, 2012). Goleman (1998) reported that 80 percent to 90 percent of the competencies that differentiate top performers are in the domain of EI, while Mount (2006) contended that EI is more than twice as predictive of business performance than cognitive intelligence, or employee skill, knowledge, and expertise.

Some studies have linked emotionally intelligent leadership with an organization's financial performance. In a study of 186 executives (Stein, Papadogiannis, Yip, & Sitarenios, 2009), researchers found a correlation between high EI test scores and company profitability. A study of a pilot project with PepsiCo executives selected for their EI competencies showed those executives outperforming their colleagues by delivering a 10 percent increase in productivity, an 87 percent decrease in executive turnover, $3.75 million added economic value, and an ROI of more than 1,000 percent (McClelland, 1998). A similar study among 358 executives of Johnson & Johnson identified a strong relationship between high-performing leaders and EI (Cavallo, 2002).

Empirical studies of specific occupations also offer some evidence of a relationship between leadership ability and EI. For example, results of a study of project managers in the United Kingdom found that individual differences in EI tend to drive those behaviors that are associated with project success (Clarke, 2010). Specifically, after controlling for cognitive ability and personality, high scores on EI ability measures and empathy, coupled with the project manager competencies of teamwork, attentiveness, and managing conflict, contributed to the leadership behaviors associated with successful project outcomes. Hutchinson and Hurley (2013) explored the extent to which enhancing leadership capability through strengthening clinical and managerial nurses' EI can reduce workplace bullying. In addition, there are case studies yielding correlations between EI and transformational leadership (Palmer, Walls, Burgess, & Stough, 2001), exploratory studies in the public service sector (Higgs & Aitken, 2003) as well as studies challenging the methodological rigor of other empirical studies that have shown strong relationships between EI and transformational leadership (Lindebaum & Cartwright, 2010).

Conceptual and empirical research continues to explore the relationship between EI and leadership, although no consensus has as yet been reached as to which EI model/measure should be the gold standard for defining the EI variables that impact leadership. Nevertheless, common to all of these studies is the conclusion that EI is a key differentiator for successful leaders and that leaders with high EI competencies tend to make better decisions, engage and influence those around them more effectively, and create a more positive environment for getting the job done than do leaders with lower EI competencies.

The second theme coming out of the research on EI in workplace settings is the relationship between EI and team effectiveness. In fact, some of these studies conclude that EI is at the heart of effective teams. For instance, a study exploring teams at companies including IDEO, Hewlett-Packard, and the Hay Group (Druskat & Wolff, 2001) found that effective teams behave in ways that build relationships both inside and outside the team, which strengthens the teams' ability to face challenges. For a team to have a high EI, it must create norms that establish mutual trust among members, a sense of group identity, and a sense of group efficacy. Druskat and Wolff deemed these three conditions to be essential to a team's effectiveness because they are the foundation of true cooperation and collaboration. Group EI is about bringing emotions deliberately to the surface and understanding how they affect the team's work.

Building on Druskat and Wolff's (2001) work on emotionally competent group norms, Koman and Wolff (2008) examined the relationships among team leader EI competencies, team level EI, and team performance in a military organization. The study results indicated that team leader EI is significantly related to the presence of emotionally competent group norms on the teams they lead and that emotionally competent group norms are related to team performance.

Jordan, Ashkanasy, Hartel, and Hooper (2002) developed a self-report EI measurement instrument called the Workgroup Emotion Intelligence Profile (WEIP-3). The instrument is specifically designed to profile the EI of individuals in work teams and was tested among undergraduate students in Australia. The instrument has also been used to examine the utility of EI for predicting individual performance, team performance, and conflict resolution styles in a study of 350 undergraduates in an introduction to management course (Jordan & Troth, 2004). The study results showed that the EI indicators in the WEIP-3 aligned positively with team performance and were differentially linked to conflict resolution methods.

In a study of 95 project teams in the IT departments of 52 distinct firms, Akgun, Kesking, Byrne, and Gunsel (2011) found that EI mediates the relationship between collaboration among team members and market success of the software products and concluded that management and regulation of the emotions acts as a platform to actualize the joint behavior toward some goal of common interest for the successful products. Other studies have focused on the link between group EI and group conflict management and resolution (Ayoko, Callan, & Hartel, 2008; Jordan & Troth, 2004; Troth, Jordan, Lawrence, & Tse, 2012).

Using the Trait Activation framework and its associated TEIQue instrument on a sample of full-time professionals and early-career managers studying in a part-time MBA program, Farh, Seo, and Tesluk (2012) sought to test the hypothesis that employees with higher overall EI and emotional perception ability exhibit higher teamwork effectiveness (and subsequent job performance) when working in job contexts characterized by high managerial work demands because such contexts contain salient emotion-based cues that activate employees' emotional capabilities. The study results affirmed the authors' hypothesis, and the authors concluded that emotional abilities and job performance are moderated by job context.

Figure 7.3 illustrates the common themes in the literature on the relationship between EI in the workplace and leadership, on the one hand, and team effectiveness, on the other. We can safely assume that organizations whose leadership displays high EI will be more likely to have teams that

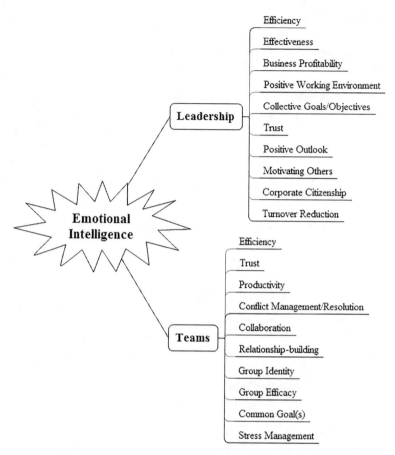

Figure 7.3 EI in the Workplace: Common Themes.

display high EI, particularly since leadership sets the tone for what goes on throughout the organization and contributes to the creation of an organizational culture in which individual employees and managers act in systematic ways that encourage positive financial performance (Wiete, 2013).

Summary

The EI landscape that emerges from the scholarly literature is complex. The definitional approaches seek to flesh out the characteristics of EI, while the models and measuring instruments focus on how to identify the extent to which individuals possess various characteristics associated with EI. Both the definitional and the model/measure approaches are consistent in recognizing a fairly broad set of emotion processing skills. However, they are not consistent in specifying the detailed components of those skills and how those skills should be measured.

Given this lack of consistency, it is no surprise that much of the criticism of the EI literature focuses on the measurement tools. For instance, questions have been raised about the reliability, construct, and predictive validity of the scales used in all the measuring tools, as well as the lack of a stringent definition within which to ground assessment measures (Dulewicz & Higgs, 2000); the potential for cultural or gender bias because the tools were developed on respondents from culturally similar backgrounds (U.S., U.K., and Australia) who speak the same language, as well as the vulnerability of self-report measurement to distortion by faking positive or socially acceptable responses (Cartwright & Pappas, 2008). There is also no shortage of criticism of the research on EI and the workplace. Criticism ranges from the use of undergraduate and graduate students as the study sample in EI research trials (Romanelli, Cain, & Smith, 2006), to exaggerated claims about the predictive power of EI in terms of individual performance in the workplace, career success. and leadership ability (Jordan, Ashton-James, & Ashkanasy, 2006). Nevertheless, the belief in EI and its ability to help an organization build its talent pool remain alive and well.

EI in the Workplace: What the Practitioners Do

A review of the practitioner literature in the fields of Human Resources Management (HRM), Human Resource Development (HRD), Talent Management, Learning and Development, and related fields yields a singular theme: EI is critical in the modern workplace. Using language that is far more passionate than any you would find in the scholarly literature, some learning professionals contend that careers can be ended if employees do not exhibit appropriate social and emotional skills at work (Nowack, 2012; Wall, 2007). In a survey conducted among more than 2,600 U.S. non-government hiring managers (Grasz, 2014), nearly three in four (71 percent) said that they value EI in an employee more than IQ. When asked what qualities and behaviors they observe to assess a candidate or employee's EI, the top mentions were (a) admit to and learn from own mistakes; (b) keep emotions in check and have thoughtful discussions on tough issue; (c) listen as much or more than talk; (d) take criticism well; and (e) show grace under pressure.

EI serves as a differentiator throughout an employee's career cycle. Employers use EI as part of the recruitment process. In a book published by the American Management Association, HR consultant Adele Lynn (2008) provided hiring managers with a primer on how to construct interview questions that reveal a candidate's self-awareness and self-regulation, ability to read others and recognize the impact of one's own behavior on others, and ability to learn from one's mistakes. For example, in probing a candidate's ability to recognize the impact of his/her own behavior on others, Lynn offered questions, such as: "Tell me about a time when you did or said something that had a negative impact on a customer, peer, or direct report. How did you know the impact was negative?" Lynn then compared the response of a candidate who was told by others that he was having a negative impact to the response of another candidate who used the other person's body language and behavior as a signal that something was wrong. The second candidate was hired. In an interview with *Staffing Management* magazine (Taylor, 2009), the chair and CEO of Texas-based staffing firm TerraHealth, Inc. stated that he uses the Bar-On EQ-i to test potential recruiters for EI because qualities such as self-confidence, sociability, empathy, assertiveness, and self-motivation help to identify the entrepreneurial "salesman-type" recruiter desired by TerraHealth, Inc.

Recently, EI assessments, along with psychological assessments, such as the Myers-Briggs personality assessment (The Myers & Briggs Foundation, 2014) and interview questions aimed at assessing EI, have been criticized for violating an individual's right to privacy and having an unintended discriminatory consequence. Federal and state fair employment laws prohibit employers from using employment practices that cause a disparate impact on the basis of race, sex, age, or other protected categories. EI assessments fall under the purview of the Uniform Guidelines on Employee Selection Procedures pursuant to Title VII of the 1964 Civil Rights Act, as well as other anti-discrimination and privacy protection laws. Legal experts offer several best practices that enable employers to use EI assessments and interviews with a lower risk of being sued, such as administering the assessments in the last phase of the hiring process and standardizing interview questions (Wirth & Gansle, 2012). Barring a major court case, it can be safely assumed that employers will continue to screen for EI as a hiring criterion.

Organizations are often willing subjects of case studies and showcase interviews that spotlight their business's best practices. Consequently, case studies and interviews focused on an organization's EI best practices are not in short supply. In a three-year case study of an international food supplier to McDonald's (Fariselli, Freedman, & Ghino, 2013), EI – as measured by a proprietary mixed model instrument – was found to be strongly correlated with individual performance, organizational engagement, and organizational performance. Moreover, the introduction of EI training to the organization's sales force yielded a 63 percent reduction in sales force turnover. The case study is considered a model for the benefits of adopting EI testing and training in the food industry.

Google has taken a different approach to fostering EI. One of its senior engineers now bears the title of "Jolly Good Fellow" – a word play on the title "Google Fellow" that is given to the highest-ranking engineers. The Jolly Good Fellow's job description is to help others learn about EI through a program called Search Inside Yourself (Bort, 2015; Tyler, 2013). The components of the program include attention training to create a quality of mind that is calm and clear, self-knowledge and self-mastery, and pro-social mental habits, such as kindness and compassion via meditation and other similar techniques. Google's program is grounded in the belief that EI can lead to more effective relationships and better leadership.

Learning professionals are no different from their HR, HRD, and Talent Management counterparts in openly advocating EI development for employees, particularly those seeking to advance their careers. Dawn Adams Miller, Director, Learning Strategy at MetLife, offers her take on the role of EI in *E-Suite Views*.

SvR: Let's turn now to everybody's favorite buzzwords and catch-phrases. If you look at the HR literature or read some of the Talent Management publications, one of the hot topics is EI. Some hiring managers have candidates take EI tests or have new hires take those tests as part of the onboarding process. Do you think EI has any relevance for instructional designers?

DAM: I do in the sense that it's about the relationships with the people you're working with that allows you to be an instructional designer. If you're an expert in a particular field, you can probably develop instruction all by yourself. But most instructional designers are not experts in the content they're designing, so they have to be able to use those relationships to be successful. So, yes, they do need to have EI, they do need to be able to recognize if they're frustrated with a person. They need to understand, first of all, why they are upset and what they can do. I'm usually the one who is the willow bending in the wind. It would be nice if other people would bend but when you're trying to dig information out of people, you've got to be the willow, you've got to understand what's going on, how you're being perceived, what battles you are willing to fight, when do you escalate, and all of those kinds of things. Also, what are the things you're taking on that you shouldn't be taking on? That's a lot of it, too. Because we're designers, we desire to help and that can be our downfall sometimes; we find ourselves doing things we really shouldn't be doing.

SvR: So you see EI in terms of cultivating relationships, in terms of what's important for instructional designers?

DAM: Yes, I think so.

SvR: Anything more? EI has as many definitions as Imelda Marcos had shoes.

DAM: I know and it's interesting, I took a look on *Wikipedia*. And, yes, knowing when an emotion hits you, if someone is being condescending, as a lot of subject matter experts can be, how do you handle that? You can't really control it but you can change it somehow. So, it's understanding your emotions but understanding the other person's emotions and, to me, that's the real interpersonal skill.

An article in *The Huffington Post* (Conley, 2014) reported the result of an unscientific but interesting poll to identify those Fortune 500 CEOs who display a high level of EI. Common to what the article calls the "Top 10 Chief Emotions Officers" is a keen self-awareness that helped them to develop as leaders at a faster rate than most CEOs and an ability to inspire those around them. Similarly, *T+D Magazine* has published spotlight stories of businesses that have implemented EI training programs and have demonstrated subsequent improvements in employee performance. Concurrent sessions and keynote speakers at annual conferences of the eLearning Guild and the Society of Human Resource Management (SHRM) have focused on EI for several years and include workshops on how to incorporate EI training into the organization's professional development curricula. In short, organizations take EI seriously. The CEO of Netflix sums it up in one word: selflessness, stating: "I want people who are ego-less and put the interests of the company above their own and are eager to share information and help their co-workers." (Hastings, 2014).

EI and How to Get It: What Would Dilbert© Do?

By now, it should be crystal clear that learning designers do have a stake in cultivating and demonstrating EI throughout their careers. Some organizations may actually test you using one of the EI instruments discussed earlier in this chapter. All organizations, whether they test or not, will watch how you conduct yourself with peers, managers, subordinates, and clients, and make judgments about your EI. So, what would Dilbert© do? We can only imagine how Dilbert's© creator would respond, but if we put on our satirical hats, here are some lessons we can learn:

- **Your opinion, while interesting, is irrelevant.** Learning designers are just like other human beings. We have a highly positive view of ourselves and of our ability to play well with others. After all, our ability to do our jobs depends on our ability to collaborate. However, how we perceive ourselves may not be how others perceive us. While we may not want to walk up and down the halls of our workplace and, emulating former New York City Mayor Ed Koch (Koch & Rauch, 1984), ask, "How'm I doin'?", we can create opportunities to solicit informal feedback from colleagues. For instance, you're in the middle of a project that seems to be going well, but you take a moment during a status meeting to ask, "Is there anything I can do to make sure that we all have a shared understanding of what we need to do to finish this project successfully? I would appreciate your input on this." Responses may range from the concrete to dead silence, but the fact that you asked the question shows that you are attuned to the thoughts and feelings of those around you, a key component of EI.

- **If you want to work alone, go off and be a hermit.** Remember how much you hated group work when you were a student? Your group always had at least one slacker who would ride the group's success wave and contribute nothing, forcing you and the other members to carry that extra load. Well, the workplace is no different. Unlike your student days, you don't get to pick your project team until you're well advanced in your career and even then, you may end up working with folks who may have the technical know-how you need but who, in your view, are short on one or more aspects of EI. Booting them off the project team or ignoring them and doing the work yourself is not an option. As Dawn Adams Miller stated in *E-Suite Views*, you have to bend like the willow in the wind and persuade the person that being an active contributor makes him/her look good by showing that person's commitment to the success of the project and ultimately, of the organization. "What's the best way to ensure we've included your expertise on this, so that we stay on track and meet our client's expectations?" Probing for what is (not) working for him/her before articulating what is not working for you is more likely to get that slacker moving.
- **Be generous with those "Atta boys!"** Everyone loves to be recognized for what they do. Organizations that regularly recognize employee accomplishments are sought-after places to work; managers who regularly compliment employees who do well and offer support to employees who are not doing as well are considered model bosses. But peer recognition is just as important as recognition by immediate supervisors or senior management, particularly when projects or activities have been more stressful than usual. Sometimes called "ego massaging" in the conflict resolution literature (Doob, 1974), acknowledging the good work of your peers, even on the smallest of tasks, demonstrates your ability to use your awareness of others to build confidence and trust, and promote a positive group dynamic, all elements of strong EI.
- **EI ≠ SU.** Being attuned to the emotions of others does not mean sucking up to others and establishing yourself as a selfless "Mr./Ms. Nice." The goal-directed use of emotion is the foundation of the "I" in EI. Using your emotions and awareness of the emotions of others to move toward your goal and doing so in a professional and courteous manner demonstrates your EI.
- **Mirror, mirror.** Workplace pressure, stress, and time constraints sometimes inhibit our ability to see how others are responding to what we say and do. Reading others is especially challenging when working in virtual teams. Even when using web conferencing systems that allow us to see team members in other locations, our focus

on the task at hand makes it difficult to scan the faces or body language of others. In addition, our reading of others can sometimes be wrong due to language, culture, or other individual differences. Of course, the reverse is also true. Others may have trouble reading us. What we can do is model the behaviors associated with EI, like listening instead of talking, reading between the lines to uncover what is meant rather than just what is said, demonstrate that we are paying attention by sustaining eye contact or nodding. If you are working with asynchronous communication tools, confirm your understanding of what someone has written by paraphrasing or by asking specific, clarifying questions. The rules of netiquette (Shea, 2014) always apply.

EI Self-Check

A colleague comes to you with a problem. He is having a bad day and nothing seems to be going right for him. He goes on to tell you a 10-minute long story about everything that has happened to him today. You have a very important meeting in 30 minutes for which you need to prepare. What do you do?

a) Show interest and be engaged in the conversation.
b) Agree with your colleague while checking your smartphone for notes you may need for your meeting.
c) Tell him you're sorry to hear he's having a bad day and would be pleased to hear more when you get back from your meeting.
d) Tell him you are sorry things are not going well but you are sure he will get through it, then walk away.

Of the four options, (a) is the optimal choice. You are showing interest, showing you are engaged and present. Your colleague will appreciate the effort you are putting into his problem and showing empathy. Your meeting will still be there in 30 minutes and your conversation does not have to take more than 15 minutes to show that you are listening. Option (b) is not a good choice. Checking your smartphone will be interpreted as checking out of the conversation and shows discourtesy as well as disinterest, even though you may not have meant it that way. Option (c) is an acceptable answer if you feel that you cannot stay engaged without jeopardizing your meeting prep time. Just make sure your colleague is fine with discussing his problem later and that you follow up with him when you return from your meeting. Option (d) is a sure way to alienate your colleague. He may perceive this as being dismissive and condescending, a take-away that may come back to bite you should you have to call on him for something in the future.

Food for Thought

1   Your supervisor approaches you with a request from the VP of Human Resources. The results of the most recent Employee Satisfaction survey indicate that most employees like their jobs but dislike their bosses; they cite a lack of support, transparency in making decisions, and appreciation of what employees do. Consequently, the VP has asked that some mandatory training be developed to enhance the EI of all those with supervisory responsibilities. How would you respond to this request?

2   Think of a person in your workplace with whom you have a strong, positive relationship. The person could be a co-worker, a supervisor, a subordinate, a client, or an external vendor. Visualize that relationship and describe it in terms of these five questions:

   • What is it like?
   • How does it feel?
   • How well do you communicate?
   • How quickly do you get things done?
   • How much do you enjoy the relationship?

3   Now, think of a person in your workplace with whom you have a relationship that is at best strained and at worst negative. The person could be a co-worker, a supervisor, a subordinate, a client, or an external vendor. Visualize that relationship and describe it in terms of these five questions:

   • What is it like?
   • How does it feel?
   • How well do you communicate?
   • How quickly do you get things done?
   • How much do you enjoy the relationship?

4   Search the Internet for a free EI test or quiz. Are the resulting scores in line with what you expected?

Up Next

In this chapter, we have (a) reviewed the definitions, models, and measures surrounding EI; (b) explored how EI is applied in various workplace settings; and (c) drawn some lessons learned about cultivating our own EI. The next sections focus on some key areas in which EI is a must-have for demonstrating the value of the learning design function and for the designer's professional success.

References

Akgun, A. E., Keskin, H., Byrne, J. C., & Gunsel, A. (2011). Antecedents and results of emotional capability in software development project teams. *Journal of Product Innovation Management, 28*(6), 957–73.

Ashkanasy, N. M., & Daus, C. S. (2005). Rumors of the death of emotional intelligence in organizational behavior are vastly exaggerated. *Journal of Organizational Behavior, 26*, 441–52.

Ayoko, O. B., Callan, V. J., & Hartel, C. E. J. (2008). The influence of team emotional intelligence climate on conflict and team members' reactions to conflict. *Small Group Research, 39*(2), 121–49.

Bar-On, R. (1996a). *The Emotional Quotient Inventory (EQ-i): A Measure of Emotional Intelligence*. Toronto, Canada: Multi-Health Systems, Inc.

Bar-On, R. (1996b). *The Era of the "EQ": Defining and Assessing Emotional Intelligence*. Paper presented at the Annual Conference of the American Psychological Association, Toronto, Canada.

Bar-On, R. E., & Parker, J. E. (2000). *The Handbook of Emotional Intelligence: Theory, Development, Assessment, and Application at Home, School, and in the Workplace*. San Francisco, CA: Jossey-Bass.

Barchard, K. A., Brackett, M. A., & Mestre, J. M. (2016). Taking stock and moving forward: 25 years of emotional intelligence research. *Emotion Review, 8*(4), 287.

Bort, J. (2015). This Google engineer's title is 'Jolly Good Fellow' and he's solving unhappiness and war. *Business Insider*. Retrieved from www.businessinsider.com/google-jolly-good-fellow-chade-meng-tan-2015-9.

Boyatzis, R. E., Goleman, D., & Rhee, K. (2000). Clustering competence in emotional intelligence: Insights from the Emotional Competence Inventory (ECI). In R. Bar-On & J. D. A. Parker (Eds.), *Handbook of Emotional Intelligence* (pp. 343–62). San Francisco, CA: Jossey-Bass.

Brackett, M. A., Rivers, S. E., & Salovey, P. (2011). Emotional intelligence: implications for personal, social, academic, and workplace success. *Social and Personality Psychology Compass, 5*(1), 88–102.

Cartwright, S., & Pappas, C. (2008). Emotional intelligence, its measurement and implications for the workplace. *International Journal of Management Reviews, 10*(2), 149–71.

Cavallo, K. (2002). *Emotional Competence and Leadership Excellence at Johnson & Johnson: The Emotional Intelligence and Leadership Study*. Retrieved from www.eiconsortium.org/reports/jj_ei_study.html.

Cherniss, C. (2010). Emotional intelligence: Toward clarification of a concept. *Industrial and Organizational Psychology, 3*, 110–26.

Clarke, N. (2010). Emotional intelligence and its relationship to transformational leadership and key project manager competences. *Project Management Journal, 41*(2), 5–20.

Conley, C. (2014, March 12). The top 10 emotionally-intelligent Fortune 500 CEOs. *The Huffington Post*. Retrieved from www.huffingtonpost.com/chip-conley/the-top-10-emotionallyint_b_911576.html.

Doob, L. W. (1974). The analysis and resolution of international disputes. *The Journal of Psychology: Interdisciplinary and Applied, 86*(2), 313–26.

Druskat, V. U., & Wolff, S. B. (2001). Building the emotional intelligence of groups. *Harvard Business Review, 79*(3), 80–94.

Dulewicz, V., & Higgs, M. (2000). Emotional intelligence: A review and evaluation study. *Journal of Managerial Psychology, 15*(4), 341–72.

Farh, C., Seo, M. G., & Tesluk, P. E. (2012). Emotional intelligence, teamwork effectiveness, and job performance: The moderating role of job context. *Journal of Applied Psychology, 97*(4), 890–900.

Fariselli, L., Freedman, J., & Ghino, M. (2013). *The Amadori Case: Supplying McDonalds-Organizational Engagement, Emotional Intelligence and Performance.* Retrieved from www.6seconds.org/2013/04/03/amadori-case-engagement-emotional-intelligence/.

Fontaine, J. R. J. (2016). Comment: Redefining emotional intelligence based on the componential emotion approach. *Emotion Review, 8*(4), 332–3.

George, J. M. (2000). Emotions and leadership: the role of emotional intelligence. *Human Relations, 53*(8), 1027–53.

Goleman, D. (1995). *Emotional Intelligence.* New York, NY: Bantam Books.

Goleman, D. (1998). *Working with Emotional Intelligence.* New York, NY: Bantam Books.

Grasz, J. (2014). Seventy-One Percent of Employers Say They Value Emotional Intelligence Over IQ, According to CareerBuilder Survey – CareerBuilder. Retrieved from www.careerbuilder.com/share/aboutus/pressreleasesdetail.aspx?id=pr652&sd=8%2F18%2F2011&ed=12%2F31%2F2011.

Hastings, R. (2014). *Netflix Culture: Freedom and Responsibility.* Retrieved from www.slideshare.net/reed2001/culture-1798664.

Haver, A., Akerjordet, K., & Furunes, T. (2013). Emotion regulation and its implications for leadership: an integrative review and future research agendas. *Journal of Leadership & Organizational Studies, 20*(3), 287–303.

Higgs, M., & Aitken, P. (2003). An exploration of the relationship between emotional intelligence and leadership potential. *Journal of Managerial Psychology, 18*(8), 814–23.

Hutchinson, M., & Hurley, J. (2013). Exploring leadership capability and emotional intelligence as moderators of workplace bullying. *Journal of Nursing Management, 21*(3), 553–62.

Jacobellis v. Ohio: The Oyez Project at IIT Chicago-Kent College of Law (1964). Retrieved from www.oyez.org/cases/1960-1969/1962/1962_11_2.

Jordan, P. J., Ashkanasy, N. M., Hartel, C. E. J., & Hooper, G. S. (2002). Workgroup emotional intelligence: Scale development and relationship to team process effectiveness and goal focus. *Human Resource Management Review, 12*, 195–214.

Jordan, P. J., Ashton-James, C. E., & Ashkanasy, N. M. (2006). Evaluating the claims. In K. R. Murphy (Ed.), *A Critique of Emotional Intelligence: What Are the Problems and How Can They Be Fixed?* (pp. 198–210). Mahwah, NJ: Lawrence Erlbaum Associates.

Jordan, P. J., & Troth, A. C. (2004). Managing emotions during team problem solving: emotional intelligence and conflict resolutions. *Human Performance, 17*(2), 195–218.

Koch, E. I., & Rauch, W. (1984). *Mayor: An Autobiography.* New York, NY: Simon and Schuster.

Koman, E. S., & Wolff, S. B. (2008). Emotional intelligence competencies in the team and team leader: A multi-level examination of the impact of emotional intelligence on team performance. *Journal of Management Development, 27*(1), 55–75.

Lindebaum, D., & Cartwright, S. (2010). A critical examination of the relationship between emotional intelligence and transformational leadership. *Journal of Management Studies, 47*(7), 1317–42.

Lynn, A. B. (2008). *The EQ Interview: Finding Employees with High Emotional Intelligence.* New York, NY: AMACOM.

Mayer, J. D., Caruso, D. R., & Salovey, P. (2016). The ability model of emotional intelligence: Principles and updates. *Emotion Review*, 8(4), 290–300.

Mayer, J. D., & Salovey, P. (1997). What is emotional intelligence? In P. Salovey & D. J. Sluyter (Eds.), *Emotional Development and Emotional Intelligence: Educational Implications* (pp. 3–31). New York, NY: Basic Books.

Mayer, J. D., Salovey, P., & Caruso, D. R. (2004). Emotional intelligence: Theory, findings, and implications. *Psychological Inquiry*, 15, 197–215.

McClelland, D. C. (1998). Identifying competencies with behavioural event interviews. *Psychological Science*, 9(5), 331–40.

Mikolajczak, M., Luminet, O., Leroy, C., & Roy, E. (2007). Psychometric properties of the trait emotional intelligence questionnaire: factor structure, reliability, construct, and incremental validity in a French-speaking population. *Journal of Personality Assessment*, 88(3), 338–53.

Mount, G. (2006). The role of emotional intelligence in developing international business capability: EI provides traction. In V. Druskat, F. Sala, & G. Mount (Eds.), *Linking Emotional Intelligence and Performance at Work* (pp. 97–124). Mahwah, NJ: Lawrence Erlbaum Associates.

Nelson, B. (2013, April). 'Come to Jesus Moment' is the most annoying business expression on earth. *Forbes*. Retrieved from www.forbes.com/sites/brettnelson/2013/04/03/come-to-jesus-moment-is-the-most-annoying-business-expression-on-earth/.

Nowack, K. (2012). Emotional intelligence: Defining and understanding the fad. *Training and Development*, 66, 60–3.

O'Boyle, E. H. J., Humphrey, R. H., Pollack, J. M., Hawver, T. H., & Story, P. A. (2011). The relation between emotional intelligence and job performance: A meta-analysis. *Journal of Organizational Behavior*, 32, 788–818.

Palmer, B., Walls, M., Burgess, Z., & Stough, C. (2001). Emotional intelligence and effective leadership. *Leadership & Organizational Development Journal*, 22(1), 5–10.

Pert, C. B. (1999). *Molecules of Emotion: The Science Behind Mind-Body Medicine*. New York, NY: Simon & Schuster.

Petrides, K. V., Pita, R., & Kokkinaki, F. (2007). The location of trait emotional intelligence in personality factor space. *British Journal of Psychology*, 98, 273–89.

Romanelli, F., Cain, J., & Smith, K. M. (2006). Emotional intelligence as a predictor of academic and/or professional success. *American Journal of Pharmaceutical Education*, 70(3), 1–10.

Ryan, G., Spencer, L. M., & Bernhard, U. (2012). Development and validation of a customized competency-based questionnaire: linking social, emotional, and cognitive competencies to business unit profitability. *Cross Cultural Management-an International Journal*, 19(1), 90–103.

Salovey, P., & Mayer, J. D. (1989–1990). Emotional intelligence. *Imagination, Cognition, and Personality*, 9(3), 185–211.

Shea, V. (2014). *The Core Rules of Netiquette – Excerpted from Netiquette by Virginia Shea – Albion.com*. Retrieved from www.albion.com/netiquette/corerules.html.

Stein, S. J., Papadogiannis, P., Yip, J. A., & Sitarenios, G. (2009). Emotional intelligence of leaders: A profile of top executives. *Leadership and Organizational Development Journal*, 30(1), 87–101.

Taylor, S. (2009). On a recruiting mission. *Staffing Management*, 5(2). Retrieved from www.shrm.org/Publications/StaffingManagementMagazine/EditorialContent/Pages/0409taylor.aspx.

The Myers & Briggs Foundation. (2014). My MBTI Personality Type – MBTI Basics. Retrieved from www.myersbriggs.org/my-mbti-personality-type/mbti-basics/.

Troth, A. C., Jordan, P. J., Lawrence, S. A., & Tse, H. H. M. (2012). A multilevel model of emotional skills, communication performance, and task performance in teams. *Journal of Organizational Behavior, 33*(5), 700–22.

Tyler, K. (2013). Google's jolly good fellow. *HR Magazine, 58*, 30–1.

Wall, B. (2007). Being smart only takes you so far. *Training and Development, 61*, 64–8.

Wiete, A. K. (2013). *Leadership and Emotional Intelligence: The Keys to Driving ROI and Organizational Performance*. White River Junction, VT: Human Capital Institute.

Wirth, G., & Gansle, G. (2012). Jump toward emotional intelligence. *HR Magazine, 67*. Retrieved from www.shrm.org/Publications/hrmagazine/EditorialContent/2012/1012/Pages/1012legal.aspx.

Wroten, C. (2014). 12 e-Learning buzzwords you need to know. Retrieved from http://elearningindustry.com/12-e-learning-buzzwords-you-need-to-know.

Yuan, B. J. C., Hsu, W.-L., Shieh, J.-H., & Li, K.-P. (2012). Increasing emotional intelligence of employees: evidence from research and development teams in Taiwan. *Social Behavior and Personality, 40*(10), 1713–24.

Zeidner, M., Matthews, G., & Roberts, R. D. (2004). Emotional intelligence in the workplace: a critical review. *Applied Psychology: An International Review, 53*(3), 371–99.

Part III

Demonstrating the Value of Learning Design and Technologies

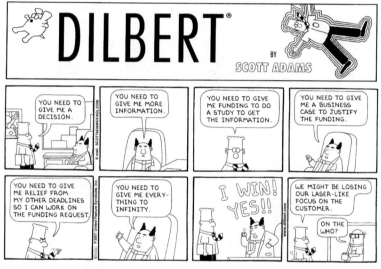

8 Business Case Writing
Offense or Defense?

In Part II, we focused on gaining a solid understanding of the workplace environment as essential to the diagnosis of performance problems. Now, we turn our attention to ways of demonstrating the value of the learning function to an organization. Demonstrating value begins with providing evidence of the contribution of learning interventions to the organization's goals for talent development. That evidence should be offered well before a particular intervention is undertaken. One of the most common methods of presenting such evidence is through a written business case. Basically, the business case is your written rationale for some new undertaking. Your business case should always describe the benefits of doing whatever it is that you are proposing. The benefits can be to the individual employee, the department, the business unit, or the entire organization. Those benefits should be observable and measurable. Your business case should include detailed information about both the financial and human resources required to complete the undertaking successfully. Importantly, your business case is a mechanism for promoting some kind of change in performance. The business case provides evidence of a solid plan for a proposed intervention with a comprehensive rationale, so that senior management will support your effort.

At this point, you may be thinking: *Isn't a business case the same thing as a proposal or a business plan?* Although you may have seen or heard the three terms used interchangeably, they differ in two key respects, namely, the target audience for whom they are written and who actually does the writing. Business plans are prepared by entrepreneurs or leaders of existing businesses with the aim of acquiring funding for their business ventures. The target audiences may be commercial banks, venture capitalists, or other types of investors who underwrite business ventures. Although specifics may vary depending on the nature of the business and of the industry sector, the business plan is intended to demonstrate that the entrepreneur or business team has thought through the various key drivers of the venture's success or failure and has assessed whether or not the venture has a sustainable business model. There is no shortage of scholarly and practitioner books and articles describing what makes a successful business plan, as well as examples from a variety of industries and regions world-wide (Chen, Yao, & Kotha, 2009; Chowdury, Azam, & Islam, 2015; De Oliveira, Shayani, & De Oliveira, 2013; Ford, Bornstein, & Pruitt, 2007; McKeever, 2014; Salman, 2008). If your future goal is to start your own business focused on learning solutions, then these and other resources will help you to prepare the business plan needed to secure funding for that business.

While the business plan is prepared by specific individual(s) for a specific purpose and is aimed at a specific audience, the proposal is much broader in nature. The dictionary definition (Proposal, n.d.) of the term is "an act of putting forward or stating something for consideration." In the education sector, proposals may be written by researchers seeking grant funding for a particular line of inquiry, with proposal requirements defined by the funding agency. Proposals may also be written by graduate students required to complete a thesis or dissertation for an advanced or terminal degree as prescribed by the relevant institution of higher education. International agencies that sponsor cross-national research projects also have their own proposal requirements. Common to all of these examples is the focus on the social or societal benefits of a proposed project or intervention. Business cases focus less on the public good and more on the benefits to the organization in terms of performance.

One particular type of proposal that looks very much like a business case is the formal response to a written Request for Proposal or RFP. Normally used by organizations that purchase products and services through a competitive bidding process, the RFP is a written document describing (a) the statement and scope of work to be done; (b) the specifications, including issues/problems to be addressed and the target audiences; (c) the schedules or timelines to which the vendor must adhere; (d) the type of contract (e.g., fixed price, time and materials); (e) the specific product or service requirements (e.g., features/functions of a software system); and (f) all other technical requirements, terms, and conditions. If you work for a vendor that provides learning content or services to external clients, your company's revenue comes from successful responses to RFPs. Federal, state, and local governments as well as K–16 public education are all required to purchase products and services above a particular cost threshold through competitive bidding. There are some key differences between a business case and an RFP response:

- The business case is targeted to an internal audience while the RFP response is targeted to the issuer of the RFP.
- The business case argues for the optimum choice among two or more alternatives while the RFP response must address the specific requirements set down in the RFP.
- The business case is normally authored by one individual, although multiple sources of information are used by that individual. In the case

of RFP responses, vendors usually employ dedicated teams of people to respond to RFPs.

- The business case argues for top priority against other projects that the organization may be considering, while the RFP pits vendors against each other for the client's business.
- Finally, if a business case fails, it does not necessarily mean the death of the proposed initiative. With RFPs, it's a win/lose situation where the vendor does or does not get the client's business.

But my job doesn't require me to write business cases and my organization doesn't expect business cases from our department. That may certainly be true, at the moment. However, even the casual observer of events in the last decade or so has noticed that the status quo is easily disrupted; what is true today may not be true tomorrow. Moreover, organizations are regularly seeking ways to remain competitive and relevant within their respective industry sectors, which requires, at a minimum, adapting to change and, optimally, anticipating change. Even in industry sectors where change is more evolutionary than revolutionary, decision-makers keep an eye out for trends that may affect organizational sustainability and growth. Finally, the ability to write persuasive business cases is among the competencies that instructional designers should possess for promotion to the managerial ranks (IBSTPI, 2014). The designer who advances beyond the functional foundations is more likely to be considered for promotion than the one who does not. In some cases, just doing your job may not help you keep your position in the event of organizational shifts and redundancies.

There are no hard and fast rules about when you need to provide a written business case. It depends partly on organizational "custom." In some organizations, it is expected that Learning and Development (L&D) professionals will write a formal business case for new opportunities that are above a specific investment threshold or address specific audiences, such as leadership. Others leave it to the judgment of the L&D professional as to when to submit a written business case. This is where you need to seek out those who know your organization well. Check with your supervisor or manager, your peers, and your organization's archives or databases for examples of when, how, and at what level of detail business cases are normally prepared. Before you begin, however, it is helpful to be clear as to what role business cases play in go/no go decisions and how to organize your thoughts as you consider when and how to build a business case. In this chapter, we will:

- Review some basic concepts of organizational decision-making that tend to drive the need for business cases;
- Explain the essentials of crafting a business case; and
- Identify some lessons learned from successful and unsuccessful business cases.

Evidence-Based Decision-Making: What Organizational Leaders (Should) Do

If your business case is to garner management's support for your initiative, the content of your business case needs to guide the decision-makers in choosing among alternatives in light of the possible consequences of those alternatives. However, the process of decision-making is far from objective:

> The process of making decisions is grounded in knowledge and expertise, and is driven by fundamental, ethical, cultural, psycho-emotional and biological principles. It reflects the psycho-emotional inner world of perception of the decision-maker, and rests on fundamentals of socio-economic principles and realities. (Chiappelli, 2010, p. 6)

Business decisions are no different from decisions we make daily in that the evidence for and against a particular decision is filtered through the lens of rational and emotional factors grounded in different and sometimes competing points of origin. As Nobel Laureate Herbert Simon once noted (Simon, 1982), decision-makers have a limited time and availability to make decisions and are limited by cognitive schema and by other limitations, such as the availability of evidence. When crafting a business case, your goal is to ensure that you have systematically gathered all of the available evidence and synthesized the best of the available evidence to support the decision-making process. Although there is no guarantee as to how much weight an individual decision-maker may give to evidence vs. emotion or gut feelings (Pfeffer & Sutton, 2006a), it is certain that the absence of evidence will send a business case to the back of the resource line if not to the dustbin.

Roots of Evidence-Based Decision-Making

Evidence-based decision-making has its roots in one of the oldest research areas in the management literature, namely, decision theory. Decision theory focuses on the development of rational methods for selecting the best among a set of alternatives in a rational, systematic manner using quantitative and qualitative descriptors. Originating in the military as part of the shift from tactical planning to strategic planning during World War II (Ives, 1973), decision theory was adopted by business and management scholars as post-war businesses sought to respond to the increasing rate of change in the environment and focus on strategic, long-term organizational problems. The theory seeks to address (a) decision-making under certainty, where a manager has too much information to choose the best alternative; (b) decision-making under conflict, where a manager has to anticipate the behavior of the competition; and (c) decision-making under uncertainty, where a manager has to obtain a lot of data to analyze and interpret what is going on and what the implications of the data mean (Simon, 1959; March, 1994). Decision-making theory focuses on how and why decisions are made, including decision-making as an economic, social, and political phenomenon in for-profit and not-for-profit organizational settings (Busenitz & Barney, 1997; Dean & Sharfman, 1993; Feldman & Kanter, 2013; Pettigrew, 2014; Simon, 1979; Steptoe-Warren, Howat, & Hume, 2011).

Emergence of Evidence-Based Decision-Making

Evidence-based decision-making emerged as a distinct research stream in the 1980s when public services were being challenged for their inconsistencies in evidence proving their effectiveness, particularly in medical science and healthcare services (Baba & HakemZadeh, 2012). Evidence-based practice (EBP) – the use of scientific research as the basis for clinical decision-making – was deemed to be the solution to curbing rising healthcare costs while offering quality care and access to services (Lockett, 1997; White, 1997). EBP seeks to combine the competencies and judgment that individual clinicians acquire through clinical experience and clinical practice with clinically relevant research, particularly patient-centered research focused on diagnostic testing and various treatment regimens to improve patient outcomes. EBP also requires the clinician to assess the validity and applicability of the research, apply it in practice, and evaluate his/her own performance against the evidence (Sackett, 1997). Given the scope and complexity of healthcare issues worldwide, it is not surprising that a robust body of knowledge about evidence-based decision-making in healthcare contexts has emerged (Adams & Drake, 2006; Birch, 1997; Clancy & Cronin, 2005).

However, it also became clear that while the leaders and managers of healthcare organizations encouraged clinicians to adopt an evidence-based approach to clinical practice, they had been slow to apply the ideas to their own managerial practice (Hewison, 1997; Kovner, Elton, & Billings, 2005; Young, 2002). Walshe & Rundall (2001) identified three main barriers to evidence-based decision-making among healthcare managers. The first barrier is related to the career path to management. Walshe and Rundall described healthcare managers as a highly diverse group drawn from different professional and disciplinary backgrounds and often lacking a shared language or terminology with which to describe and discuss what they do. Furthermore, there is no specified formal body of knowledge, training, or registration required to become a healthcare manager, and many clinicians took on healthcare management roles with little or no formal management training. Personal experience and self-generated knowledge played a much larger part in determining how managers approach their jobs, and there was less reliance on a shared body of formal knowledge in decision-making. Walshe and Rundall described the managerial culture as intensely pragmatic, valuing the application of ideas in practice more than the search for knowledge about those ideas. Another barrier that Walshe and Rundall identified focuses on manager experiences with research and evidence, noting that managers may come from an academic discipline in which observational methods are used, qualitative research is more accepted and may be the norm, and there may be a greater focus on theoretical development than on empirical theory testing. Also, the loosely defined, methodologically heterogeneous, widely distributed and hard to generalize research base for healthcare management was difficult for healthcare managers to use. Finally, Walshe and Rundall pointed to how healthcare managers make decisions, using no explicit decision process and having no decision support infrastructure.

If this sounds familiar, that is because it is not uncommon to find L&D managers from backgrounds and disciplines unrelated to L&D, with a "get-the-job-done" attitude and preference for those who learn by doing rather than those who have theoretical knowledge of the field governing their decision-making.

Evidence-Based Decision-Making across the Disciplines

Evidence-based decision-making as a stream of scholarly research thrives in the education policy literature (Biesta, 2007; Honig & Coburn, 2008; Kowalski & Lasley, 2009), as well as in the literature of criminal justice (Drake, Aos, & Miller, 2009; MacKenzie, 2000) and public administration (Head, 2008; Jennings & Hall, 2012). In the management literature, the practice of evidence-based decision-making in management (sometimes referred to as Evidence-based Management or EBMgt) emphasizes a rational, objective, and empirical approach to addressing business issues, particularly (a) learning about cause-effect connections, (b) isolating the variations that affect desired outcomes, (c) creating a culture of evidence-based decision-making and research participation, (d) using information-sharing communities to ensure good use of specific practices, (e) building decision support tools and systems to promote practices that the evidence validates, and (f) having individual and organizational factors promote access to and use of knowledge (Rousseau, 2006).

Similar to many of the findings about evidence-based decision-making in healthcare contexts, the research on evidence-based decision-making in private sector businesses indicates a gap between research and practice due to lack of exposure to the research on evidence-based decision-making, the absence of a shared body of knowledge among practicing managers, the misapplication of organization-specific practices to dissimilar organizational contexts, and individual manager tendencies to manage-by-anecdote (Leslie, Loch, & Schaninger, 2006; Pfeffer & Sutton, 2006b; Rousseau, 2006). The good news is that L&D managers are becoming more evidence driven, moving toward training program evaluations that are expressed in terms of financial results or measures of performance (Cascio, 2007; van Rooij & Merkebu, 2015). For L&D professionals outside of the C-suite, most evidence is gathered to inform organization-specific decisions, as exemplified by root cause analysis and other fact-based approaches related to organizational decision-making.

Barends, Rousseau, and Briner (2014) sought to provide guidance to managers on what is required to apply evidence-based decision-making to daily practice, describing the following main skills required to practice in an evidence-based way:

1   Asking: translating a practical issue or problem into an answerable question;
2   Acquiring: systematically searching for and retrieving the evidence;
3   Appraising: critically judging the trustworthiness and relevance of the evidence;
4   Aggregating: weighing and pulling together the evidence;
5   Applying: incorporating the evidence into a decision-making process; and
6   Assessing: evaluating the outcome of the decision taken.

The sources of evidence should include findings from published research, data, facts, and figures gathered from inside the organization, the professional experience and judgment of practitioners, and the values and concerns of people who may be affected by the decision (i.e., stakeholders).

Figure 8.1 graphically illustrates the evolution of evidence-based decision-making as a field of research and scholarship across the disciplines. At this point, you may be thinking: *There is no way my manager is going to spend time collecting and analyzing multiple sources of data in order to make a decision.* You're probably right. There is a considerable

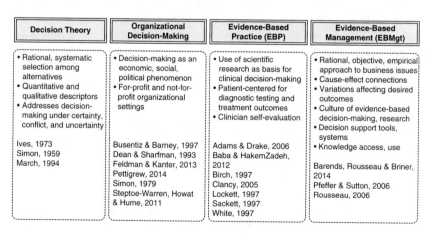

Decision Theory	Organizational Decision-Making	Evidence-Based Practice (EBP)	Evidence-Based Management (EBMgt)
• Rational, systematic selection among alternatives • Quantitative and qualitative descriptors • Addresses decision-making under certainty, conflict, and uncertainty	• Decision-making as an economic, social, political phenomenon • For-profit and not-for-profit organizational settings	• Use of scientific research as basis for clinical decision-making • Patient-centered for diagnostic testing and treatment outcomes • Clinician self-evaluation	• Rational, objective, empirical approach to business issues • Cause-effect connections • Variations affecting desired outcomes • Culture of evidence-based decision-making, research • Decision support tools, systems • Knowledge access, use
Ives, 1973 Simon, 1959 March, 1994	Busentiz & Barney, 1997 Dean & Sharfman, 1993 Feldman & Kanter, 2013 Pettigrew, 2014 Simon, 1979 Steptoe-Warren, Howat & Hume, 2011	Adams & Drake, 2006 Baba & HakemZadeh, 2012 Birch, 1997 Clancy, 2005 Lockett, 1997 Sackett, 1997 White, 1997	Barends, Rousseau & Briner, 2014 Pfeffer & Sutton, 2006 Rousseau, 2006

Figure 8.1 Evolution of Evidence-Based Decision-Making Research.

body of international research about the types of tasks and activities that managers delegate to their direct reports (Ardichvili & Kuchinke, 2002; Armstrong, 2011; Harrison & Pelletier, 2000; Oshagbemi & Ocholi, 2006). The research suggests that most managers will delegate the actual data collection, synthesis, and analysis activities, and then use the data as an input to decision-making. Consequently, acquiring the ability to produce a well-crafted business case is a sound career move.

The Thinking Behind Your Business Case

Nature of the Challenge/Opportunity: Gathering Your Thoughts

Crafting a sound business case begins not with structure or presentation but with the thought processes that bring you to the realization that a business case would help you to either solve an existing L&D challenge or identify a L&D opportunity. Importantly, a business case will help you to sell your ideas to decision-makers. Whether you have been asked to write a business case or you come up with a challenge or opportunity on your own, you still need to think through the idea systematically before drafting your business case document. Start by jotting down the answers to the following orienting questions:

1   Does this challenge/opportunity address a current or potential performance issue that my boss and my boss's boss deem to be critical?
2   Does addressing that performance issue have tangible benefits (e.g., revenue) or intangible benefits (e.g., customer satisfaction)?
3   Do those benefits align with the strategic goals of my organization?
4   Do I know who inside my organization can help me to identify any factors or circumstances inside and outside my organization that could influence the decision (not) to address the challenge or opportunity?

Next, use the answers to these orienting questions to draft a one-sentence statement that describes at a high level the challenge/opportunity in terms of its business benefits.

Let's take an example by way of illustration. You are a member of ABC Company's L&D group. John Jones, your supervisor, comes to you and says that the L&D group needs to come up with ways to speed up new employee productivity. He recently attended a conference presentation given by one of your competitors and learned that their new employees were reaching full productivity in only three months, down from the previous norm of nine months, due to a new online training program. He asks you to help him write a business case for a similar initiative at your organization.

This request has come from your direct supervisor, so it is very tempting to go back and start researching ways to develop a new online training program for new employees. Resist the temptation of Beginner's Blind Obedience! In articulating the problem of new employee time-to-productivity, John has offered a solution that may not solve the problem. Consequently, he may miss out on considering a variety of alternative solutions to that problem. Instead of starting with a solution, start with your orienting questions. Based on what you already know about your organization, conversations with colleagues, as well as a quick search of publicly available information in- and outside of your organization, your answers may look something like this:

1 ABC's leadership is concerned about getting new employees fully productive faster so that it can recover the costs of new hires faster, increase the capacity of the departments to which those new employees are assigned, and decrease the workload of existing employees.
2 There are tangible benefits, such as a smaller portion of the relevant departmental budgets spent on onboarding, and intangible benefits, such as increased employee satisfaction and employee retention.
3 A quick read of the organization's strategic plan indicates that these benefits are in line with the organization's strategic goals of creating reliable internal sources of talent to achieve higher performance across all levels and functions, and having experienced and trained employees prepared to assume leadership roles as soon as those roles become available.
4 The people inside my organization who can identify things about this issue that I have not thought of are John Jones, L&D Manager; Mary Smith, HR Director; Roger Thomas, Finance Manager; Lydia Gomez, Information Systems Manager; and Harold Evans, Director of Operations.

Using these answers, your one-sentence statement might read:

> The L&D group will help ABC to more quickly expand its pool of trained, high-performing employees by enabling ABC to move to a more efficient and effective onboarding approach.

In looking at this example of a challenge/opportunity statement, note what the statement does **not** do. It does not describe:

- A specific solution;
- What employees need to learn; or
- How instruction will be used.

Instead, a good challenge/opportunity statement focuses on how spending resources to address your challenge/opportunity will help the organization to achieve its strategic goals.

Preliminary Temperature Check

Before you invest time and energy in data gathering, you will want to gauge whether or not your idea has any chance of being heard among the many other new ideas competing for your organization's finite resources. Here is an opportunity to apply what you learned about needs assessment and stakeholder analysis in Chapters 4 and 6 of this book. Look at the list of stakeholders you created in response to orienting question number 4. Feel free to add names and, based on any previous dealings you may have had with these individuals, provide your best guess as to whether they would be receptive, neutral, or skeptical about your proposed initiative. You will want to validate your idea with a small sampling of these stakeholders. A technique often used to gauge potential support is the focus group. The focus group format would work well because participants can interact with one another in a more informal, conversational pattern than would be the case with a one-on-one interview or a survey. Given the ubiquity of web conferencing tools in most workplaces, you could conduct your focus group online for easier and faster access to participants. Eight to ten is a manageable number and should include representation from management, subject matter experts, and anyone else you believe may be willing to think along with you about the idea. This will increase buy-in if the business case is approved.

To make the most efficient and effective use of stakeholder time, you will need a more condensed instrument for facilitating your session than the traditional focus group discussion guide. As shown in Figure 8.2, moving through your orienting questions with specific probing questions should generate enough feedback to not only refine the responses to those questions but strengthen the challenge/opportunity statement that will describe the purpose of your business case. As your focus group session proceeds, more sub-questions may arise under any or all of the four

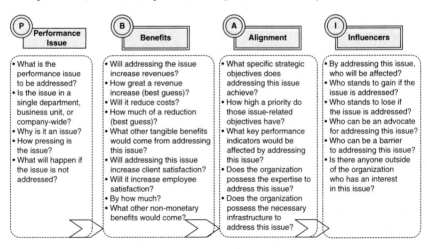

Figure 8.2 Preliminary Testing of Challenge/Opportunity Idea.

orienting questions. The outcomes of your session should include (a) a list of the most relevant business objectives the organization will achieve by addressing the challenge/opportunity, (b) the priority of these objectives from an organizational perspective, and (c) the metrics to measure the impact of the alternatives that your business case will evaluate.

Before concluding your focus group session, invite the focus group participants to be members of a stakeholder panel for your challenge/opportunity. A decades-old mechanism used to inform policy in various sectors, such as environmental science (Bunting, 2010), education (Brown & Hunter, 2006), as well as business and management (Spitzeck & Hansen, 2010), stakeholder panels generally consist of a group of individuals who are interested in the purposes for which the panel was established and have an ability to affect, either directly or indirectly, the progress and outcomes of those purposes. Make it clear that the panel will serve as an issue-specific source of ideas for identifying alternative solutions to the challenge/opportunity discussed in the focus group and will contribute to select the solution recommendations in your business case. Importantly, discuss and agree on frequency and methods of communication so that expectations about anticipated demands on panel members' time are clear.

In sum, the focus group will help to guide your due diligence efforts, so that you and your stakeholders can flesh out any faulty assumptions, knowledge gaps, unacceptable risks, or other barriers to success early on. If your preliminary temperature check reveals the need to make revisions to your challenge/opportunity statement, the panel enables you to get feedback on those revisions without having to repeat the entire focus group process. It will also provide you with an ongoing pool of "critical friends" (Forstater et al., 2007) to help you find the evidence you need to build a persuasive, data-driven business case.

Crafting Your Business Case

The Search for Solution Alternatives

Now that you have defined the challenge/opportunity, you will need to generate a list of options for addressing your challenge/opportunity. You should have a general idea of what solution alternatives would be worth considering based on your experience inside the organization as well as a review of secondary information sources, such as previous initiatives aimed at similar challenges. In our ABC Company example, you would look at current programs, processes, and procedures for onboarding new employees, as well as any internal surveys that include new employee feedback on their experiences with the onboarding process. You may also want to include approaches that you have seen or heard about at professional association events or in practitioner publications.

Here is where the Delphi method discussed in Chapter 6 will help you to get the feedback you need to identify your suite of alternatives. Once you have your initial list of solution alternatives, send your list to your panel of stakeholders and ask them to add their own ideas to the list. At this point, your goal is to generate as many potential alternatives as possible without expressing a preference for one alternative or another. Next, compile the results of this first round of feedback and create a scale to assess levels of agreement among the panel members. For instance, you might ask the panelists to rate each solution alternative collected in the first round on a 7-point Preference scale. To help you understand the reasons behind the ratings, include a comment area in which stakeholders explain their reasons for rating a particular idea at the top of the Preference scale, particularly in terms of the idea's ability to help meet the organization's business goals. Then, compile the results from the second round of data collection and see which solution alternatives stand out. Did most panelists rate a particular alternative as most preferred? Were there any alternatives that were primarily rated at the opposite end of the Preference scale? If no clear winners emerge, distribute the results of this second round of data collection and ask the panelists to share a story from their own, firsthand experience with the challenge/opportunity, and describe what went wrong and what went right. Using our ABC Company example, ask for a story about a new hire whose time to productivity was longer than expected and the reasons why it was longer; then, identify common themes across the stories.

Your three rounds of data collection should enable you to narrow down your list of alternatives to two or three options that will best address your challenge/opportunity. If your list is particularly long, eliminate the highest risk options first and focus on those that are most likely to address business goals and are most feasible for your organization to undertake. A quick conversation with your supervisor or, if you have some time, a review by your stakeholder panel, should provide enough feedback to firm up the list. Your final list should also include the option of maintaining the status quo – the "do nothing" option – and serve as the baseline against which the pros and cons of all the other options should be evaluated. Returning to our ABC Company example, your final list of alternatives might contain the following options:

1   Do nothing.
2   Convert the current onboarding program to an online format.
3   Build an online supplement to the current onboarding program.
4   Purchase a commercial, off-the-shelf onboarding training package.

Assessing Each Alternative

In order to identify the optimal solution, you need to provide an evidence-based assessment of each alternative. Your assessment should clearly describe the pros and cons of implementing each alternative, the assumptions and risks associated with each alternative, the tangible and intangible costs and timeline of each alternative, and the impact on the business of implementing each alternative. The evidence you provide should be grounded in the three outcomes achieved at the end of your stakeholder focus session: (a) the list of the most relevant business objectives the organization will achieve by addressing the challenge opportunity; (b) the priority of these objectives from an organizational perspective; and (c) the metrics to measure the impact of the alternatives that your business case will evaluate.

Collecting the data for this assessment process will probably be the most labor-intensive portion of your business case because the data you need will most likely come from multiple sources. If at all possible, begin by collecting historical data from in-house to use as a benchmark against which to estimate the changes that each alternative solution would bring, should that solution be implemented. Here is where a data collection planning worksheet similar to the one shown in Table 8.1 can help you focus your data gathering and ensure that you collect comparable data for all of your solution alternatives. As you gather data and talk with colleagues, you will probably add to the list of data points. Your completed worksheet may be included in the Appendix section of your business case document to serve as evidence of where, how, and when you got your data.

Once you have gathered the data on your alternatives, you need to analyze and compare your alternatives against the organization's business objectives and the metrics that you and your stakeholders agreed would best measure the impact of your solution on those objectives. A core component of your comparative analysis will focus on the financial implications of each alternative, such as the direct costs of any products/services associated with the alternative or cost savings from implementing a particular

Table 8.1 Data Collection Planning Worksheet

Information Needs	Alternative 1	Alternative 2	Alternative 3	Alternative 4
General Description				
Business Objectives Addressed				
Data Types Required				
Metrics/KPIs				
Implementation Timelines				
Data Sources (Who, When, How)				

solution. If financial analysis is not your strong suit, this is where your stakeholder(s) from the Finance group become powerful contributors to the credibility of your business case by doing the analysis for you (more on the financial component in Chapter 9). Your analysis should also include the non-financial, intangible benefits you and your stakeholders deemed relevant when you were first fleshing out your challenge/opportunity idea.

Table 8.2 shows an extract of what your comparative assessment might look like for our ABC Company example. For each alternative, including

Table 8.2 Comparison of Solution Alternatives: ABC Example

Criteria	Do Nothing	Convert to Online Format	Build Online Supplement	Purchase Commercial Product
Advantages	No cost, no effort	Customized to needs Easy access for new hires	Easy access to resources New information not covered in current program	Ready to use immediately No internal human resources required
Disadvantages	Does not address goal of onboarding efficiency and effectiveness	Time- and labor-intensive Take resources away from other L&D projects in flight	Increases onboarding process from one to two steps Requires L&D resources	Does not meet all needs High upfront costs No ability to update as needed
Costs	None	Development: $25,000 (est.) Maintenance: $2,000/yr.	Development: $10,000 Maintenance: $1,000/yr.	Annual subscription: $15,000
Assumptions	Satisfaction with status quo	In-house development Defer/re-prioritize existing projects	In-house development Defer/re-prioritize existing projects	Vendor/product selection in 30 days or less Compatibility with in-house systems
Risks	Failure to meet onboarding goals leads to lower employee productivity rates and higher employee attrition	New hires may not be comfortable with online learning	Two-step process may increase time to productivity	Vendor may go out of business

the "do nothing" alternative, you see the advantages and disadvantages in terms of addressing business objectives, financial information for each alternative, your assumptions about the conditions that must exist in order for the solution to be implemented, along with the risks associated with implementing each alternative.

Selecting the Best Alternative

Once you have analyzed and compared your alternatives, you will need to select the alternative that best addresses the challenge/opportunity for which you are creating the business case, and where the benefits outweigh the costs and risks. It sometimes happens that there is a clear winner among the alternatives, and the data from your comparative analysis enable that alternative to more or less sell itself. In most instances, however, the optimal choice does not jump off the page. In making your final selection, jot down the answers to the following questions:

- Which of my alternatives best supports my organization's business objectives?
- Which of those objectives are most important to my organization?
- Which alternative will be easiest to implement?
- What are the top three reasons why I selected this alternative?
- What are the risks associated with this alternative?
- How can I mitigate the risks associated with this alternative?
- How likely are the desired outcomes of this alternative to occur?

The answers to these questions will either affirm your initial selection or point toward another of the alternatives or even a combination of alternatives.

From Idea to Action

Now that you have identified your challenge/opportunity, evaluated various solution alternatives, and selected the optimal alternative, you need to demonstrate that you know how to convert your solution into reality by developing a high-level implementation and evaluation plan. The plan identifies the major milestones, responsibilities, material and human resources, timelines, and success measures for your chosen alternative.

Returning to our ABC Company example, let's say you selected Alternative 3, "build an online supplement to the current onboarding program." Your high-level implementation and evaluation plan might contain the information shown in Table 8.3. Note the following:

- Major milestones are observable and measurable;
- Dates are non-specific;
- Timelines are generous without appearing to be "padded"; and
- Human resources list specific names rather than function areas to ensure accountability and commitment.

Table 8.3 Summary Implementation and Evaluation Plan: ABC Example

Task	Staff Resources	Deliverable	Est. Time to Completion
Requirements gathering	Liz Anderson, Talent Mgmt. Harry Evans, IT/LMS Admin. Sarah Long, Onboarding Specialist	Preliminary product specifications	30 days
Milestone: Specification review and approval	Everett Chase, Sam Wills, & Lou Aaron, HR Managers	Final product specifications document (with signed approvals)	5 days after formal review meeting
Supplement design	Mary Wills, Instructional Designer Sarah Long, Onboarding Specialist Larry Jones, Recent Hire	Final iteration (with written approval)	10 days after receipt of formal specifications
Development, testing			
Pilot			
Rollout			
Follow-up (Pre- vs. post-avg. time to productivity)			

You may also want to include explicit communication check points so that the stakeholders remain aware of the project's progress and can step in to assist you, should any mid-project shifts be required. The tabular format also enables you to get some quick feedback from a sampling of your stakeholders.

Presenting Your Case

Organizations tend to have their own requirements for the format and layout of written business cases. If there is no required format, check with your supervisor, Finance, or HR for examples of previously written business cases. It is highly unlikely that you will be the first person in your organization to present a business case; so, ask for a couple of examples of business cases that were approved and business cases that were not approved. When looking at the examples, consider the following:

- Does the case grab your attention by clearly stating the opportunity/ challenge up front and reinforcing the importance of the opportunity at the end of the document?
- Is the rationale for the recommended alternative clear and a logical result of the data presented?
- Is it concise and free of jargon?
- Is it clear what the business case is asking decision-makers to do?
- Are there any errors – language, mathematical, etc. – in the document?

These considerations will provide you with insights about what (not) to do when writing up your business case.

No matter what format or layout is used, all business cases tend to have the following elements in common:

1 Executive Summary: The Executive Summary condenses the entire business case document for someone who will not read it in its entirety. That is key because the individual who ultimately makes the decision might only have read the Executive Summary, not the entire document. The decision-maker might ask others to read the document in-depth and report on any issues of which the decision-maker should be aware. Consequently, the Executive Summary must provide the highlights and key conclusions, not a listing of topics covered.

2 Nature of the learning challenge or opportunity: This section provides business case readers with a brief background of the need driving your request. You should clearly state how your need is strategically aligned with the organization's goals, so that your readers understand the importance of addressing the learning challenge or opportunity you are describing.

3 Assessment of alternatives: Create a clear description of alternative approaches to address the learning challenge or opportunity and explain how you identified those alternatives and your efforts to determine what each alternative will in fact cost the organization. This provides decision-makers with a measure of assurance that your recommendations are well-considered ones. Include all assumptions and risks associated with each alternative. No one can predict the future; so, you need to indicate what conditions or ingoing assumptions and potential risks helped frame your business case arguments.

4 Financial metrics and measures: After anticipating the costs associated with alternatives, consider the returns that each might provide. You should link the manner in which you calculate returns with the business objective of the project. For example, if the business objective relates to generating revenue, then the returns should indicate how the

alternative will generate revenue. If the business objective relates to containing expenses (reducing expenses or, at the least, having them grow more slowly than under the status quo), then the returns should indicate how the alternative will contain expenses. If the business objective relates to conforming to an organizational, industry, or government regulation, then the returns should describe this compliance.

5 Business impact of each alternative: This element describes the observable, measurable benefits and outcomes of each alternative, along with who will be affected and how should the alternative be implemented.

6 Conclusions and recommendations: This is where you clearly state which specific alternative is optimal, along with the evidence-based rationale for your recommendation.

7 High-level implementation and evaluation plan: Here, you state explicitly who is going to do the work, how long will it take, and how you will know the initiative has been successful.

Summary

Figure 8.3 provides a graphical display of the business case development process, from initial thoughts to final write-up. The business case enables you to demonstrate the value of your initiative up front and capture and retain support for your initiative from idea to implementation.

As with all new efforts, your first business case may be the hardest but will certainly enrich the business skill set that today's employers demand

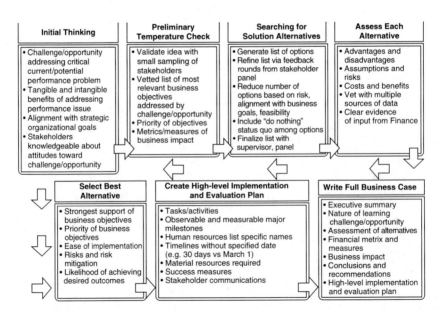

Figure 8.3 Business Case Development Process.

of their learning professionals. Stuart Belle, Director of Knowledge Management and Learning Strategy with the non-profit Pact, shares his journey from novice to seasoned business case writer in *E-Suite Views*.

SvR: One of the skill sets that we find difficult to teach folks with an education background is how to write an effective business case and I note that in the not-for-profit world, business cases are sometimes even more important than they are in the for-profit sector. Share a little bit about your experiences with business cases.

SB: There was a time when I was thinking about a career shift and I was looking at some of the ways that I could strengthen my skills. One of the things that I was told in a sort of informal interview is that a business case lets you sell to the market. In my world, what that business case is, is called a concept note. I've had to write a hundred of those and I've really been able to conceptualize what it is I want to be able to do, why is it important, how is it going to get done, what roles we will need to support this and over what time frame, and what is the expected output. It is similar to a business case, just referred to as a concept note. What I have learned about how to do that is, you know, the importance of – I am going to go philosophical on you here – the importance of imagination and trying to really project and say, *what if, what if we could to do this, what would it look like?* So, that's the reach, reaching out and trying to get people to kind of **visualize** what it is you want to do.

The second thing around a concept note and me learning how to do that is really around the whole idea of linkages and connection. Many times, we are having to learn how to make a case, like a business case, that connects one idea to the others in an organization. So, this is about how this is going to enhance something else or how another business process is going to feed into what you want to do. So, you are trying to sort of gain the efficiency to maximize resource allocation but you're also showing a strategic connection in a way. How is this a stepping stone to something else and not just a one-off training? What is the engagement with the participants after they leave the training room? What kind of ongoing network building is going to be helpful? What kind of ongoing communication plan will help you keep the energy up, keep the awareness up, keep the stories of success and failure coming so that the next time we do this, we have a track record history – what is the word I am looking for – we have a trail of experiences that we can look back to and say, *and this is why this is important.*

SvR: Right.

SB: This is what we've learned since doing this thing last time. What one is trying to show in the business case is: Here is what the **cost** is going be, here is what the **return** is going to be, and here is how we are going to **manage risk**. Sure enough, but you know, particularly in my work, my work is with the public sector, it's government money and tax payers' money and all of the above. Making the business case means: Give me your vision for this thing and how does it leverage resources that we have so that we get this new thing that we are talking about. I don't know if I have answered your question, but that's how I have learned about the shifting nature of making a business case.

SvR: That was my next question. Please proceed.

SB: I will tell you a little about the visioning and the strategic connection. What donor agencies and what NGOs are looking for is the whole question around sustainability. How is this going to continue in its current shape or another form? How is this going to get us farther, faster, and then, how are we going to make sure that even if we do have enough people trained, how do we set up the mechanisms to support the knowledge transfer? This is where the learning systems and training systems come in. Once we are training and we are putting in learning systems, we are putting in capacity-building interventions. How are we going to sustain this and then, how are we going to get the knowledge moving around the organization because not everybody can be trained, but how do we get them to transfer and sort of hand off to the next cohort of staff and the orientation system? What I am saying is initially, the training function is moving somewhat out of a traditional training mode into more of a knowledge transfer mode. How do we get peer to peer, how do we get mentoring, how do we get coaching, how do we get observational field site visits, you know, learning while doing? It's more than a two-day workshop where they lock you in a room and show you 100 slides of this thing. It's more dynamic, more real time than that, and it is more experiential than that.

SvR: Right. Thinking about the very first concept note that you wrote, how do you go about getting the information you need? What was the process you used for the very first one, if you can remember back then?

SB: First concept note. Beyond reading documents, like in the 100th position, the intervention with the organization so I can demonstrate my awareness of a bigger picture. In addition, talking to people to get their advice about who the audience is and how to understand the reader of the concept note. Maybe the third thing is really listening and observing and making sure that I had enough exposure personally, personal exposure and just enough presence in situations where I can see the application of what we are trying to do, so I could use examples. I can get a reference in that situation, a real problem that exists in the organization, and I have been able to help people, help leaders, help the decision-makers to see what it was like to not have a solution to that problem. For example, we would say something like: So in order to address the challenge of alignment in finance, the finance department and the supply chain management department – because they had a breakdown and sequencing or scheduling or, you know, understanding the context and the cost of doing business in this context – what we need to do is get people to have a sense of appreciation for what would it be, a framework. It is helping them see how they contribute to the overall program, so they can get out of their departmental silos. Training would be something around, you know, integrated program design.

SvR: Okay, that is really great. The next thing I want to know is: You said earlier that one of the things you were doing was talking to people. How did you know who to talk to?

SB: Right. I look at the job title.

SvR: And that is fair.

SB: I get a list of them and most of the time it is from workshops. You go to a workshop and you get a list of the participants as part of, you know, the package for participants, and you look at those people and you look at what office they came from and all that.

SvR: Okay.

SB: And that is how you are going to get to know who they were. Back in those days, there was not this information on social networking and social media and all of that. The lack of virtual technology and stuff like that, you had to basically find people at events. So, regional meetings, workshops, conferences, or you just jump on a plane and just do the rounds. I remember doing that earlier. But that was mostly how it happened, yeah, on paper, get to know what they did and then who might be best to talk to about this issue.

SvR: Right. Okay. Getting back to the notes that you have either written or that you have seen, I am sure that of the 100 or so that you have written, some were successful and some were not. What were the lessons learned from the ones that were not successful vs. the ones that were successful?

SB: Yeah, I am in the middle of utilizing a couple of them right now because the initial concept was, it was good but could be better. And the feedback is, "we are not sure what problem this is going to solve. We know what we are going to do but what is the problem this is going to address?" That is one thing. Number two, "let us think about making timelines that are more realistic." So, it wasn't that these were deal breakers or they just killed the whole thing but do a better job of convincing us through these few things. So, one is, what is the real problem we are trying to address and can you help us with the issue to assess what the problem is? Two, let us get some realistic timelines built in here because there are lots of things happening in this organization. Now, how do we avoid being overcome by events and doing this at the right time? And then maybe another, third lesson really is the language. The jargon really doesn't help, long sentences don't help, keep it simple and use examples. Another lesson I would say that I have taken away is: A picture is worth a thousand words. And as much as you can, alongside the text that you are writing in this concept note, how about a picture to help us see what this actually looks like? Yeah, so that and doing that has made some of these really successful.

SvR: When you say picture, you mean like an image or a graphic or something like that?

SB: A graph, a flowchart, or a table, you know, with milestones, that kind of things. So, it is not going to replace the narrative but it is another way to organize what you are trying to say and how you are trying to get it done.

SvR: That was great. Thanks so much for sharing.

Whether you are working in the for-profit or the not-for-profit sector, Dr. Belle's lessons learned make it clear that the business case addresses a problem that the organization needs to solve in order to achieve business goals and should be written in clear, to-the-point language with evidence to support what is being proposed.

Dilbert's© Lessons Learned from Failed Business Cases

Despite the most thorough preparation, decision-makers might choose an alternative other than the one you recommended. They might choose to do nothing, or, like Dilbert's© boss, they might choose to defer decision-making but not offer any time frame for when the decision will be made. Don't beat yourself up! Sometimes, decision-makers choose another alternative because they have a different perspective on the situation than you do. In most of those instances, they have access to different information than do those who prepared the business case. The possible lesson to learn from such an experience is: *Could I have anticipated this?* Learn from the experience so that you can conduct deeper analyses with the next business case. Other times, decision-makers choose a different alternative because it requires less of an initial outlay. The lesson to learn in such instances is to better assess the financial capabilities of the organization. In some cases, the organization simply cannot afford some alternatives. Even though such alternatives might provide the best returns, the organization cannot afford the initial investment in them.

What you can do is ensure that your business case does not have built-in failures. In most cases, business cases fail for one or more of the following reasons:

- **No alignment, no go:** Failure to demonstrate alignment with organizational strategic goals pretty much guarantees that your business case will be rejected. No matter how innovative or even potentially profitable your proposed project may be, it must align with the organization's strategic goals in order to be considered.
- **Over-reliance on the warm-and-snugglies:** Even intangible benefits need to be specific, measurable, achievable, realistic, and time-bound (SMART). Emotional benefits, such as "all employees will be happier" or "will do their jobs better," meet none of these criteria. Employee happiness, expressed in terms of reduced rates of attrition or job performance in terms of productivity increases, helps make your warm-and-snuggly benefits real, concrete.
- **No worries, mate:** Business cases that do not identify risks also tend to collapse. There are few solutions to problems that do not have risks. If there are no risks, then why are you writing a business case?
- **THE one and only:** A business case that does not contain alternative solutions is also a non-starter. The decision-maker needs to know that you have done your due diligence and that there's a solid rationale for your recommendation. When discussing alternatives, one alternative you should always address is the option of doing nothing. In many instances, learning professionals present one and only one option to decision-makers and decision-makers reject that choice. In such instances, decision-makers have essentially chosen "no," even though no one has formally presented "no" as an option, let alone explored the consequences of choosing "no." In fact, choosing "no" might appear to incur no cost. But doing nothing might allow a bad situation to become worse, causing significant emergency costs. For completeness, a business case should also present the implications of doing nothing and raise awareness of costs that might arise as a result.
- **The missing money:** Lack of financial information, either in terms of direct costs of your solution or the impact of your solution on existing costs, is a fatal flaw. Listing a series of numbers without any analysis of what those numbers mean is also a fatal flaw. Your critical friend from Finance is your best defense against this built-in failure. Remember: "business cases and blue skies do not mix well" (Gambles, 2009, p. 27).

- **The TBD flaw:** In failed business cases, the TBD (to be determined) designation is often seen in the section devoted to implementation and evaluation of the solution. Although the business case does not decompose the work to be done down to the granular, individual task level, it should have specific observable and measurable milestones, time frames, and named resources for doing the work associated with implementation and evaluation. That is how your decision-maker knows that you have determined the feasibility and sustainability of your chosen solution.
- **Spellcheck-dependence:** At the risk of stating the obvious, the business case with typos and language errors is guaranteed to receive a poor reception. The spelling and grammar check tools built into the word processing software is far from full-proof, and errors make the decision-maker wonder about the thoroughness of your efforts.

The net take-away from a failed business case is to find out why it failed. In most instances, you will find that it had one or more built-in failures. Whatever the reasons, consider those reasons the next time you prepare a business case. You might even want to clean up that failed business case and re-submit it at a later date, should conditions in- or outside of the organization make the need to address your challenge/opportunity even more pressing than it already is.

Business Case Self-Check

LunchandLearn is a regional advocacy organization dedicated to instilling nutritional eating habits throughout a person's life span. The organization's new strategy will require that its 100 campaign developers in North America – those that design and develop nutrition-related education curriculum for the public in Canada, the U.S., the Caribbean, Central America, and Mexico – find new ways of identifying information needs and define the best solutions to meeting those needs. Elizabeth Standing heads the L&D group at LunchandLearn and you are the more senior of the two learning designers in her group. The group is already fully tasked with current projects and Elizabeth's boss, the VP of Program Outreach, has stated that none of the current projects can be delayed or canceled. Elizabeth has asked her L&D team to come up with ideas to support the new strategy. She's given the team 30 days to do so. What would you do?

a) Wait for her instructions as to the next steps.
b) Start researching information sources outside of North America to see if they could be useful.
c) State that you would like to take the lead in preparing a business case for a solution, then begin working on getting the answers to some basic orienting questions.
d) Ask her for more information about what she expects from the team in the next 30 days.

Of the four options, (c) is the optimal choice. You are taking the initiative and proactively seeking an opportunity to demonstrate your business acumen. Options (a) and (d) leave you in the role of order-taker and will certainly come back to haunt you as you work toward a career advancement, while option (b) has you gathering data with no grounding in the organization's goals and strategies or clear definition of the problem to be solved.

Food for Thought

1   Identify and interview someone in your workplace who has written at least two business cases. (The person need not work in your group or department.) Ask the person to describe his/her most successful business case and why it was successful; then do the same with his/her least successful business case. What common themes can you identify from his/her comments?
2   You are asked to write a business case about an issue but you know in advance that senior management has already made a decision about the issue. What do you say to the person requesting the business case?
3   You are asked to write a business case justifying the costs for a holiday party the following winter. What do you do?

Up Next

In this chapter, we have (a) reviewed some basic concepts of organizational decision-making that tend to drive the need for business cases; (b) stepped through the essentials of crafting a business case; and (c) identified some lessons learned from successful and unsuccessful business cases. One of the more powerful lessons learned was the need to include a clear definition and explanation of the costs associated with our solution alternatives, and the weight given to financial metrics in the decision to select one alternative over another. For those with a limited business background, the financial component of the business case can be the most challenging. The ability to present the financial impact of your solution clearly and accurately requires an understanding of how budgeting works in your organization, which is the subject of the next chapter.

References

Adams, J. R., & Drake, R. E. (2006). Shared decision-making and evidence-based practice. *Community Mental Health Journal*, 42(1), 87–105.

Ardichvili, A., & Kuchinke, K. P. (2002). Leadership styles and cultural values among managers and subordinates: a comparative study of four countries of the former Soviet Union, Germany, and the US. *Human Resource Development International*, 5(1), 99–117.

Armstrong, M. (2011). *How to Be an Even Better Manager: A Complete A to Z of Proven Techniques and Essential Skills* (8th edn.). London, UK: Kogan Page.

Baba, V. V., & HakemZadeh, F. (2012). Toward a theory of evidence based decision making. *Management Decision*, 50(5), 832–67.

Barends, E., Rousseau, D. M., & Briner, R. B. (2014). *Evidence-based Management: The Basic Principles*. Amsterdam, the Netherlands: Center for Evidence-Based Management.

Biesta, G. (2007). Why "what works" won't work: Evidence-based practice and the democratic deficit in educational research. *Educational Theory*, 57(1), 1–22.

Birch, S. (1997). As a matter of fact: Evidence-based decision-making unplugged. *Health Economics*, 6(6), 547–59.

Brown, F., & Hunter, R. C. (Eds.). (2006). *No Child Left Behind and Other Federal Programs for Urban School Districts*. San Diego, CA: Elsevier.

Bunting, S. W. (2010). Assessing the stakeholder Delphi for facilitating interactive participation and consensus building for sustainable aquaculture development. *Society & Natural Resources*, 23(8), 758–75.

Busenitz, L. W., & Barney, J. B. (1997). Differences between entrepreneurs and managers in large organizations: Biases and heuristics in strategic decision-making. *Journal of Business Venturing*, 12(1), 9–30.

Cascio, W. F. (2007). Evidence-based management and the marketplace for ideas. *Academy of Management Journal*, 50(5), 1009–12.

Chen, X.-P., Yao, X. I. N., & Kotha, S. (2009). Entrepreneur passion and preparedness in business plan presentations: A persuasion analysis of venture capitalists' funding decisions. *Academy of Management Journal*, 52(1), 199–214.

Chiappelli, F. (2010). *Sustainable Evidence-Based Decision-Making*. New York, NY: Nova Science Publishers.

Chowdury, M. S. A., Azam, M. K. G., & Islam, S. (2015). Profiles and prospects of SME financing in Bangladesh. *Asian Business Review*, 2(2), 51–8.

Clancy, C. M., & Cronin, K. (2005). Evidence-based decision making: Global evidence, local decisions. *Health Affairs*, 24(1), 151–62.

De Oliveira, L. S., Shayani, R. A., & De Oliveira, M. A. G. (2013). Proposed business plan for energy efficiency in Brazil. *Energy Policy*, 61, 523–31.

Dean, J. W., & Sharfman, M. P. (1993). The relationship between procedural rationality and political behavior in strategic decision making. *Decision Sciences*, 24(6), 1069–83.

Drake, E. K., Aos, S., & Miller, M. G. (2009). Evidence-based public policy options to reduce crime and criminal justice costs: implications in Washington state. *Victims & Offenders*, 4(2), 170–96.

Feldman, J., & Kanter, H. E. (2013). Organizational decision making. In J. G. March (Ed.), *Handbook of Organizations*. New York, NY: Routledge.

Ford, B. R., Bornstein, J. M., & Pruitt, P. T. (2007). *The Ernst & Young Business Plan Guide* (3rd edn.). Hoboken, NJ: John Wiley & Sons.

Forstater, M., Dupree, S., Oelschlaegel, J., Tabakian, P., & de Robillard, V. (2007). *Critical Friends: The Emerging Role of Stakeholder Panels in Corporate Governance, Reporting and Assurance*. Retrieved from www.accountability.org/images/content/3/1/318/Critical%20Friends_StakeholderPanels_report.pdf.

Gambles, I. (2009). *Making the Business Case: Proposals that Succeed for Projects that Work*. Surrey, UK: Gower Publishing.

Harrison, E. F., & Pelletier, M. A. (2000). The essence of management decision. *Management Decision*, 38(7), 462–70.

Head, B. W. (2008). Three lenses of evidence-based policy. *Australian Journal of Public Administration*, 67(1), 1–11.

Hewison, A. (1997). Evidence-based medicine: What about evidence-based management? *Journal of Nursing Management*, 5(4), 195–8.

Honig, M. I., & Coburn, C. (2008). Evidence-based decision making in school district central offices: Toward a policy and research agenda. *Educational Policy*, 22(4), 578–608.

IBSTPI. (2014). *Instructional Designer Competencies — Welcome to ibstpi*. Retrieved from http://ibstpi.org/instructional-design-competencies/.

Ives, B. D. (1973). Ideational items decision theory and the practicing manager. *Business Horizons*, 16(3), 38–40.

Jennings, E. T., & Hall, J. L. (2012). Evidence-based practice and the use of information in state agency decision making. *Journal of Public Administration Research and Theory*, 22(2), 245–66.

Kovner, A. R., Elton, J. J., & Billings, J. D. (2005). Evidence-based management. *Frontiers of Health Services Management*, 16(4), 3–24.

Kowalski, T. J., & Lasley II, T. J. (Eds.). (2009). *Handbook of Data-Based Decision Making in Education*. New York, NY: Routledge.

Leslie, K., Loch, M. A., & Schaninger, W. (2006). Managing your organization by the evidence. *The McKinsey Quarterly*, 2006(3), 64–75.

Lockett, T. (1997). *Evidence-Based and Cost-Effective Medicine for the Uninitiated*. Oxford, UK: Radcliffe Medical Press.

MacKenzie, D. L. (2000). Evidence-based corrections: identifying what works. *Crime & Delinquency*, 46(4), 457–71.

March, J. G. (1994). *Primer on Decision Making: How Decisions Happen*. New York, NY: The Free Press.

McKeever, M. P. (2014). *How to Write a Business Plan*. Berkeley, CA: Nolo.

Oshagbemi, T., & Ocholi, S. A. (2006). Leadership styles and behaviour profiles of managers. *Journal of Management Development*, 25(8), 748–62.

Pettigrew, A. M. (2014). *The Politics of Organizational Decision-Making*. Oxon, UK: Routledge.

Pfeffer, J., & Sutton, R. I. (2006a). Evidence-based management. *Harvard Business Review*, 2006 January, 63–74.

Pfeffer, J., & Sutton, R. I. (2006b). *Hard Facts, Dangerous Half-Truths, and Total Nonsense: Profiting From Evidence-Based Management*. Boston, MA: Harvard Business Press.

Proposal. (n.d.). In *Merriam-Webster Online Dictionary*. Retrieved from www.merriam-webster.com/dictionary/proposal.

Rousseau, D. M. (2006). Is there such a thing as "evidence-based management"? *Academy of Management Review*, 31(2), 256–69.

Sackett, D. L. (1997). Fatal and neonatal hematology for the 21st century evidence-based medicine. *Seminars in Perinatology*, 21(1), 3–5.

Salman, W. A. (2008). *How to Write a Great Business Plan*. Boston, MA: Harvard Business Press.

Simon, H. A. (1959). Theories of decision-making in economics and behavioral science. *The American Economic Review*, 49(3), 253–83.

Simon, H. A. (1979). Rational decision making in business organizations. *The American Economic Review*, 69(4), 493–513.

Simon, H. A. (1982). *Models of Bounded Rationality*. Cambridge, MA: MIT Press.

Spitzeck, H., & Hansen, E. G. (2010). Stakeholder governance: How stakeholders influence corporate decision-making. *Corporate Governance: The International Journal of Business in Society*, 10(4), 378–91.

Steptoe-Warren, G., Howat, D., & Hume, I. (2011). Strategic thinking and decision-making: Literature review. *Journal of Strategy and Management*, 4(3), 238–50.

van Rooij, S. W., & Merkebu, J. (2015). Measuring the business impact of employee learning: A view from the professional services sector. *Human Resource Development Quarterly*, 26(3), 275–97.

Walshe, K., & Rundall, T. G. (2001). Evidence-based management: from theory to practice in healthcare. *The Millbrook Quarterly, 79*(3), 429–57.

White, S. (1997). Evidence-based practice and nursing: The new panacea? *British Journal of Nursing, 6*(3), 175–8.

Young, S. K. (2002). Evidence-based management: A literature review. *Journal of Nursing Management, 10,* 145–51.

9 Budgeting and Cost Management
Show Them the Money

For those outside of the world of finance and accounting, budgeting may seem to be an opaque, almost mystical process that requires a combination of advanced numeracy skills, the concentration of an Indian yogi, and a touch of hocus pocus. Nevertheless, if we think about the simplest definition of budget – "an amount of money available for spending that is based on a plan for how it will be spent" (Budget, n.d.), budgeting as an activity is something that nearly every adult on the planet has probably done. Have you ever created a budget for household expenses or a vacation or that special purchase? The scope of budgeting activities can range from personal finances to small business budgeting to long, complex processes such as creating the budget for the Federal Government, or the budget of a large, multinational corporation. Budgeting is a part of the activities of any organization of any size and in any industry sector. Whether you are a freelancer or work for an organization, any initiatives that you and your Learning and Development (L&D) colleagues undertake require budgeting and cost management at some level. Once a budget is created and approved, you need to monitor that budget on a regular basis to ensure that your L&D project is completed within the approved budget. The entire process of planning and controlling the budget is called cost management (Shim, Siegel, & Shim, 2012).

But we didn't learn about budgets in grad school! You may be thinking. It is true that budgeting and cost management are not part of the traditional instructional design curriculum in higher education. This could reflect a clash of cultures and philosophies between schools of Education, the locus of most instructional design degree programs, and schools of Business, where nearly all programs include some elements of budgeting and cost management. Evidence of this "clash of logics" (Ezzamel, Robson, & Stapleton, 2012) has become more apparent as public education turns increasingly to business models to fill the gaps created by ever-declining federal and state funding. Another reason why financial issues associated with L&D are not part of the education curriculum is time. Courses covering instructional design methods and models, adult learning theory, research, and other related topics already consume the circa 30 credits associated with most Master's degree programs. The relatively fewer undergraduate degree programs in our field are also limited in their ability to accommodate new courses due to the need to combine the basic arts and sciences courses with courses in instructional design. Adding a course on budgeting and cost management would mean either lengthening the program or giving up one or more courses in the current program. In addition to the challenge of obtaining stakeholder consensus inside the institution, such a program change would also require recruiting faculty with budgeting and cost management expertise to teach in the instructional design programs, raising challenges due to differences in compensation, rewards, and recognition between schools of Education and Business, respectively.

Despite this gap in the traditional instructional design curriculum, budgeting and cost management experience is essential to your career advancement and is explicitly stated among the must-have competencies for instructional designers seeking to move to management (IBSTPI, 2014). In the previous chapter, we noted that a detailed explanation of the costs of your solution alternatives was a core component of the business case, and that a clear description of the tangible and intangible costs and benefits associated with each of those alternatives was a key selling point for your preferred solution choice. Once your business case is approved, those same costs and benefits will serve as inputs to the monitoring of the budget throughout your solution's project life cycle.

Unlike many of the topics we have covered thus far, budgeting and cost management are not grounded in a variety of theories and models but instead are based on a common set of accounting principles, standards, and procedures set down by national accounting policy and standards boards that define how organizations record and report financial data. Consultants and learning vendors offer their own versions of costing models (usually for a fee) and there are a few case studies that assess the accuracy of the specific cost models used in e-learning projects (Mohamed & Kamal, 2015 Mosely & Valverde, 2014). However, there are no generally accepted standards or models of budgeting and cost management for L&D initiatives. Consequently, you will need to learn the basics of budgeting and cost management from multiple sources. This task is not as daunting as it seems. Just as you read, network, and attend events to keep pace with developments in the field, you can also capitalize on your self-directed efforts to learn and apply the principles of budgeting and cost management. Although you will not be expected to have the same breadth and depth of financial knowledge as someone who specializes in budgeting and finance, you will be expected to know some of the basic concepts, so that you can ask the right questions of your financial stakeholders when creating and managing your L&D projects. Consequently, in this chapter we will:

- Review some basic concept and approaches to budgeting for L&D projects;
- Discuss considerations associated with collecting financial data for creating the project budget; and
- Examine the various ways of planning for cost management once your project business case has been approved.

The Basics: Never Lost in Translation

The One Thousand-Foot View

All organizations – for-profit, non-profit, government – have budgets and, thus, engage in the budgeting process. How the budget for the organization as a whole is created influences how the various departments or business units inside the organization create their budgets and ultimately, how departments and business units create budgets for their individual initiatives. Budgeting is a collaborative process in which the organization's various business units build their budgets to align with organizational goals. Budgets include elements, such as expected revenue or sources of income, costs, profits (for private sector organizations), fundraising, programs and grants (for non-profit organizations), cash flow, or the difference between the amount of cash available at the beginning of a period of time (usually the calendar or fiscal year) and the amount available at the end of that period, and so on. In other words, the budget is the financial plan that provides targets and directions for future operations; "budgeting is planning for a result and controlling to accomplish that result" (Shim, Siegel, & Shim, 2012, p.4).

All organizations have a master budget. The master budget is the aggregation of all of the budgets created by the various business units or departments in the organization and serves as the central planning tool that the organization's senior leadership uses to direct the organization's activities for the upcoming year, as well as to judge the performance of the individual business units or departments. The format of the master budget depends on organizational size and industry sector but often includes some explanatory text about how the master budget will contribute to achieve specific goals and the management actions needed. Master budgets also tend to go through several iterations until senior leadership arrives at a budget that allocates funds to achieve the desired results (Bragg, 2014).

Budgeting Approaches

Before you can build a budget for your solution or project, you need to understand how your organization approaches project budget derivation. Budget derivation refers to the basis on which a project budget is constructed (Gambles, 2009) and that basis is either bottom-up or top-down. The bottom-up budgeting approach gathers a detailed cost estimate for all of the activities (labor, course-building software, etc.) and deliverables (e.g., web-based modules, job aids) associated with the full life cycle of your project. With this approach, you and your team will identify the tasks and activities required for each phase and then add those costs to arrive at the total project cost. At the business case phase, the costs are approximations of the costs of all the human and material resources you will need to complete the project. Once the business case is approved, you will allocate the project cost estimate to actual tasks over time. That allocation is your budget. The bottom-up approach is the most commonly used approach for individual initiatives because the group that is actually going to do the work is the one building the budget. Consequently, bottom-up budgeting – also called participative budgeting (Heinle, Ross, & Saouma, 2014) – tends to be fairly accurate. It also serves as a contributor to team cohesion since all team members are involved in the budget creation process. However, bottom-up budgeting can lead to underestimation of costs if the team does not have a full and comprehensive list of tasks and activities needed to complete the solution (Shim, Siegel, & Shim, 2012).

Conversely, top-down budgeting is based on an allocation of funds that reflects senior management's prioritization of your project in the context of available resources and competing demands on those resources. In other words, senior management provides your team with a predetermined amount of money. It is then up to you and your team to figure out how to complete the project within that pre-determined amount. Top-down budgeting forces your team to maximize efficiencies throughout the project life cycle. The challenge associated with top-down budgeting is an unrealistic budget due to insufficient knowledge of the work involved to create a reasonable estimate. If experience from prior L&D projects indicates that the budget is unrealistic, you and your team should provide a rationale as to why it is unrealistic and what trade-offs would have to be made (e.g., time and scope of work), should that budget remain unchanged.

Organizations may also take a case-by-case approach, with some initiatives based on bottom-up budgeting and others on top-down budgeting. Your stakeholders in Finance as well as other members of your stakeholder panel can provide insights as to which budgeting approach is used in your organization and how best to integrate that knowledge into the financial component of your business case.

Types of Costs

Building a budget requires estimating the costs of everything required to complete the project. Much of the number-crunching associated with budgeting and cost management can be accomplished using simple tools, such as spreadsheets with macros, to accommodate your organization's formulas for calculating costs. At the most basic level, you want to characterize your costs as direct or indirect (Rachlin & Sweeny, 1996).

Direct costs are those that are easily attributable to the specific project and are charged on an item-by-item basis. Labor tends to be the most significant cost for L&D projects. The costs associated with the members of your project team would most likely be the largest component of the costs of labor. Examples of other direct costs would include license fees for software purchased specifically for your project, fees for external consultants to the project, or travel expenses to discuss project progress at the client site. Indirect costs are the costs for items that benefit multiple projects, and only a portion of their total cost is charged to the specific project. Moreover, it would be extremely difficult to parse out indirect costs to individual projects. Examples of indirect costs include telephone charges, office equipment, and office space rent.

In addition to the main categories of direct and indirect costs, costs can also be fixed or variable. Fixed costs are one-time costs that are unaffected by changes in project activity. For example, your salary is a fixed cost. However, your organization may use a formula to charge a portion of fixed salary costs to individual projects. Variable costs change with activity levels. For example, the cost of participant incentives for usability testing can change, depending on which participants do (not) complete the testing.

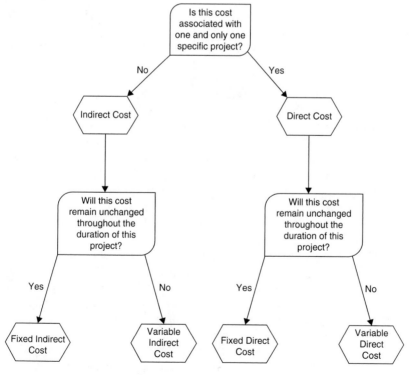

Figure 9.1 The Basics of Cost Categorization.

Although a cost is either direct or indirect, fixed or variable, both direct and indirect costs can be either fixed or variable. As illustrated in Figure 9.1, the simplest way to determine what kind of cost you are dealing with is to first ask yourself whether the cost is attributable to one specific project and then ask whether the cost will remain unchanged throughout the duration of the project. The responses to those questions show the overlaps across the cost categories.

Financial Analyses for L&D Initiatives

As we noted in the previous chapter, an organization's decision-makers tend to approve business cases based on the compatibility of the proposed initiative with the organization's goals and strategies. To increase the chance of your business case being approved, you should be familiar with the most common methods used to assess the relative strength of a proposed solution. The five most common methods for L&D initiatives are cost avoidance, cost-benefit analysis, break-even analysis, net present value, and return on investment.

Cost avoidance identifies how much money will be saved using the new or proposed initiative vs. maintaining the status quo. Examples of savings could be in the number of hours required to complete a set of tasks, lost productivity as measured in absence rates, or dollars spent in reworking completed instructional materials. Cost avoidance is used regularly to evaluate initiatives in the healthcare sector (Branham et al., 2013), higher education (Kirwan, 2007), and public services (White, 2010). Cost avoidance also takes into account intangible benefits that cannot be measured in monetary units. Improved image of the organization, enhanced growth potential, or improved client satisfaction are examples of intangible benefits. Some organizations do monetize intangible benefits. For example, client satisfaction can be quantified by means of surveys or anecdotal feedback, such as compliments sent via email. One could argue that increased client satisfaction means more referrals of new clients and more repeat business from existing clients. It could also mean fewer lost clients. Consequently, the image of the organization improves, more products or services are sold, and the growth potential of the organization is enhanced.

Cost-benefit analysis (CBA) focuses on the relationship between costs and benefits over the life of a product or service. Broadly speaking, it involves adding up the benefits of a course of action and comparing those benefits with the costs associated with that course of action. CBA is a mathematical analysis and, thus, requires monetization of intangible benefits. Here is where input from your stakeholders in Finance is essential because they are the ones who know how your organization calculates variables, such as lost productivity, improved task performance, and other intangibles, the monetization of which can vary from organization to organization. Like CBA, break-even analysis (BEA) is a mathematical analysis requiring monetization of all variables. BEA identifies the point at which the cash outflow for an initiative or project equals the related cash inflow. After the break-even point, the organization has recovered the development costs for the initiative and begins making a profit. BEA is common among companies that sell learning solutions (courses, workshops, etc.) to external clients.

Net present value (NPV) is primarily used for initiatives that have a development cycle covering multiple years. In the L&D field, examples of multiyear projects include the establishment of a corporate university, the creation of a new degree program at a college or university, or the creation of a digital public information library by a nonprofit organization. NPV analysis includes factors such as cash outflows early in the life of the initiative, the expected rate of inflation, and the expected rate of return. If and when NPV calculations are required will be determined by your Finance colleagues. However, it helps to be aware that if your proposed initiative requires effort over multiple years, the financial section of your business case will undergo a greater degree of senior management scrutiny than an initiative with a shorter development cycle.

Probably the most familiar financial analysis method is return on investment (ROI). However, ROI has different meanings in different disciplines. In accounting, ROI refers to the relationship between the gains made by an investment and the costs of that investment. In the applied sciences and technology, it is similar to a cost-benefit analysis but without the intangibles. In L&D, ROI is epitomized in the Phillips methodology designed to evaluate the business impact of an L&D initiative (more about evaluation in Chapter 11). However, ROI as applied in L&D tends to be backward-looking rather than a method of predicting how much of an impact a proposed initiative will have on the business.

Using the business case for a new approach to employee onboarding for ABC Company discussed in the previous chapter, Table 9.1 contains an example of a high-level financial analysis. The table shows all of the options, including the "do nothing" option, the total of the direct and indirect costs for each solution alternative, the cumulative savings over a 5-year period, the break-even point, and the ROI timeline. It also shows the measures and metrics for the non-monetized benefits of each solution. You'll note that Option 3 has the highest cumulative savings, the shortest break-even period, and the fastest ROI. It also has the strongest projected increase in training satisfaction. Consequently, Option 3 is the clear winner based on this data.

In preparing your business case, you may discover that one option's intangible benefits may exceed those of all the other alternatives, but the tangible benefits may not be different from or even lower than one of the other alternatives. In such cases, you and your stakeholders will need to review the business objectives, then decide what trade-offs would be the most acceptable, given those objectives.

Table 9.1 Financial Summary: ABC Example

	Option 1: Continue with Current Program	Option 2: Convert Current Program to Online Format	Option 3: Build Online Supplement to Current Program	Option 4: Purchase Commercial Onboarding Training Package
Tangible Benefits				
Total direct and indirect costs	N/A	$110,100	$130,000	$166,000
Annual operational costs	$124,000	$126,000	$40,000	$38,000
Cumulative savings (5 years)	N/A	($112,100)	$290,000	$264,000
Break-even (years)	–	–	2.6	3.2
ROI achieved (years)	N/A	–	3	4
Intangible Benefits				
Projected increase in employee retention (5 years)	(11%)	3%	6%	6%
Projected increase in training satisfaction score (5 years)	0%	10%	15%	5%

Summary

Creating a budget for a business case occurs within the larger context of how your department or business unit and your organization as a whole conduct the budgeting process. Budgeting at all levels of the organization is intended to indicate the contribution to the achievement of organizational goals. Once approved, the budgets become the road map for operations for the coming year. Furthermore, the budgets become the benchmark against which the performance of the organization and all of its operations are judged. A basic knowledge of your organization's approach to budgeting, costing, and financial analyses helps you to understand the mindset of your finance stakeholders so that you not only know what questions to ask, but also how to ask your questions in a language that is understandable to them. It ensures that the responses you receive address your needs as you proceed to construct your budget.

Collecting Financial Data: The Need to Know

You will use the same planning approach for collecting data regarding solution alternatives to address your business case challenge/opportunity and for planning out data collection for the financial section of your business case. In other words, determine who will collect what data, when, and from where/whom. The answers to these questions may have already surfaced in your exploration of potential alternative solutions with your stakeholders, enabling you to begin classifying the resources needed for each solution into broad categories. To facilitate an apples-to-apples comparison of the financial data for each solution, you will need to take the following into account:

- Measurement unit consistency: For each of the resources needed, clearly define the units of measurement (e.g., number of staff hours, frequency of third-party fees) and make sure to use the same units across all solutions.
- Numerical precision: This states whether or not your cost estimates are rounded up (e.g., $995.55 to $996). This would also apply to time measurements, such as the number of staff hours.
- Estimation accuracy: This refers to the acceptable margin of error based on known risks and historical practice. For example, in the project management profession, a best practice is to add ± 10 percent for contingencies or unexpected costs that may arise during the project (Project Management Institute, 2013).

What if my organization does not share financial data? This is a common concern, particularly among early-career practitioners who have asked for financial information and been told that such data is provided on a need-to-know basis. In many instances, that need-to-know reaction is based on (a) unclear explanations of what data is needed and why; (b) who is going to be viewing the data; and (c) how the data is going to be used over time. Situations in which the stakeholder panel has no representation from Finance or the Finance representative hands off your request for financial data to a colleague who has little or no awareness of your efforts to construct a business case are likely to meet with resistance to providing you with the company's financial data. Imagine a co-worker coming up to you out of the blue and asking you your annual salary. Unless you work in the public sector where staff salaries are posted on the organization's intranet, chances are you will give that co-worker some form of need-to-know response. That is why it is essential to have representation from your organization's Finance group in your stakeholder panel so that Finance is involved from the very beginning and consequently, has a thorough understanding of what business objectives you are seeking to achieve and what data sources can provide the evidence you need to vet each of

Table 9.2 Financial Data Collection Plan

Information Needs	Alternative 1	Alternative 2	Alternative 3	Alternative 4
Cost Factors • Direct costs • Indirect costs				
Data Types Required • Labor units of measurement • Material units of measurement • Overhead measurement • Estimation precision				
Cost distribution formulas/ allocation				
Data Sources (Who, When, How)				

your solution alternatives. Table 9.2 is an example of things to take into account when seeking out the data you need to estimate your costs.

If you set the stage with your Finance stakeholders by explaining the rationale behind your data collection, do not be surprised at how eager they will be to help you. Mike Beitler, President of Beitler and Associates, offers his insights on what learning professionals with little or no background in Finance need to know about budgeting and cost management in *E-Suite Views*.

SvR: From your perspective, has the role of L&D changed over the past decade, and particularly as that relates to what non-managers need to know about finance?

MB: Yeah, I think that's a great place to start, with non-managers, because I don't think you can wait until you're one step away from the C-suite to start thinking about this stuff. I would say even if you're a non-manager, you have to understand how you add value to the organization. Meaning, you have to understand concepts like incremental cost, and variable cost, and fixed costing, cost allocation between projects, or why, etc. So,

I think even non-managers need to start thinking about these concepts at the beginning of their career.

SvR: So, right from the start, early on, and not waiting until they've got experience?

MB: I think so. They need to be introduced to it right away, to understand that that's what the department chair or the CLO [Chief Learning Officer] is already thinking about.

SvR: Right, that makes sense. Going back to the point you made at the beginning about the different types of financial concepts, sort of basic concepts that should be known, one of the competencies for an instructional designer is the ability to either construct a budget for a proposed learning intervention, or manage a budget that they are given for a particular project. Short of going out and getting an MBA, how would you recommend that these folks acquire the basics of budgeting and cost management?

MB: I'm thinking they quickly need to get to a place where they think of themselves as an L&D professional, or a learning and performance internal consultant, and they can already start to think in terms of what are the concerns of people at the C-level. They have to look for, maybe, online opportunities where they can learn about budgeting and cost management, and maybe even forums where people are talking about these issues. Just get familiar with the concepts, and what the concerns are at the C-level.

SvR: Right. Any other ideas that you would offer about how to get the basics?

MB: I was thinking, where do they hang out on the web to find some like-minded people, or just offer up things like, what good books have you read lately, and what websites do you recommend, which chat groups do you belong to, and that sort of thing. There are lots of things out there. Formal programs are certainly great places, not just to get the knowledge, but to do some networking as well.

SvR: Basically, what I'm hearing is that the learning professional needs to really be proactive, and get this knowledge on his or her own.

MB: That's exactly the word that I would use, because we all own our own careers now, so you really do have to be proactive, you have to go to your supervisor and say, "I think this is what I need." It's in your court here, as opposed to the supervisor coming to you and saying, "This is where I think I want you to go."

SvR: Right, and that goes back to the point that we were talking about earlier, about language. One of the challenges that a lot of the folks in L&D have, particularly those at the lower levels have, is not really knowing how to ask questions, or how to ask the right questions to the people in Finance.

MB: It's true, I think it's a really good point; just learning the language, if you can speak that language, you may have to translate how you would naturally say it, but you can sell your idea a lot better if people actually understand the terminology that you're using.

SvR: Okay, and if you don't know the language, would plain English do?

MB: I think so. Yeah, it's just like if I'm coming from an accounting and finance point of view, I wouldn't throw around terms like "indirect method conversion," those kinds of things. L&D people need to do the same thing. They can't throw around terms like "deliverables" or something like that where the CFO's head would spin and think, "What does that mean?" It's like you're saying, even if you don't know what the equivalent is in financial term, you can do it in plain English, the common language.

SvR: The common language is probably the best bet. I once heard a Director of Finance tell his L&D people, "If you don't know how to do the financial component, just send your information to us, and we'll do it for you." Aside from the fact that that kind of generosity isn't prevalent across all companies, is that a good thing or a bad thing for an L&D person? Will that help or hinder their learning about budgeting and cost management?

MB: Like you said, it sounds like a delicious offer that you can't pass up, but I think the L&D person should always insist on, "Let me be part of this so I can get better at this myself." I mean certainly take up the offer but, yeah, you really have to be able to get inside the CFO's head to be able to understand, "Hmm, okay, that's what she thinks is important or that's completely irrelevant in her world." It will be really valuable just to watch the process.

Managing Costs: Avoiding Dilbert©-Like Dilemmas

When you created your budget estimates for your business case, those estimates were based on the need for specific human and material resources in specific quantities for specified periods of time. Once your business case is approved and your L&D project begins, you need to keep an eye on the actual costs incurred during the project life cycle to ensure that the project is completed on or within budget. We will examine project management tools and techniques in the next chapter. For now, however, here are some potential issues for which you need to plan, in order to be able to monitor and control your costs and avoid any unpleasant Dilbert©-like surprises:

• **Time and cost accounting procedures:** When collecting your financial data, you want to learn how your organization tracks and reports project time and costs, so that you can compare your budgeted costs and time with the actual cost and time spent during the project life cycle.

Ideally, you want to obtain agreement in advance as to what kinds of reports can be generated or what approval procedures must be followed in order for you to monitor actual costs and time.

- **Impact of "hidden" work:** Occasionally, a team member may come up with a bright idea that he/she simply undertakes without discussing it with the rest of the team. Although team member creativity should be highly valued, tasks and activities that were not in your approved budget can adversely affect the accuracy and effectiveness of your ability to monitor and control your costs. If you receive frequent reports of the actuals for time and cost, you can nip hidden work in the bud before it makes a dent in your budget.

- **Expect the unexpected:** The contingency that you built into your budget was intended to cover unexpected events, such as a rise in prices or fees that may affect your original budget estimates. However, the section of your business case that describes your high-level implementation plan should explain (a) who gets alerted when deviations from the approved budget occur; (b) the processes and procedures for preventing, detecting, and addressing variance from the approved budget; and (c) the criteria, processes, and procedures for updating estimates to reflect actual costs and changes.

- **Where the buck stops:** Your high-level implementation plan should have indicated who would be managing your L&D project. If someone other than yourself will serve as the project manager, the process for handing off the approved business case and approved budget to that person should be clearly described in the implementation section of your business case.

Bottom line: The creation of the budget and the ongoing management of costs once a project begins require close collaboration between L&D and Finance. This will enable those in Finance to relate your expenditures to the actual operational progress, so that both L&D and Finance have a shared understanding of the extent to which your work is on schedule and within budget.

In an effort to explain how operational areas like L&D think differently from those in Finance, a faculty member at the University of Aberdeen in Scotland stated the following:

> Accountants on the other hand, tend to think in terms of time periods and cost types – they ask, "What did we spend on labour in May?" rather than, "What did it cost us to build module 4?" When they think of flexible budgeting and forecasting, they tend to refer to manufacturing models which can only cope with volume changes within an accounting period, and cannot deal directly with task timing changes…. They think that what things have cost so far is the most important measurement, because it is based on the accounting facts, and doesn't depend on "speculation." (Arthur, 2000, p. 20)

Knowing the basics will help to ensure that your interactions with those in Finance will never get lost in translation.

Budgeting and Cost Management Self-Check

Based on feedback from your stakeholders, you have identified four potential solutions to the learning challenge that your business case addresses. One of your stakeholders represents the Finance group and mentioned that for a previous L&D project, they allocated a fixed rate of 15 percent of team member salaries to overhead and recommended that you do the same for your proposed project. You have a meeting with another member of the Finance group tomorrow to request the financial data you need to complete the financial section of your business case. What should you do to ensure you get the most out of tomorrow's meeting?

a) Prepare a spreadsheet with the 15 percent rate for team member labor already filled in so that you can focus on collecting all the other financial data needed for the business case.
b) Mention what your stakeholder has said about the 15 percent rate and confirm whether or not that rate would apply to your specific project.
c) Ignore what your stakeholder said about the 15 percent rate and start your meeting as though you know nothing about your organization's approach to cost estimation.
d) Ask your supervisor whether or not you should follow the stakeholder's recommendation.

Of the four options, (b) is the optimal choice. The members of the Finance group with whom you are to meet tomorrow may not know the similarities/ differences between the level of expertise required of the team in your business case vs. that of the previous L&D project. Applying a standard percentage rate across the board to all team members can lead to an underestimation of labor costs. Options (a) and (d) relegate you to the role of order-taker and enhance the risks of inaccurate estimates, while option (c) risks alienating a key member of your stakeholder coalition because it is very likely that those in tomorrow's meeting will tell that stakeholder what was (not) discussed.

Food for Thought

1 Explore two or three of the many free training cost calculators available on the Internet. What are the strengths of these tools? What are the tools' weaknesses?
2 Your organization places more value on quantitative data than qualitative data. However, there does not appear to be any standard practices or guidelines for monetizing intangible benefits. How would go

about eliciting "hard" data regarding the intangible benefits of the solutions identified in your business case?

3 Your business case has been approved. However, you have just learned that although you will be a member of the project team, someone else will be the project team leader. How would you go about ensuring a smooth transition from business case to project?

Up Next

In this chapter, we have (a) reviewed some basic concepts and approaches to budgeting for L&D projects; (b) discussed considerations associated with collecting financial data for creating the project budget; and (c) examined the various ways of planning for cost management once your project business case has been approved. One of the most critical take-aways was the need to actively involve representatives from your organization's Finance group to make sure that financial measures and metrics used to evaluate your solution alternatives and, consequently, to select the best alternative are grounded in the accounting principles and practices of your organization. That grounding enables to you clearly demonstrate the extent to which the solution to the learning challenge/opportunity presented in your business case contributes to the organization's business objectives. Moreover, it ensures that you will be able to compare your estimates with what is actually spent throughout the project life cycle. The ability to monitor and control project costs is one of the critical competencies in effective project management, which is the subject of the next chapter.

References

Arthur, A. (2000). How to build your own project budget. *Management Accounting*, 78(4), 20–2.

Bragg, S. M. (2014). *Budgeting: A Comprehensive Guide* (3rd ed.). Centennial, CO: AccountingTools, Inc.

Branham, A. R., Katz, A. J., Moose, J. S., Ferreri, S. P., Farley, J. F., & Marciniak, M. W. (2013). Retrospective analysis of estimated cost avoidance following pharmacist-provided medication therapy management services. *Journal of Pharmacy Practice*, 26(4), 420–7.

Budget. (n.d.). In *Merriam-Webster Online*. Retrieved from www.merriam-webster.com/dictionary/budget.

Ezzamel, M., Robson, K., & Stapleton, P. (2012). The logics of budgeting: theorization and practice variation in the educational field. *Accounting, Organizations and Society*, 37, 281–303.

Gambles, I. (2009). *Making the Business Case: Proposals that Succeed for Projects that Work*. Surrey, UK: Gower Publishing Limited.

Heinle, M. S., Ross, N., & Saouma, R. E. (2014). A theory of participative budgeting. *The Accounting Review*, 89(3), 1025–50.

IBSTPI. (2014). Instructional Designer Competencies – Welcome to ibstpi. Retrieved from http://ibstpi.org/instructional-design-competencies/.

Kirwan, W. E. (2007). Higher education's "accountability" imperative: How the University System of Maryland responded. *Change: The Magazine of Higher Learning, 39*(2), 21–5.

Mohamed, A., & Kamal, M. (2015, October). *e-Learning Capital Budgeting Decision Models: A Comparative Analytical Study.* Paper presented at the 2015 Fifth International Conference on e-Learning (econf), Manama, Bahrain.

Project Management Institute. (2013). *A Guide to the Project Management Body of Knowledge* (5th ed.). Newton Square, PA: Project Management Institute.

Rachlin, R., & Sweeny, A. (1996). *Accounting and Financial Fundamentals for Nonfinancial Executives.* New York, NY: AMACOM, a division of the American Management Association.

Shim, J. K., Siegel, J. G., & Shim, A. I. (2012). *Budgeting Basics and Beyond* (4th ed.). Hoboken, NJ: John Wiley & Sons.

White, L. N. (2010). Assessment planning for distance education library services: strategic roadmaps for determining and reporting organizational performance and value. *Journal of Library Administration, 50*(7–8), 1017–26. doi:10.1080/01930826.2010.489007.

10 Project Management
People + Process = Results, Sometimes

Anyone who has ever been involved in a project – be it in the workplace or at home – has had a Dilbert©-like project experience. There's the home improvement contractor who didn't complete your renovation on time and on budget as you expected; the roll out of your employer's new software system that was full of "bugs"; the new school website full of broken links or pages that took forever to download. Statistics about project success – or lack thereof – abound. For example, the Project Management Institute (PMI), a US-based professional association with more than 700,000 members worldwide, defines project success as meeting the original goals and business intent, completed within original budget, and completed on time. In 2016, only one in two projects met all three success criteria, while nearly one in five failed on all three criteria:

> More critical is the money that continues to be wasted when projects aren't managed well. We see US$122 million wasted for every US$1 billion invested due to poor project performance, a 12 percent increase over last year. (Project Management Institute, 2016)

Published research studies of why projects fail are also abundant. Although there are myriad reasons why projects fail, there are four characteristics of failed projects that are common to projects of any size or level of complexity in any industry sector: (a) lack of a clear project definition and scope; (b) little or no systematic application of project management processes; (c) unclear or unrealistic stakeholder expectations; and (d) lack of concrete senior management support. These four factors appear consistently in literature reviews focused on project failures in the IT sector (Jorgensen, 2014; Nelson, 2005; Rajkumar & Alagarsamy, 2013), in a variety of industry sectors other than IT (Nixon, Harrington, & Parker, 2012), and in performance improvement consulting (Bolin, 2012).

But I'm an instructional designer and never work on multi-million dollar projects, so why can't I just stick to my instructional design models? you ask. The answer is: It depends on whether or not you want to remain employable and marketable. The ability to manage and eventually lead instructional design (ID) project teams is a critical skill set for building your career. The International Board of Standards for Training, Performance and Instruction/IBSTPI (IBSTPI, 2014) describes the ability to plan and manage instructional design projects in terms of the following six performance statements:

- Establish project scope and goals;
- Write proposals for instructional design projects;
- Use a variety of planning and management tools for instructional design projects;
- Allocate resources to support the project plan;
- Manage multiple priorities to maintain project time line; and
- Identify and resolve project issues.

Similarly, the foundational competencies included in the ATD Competency Model (ATD Certification Institute, 2017) integrate project management under the business skills required of all learning professionals. Some instructional design textbooks are beginning to devote entire chapters to project management (Morrison, Ross, Kalman, & Kemp, 2013; P. L. Smith & Ragan, 2004), and case studies around the application of project management principles in instructional settings have also gained visibility (Allen & Hardin, 2008; Benson, Moore, & Williams van Rooij, 2013; Williams van Rooij, 2014).

The importance of project management to a designer's success is clear. All initiatives in which the designer may play a role – contributing to the organization's human resource development (HRD) plan, enacting an organizational development (OD) intervention, producing a new training curriculum, or supporting an employee's on-the-job learning – are most often organized into projects. With a few exceptions, however, project management remains absent from the instructional design core curriculum in higher education and in professional association instructional design certification programs (Pan, 2012; Williams van Rooij, 2011). In a perfect world, this gap would be filled by employers. Once on the job, the designer would be given an opportunity to learn the skills needed to be an effective project manager. A coaching or mentoring program whereby the designer undertakes an assistant's role to an instructional design project manager and learns through direct observation and interaction with team members would provide guidance, support, and experience to the designer seeking to become a project manager. Opportunities to attend project management seminars, workshops, and training courses would also enable the designer to learn how to run a project and use specific project management processes, tools, and techniques.

However, organizations are not always willing to fund such learning opportunities. Organizational support tends to be weakest in industry sectors where project management practices are less mature and where formal project management has a limited history. Consequently, the designer may be called upon to manage a project because of his/her solid instructional design skills but may be lacking in other skills and knowledge required to effectively manage a project. The designer then becomes an "accidental" project manager (Darrell, Baccarini, & Love, 2010), thrown into the deep end of the pool to sink or swim through luck, perseverance, or the survival instinct, all while maintaining his/her full-time design responsibilities.

That's a great incentive to buy a book on project management and learn on my own, you say. Yes, it is but when you are managing a project, your actions and decisions have greater visibility and accountability than when you were not in a leadership role. You are now responsible not only for your own work but for the work of the entire project team. When things go wrong, as they sometimes do, you will be the first in the line of fire. No matter how self-directed and self-motivated you may be, learning project management by doing project management is not always wise and/or feasible. Depending on the organizational context in which you work, the tolerance for mistakes or the project timetable may make it too risky to be an accidental project manager who learns the basics of project management at his/her own pace, acquiring just enough project management knowledge to be dangerous.

This chapter will help move you from the accidental to the intentional management of projects by honing in on what Project Management as a discipline – separate and distinct from Instructional Design – is all about and what touchpoints exist between the two. In this chapter, we will:

- Review the current state of project management as a field of study;
- Examine the synergistic relationship between project management and instructional design;
- Identify the skill sets common to both the instructional designer and the project manager; and
- Summarize some key considerations for successful instructional design project management.

The Current State of Project Management Research: In Flux but Progressing

If we take as our starting point the dictionary definition (Oxford or Webster) of a project as a temporary endeavor with a definite beginning and end, undertaken to create a unique product, service, or result, then the need to manage projects to successful completion has existed since the Neolithic age when humans built structures out of bone, wood, animal skin, and stone. It is no surprise, then, that project management as an occupation and as a field of study originally focused on construction and engineering projects. Fortunately, for those in other industry sectors, it has expanded over time into other contexts and settings.

Projects are often utilized as a means of achieving an organization's strategic goals. Projects are typically authorized because of market demand, such as authorizing a new brand of learning management system (LMS) in response to market dissatisfaction with existing brands; organizational need, such as a training company authorizing a project to create a new course to increase company revenue; client request, such as a sales division asking the training department to create a workshop for new sales reps; technology advances, such as cloud computing as a means of hosting teaching and learning applications; and legal requirements, such as mandatory compliance training at the federal, state, or professional certification level.

Like instructional design, project management is about achieving a specific end result; so, it could be expected that project management, like instructional design, would be well grounded in theories drawn from a variety of disciplines. Such an expectation has not (yet) been fully realized. Project management has a relatively unique history that has affected its treatment in the scholarly literature and its adoption in professional settings. A high-level review of that history, along with the various project management models and theories, merits consideration before thinking about how project management applies to the work of the designer.

Roots of Project Management

In their analysis of peer-reviewed journal articles that take a historical perspective of project management, Carden and Egan (2008) identified four distinct periods in the history of project management. First came the Emergence period in the early 1900s in which project management as an organized work-related approach was established. Planning and management tools, such as the Gantt chart – a graphical representation of a project schedule that includes all deliverables and progress toward their completion – and the harmonogram – a workflow network diagram – were developed and adopted by the military and by the manufacturing sector. Next came the period of Refinement in the 1950s when project management became a theoretical field grounded in algorithm-based mathematical research. Additional planning tools and techniques, such as program evaluation and review techniques (PERT) and critical path methods (CPM), were introduced. PERT was developed by the US Navy as a statistical tool for measuring and forecasting progress in research and development projects and was first used in the development of the Polaris submarine weapons system. CPM is an algorithm-based scheduling technique that enables you to calculate the longest possible duration of a sequence of activities so that you know in advance that any delay in activities along that critical path will adversely impact the project completion date.

The Human Resources period of the 1960s emphasized individual, team, and organizational effectiveness in executing projects successfully.

Carden and Egan particularly noted an increase in the number of journal articles focusing on project manager competencies, resource allocation, project team issues and challenges, and the alignment of human resources, authority, and leadership for successful project management. The Performance period, the fourth and current period, began in the 1980s and focuses on project management successes and failures and their impact on the organization as a whole. In addition to a focus on critical success factors, the current period addresses the impact of technology-based support tools and project management's strategic benefits to the organization.

In a similar vein, Garel (2013) viewed the history of project management as yielding "an articulated collection of best practices" (p. 663) that draw largely on the study of large-scale, complex North American engineering projects. Garel viewed project management as initially indistinct from the history of techniques or professions. It was not until the 1950s and 1960s that Garel deemed project management to be a true management model, independent and standardized, to assist engineering contractors in rationalizing their efforts.

While Carden and Egan (2008) and Garel (2013) sought out themes in their historical analysis of project management, Pollack and Adler (2015) applied quantitative techniques to identify trends in project management-related research published between 1962 and 2012. Using a software program that creates graphic renderings of bibliographic data from some 94,000 records stored in scholarly databases across multiple fields, Pollack and Adler conducted keyword and abstract searches by frequency of occurrence, to track the various changes in the data over time. The software's burst detection algorithm – an algorithm that identifies words/themes that occur with high intensity over a limited period of time – confirmed other authors' observation about the influence of engineering on the early development of project management. However, more recent "bursts" in research included keywords related to environmental issues, strategic planning, project managers, knowledge management, business, and innovation. The authors stated that this suggests a movement from technical and industry-specific issues to an emphasis on the interpersonal aspects of project management and the role of the field in the broader organizational context. The authors also noted that recent bursts in research-related keywords suggest an increasing focus on project management as an independent field of research.

Other keywords have gradually faded from the project management research literature, a phenomenon that Pollack and Adler called "evanescence." The use of keywords related to education was popular from 1999 to 2005, while keywords related to cost, contracts, and investment were popular from 2001 to 2006. Keywords related to computer networks and information systems were popular from 2008 to 2012, while keywords related to new product development and economics were popular from

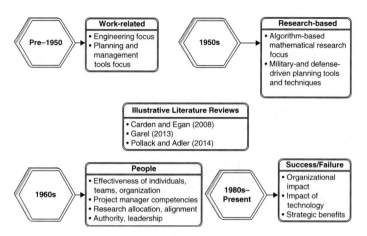

Figure 10.1 The Roots of Project Management.

2009 to 2012. A network analysis based on the frequency of keywords that were related (keyword co-occurrence) revealed that issues associated with decision-making are central to project management research. Keywords related to cost and contract management were more strongly associated with the construction industry than the IT industry, while issues associated with education have been more strongly associated with IT than with construction. Figure 10.1 offers a graphical illustration of the roots of Project Management from a historical perspective.

Project Management Models

Like Instructional Design, Project Management has no single, agreed-upon model that is used in the field. Early practitioners of project management formed professional associations focused on creating a standard set of project management processes. Today the largest project management associations are the Europe-based International Project Management Association (IPMA), a federation of 50 national associations, with the U.K. and Germany representing the largest proportion of members, and the US-based Project Management Institute (PMI), representing more than 700,000 project management professionals worldwide. IPMA focuses on the technical, contextual, and behavioral competencies of a project manager (International Project Management Association, 2015) and PMI focuses on project management practices and processes (Project Management Institute, 2017). However, there are a few models that are recognized worldwide, namely, the (a) traditional models as exemplified by PMI and the PRINCE2 methodologies, (b) Agile Project Management model, (c) Benefits Realization Management model, and (d) Project Management Maturity models.

Traditional Models

The traditional models define a sequence of stages that may be completed either sequentially or iteratively, depending on project complexity, the clarity of project requirements, time, and resources (Wysocki, 2011). The basic stages include: (a) initiating, consisting of all of the processes and procedures for obtaining authorization to start the project; (b) planning, to establish the total scope of the project, define and refine the objectives, and develop the course of action required to achieve those objectives, all of which is documented in a project plan; (c) executing, to complete the work that is defined in the project plan to satisfy project specifications and that involves coordinating people and resources, as well as integrating and performing the activities in accordance with the project plan; (d) monitoring and controlling, to track, review, and regulate the progress and performance of the project work, as well as identify any areas in which changes to the plan are required; and (e) closing, to finalize all activities to formally complete the project, such as obtaining client acceptance of the final deliverable(s), post-project reviews, and documentation of lessons learned, and close out of any external contracts with vendors and suppliers. Not all projects will have every stage, but most industries use variations of these stages.

Effective project management requires knowledge of the characteristics of the project's environment (e.g., technology, industry, etc.) as well as general management knowledge and skills, and interpersonal skills. Those interpersonal skills – particularly communication skills and leadership skills – are deemed essential to successful project management in the digital age (Horine, 2005). PMI's PMBOK® Guide (Project Management Institute, 2013) describes the knowledge and practices that are applicable to most projects most of the time and indicates consensus about the value and usefulness of those practices. The PMBOK® Guide also provides and promotes a common vocabulary within the project management profession for using and applying concepts.

PRINCE2 is another traditional, structured approach to project management. Originally developed as a UK Government standard for information systems (IT) project management, PRINCE is an acronym for Projects in a Controlled Environment. PRINCE2 was released in 1996 as a generic project management method and is now a *de facto* standard for project management in many UK government departments and among some members of the European Union. PRINCE2 describes procedures to coordinate people and activities in a project, how to design and supervise the project, and what to do if the project has to be adjusted if it does not develop as planned. Each process is specified with its key inputs and outputs and with specific goals and activities to be carried out. This allows for automatic control of any deviations from the plan. Divided into manageable stages, the method enables an efficient control of resources. Based on close monitoring, the project can be carried out in a controlled and organized way. PRINCE2 provides a common language for all participants in the project. The various management roles and responsibilities involved in a project are fully described and are adaptable to suit the complexity of the project and skills of the organization (PRINCE2.com, 2017).

Agile Project Management

In contrast with the traditional project management models, the Agile model views a project as a series of relatively small tasks conceived and executed as the situation demands in an adaptive manner, rather than as a completely pre-planned process (Highsmith, 2009). The assumption underlying the Agile approach is acceptance that project requirements are likely to change and, as such, the project processes must be able to respond accordingly. Agile employs iterative life cycles focused on delivering the highest priority business features, so that the project team can reflect back and adapt the process at regular intervals. Greater emphasis is placed on communications and collaboration than on documentation. Agile project management is most often used in the software, website development, technology, creative and marketing industries where competition is intense and first mover advantage is paramount (Larman, 2003). However, as more organizations apply the Agile philosophy to learning design (see, for example, Allen & Sites, 2012; Ellis, 2015; Neibert, 2014), Agile project management is gaining traction, particularly for design projects with uncertain requirements, shifting business needs shift, and complex decision-making.

The problem is, however, that the word "agile" has been slapped onto many ideas and concepts with the intent of indicating flexibility. In reality, however, it has often been translated to mean quick, dirty, and cheap. So, what is Agile Project Management? Formalized by a group of developers who formed the Agile Alliance back in 2001 and documented in the Agile Manifesto (Highsmith, 2001), Agile is not one thing but rather an umbrella term for a group of methodologies that employ iterative methods. The product is developed in iterations or small boxes of time that allow the team to design and develop small "chunks" of product that can be evaluated and refined after each iteration. Agile methodologies are adaptive, meaning that they accept that product requirements are likely to change. They work to deliver the highest priority features first, focusing on the "must have" content areas. They emphasize communication and collaboration among team members, so that teams are empowered to make decisions about change. Finally, Agile methodologies are retrospective, enabling team members to reflect back at regular intervals and adjust their work. Agile methods can be used for creating a product as well as for the processes involved in creating that product.

Agile is more than just a set of methods. It is a mindset defined by values, guided by principles, and manifested through many different practices. The Agile mindset encompasses collaboration, build, and feedback; is value-driven; and welcomes and responds to change and the continuous delivery of must-have product features as small value-added slices. The Agile project practitioner internalizes the Agile mindset, values, and principles, then applies the right practices and tailors them to different situations as they arise. But applying the practices and applying them without knowing the mindset and principles to know when to tailor and how to select the appropriate processes is a recipe for project failure. In fact, Agile projects suffered a 9 percent failure rate according to the 2015 Standish report (Hastie & Wojewoda, 2015). This is certainly lower than the failure rate for traditional projects, but it should be noted that both Agile and traditional projects experienced similar rates of challenge or project difficulties in 2015. In other words, Agile does not in and of itself guarantee project success.

Benefits Realization Management Model

First developed in the U.K., Benefits Realization Management (BRM) enhances traditional project management models by focusing on agreement as to what outcomes should change (the benefits) during the project, and then measuring to see if that is happening to help keep a project on track. Outcomes are changes identified as important by stakeholders and can be strategic or non-strategic. A benefit is a measurable positive impact of change (Jenner, 2012). In short, rather than attempting to deliver agreed requirements, the aim is to deliver the benefit of those requirements. An example of delivering a project to requirements could be agreeing on a project to deliver a computer system to process staff data with the requirement to manage payroll, holiday, and staff personnel records. Under BRM, the agreement would be to use the suppliers' suggested staff data system to see an agreed reduction in staff hours processing and maintaining staff data (benefit: reduce HR headcount).

In an effort to address increasingly tight budgets, state and local governments in the U.S. have been adopting BRM as the model for effective project management. For example, the state of Texas has adopted BRM as the framework for information technology projects in government and education (Department of Information Resources, 2014).

Project Management Maturity Model

Given the various approaches to project management, the question arises as to the extent organizations systematically adopt and apply one or more of those approaches. In other words, the question is: How mature is the level of project management in an organization? Project management maturity refers to the progressive development of an enterprise-wide project management approach, methodology, strategy, and decision-making process (Crawford, 2007). The appropriate level of maturity will vary for each organization based on its specific goals, strategies, resource capabilities, scope, and needs. Most project management maturity models place organizations on a continuum ranging from a low level of maturity, where project management is hit and miss, to a high level of maturity, where project management is consistent and systematic throughout the entire enterprise (Ibbs & Kwak, 2000; Kerzner, 2005).

Thomas and Mullaly (2008) offered a five-level model of project management implementation maturity in organizations derived from case studies of 65 organizations in a variety of industry sectors worldwide. Drawing on Humphrey's (1992) Capability Maturity model for software development, Thomas and Mullaly assessed the project management maturity of an organization as follows:

- Level 1 (ad hoc), with no organizational implementation of project management; any use of project management processes depends on the expertise of individual project managers;
- Level 2 (some practices), with incomplete or inconsistent application enterprise-wide;
- Level 3 (consistent practices), with a complete project management process in place and applied consistently enterprise-wide;
- Level 4 (integrated practices), with project management as an integral management capability that is fully integrated with the organizational life cycle; and
- Level 5 (continually improving practices), with a holistic, fully integrated approach to managing projects with a formal and consistently followed process of evaluating, assessing, and improving project management implementation.

Table 10.1 summarizes the four project management models discussed in the literature. Common to all of the models is a focus on project management efficiencies and best practices for successful project completion.

Project Management Theories

Much of the literature on project management theory consists of critiques about the lack of a rigorous body of theory. One stream of criticism argues that project management research has a practice-based focus that is the antithetical to theory-building or theory-testing. For instance, Soderlund (2004) characterized much of the project management literature as focused on problem-solving, models-for-management approaches, and calls for more empirical research that includes in-depth case studies, studies of processes, and studies in real time as beneficial in building

Table 10.1 Project Management Models

Key Features	Traditional	Agile	Benefits Realization	Project Management Maturity
Specific industries	• Industry-neutral	• Software development • Website development • IT • Creative services • Marketing	• IT	• Industry-neutral
Approach	• Defined sequence of steps • Documentation and standardization • Emphasis on context/environment, as well as general management and interpersonal skills	• Series of small tasks/deliverables • Executed iteratively from highest priority business features • Communication and collaboration focus	• Enhancement to traditional models • Change-focused, measurable positive impact of change • Outcome-oriented – i.e., what the final deliverable does for the business	• Focus on systematic adoption, application at the enterprise level • Continuum of low to high maturity
Methodologies	• PMI PMBOK© • PRINCE2	• Ad hoc, informal, project-by-project	• Used with PMI PMBOK©, PRINCE2	• Methodology-neutral • Focus in ability to implement
Illustrative Authors	• Horine (2005) • Wysocki (2011)	• Allen & Sites (2012) • Ellis (2015) • Highsmith (2009) • Neibert (2014)	• Jenner (2012)	• Crawford (2007) • Thomas & Mullaly (2008)

theories for understanding fundamental issues of projects and project organizations.

Somewhat harsher is the criticism offered by Pollack (2007), stating that project management research is biased toward what he calls the "hard" systems approach. Pollack started from the premise of the hard vs. soft paradigm, where the hard paradigm is associated with a positivist epistemology, deductive reasoning, and quantitative or reductionist techniques, and the soft paradigm is associated with an interpretive epistemology, inductive reasoning, and exploratory, qualitative techniques. He argued that project management research has been developed as a purposeful, functionalist activity, aligning with the hard systems paradigm in terms of tendencies toward positivist and realist philosophies and emphasizing quantitative techniques in project planning, scheduling, and controlling, and dominated by systems methodologies, such as systems analysis, systems engineering and cybernetics, and operations research.

A second stream of criticism is more positive, seeing the potential benefit of practice-based research to contribute to theory. Kwak and Anbari (2009) conducted a review of the business and management literature to explore linkages between project management research and research in allied fields such as IT, engineering and construction, and operations research/decision sciences. The authors saw the integration of project management in the research of those fields as a positive step toward the development of project management as a discipline, not just a practice. Lalonde, Bourgault, and Findeli (2010) identified four types of theory-practice relationships in the project management literature, all of which have contributed to project management research:

- Practice as a heuristic, where theory is minimal. The focus is on concrete outcomes of project management activities (new products, competitive differentiation, etc.) with no new knowledge produced with which to build a theoretical and scientific framework for project management. The goal is not theory-building, but rather action.
- Practice as an applied science, with prescriptive models. The focus is on tools and techniques, and theorization stems from mainstream project management practice.
- Theory as an interpretive framework, with descriptive models. New perspectives are added to the traditional vision of the project and consider not only the financial and economic aspects of projects but also the political, strategic, social, environmental, technological, and communicational aspects. Theory is a lens by which practitioners can enrich their understanding of a project from different angles (e.g., project-generated anxiety, power relations between actors) and assisting practitioners in making better decisions grounded in multiple disciplinary lenses.

- Reflective practice and situated theorization. This implies that the theorization effort literally ensues from reflective practice, whereby reflective practice becomes the main empirical ground on which to sketch theories of project management practice. As such, this type of theory-practice relationship has the strongest potential for project management theory-building and theory-testing.

An example of situated theorization can be seen in the work of Cicmil, Williams, Thomas, and Hodgson (2006), who viewed projects as complex social processes that play out at various levels. Understanding those social processes will benefit both theory development in the field of project management and practical action for more satisfactory project outcomes.

A third stream of criticism calls for a shift toward a theoretical lens specifically grounded in the social sciences. Floricel, Bonneau, Aubry, and Sergi (2014) characterized much of the project management research as grounded in decision rationality as expressed in decision theory, economics, and finance, whereby a decision-maker imagines alternatives for action, anticipates future developments, and emphasizes the logical consistency of the choice among these alternatives in light of the values and probabilities attributed to the various possible outcomes of each action alternative. Using the decision rationality lens, project planning is a series of decision moments in which planners choose between alternative projects or parameters, then move to operational planning guided by prescribed tools and techniques. Floricel et al. saw the prevalence of project failures as evidence of the shortcomings of decision theory and advocated turning to social science theories, such as activity theory, structuration theory, and actor-network theory to inform the investigation of project organizations.

The call for the adoption and adaptation of social science theories to project management research was also made by Blomquist, Hollgren, Nilsson, and Soderholm (2010), who argued for a deeper and more insightful understanding of how people actually use project management tools, how they react and respond to various changes in circumstances, and how they think creatively to promote and offer support when needed. Figure 10.2 offers a graphic representation of the current state of project management theory.

Summary

Project management as a field of research is in a state of flux but is making good progress. The scholarly literature is beginning to move beyond the tools and techniques of individual project practice to include consideration of new theories and the application of existing theories from other disciplines. Empirical research focused on theory-building about applying lessons learned from project management practice (Jugdev & Wishart, 2014), project initiation (Mullaly, 2014), as well as case studies grounded in social sciences theories, such as Appreciative Inquiry (Mathiassen &

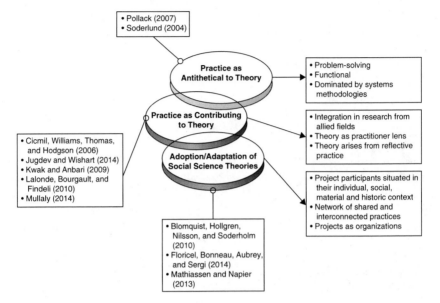

Figure 10.2 Project Management Theories.

Napier, 2013), are just a few examples from the growing base of robust theory-based project management research. As the scope and incidence of project failure continue to haunt businesses worldwide, we can expect further advances in research that seek solutions in a broader and deeper context than the traditional processes, procedures, tools, and industry sectors.

Project Management and Instructional Design

Although the importance of project management is strongly advocated in the Learning and Development (L&D) field, the Instructional Design literature offers a mixed picture of project management. Furthermore, as project management research and practice continue to evolve to address the challenges and opportunities associated with managing projects and project teams in virtual environments, these same issues will impact the specific project management skills that designers need to successfully manage virtual design teams. Consequently, understanding the synergy between Instructional Design and Project Management requires an examination of the various models of instructional design (ID) project management. We can then compare those models to what learning designers who manage projects deem the role of project management to be.

Instructional Design as a Non-Traditional Project Management Area

In reviewing the Project Management literature, it was clear that research outside of the traditional sectors of focus – construction, engineering, IT, utilities – is just getting underway. Nevertheless, instructional design projects often face some of the same challenges as their larger, more complex counterparts in the traditional sectors. For instance, anecdotal evidence suggests that instructional design (ID) projects tend to be constrained by limited staff, funding, and quick turnaround times. Unlike projects in the traditional sectors, however, ID projects tend to be smaller, less complex, and less resource-intensive and they often fall into what the project management literature describes as "small" projects. Small projects are characterized by (a) a duration of less than 6 months; (b) fewer than 10 team members; (c) a small number of skill areas; (d) a single objective and a readily achievable solution; (e) straightforward deliverables with few interdependencies among skill areas; and (f) a budget of $75,000 or less (Rowe, 2007). There are, of course, examples of large (six to seven figures) instructional design projects, particularly when they are part of a broader suite of performance improvement solutions.

Project failure or the potential for failure is every designer's worst nightmare. Threats to project success range from communication breakdowns to changes in human or financial resource availability to poor planning. The managers of ID projects must meet the same constraints of time, money, quality, and stakeholder acceptance as their counterparts who manage multi-million dollar projects. Even when the roles of designer and ID project manager are filled by the same individual, using project management processes enables the ID project manager to (a) clearly define the project, develop realistic schedules, and manage change; (b) choose those processes, levels of detail, and methodology components appropriate to the specific project; (c) operate in an organized and efficient manner; and (d) have more time to devote to the management of interpersonal skills, such as team building.

ID projects also involve managing the product development life cycle, the phases that produce the project deliverable. The product development life cycle represents a specific industry, product, or service, and defines the end-to-end methodology for creating that deliverable. For example, in the software development industry, product development methodologies include (a) waterfall, a sequential process where one phase is completed before another phase can begin; (b) spiral or iterative, consisting of partial deliverables with each deliverable having incrementally more functionality than the previous deliverable, and the last iteration consisting of the final, complete product; (c) agile, where the product is developed in a series of time-boxed stages or "sprints" that are completed and added to the product each sprint, and the product is released as soon as it is determined to provide added value to users; and (d) open source, where volunteer-developers share their source code with other developers who can add more functionality and share with the developer community (Okoli & Carillo, 2012). Instructional design models, such as the generic ADDIE model (Conrad & TrainingLinks, 2000), the Dick and Carey model (Dick,

Carey, & Carey, 2005), the Smith and Ragan model (Smith & Ragan, 2004) or the Morrison, Ross, Kalman, and Kemp model (Morrison et al., 2013), define the product development life cycle for developing instruction in a variety of settings. The complexity of each model phase depends on the complexity of the instructional deliverable, with some phases shortened or lengthened as needed. In short, the product development life cycle describes **what** you are going to build.

Project management complements the design process by offering a set of repeatable processes with which to describe, organize. and complete work required for each phase of the product life cycle, with deliverable complexity also determining how much process is used at each phase (Williams van Rooij, 2010). In other words, project management describes **how** you are going to build your product. Figure 10.3 illustrates those repeatable processes using a traditional waterfall project management model and the generic ADDIE model. In order to do anything in instructional design, you have to have a project and to get a project, the Initiating process or authorization of that project – shown in the outer circle – has to take place. Following project initiation is the Analysis you need to do or the first iteration of the analysis you would do in instructional design, shown in the inner circle. This becomes part of the Planning process in project management, including any preliminary design work you may do. The actual Development of your instructional product falls into the Executing

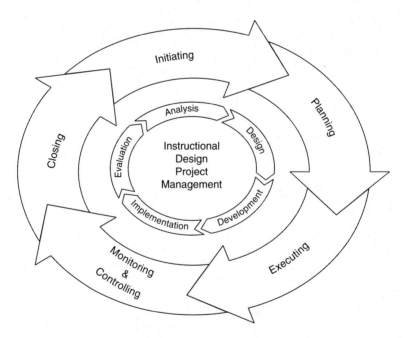

Figure 10.3 Instructional Design Project Management: ADDIE and Waterfall PM.

project management process group, while product Implementation falls under Monitoring and Controlling. Finally, evaluation is part of the closing process.

Notice that there is not a one-to-one correspondence between the project management process groups and the instructional design processes. That's because the starting points vary, depending on the point at which you have an official project. Furthermore, just as instructional design is not a linear process, project management is not linear.

Let's take two concrete examples to move through the two concentric circles. Our first example is an internal request for training. The head of the Customer Service department at your organization tells your manager that the organization is experiencing problems with customer service response time and accuracy. The department head thinks training is the answer. Your manager informs you of any allotted budget and timeline in which to conduct a front-end analysis (discussed in Chapter 4) to make sure that training is the right solution. If your organization treats front-end analyses as projects, then you would apply the project management processes shown in the outer circle to the work needed to create the front-end analysis. Once it is determined that instruction is the solution (or part of it), then the next project would be the creation of the instructional design document (IDD), represented by the "design" segment of the inner circle. Once that IDD is approved, then a plan for the execution of the content of the IDD, represented by the remaining segments of the inner circle, would be made.

For our second example, let's assume that you work for an e-learning vendor and that you've been awarded a project as the result of a contract with a statement of work (SOW) that your team or some other team has created. That SOW serves as a preliminary instructional design document. Most e-learning vendors differentiate between pre-contract work and post-contract (or project work). Pre-contract work, the work needed to win the business, tends to consist of a high-level IDD and rudimentary prototype that would provide the potential client with just enough to get a picture of what the company can do (but not enough to take the information and create the instruction in-house or with another vendor) along with a cost and time estimate to actually do the work. Large learning solution vendors have whole teams dedicated to pre-contract work/proposals in which you, as instructional designer, may not be involved until you either are at a very high level or have worked on projects for the same client in the past.

Once the contract is signed, that contract then serves as your Project Charter and you begin documenting your project plan, including (a) who is going to do the work (and when) of fleshing out/finalizing the IDD; (b) how you will obtain client approval of the full IDD, and specifically, whose signature(s) is/are required for approval; then (c) who is going to actually do the work (and when) needed to execute the IDD. If the project is relatively large and complex, some learning solution vendors will break this up into separate projects each with its own plan – i.e., project 1, IDD finalization and approval; project 2, execution of the IDD and creation of the instructional product.

Common to both of these examples is the application of project management processes to clearly define your project, be it determining what the product(s) should be via front-end analysis or creating an instructional intervention. In sum, the outer circle of project management can be "wrapped" around any deliverable, from definition of solution to intervention(s).

Models of Instructional Design Project Management

In recognition of the synergy between project management and instructional design, there have been several efforts to create project management models that are specific to instructional design, rather than simply layering on the models developed in the traditional IT, engineering, and construction industry sectors. Most of those models were constructed back in the 1990s in response to the changing demands on instruction and, thus, the instructional designer, created by the Internet and advanced network technologies. One of the first models recognizing the importance of project management in instructional design was Greer's (1992) ten-step Instructional Design Project Management (IDPM) model. The first two steps occur in the project planning phase and consist of project scope definition and project organization. The instructional development phase includes the next five steps, namely, information gathering, blueprint development, draft material creation, draft material testing, and production of master materials. The last three steps are part of the follow-up phase and consist of production, distribution, and evaluation. However, the model is linear in nature and focuses on managing the development effort for delivering specific instructional products.

Another model that embeds project management within the instructional design process was Gentry's Instructional Project Development and Management (IPDM) model (Gentry, 1994). This model identified eight primary instructional design processes – production, design, adoption, needs assessment, evaluation, operation, installation, and prototyping – and seven supporting processes that include management, facilities, personnel, resource acquisition and allocation, information handling, and communication. Supporting processes are interdependent on and interrelated with the primary processes, making project management skills an essential part of effective instructional design. Nevertheless, the model categorized management as a process distinct from the other project management processes and, thus, offers a limited view of the breadth and depth of project management processes. Yang, Moore, and Burton (1995) sought to adapt project management principles used in software engineering by creating an instructional design workflow and project checklist for courseware production. The resulting model included a procedural flow that regulates the production activities, a task definition component that describes the scope and type of each production actvity, and a role explanation component that defines the responsibilities of team members for each procedure. However, this model does not address the depth and breadth of either instructional design or project management, nor does it indicate the relationship between the two sets of processes.

McDaniel and Liu (1996) provided a practitioner perspective by conducting in-depth interviews with five instructional multimedia developers on their project management processes. Using Greer's IDPM (1992) model, the authors probed participants about their processes for funding and proposal writing, team assembly and management, instructional design, evaluation, marketing and support, and management. However, the limited number of study participants as well as the focus on a small subset of processes prohibits any generalizations about the role of project management in instructional design. Layng (1997) used Dick and Carey's model for instructional design as the framework for drawing parallels between instructional design and project management. Layng saw project management as a tool to help instructional designers develop detailed outlines of instructional materials and learn a method of managing those outlines. She also viewed project management as a means of obtaining management buy-in to the instructional design process, to avoid shortcuts intended to save time but usually resulting in poorly designed training and expensive revisions. By focusing only on instructional materials, however, Layng provides a rather limited view of the impact of project management in instructional design.

There are also empirical sudies offering insights into the instructional design project best practices of individual organizations. A case study in medical education (Koller, Frankenfield, & Sarley, 2000) documented how project management techniques, such as selecting project team members and criteria for selecting projects, were combined with instructional design principles to undertake an educational multimedia project at a teaching hospital. Although providing insights into the real-world impact of some specific practices, the case study provides little insight into the process contexts surrounding those practices. Similarly, Stubbs (2002) described a process developed in the instructional technology center of an institution of higher education that draws on project management processes used by organizations such as Disney Imagineering, as well as software engineering best practices for succesful project management. While illustrating the cross-disciplinary nature of project management, this case study does not clearly indicate which of the processes discussed are project management and why those specific processes vs. all of the processes in project management were selected for adoption.

In describing the process for transforming face-to-face courses into online Web-based courses, Li and Shearer (2005) stressed the importance

Table 10.2 Overview of Instructional Design Project Management Models

Author(s)	Model/Year	Strengths	Limitations
		Research	
Greer	Instructional Design Project Management (IDPM)/1992	• Stresses project scope definition and organization	• Assumes linear processes • Focuses on product production
Gentry	Instructional Project Development and Management (IPDM)/1994	• Clearly delineates instructional design (ID) vs. project management (PM) processes • Emphasizes inter-dependence of processes	• Limited view of PM breadth and depth
Yang, Moore, & Burton	Instructional Design Workflow & Checklist/1995	• At-a-glance visual representation of selected processes	• Addresses only a subset of ID and PM processes • Does not address ID/PM relationships
McDaniel & Lu	Greer's IDPM Applied/1996	• Provides a practitioner's perspective	• Small number of participants (5) • Focuses on a subset of ID/PM processes
Layng	Dick & Carey's ISD Model Applied/1997	• Focuses on ID/PM synergy • Emphasis on PM as tool for strengthening ID process credibility	• PM limited only to instructional materials

Discipline-Based Practices

		Discipline-Based Practices	
Koller, Frankenfeld, & Sarley	Medical Education Case Study/2000	• Real-world success with specific PM processes	• Examines a few specific PM practices rather than processes surrounding those practices
Stubbs	Higher Education Instructional Technology Center Best Practices/2002	• Illustrates cross-disciplinary nature of PM	• Unclear as to which PM processes were adopted and why
Li & Shearer	Tool Best Practices/2005	• Stresses schedule management, communication, and subject matter expert guidance	• Little insight into process context • Examines a few specific PM practices
Byers	Leadership Roles/2005	• Addresses real-world scenario of designer required to serve as project manager	• Limited discussion of specific skills required of each role, and of how missing skills are acquired
Giller & Barker	Multimedia Courseware/2006	• Advocates using PM throughout project life cycle	• Unclear differentiation between instructional design and project management
Huang	Multimedia Instructional Materials/2005	• Recognition of on time/on budget as critical to ID projects • Emphasis on project manager as "communicator" to/with internal and external stakeholders • Acknowledgment of PM as cross-disciplinary	• Limited discussion of specific skill sets

of project management scheduling tools, such as Gantt charts, along with clear communication plans and detailed guidelines for faculty subject matter experts. However, no process context is provided for these best practices. Byers (2005) discussed the challenges associated with having the roles of project manager and instructional designer fulfilled by a single individual and emphasized the need for solid project management by the project leader. The discussion acknowledged that each role requires a different skill set, but did not discuss those differences nor how the individual tasked with both roles should acquire missing skills. Giller and Barker (2006) noted that many of the problems associated with multimedia courseware projects can be attributed to poor project management policies and that project management should be carried out throughout the project life cycle. However, both the Byers and the Giller and Barker studies appear to view project management as synonymous with the effective use of instructional design models.

Huang (2005) embedded elements of the project management methodology in her model for creating multimedia educational materials. Although Huang's model included elements common to other instructional design models, Huang emphasized the importance of planning, teamwork, and flexibility throughout the project life cycle, so that the project can remain on target with deadlines while meeting user needs. Huang's model also stressed the role of the project manager as liaison between the various stakeholders and the project team, along with responsibility for task allocation, milestones and deadlines, and project deliverables, all within the agreed-upon budget and timetable. Although Huang stated that the successful project manager should have a strong background in the sciences, technology, and education in order to provide the leadership for an interdisciplinary project team, it is not clear whether the background she described is acquired through formal education or on-the-job experience.

Table 10.2 summarizes the instructional design project management models discussed in this section. Common to all of the models is the explicit contention that (a) a formal, documented process of project management is essential to the success of any instructional design project; (b) those who manage instructional design projects must be skilled project managers as well as skilled instructional designers; and (c) project management is embedded in the successful execution of the various phases and stages of the instructional design process. What is missing, however, is a clear and consistent definition of what constitutes project management and the empirically grounded competencies required for successful management of instructional design projects.

Summary

Project management and instructional design are different but complementary processes and professions. Nevertheless, the Instructional Design literature has tended to treat project management as phases within the larger process of instructional design. Pan (2012) attributed this integrated view of instructional design and project management to the fact that instructional designers tend to work in various settings, many of which involve small-scale instructional design projects where the designer is less likely to take on duties beyond instructional design and, as such, can focus on a select set of project management ideas or concepts as supporting tools and techniques.

However, there has been a growing number of medium- and large-scale instructional design projects – particularly in the government and private sectors – where the instructional designer is delegated more responsibility than design and may be responsible for selecting and managing project human and financial resources, along with stakeholder relationships beyond the project team. Furthermore, instructional designers are now responsible for creating learning opportunities that do not automatically include instruction and find themselves working with function area specialists and stakeholders with whom they previously may have had limited involvement. As such, twenty-first-century designers need to be aware of the project management-specific skill sets required to effectively lead any type of L&D project.

Project Management Skills and Instructional Design Skills: The Shared Must-Haves

So, what does managing an L&D project include? It includes identifying requirements, what it is that has to be done in order to complete the project successfully. It includes addressing the stakeholder's expectations. Each stakeholder may have different expectations of the project; so, it is up to the L&D project manager to help set and address the stakeholder's expectations. Importantly, managing an L&D project includes balancing competing project constraints, such as scope, quality, schedule, budget, resources, and risks. In short, the L&D project manager is the person accountable for accomplishing project objectives. This does not mean that he/she does all of the work for the project but that he/she has bottom-line responsibility for successfully completing the project's objectives.

Although professions tend to be defined by (a) a unique body of knowledge that can be studied and learned through formal education; (b) a commitment to ethical behavior as defined within the characteristics of the profession; and (c) a set of defined minimum standards that must be met for entry into the profession (Smith, 2003), the boundaries between the design professional and the project management professional are often unclear, with conflicting and overlapping roles and responsibilities (Dobrovolny, Lamos, Sims, & Spannaus, 2002; Greer, 1992; Layng, 1997). At the beginning of this chapter, we noted the specific performance indicators that IBSTPI and ASTD/ATD attribute to the instructional/learning designer who can manage a project successfully. But how do those performance indicators compare with those of the professional whose sole occupation is project management?

A Tale of Two Skill Sets: People First, Then Process

Scholars and practitioners in the Instructional Design world have been trying to figure out just how much project management knowledge an instructional designer needs to manage effectively the project and the project team. Knutson, Cain, Hurtubise, and Kreger (2006) noted that the knowledge area skills required to apply project management processes are distinctly different from those of an instructional designer. Brill, Bishop, and Walker's (2006) study of 147 alumni of a private Research university in the northeast who are practicing instructional design project managers included the ability to apply PMI processes and principles among the core success criteria for educational/training product development projects. In a survey of 142 practicing professionals in academic and corporate settings, Cox and Osguthorpe (2003) sought to determine how instructional designers spend their time when working on individual projects, particularly in terms of time spent on managing the project rather than on the design process. The results of their study showed that instructional designers spent a great deal of time on project management, particularly in the management of the clients' and other stakeholders' expectations.

Looking at the corporate training market, Fabac (2006) made the case for acquiring project management skills as defined in the PMBOK® Guide, to provide the necessary control functions needed to update the ADDIE model of instructional design. The eLearning Guild, a Community of Practice (CoP) composed of working professionals employed in the design, development, and management of web-based instructional content for educational, government, and corporate settings, emphasized the importance of project management skills and practices as outlined in the PMBOK® Guide to increase efficiencies and reduce risk in the courseware development process (Dickinson, 2006).

A more recent study seeks to compare employers' expectations about the skills/competencies of instructional design project managers with the perceptions of instructional design practitioners with little or no formal project management training, and of project management professionals with little or no formal instructional design training (Williams van Rooij, 2011). The study collected data via a web survey of 103 respondents from public and private sector organizations worldwide that develop educational/training products for internal use and/or for external clients. The respondents were presented with a consolidated list of 24 IBSTPI and PMI skills and competencies and were asked to rate whether each is more essential for the project manager, the instructional designer who is a member but not the manager of the project team, or both equally, using a 7-point scale where "1" means "always the project manager" and "7" means "always the instructional designer." The respondents' mean ratings, along with the results of an exploratory factor analysis, revealed that the instructional designer was expected to demonstrate proficiency in the following IBSTPI competencies:

- Select and use a variety of techniques for determining instructional content (Content);
- Select and use a variety of techniques to define and sequence the instructioal content and strategies (Sequencing);
- Apply fundamental research skills to educational/training product development projects (Research);
- Evaluate and assess instruction and its impact (Assessment);
- Select, modify, or create a design and development model appropriate for a given educational/training product development project (Design Models);
- Conduct a needs assessment to identify the perceived gap between an existing situation and the desired situation (Needs Assessment);
- Analyze the characteristics of existing and emerging technologies and their use in an instructional environment (Technologies); and
- Apply current theory to solve practical problems (Theory).

At the other end of the spectrum, project managers are expected to possess the following PMI-based competencies:

- Plan, estimate, budget, and control costs so that the project can be completed within the approved budget (Costs);
- Organize and manage the project team so that team member competencies and interactions enhance project results (Team Management);
- Define, resource and schedule all activities required to accomplish timely project completion (Activities Scheduled);
- Ensure timely and appropriate collection and distribution of project information to stakeholders (Information Distribution);
- Identify and manage risks that may impact the project (Risk Management);
- Plan and manage educational/training product development projects, including scope, budget, schedule, and resources (Project Management);
- Promote collaboration, partnerships, and relationships among the participants and stakeholders (Collaboration);
- Define and control what is (not) included in the project (Scope); and
- Analyze the characteristics of the project environment (Project Environment).

Skills/competencies that are expected of both the instructional designer and the project manager are:

- Communicate effectively in visual, oral, and written form (Communicate);
- Identify and apply the relevant quality standards so that the results satisfy the project requirements (Quality);
- Provide for the effective implementation of educational/training products and programs (Implementation);
- Identify and resolve ethical and legal implications of educational/ training product development in the workplace (Ethical/Legal);
- Make trade-offs among competing objectives and alternatives (Trade-offs); and
- Anticipate and address potential issues before they become critical (Issues).

In a qualitative study designed to identify the "must have" skills/ competencies for instructional design project managers from the perspective of employers in the professional services sector (Williams van Rooij, 2013), an expert panel of Chief Learning Officers (CLOs) from finance and insurance, training/coaching services, IT services, healthcare services, and management consulting services ranked people-management skills that focus on listening and communicating as the top "must have" instructional design competencies for designers seeking to lead project teams, with "ability to listen to clients and team members" ranked highest in priority. Similarly, people management skills were at the top of the "must have" list in terms of project management competencies, with client and stakeholder management skills vying for first place, followed closely by accountability, the clear setting of expectations, and the ability to keep projects moving forward. The experts' emphasis on people skills suggests that although "hard" instructional design skills provide the ticket to entry into the field of instructional design, those occupational skills must be supplemented with strong interpersonal skills to advance to a team leadership position. This emphasis aligns with the interpersonal skills included in IBSTPI's instructional design competencies and with the expansion of the PMBOK® Guide to include a section on interpersonal skills (Creasy & Anantatmula, 2013). Interpersonal skills are also among the most desirable employee attributes in the global labor market (Schramm, Phil, Coombs, & Boyd, 2013).

Figure 10.4 offers a graphical representation of the skills/competencies for effective instructional design project management. At the core are the universal "soft" skills needed to be successful in any occupation that requires working well with others to get the job done. Examples of those skills – active listening, collaboration, communication, ethical behavior, and knowing how to make trade-offs based on priorities – hark back to the discussion of emotional intelligence in Chapter 7 of this book.

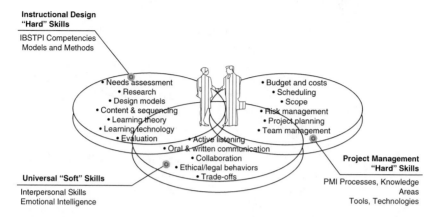

Instructional Design "Hard" Skills

IBSTPI Competencies
Models and Methods

- Needs assessment
- Research
- Design models
- Content & sequencing
- Learning theory
- Learning technology
- Evaluation
- Active listening
- Oral & written communication
- Collaboration
- Ethical/legal behaviors
- Trade-offs
- Budget and costs
- Scheduling
- Scope
- Risk management
- Project planning
- Team management

Project Management "Hard" Skills

PMI Processes, Knowledge Areas
Tools, Technologies

Universal "Soft" Skills

Interpersonal Skills
Emotional Intelligence

Figure 10.4 Instructional Design Project Management Skills/Competencies.

The instructional designer complements these universal "soft" skills with the "hard" occupational skills of his/her profession but must also acquire the "hard" skills of project management to successfully manage and lead an instructional design project.

As a design practitioner, you have the "must have" instructional design skills and competencies. You also focus on improving and applying your "soft" skills at every opportunity (or at least, you should). Do you now have to become a certified Project Manager as well? Chris Daniel, Principal and Founder of Regroup Consulting, offers his take on getting those project management "hard" skills in *E-Suite Views*.

SvR: Let's start with the role of project management in instructional design. My key question is: If someone is credentialed in instructional design and working, can they learn project management "on the fly" or should they have had formal training?

CD: Can they? Yes. Should they take that approach? No. I like the question because I went the alternate route. I got the PMP® first; then, I got the instructional design and it helped so much to frame projects for me. You also asked another question, which I see as the second part to this question, which is: Can you be as successful? Yes, you can but it's a lot harder to go backwards than it is to learn the PMI framework. You should first learn to manage projects, and then you can drop instructional design into that framework. So, my recommendation would be to really be versed in project management principles and the framework, and that way, you can look at anything, especially instructional design, to have a great product at the end.

SvR: Now, suppose my budget is $10,000 for the whole training program. Is it worth my while as an instructional designer to get involved in the project management processes and documentation or am I better off winging it? What do you think?

CD: First, you've got to grow that "consulting nerve" and go back to the table and talk about the value-based proposition. If we have $10,000 and that's all we have, what is the expectation from that? If I've got $10,000 and you want me to train 100 people, just know that I'm going to put together a 2-hour focus group and a list of recommendations for the next steps. Unless that work has been done and the data immediately relevant, that's the misstep I observe with most training organizations who want to grow. $10,000 may not get you a full-day session. But being able to say, let's look at the value of this. If you want me to train 100 people, let's look at their salaries. Let's say they make on average $50,000 each, so I've got $5 million in the room. How much is it worth to develop $5 million? How much revenue do they currently bring? How much do you expect them to bring after they're trained? Is it worth $10,000 or are you willing to invest a little more to get the outcome that you want? These 100 people, do they not have the skills that you need them to have? So, if I help them to develop those skills, how much is it going to improve your organization? Are you going to go up $1 million just from this one session? So, you want to invest $10,000 to get $1 million return. You see what I mean? So, being able to talk the value proposition, that's what you learn in the project management piece, combined with a little consulting savvy.

SvR: What advice would you give to early and mid-career instructional designers about ways to acquire and strengthen their project management skills? What would you tell them to do and importantly, what would you tell them NOT to do?

CD: Let me start with the "not": Don't wing it any more. The thing to do is to develop that project management side. Now, this doesn't mean you've got to pay $3,000 for a PMP® boot camp; that's not what I'm talking about. I'm talking about all of the webinars, all of the podcasts, all of the things that make sense FOR YOU. Books, articles – read it; then, start to apply it. Another thing is to develop IP – intellectual property. That's one of the things I think instructional designers don't do a lot of or enough of. Whatever your process is that works, I can almost guarantee that it's going to help somebody else. There's also a lot of space for what doesn't work. We call them lessons learned. Remember those? Develop IP and if you resell it, that's fine. If you share it for free, that's fine. Just like you've asked these questions of me, I'm sure that someone has a process that's working for them that can benefit a lot of us. Just continue to develop yourself, your working knowledge, and contribute to the profession.

SvR: So, their personal IP, meaning their intellectual property?

CD: Absolutely. Copyright it, put it out there for the world to see; talk about pros and cons, benefits to doing it your way, and have someone add on to it, their way and, before you know it, you'll have some pretty good things to share out there.

A keyword search of instructional/learning designer positions on job boards, such as SimplyHired.com and Indeed.com, confirms what Chris Daniel says about the importance of learning the "hard" project management skills. Positions that require five or more years of instructional design experience mention project management skills explicitly, with some of the most senior positions mentioning some type of certification or coursework in project management. The combination of instructional design and project management expertise – acquired through training and experience – will give your career that extra boost.

Key Considerations: Avoiding the Dilbert© Project Experience

Now that you know what skills and competencies you need to be a successful L&D project manager, how can you get started so that you don't create or contribute to a Dilbert©-like project experience? Here are some considerations to keep in mind:

- **Why are we doing this?** Whether you are leading your first or your tenth project, it is essential to know what business problem that particular project is intended to solve. If you are creating an instructional intervention, what are the knowledge/skill/ability challenges being addressed? How was the need for this project identified? What benefits will this project provide the organization? Asking these questions will not only demonstrate your professionalism but also your ability to link what you do to the needs and goals of the organization. It is that "bigger picture" ability that separates the entry-level from the advanced practitioner.
- **Friend or foe.** In design, your Context Analysis helps you to identify the various stakeholders of your project. These are the folks who are ultimately affected – positively or negatively – by the project. However, as we saw in Chapter 6, stakeholder identification is often one of the most challenging tasks because new stakeholders may suddenly appear late in the project life cycle, when the costs of change are higher, both in terms of time and resources. At the start of your project, conduct

one or two brainstorming sessions with your team and with the client to generate a preliminary list of stakeholders. You can ask known project stakeholders to point out who they think other project stakeholders would be and why they should be on your list. If this project is repeat business from an existing client, review any documented lessons learned to gauge previous experiences with specific stakeholders. Importantly, determine whether each of the stakeholders has the power and legitimacy to sink or boost your project. A basic table or spreadsheet – called a stakeholder registry – with a list of names in the first column, followed by additional columns with contact information, project knowledge, interest in the project, power/influence, and project expectations is a good start. However, be careful with whom you share your stakeholder registry. Imagine what would happen if your key client contact finds out that you have categorized him/her as "foe"?

- **Documentation prevents *memoritis interruptus*.** Paperwork is probably not one of your favorite pastimes. Nevertheless, human memory is not the most reliable way of keeping track of your project. You may already be working with detailed instructional design documents but you still need to be clear and specific about the work required to convert that instructional design document into a concrete deliverable. What to document is dictated by project size and scope, as is the level of detail in each document. Even Agile projects have some documentation. In addition, traditional patterns of documentation in your organization will determine the layout of your documents, along with the technology systems used to capture and archive project documentation. Whether your organization has its own set of templates for project documentation or you adopt one of the many publicly available project management templates, the basic documentation must-haves include (a) project description, scope, requirements/specifications, and desired project outcomes (success/failure criteria with metrics) with a formal sign-off from the person(s) authorizing the project; (b) the resources – people, technology, processes, budget – needed for the project and how those resources will be secured; (c) potential project risks and how often those risks will be monitored; (d) stakeholder communication frequency and methods; (e) formal sign-off on deliverables so that you know when you are done; and (f) lessons learned, for the benefit of future projects. The L&D project manager's job is to ensure not only high-quality deliverables but the management of those deliverables from start to finish. The simplest documentation is far better than relying on remembering who said what to whom.

- **Design team as stakeholder.** How design teams are managed, how project documents are organized for quick and efficient access by project team members, and how team members communicate with each other as a workgroup can sink or boost a project as much (if not more) than a challenging client or unengaged project sponsor. By the same token, building unity and trust among team members takes time, and L&D projects sometimes have a completion date of "yesterday." The same "soft" skills and emotional intelligence attributes we use with clients to establish and maintain a shared understanding of project goals and outcomes are also instrumental for project team cohesion and performance. This is where the designer can not only get down in the weeds with details of project progress vs. end goals, but it is also an opportunity to reinforce the value of each team member's contribution to the project's success.

- **Learn from the best.** How do you recognize a top-notch L&D project manager? He/she determines the appropriate processes for each project, maintains continuous communications within the team as well as across the various stakeholders, and creates an environment of trust. He/she demonstrates a commitment to team success by keeping the project sponsor informed and engaged so that the team retains the resources, support, and skills necessary for effective project completion. Finally, he/she creates a shared vision of the outcome so that all stakeholders – internal and external – are singing from the same songbook when it comes to perceptions of what the ultimate outcome of the project is going to be. If there is one or more of these exemplary L&D project managers in your organization, pick their brains, ask to work with them on a project. Share your mutual strengths and weaknesses; it is an excellent opportunity for you both to develop professionally.

- **Stuff does happen.** The most experienced L&D project manager will get hit by some unforeseen event or circumstance. The green status light turns to amber and the urge to internalize and stress takes over. This is where the project manager as strategic thinker takes over. Taking that step back and brainstorming with your team to determine what is happening and why, along with feasible options to get back on track, not only helps resolve the unexpected issue but contributes to team cohesion and trust. *But what if my team and I can't resolve the issue?* Unless you and your team members are all-knowing superheroes, there will be times that no viable alternative comes to mind. In such cases, there is nothing wrong with going to the project sponsor or your department head to pick his/her brain. The person who authorized this project in the first place has a vested interest in the project's success, even if it's just a question of failure reflecting negatively on him/her. He/she may also have deeper insights into the issue at hand. Framing your request for help in terms of the desire for project success enhances your credibility as a business-focused professional.

Project Management Self-Check

You are managing an L&D team that is creating a mentoring program for an external client. The program is part of the client's succession planning strategy to identify and groom the next generation of the organization's senior management. You are having difficulty communicating with the client-designated subject matter expert (SME) who is providing important content for your team's project. According to your stakeholder registry, the SME prefers email communications, but has not replied to your last two emails requesting content. As the project manager, what strategy might you use to help improve communications?

a) Put all communications in writing;
b) Put all communications on your project website;
c) Use several different methods to communicate with this person; or
d) Ask the project sponsor or your boss to find a better person to provide the content.

Of the four options, (c) is the optimal choice. The SME is a critical stakeholder who is also probably a very busy person whose attention is difficult to capture. Text message, voice mail, or a request to one of the SME's colleagues to help you contact the SME are some viable alternatives. At the same time, you should be checking whether or not your emails are communicating the relevant information as described in your stakeholder registry. Do your email messages have an attention getting subject line? Is the body of each message succinct, easy to understand, and free of design jargon? For instance, a SME may not know the meaning of *terminal and enabling objectives* but does know the meaning of *performance outcomes*. Finally, have you reinforced the project's benefits from the SME's perspective? The "what's in it for me" (WIFM) factor speaks to the reasons for the SME's involvement in the project and what project success means to him/her.

Food for Thought

1 Your supervisor has just placed you in charge of a new project to review and evaluate all of the compliance training housed in your organization's learning management system (LMS). She has assigned two SMEs and one entry-level instructional designer to your project team. The LMS administrator is your technical point of contact. You have never worked with any of these individuals before. In that case, how would you go about building a cohesive project team?

2 Think back to the L&D projects on which you have worked – **but not managed** – in the past five years. Select one that you believe to have been a clear success. Describe that project in terms of the following questions:
   • Why do you think the project was a success?
   • How did the project manager build and manage the project team?
   • How well did the project manager establish and maintain a shared vision of project outcomes with all stakeholders?
   • How can others in the organization tap into the lessons learned from that project?

3 Now, think back to the L&D projects that **you** have managed in the last five years. Select one that was the most successful. Describe that project in terms of the following questions:
- Why was that project the most successful of all the projects you have managed?
- How did you build and manage the project team?
- How well did you establish and maintain a shared vision of project outcomes with all stakeholders?
- How can others in your organization tap into the lessons learned from that project?

4 How would you summarize some of the lessons you have learned from projects that have failed? The lessons could be from projects that you managed or projects in which you participated but did not manage.

Up Next

In this chapter, we have (a) reviewed the current state of Project Management as a field of study; (b) explored the relationship between project management and instructional design as separate but complementary processes and professions; (c) identified the must-have skills and behaviors of the effective L&D project manager; and (d) identified some key considerations in developing our own project management abilities to avoid a Dilbert©-like project experience. The next chapter addresses another results-focused area that is essential for professional success. That area is evaluation of learning's impact on the business with metrics and measures.

References

Allen, M., & Sites, R. (2012). *Leaving ADDIE for SAM: An Agile Model for Developing the Best Learning Experiences*. Alexandria, VA: ASTD Press.

Allen, S., & Hardin, P. (2008). Developing instructional technology products using effective project management practices. *Journal of Computing in Higher Education, 19*(2), 72–97.

ATD Certification Institute. (2017). The ATD Competency Model™. Retrieved from www.astd.org/Certification/Competency-Model.

Benson, A. D., Moore, J. L., & Williams van Rooij, S. (Eds.). (2013). *Cases on Educational Technology Planning, Design, and Implementation: A Project Management Perspective*. Hershey, PA: IGI Global.

Blomquist, T., Hollgren, M., Nilsson, A., & Soderholm, A. (2010). Project-as-practice: In search of project management research that matters. *Project Management Journal, 41*(1), 5–16.

Bolin, A. U. (2012). Salvaging value from project failure. *Performance Improvement, 51*(5), 12–16.

Brill, J., Bishop, M., & Walker, A. (2006). The competencies and characteristics required of an effective project manager: A web-based Delphi study. *Educational Technology Research and Development, 54*(2), 115–40.

Byers, C. (2005). Multi-level alignment model: transforming face-to-face into e-instructional programs. *Journal of Workplace Learning, 17*(5/6), 346–58.

Carden, L. L., & Egan, T. M. (2008). Human resource development and project management: Key connections. *Human Resource Development Review, 7*(3), 309–38.

Cicmil, S., Williams, T., Thomas, J., & Hodgson, D. (2006). Rethinking project management research: researching the actuality of projects. *International Journal of Project Management, 24*(8), 675–86.

Conrad, K., & TrainingLinks. (2000). *Instructional Design for Web-Based Training.* Amherst, MA: HRD Press.

Cox, S., & Osguthorpe, R. (2003). How do instructional design professionals spend their time? *TechTrends, 47*(3), 45–7.

Crawford, J. K. (2007). *Project Management Maturity Model.* Boca Raton, FL: Auerbach/CRC Press.

Creasy, T., & Anantatmula, V. S. (2013). From every direction – How personality traits and dimensions of project managers can conceptually affect project success. *Project Management Journal, 44*(6), 36–51.

Darrell, V., Baccarini, D., & Love, P. E. D. (2010). Demystifying the folklore of the accidental project manager in the public sector. *Project Management Journal, 41*(5), 56–63.

Department of Information Resources (2014). Benefits Realization Review Gate. Retrieved from www.dir.texas.gov/management/projectdelivery/projectframework/benefits/Pages/Overview.aspx.

Dick, W., Carey, L., & Carey, J. (2005). *The Systematic Design of Instruction* (6th ed.). New York, NY: Prentice-Hall.

Dickinson, M. (2006). Evolution of an e-learning developers guide: Do you really need one? Learning Solutions e-Magazine, 1–8.

Dobrovolny, J., Lamos, J., Sims, R., & Spannaus, T. (2002). Should instructional designers be project managers? Paper presented at the World Conference on Educational Multimedia, Hypermedia and Telecommunications, Denver, CO.

Ellis, R. K. (2015). Understanding agile instructional design. Retrieved from www.td.org/Publications/Newsletters/Links/2015/01/understanding-agile.

Fabac, J. (2006). Project management for systematic training. *Advances in Developing Human Resources, 8*(4), 540–7.

Floricel, S., Bonneau, C., Aubry, M., & Sergi, V. (2014). Extending project management research: insights from social theories. *International Journal of Project Management, 32*(7), 1091–1107.

Garel, G. (2013). A history of project management models: From pre-models to the standard models. *International Journal of Project Management, 31*(5), 663–9.

Gentry, C. (1994). *Introduction to Instructional Development: Process and Technique.* Belmont, CA: Wadsworth.

Giller, S., & Barker, P. (2006). An evolving methodology for managing multimedia courseware production. *Innovations in Education and Teaching International, 43*(3), 303–12.

Greer, M. (1992). *ID Project Management: Tools and Techniques for Instructional Designers and Developers.* Englewood Cliffs, NJ: Educational Technology.

Hastie, S., & Wojewoda, S. (2015). Standish Group 2015 CHAOS report – Q&A with Jennifer Lynch. Retrieved from www.infoq.com/articles/standish-chaos-2015.

Highsmith, J. (2001). History: The Agile Manifesto. Retrieved from http://agilemanifesto.org/history.html.

Highsmith, J. (2009). *Agile Project Management: Creating Innovative Products* (2nd ed.). Boston, MA: Addison-Wesley Professional.

Horine, G. M. (2005). *Absolute Beginner's Guide to Project Management.* Indianapolis, IN: Que Publishing.

Huang, C. (2005). Designing high-quality interactive multimedia learning modules. *Computerized Medical Imaging and Graphics, 29*, 223–33.

Humphrey, W. S. (1992). *Introduction to Software Process Improvement.* Pittsburgh, PA: Carnegie Mellon University.

Ibbs, C. W., & Kwak, Y. H. (2000). Assessing project management maturity. *Project Management Journal, 31*(1), 32–43.

IBSTPI. (2014). Instructional Designer Competencies – Welcome to ibstpi. Retrieved from http://ibstpi.org/instructional-design-competencies/.

International Project Management Association. (2015). About IPMA | IPMA: International Project Management Association. Retrieved from http://ipma.ch/about/.

Jenner, S. (2012). Advances in project management: Benefits realization – Building on (un)safe foundations. *PM World Journal, 1*(1), 1–6.

Jorgensen, M. (2014). Failure factors of small software projects at a global out-sourcing marketplace. *Journal of Systems and Software, 92*, 157–69.

Jugdev, K., & Wishart, P. (2014). Mutual caring – resolving habituation through awareness: supporting meaningful learning from projects. *Project Management Journal, 45*(2), 66–82.

Kerzner, H. R. (2005). *Using the Project Management Maturity Model: Strategic Planning for Project Management.* Hoboken, NJ: John Wiley & Sons.

Knutson, D., Cain, T., Hurtubise, L., & Kreger, C. (2006). Lessons learned: Developing e-learning to teach physical examination. *The Clinical Teacher, 3*(3), 163–9.

Koller, C., Frankenfield, J., & Sarley, C. (2000). Twelve tips for developing educational media in a community-based teaching hospital. *Medical Teacher, 22*(1), 7–10.

Kwak, Y. H., & Anbari, F. T. (2009). Analyzing project management research: Perspectives from top management journals. *International Journal of Project Management, 27*(5), 435–46.

Lalonde, P. L., Bourgault, M., & Findeli, A. (2010). Building pragmatist theories of PM practice: Theorizing the act of project management. *Project Management Journal, 41*(5), 21–36.

Larman, C. (2003). *Agile and Iterative Development: A Manager's Guide.* Boston, MA: Addison-Wesley Professional.

Layng, J. (1997). Parallels between project management and instructional design. *Performance Management, 36*(6), 16–20.

Li, D., & Shearer, R. (2005). Project management for online course development. *Distance Learning, 2*(4), 19–23.

Mathiassen, L., & Napier, N. P. (2013). Exploring win-win contracts: an appreciative inquiry into IT project management. *Journal of Information Technology Theory and Application (JITTA), 14*(3), 5–29.

McDaniel, K., & Liu, M. (1996). A study of project management techniques for developing interactive multimedia programs: A practitioner's perspective. *Journal of Research on Computing in Education, 29*(Fall), 29–48.

Morrison, G. R., Ross, S. M., Kalman, H. K., & Kemp, J. E. (2013). *Designing Effective Instruction* (7th ed.). Hoboken, NJ: John Wiley & Sons.

Mullaly, M. (2014). The role of agency in project initiation decisions. *International Journal of Managing Projects in Business, 7*(3), 518–35.

Neibert, J. (2014). Effective performance with A.G.I.L.E. instructional design. Learning Solutions Magazine. Retrieved from www.learningsolutionsmag.com/articles/1346/effective-performance-wotj-agile-instructional-design.

Nelson, R. R. (2005). Project retrospectives: Evaluating project success, failure, and everything in between. *MIS Quarterly Executive, 4*(3), 361–72.

Nixon, P., Harrington, M., & Parker, D. (2012). Leadership performance is significant to project success or failure: A critical analysis. *International Journal of Productivity and Performance Management, 61*(2), 204–16.

Okoli, C., & Carillo, K. (2012). The best of adaptive and predictive methodologies: Open source software development, a balance between agility and discipline. *International Journal of Information Technology and Management, 11*(1–2), 153–66.

Pan, C. C. (2012). A symbiosis between instructional systems design and project management. *Canadian Journal of Learning & Technology, 38*(1), 1–15.

Pollack, J. (2007). The changing paradigms of project management. *International Journal of Project Management, 25*(3), 266–74.

Pollack, J., & Adler, D. (2015). Emerging trends and passing fads in project management research: a scientometric analysis of changes in the field. *International Journal of Project Management, 33*(1), 236–48.

PRINCE2.com. (2017). PRINCE2 Processes | PRINCE2.com. Retrieved from www.prince2.com/usa/what-is-prince2.

Project Management Institute. (2013). *A Guide to the Project Management Body of Knowledge* (5th ed.). Newton Square, PA: Project Management Institute.

Project Management Institute. (2016). Pulse of the profession: the high cost of low performance. Retrieved from www.pmi.org/~/media/PDF/Business-Solutions/PMI_Pulse_2014.ashx.

Project Management Institute. (2017). About PMI. Retrieved from www.pmi.org/about.

Rajkumar, G., & Alagarsamy, K. (2013). The most common factors for the failure of software development projects. *International Journal of Computer Science & Applications (TIJCSA), 1*(11), 74–7.

Rowe, S. (2007). *Project Management for Small Projects.* Vienna, VA: Management Concepts.

Schramm, J., Phil, M., Coombs, J., & Boyd, R. (2013). The top workplace trends according to HR professionals. Retrieved from www.shrm.org/ResourcesAndTools/hr-topics/behavioral-competencies/Documents/13-0146%20workplace_forecast_full_fnl.pdf.

Smith, A. (2003). Surveying practicing project managers on curricular aspects of project management programs: A resource-based approach. *Project Management Journal, 34*(2), 26–33.

Smith, P. L., & Ragan, T. J. (2004). *Instructional Design* (3rd ed.). Hoboken, NJ: John Wiley & Sons.

Soderlund, J. (2004). Building theories of project management: Past research, questions for the future. *International Journal of Project Management, 22*(3), 183–91.

Stubbs, S. (2002). How did you manage to do that? An instructional multimedia production management process. *Journal of Interactive Instruction Development, 14*(4), 25–32.

Thomas, J., & Mullaly, M. (2008). *Researching the Value of Project Management.* Newtown Square, PA: Project Management Institute.

Williams van Rooij, S. (2010). Project management in instructional design: ADDIE is not enough. *British Journal of Educational Technology, 41*(5), 852–64.

Williams van Rooij, S. (2011). Instructional design and project management: complementary or divergent? *Educational Technology Research and Development, 59*(1), 139–58.

Williams van Rooij, S. (2013). The career path to instructional design project management: An expert perspective from the US professional services sector. *International Journal of Training and Development, 17*(1), 33–53.

Williams van Rooij, S. (2014). Jack Waterkamp: Managing scope change in an instructional design project. In P. A. Ertmer, J. A. Quinn, & K. D. Glazewski (Eds.), *The ID Casebook: Case Studies in Instructional Design* (pp. 259–70). Upper Saddle River, NJ: Pearson Education.

Wysocki, R. (2011). *Effective Project Management: Traditional, Agile, Extreme* (6th ed.). Indianapolis, IN: Wiley Publishing.

Yang, C., Moore, D., & Burton, J. (1995). Managing courseware production: an instructional design model with a software engineering approach. *Educational Technology Research and Development*, 43(4), 60–70.

11 Evaluation
Metrics, Measures, Dashboards

Why do we spend so much on training?
How do we know that this coaching program is paying off for us?
What's the return on our investment for that learning management system?

If you have ever heard these questions about a learning initiative or a learning technology software application, you are not alone. Most learning professionals have experienced that "Dilbert© vs. The Boss" moment at some point in their careers, often on more than one occasion. Like Dilbert©, you may feel that you spend a great deal of time trying to articulate the value of your work to a stakeholder or stakeholders who seem(s) determined **not** to understand.

For the entry-level and mid-career learning designer, the idea of having to "defend" your work may seem puzzling. On the one hand, news from the Learning and Development industry suggests that organizations continue to invest in their employees by offering opportunities for learning. For example, in its 2016 report on the state of the industry, ATD estimated that organizations spent $1,252 per employee on direct learning expenditure (direct costs associated with learning programs) for 2015, a slight increase over the previous year (Ho, 2016). The majority (61 percent) of this was spent internally, with external services (28 percent) and tuition reimbursement (11 percent) accounting for the balance of expenditures. Moreover, the proportion of total expenditure allocated to internal learning and development has been increasing, while external services and tuition reimbursement allocations have been declining. This suggests that organizations are focusing more on strengthening the skills/competencies that will directly benefit the organization rather than on degree programs and general skills courses.

Not surprisingly, the growth in internal learning and development was largely attributable to an increase in online learning opportunities at the expense of face-to-face classroom-based training.

In addition to investments in learning and development, organizations remain eager to tout their recognition of the relationship between learning and business performance. A scan of the scholarly and practitioner literature on the topic of employee learning and development suggests that organizations recognize the importance of a knowledgeable workforce to organizational success, with training as the most studied mechanism for promoting learning. For example, a search of the journal *Human Resource Development Quarterly* from 2000 to 2016 using the keyword "training" yields 460 articles focusing on the business impact of training. Other publications have also devoted attention to the business benefits of training. In their review of the training literature from 2000 to 2008, Aguinis and Kraiger (2009) outlined the benefits of training in terms of job performance, organizational performance (effectiveness and profitability), and national economic performance, themes that recur in studies conducted in international contexts as well as US contexts (Aragon-Sanchez, Barba-Aragon, & Sanz-Valle, 2003; Bartel, 2000; Zwick, 2006).

Despite the ongoing investment in learning and development, decision-makers continue to ask for evidence of learning's contribution to the bottom line. Some argue that C-level decision-makers have not been presented with meaningful evidence about the positive relationship between learning activities and business success (O'Leonard, 2013; Short & Harris, 2010), while others criticize the application of a one-size-fits-all approach to measurement for all learning and development programs, regardless of the impact of these programs on the business or the industry sector in which the business operates (Barnett & Mattox II, 2010).

Nevertheless, metrics, measures, and dashboard-style executive reporting models designed to demonstrate the business impact of learning have been available for years. The scholarly literature offers several strategies for mapping employee learning to business performance, including focusing on learning transfer (Brinkerhoff & Apking, 2001), designing instructional interventions with specific business, performance, and learning objectives in mind (Hodges, 2002), return-on-investment (ROI) models (Phillips, 1994; Phillips, 1997a, b) or descriptions of what organizations should be doing to ensure that investments in employee learning yield concrete business results (Wick, Pollock, & Jefferson, 2010). However, studies vary in terms of how learning and business impact are defined and, consequently, how they are measured, offering little insight as to whether definitional consensus exists within a particular industry sector let alone across industries. On the practitioner side, *Chief Learning Officer* magazine regularly features articles focused on learning metrics and measurement, particularly as related to the alignment of learning with business needs. Digital dashboards – graphical representations of business performance on key indicators, such as revenue, number of new contracts, and number of new employees, constructed from data points collected across the organization – provide an organization's leadership with an at-a-glance view of the business, enabling leaders to make data-driven decisions. Consultants have developed entire practices dedicated to helping organizations identify, collect, and analyze data that demonstrate the business impact of learning.

Despite all of this activity, there is no universal consensus as to how learning's impact should be measured. Moreover, there are few examples of organizations that are doing it successfully. In fact, most organizations appear to rely on indirect measures, such as customer satisfaction or employee engagement, along with operational throughput data (e.g., number of training events offered and number of training participants per event), to measure impact rather than on financial metrics, such as revenue or market share (HCM Advisor Group, 2012). The primary barriers to more vigorous impact measurement have included, among others, a lack of personnel skilled in measurement and statistical analyses, and a systematic way of collecting and storing the data needed for business impact measurement.

But measurement is an integral part of the instructional design process, you say. Yes, you are right. The instructional design process includes three types of evaluation: formative evaluation, used throughout the design process as a diagnostic for making improvements to the instructional product prior to launch; summative evaluation, to determine the efficiency and effectiveness of the instructional product right after instruction is completed, along with attitudes and reactions; and confirmative evaluation, to affirm instructional efficiency and effectiveness after some time has passed (Morrison, Ross, Kalman, & Kemp, 2013). But designers use evaluation primarily from a training and development perspective. As we have seen in previous chapters, designers now work on a variety of projects, not just training projects. Just as the scope of your work as a designer has changed, so must the scope of your evaluation efforts.

Does this mean that I have to learn a whole new set of evaluation models for every learning opportunity other than training? you ask. Thankfully, no. The same evaluation models that are prevalent from an instructional design and program evaluation perspective are also the basis for evaluating learning opportunities that do not include formal instruction. This chapter will help you capitalize on what you already know about evaluation so that you can apply that knowledge to any performance improvement effort you design. In this chapter, we will

- Examine the current landscape of evaluation models, metrics, and measures that tend to dominate the scholarly and practitioner literature;
- Describe some tips for applying the same evaluation tools and techniques to a variety of learning and performance imporvement opportunities; and
- Summarize some key lessons learned for the effective use of evaluation.

The Evaluation Landscape

When evaluating anything – be it a learning initiative, a computer software package, or a new investment opportunity – you need to have a very clear idea of (a) why you want to evaluate (the purpose); (b) what you are going to evaluate (the components); (c) which criteria to use for comparison (the benchmarks); (d) how you are going to evaluate (the model or method); and (e) what mechanisms you are going to use to make the results of your evaluation actionable (data-driven decision-making). This requires a fairly clear and accepted definition of the thing that you are evaluating. For tangible products like a computer software package or investment opportunity, features/functions, costs, and other components tend to have industry-standard, accepted definitions and, thus, are observable, measurable, and can be analyzed in ways that facilitate buying decisions. Unlike tangible products, learning has no industry-standard, accepted definition. As we saw in Chapter 3, learning is one of those broad, abstract constructs that has been defined and redefined for more than a century. Because of the challenges associated with defining when and how learning occurs, measurement and evaluation models of business impact are in no short supply.

Given the many approaches to and definitions of measurement and evaluation, let's work with Wang and Spitzer's (2005) relatively broad definition of measurement as the collection and analysis of data according to a specific standard, and evaluation as the making of judgments based on the measurement results. Studies of learning measurement and evaluation have largely focused on two target audiences: Learning and Development (L&D) practitioners responsible for the design, development, deployment, and evaluation of the outcomes of learning initiatives, and organization decision-makers charged with evaluating the extent to which all L&D initiatives map to strategic goals and, thus, determine the funding of such initiatives. Although all evaluation models have decision-making as their intended output or usage (Holton & Naquin, 2005), the L&D practitioner conducts evaluation for program and process improvements, as well as for determining the merit or worth of the learning initiative (Scriven, 1996).

Models for L&D Practitioners

The roots of measurement and evaluation of learning initiatives lie in the literature on training evaluation, where the target audience for the evaluation is the L&D practitioner and the goal of evaluation is to determine whether or not a particular training intervention accomplished what it was designed to accomplish based on a combination of objective learner assessments, such as quizzes conducted during training and subjective post-training assessments, such as satisfaction surveys. Kirkpatrick's Four Level Evaluation Model – Reaction or how well the learners liked the learning process; Learning or the extent to which the learners gained the knowledge and skills the training was supposed to provide; Behavior or the degree of performance of the newly learned skills; and Results or the tangible outcomes for the business in terms of reduced cost, increased production, etc. (Kirkpatrick, 1959, 1996) – is probably the most well known of these models. Some training professionals contend that the model is not just for training but can also be used to assess a variety of employee development activities, such as performance reviews or informal learning activities (Craig, 1996; Nadler, 1984).

Although more than 50 years old, the Kirkpatrick model remains the most popular for evaluating training. However, the model is not without criticism, including studies that show: (a) there is little correlation between how learners react to training and how they actually perform on the job after the training (Alliger & Janak, 1989); (b) the model does not take into account other variables that affect post-training performance (Holton, 1996); and (c) the model does not reflect twenty-first-century socio-economic realities or cost and value considerations (Giangreco, Carugati, & Sebastiano, 2010). Kirkpatrick sought to address the cost-value criticism by updating the model to include Return on Expectations (ROE), which involves a dialogue with senior management to set a clear definition of what management perceives as value and how that perception can be operationalized into concrete behaviors (Kirkpatrick & Kirkpatrick, 2010). Nevertheless, Wick, Pollock, Jefferson, and Flanagan (2006) noted that evidence of the use of the Kirkpatrick model to demonstrate business impact – defined as the extent to which the resources spent on training contribute to the overall health and prosperity of the organization – is sparse at best.

Holton's (1996) model bypasses learner reactions and takes a deeper dive into individual performance and mediating variables that affect outcomes, such as motivation to learn, perceptions of training, and transfer climate. Holton's model also proposes linkages between learning, individual performance, and organizational performance. Kraiger's decision-based model (2002) focuses on three target areas for evaluation: training content and design as measured by participant reactions; changes in learner attitudes, knowledge, and behavior; and training benefits to the organization in terms of learner job performance, training transfer climate, and results. The model stresses measurements focused on the intended purpose for evaluation (decision-making, marketing, feedback to participants, instructors, instructional designers). The model provides examples of the types of measures to be used for each evaluation target (e.g., changes in participant behavior) and a taxonomy that includes assessing the training program, changes in the learner, and changes in the organization. There are also step-by-step guidelines and a checklist for evaluating in-house employee development programs (Peterson & Kraiger, 2003). There are a few empirical studies that incorporate Kraiger's use of trainee reactions to online training programs (Long, DuBois, & Faley, 2008), healthcare training (Beech, 2008), and sales training (Kauffeld & Lehmann-Willenbrock, 2010). However, there is little evidence that Kraiger's model has been used by either scholars or practitioners to measure business impact beyond training participant perceptual measures.

The Brinkerhoff Success Case Method has been offered as an alternative to Kirkpatrick. The Success Case Method is a quasi-mixed methods approach that combines comparative analysis of high vs. low post-training performance with case study and narrative storytelling. The essential purpose of a Success Case study is to find out how well an organizational initiative (e.g., a training program, a new work method) is working, as well as identify and explain the contextual factors that differentiate successful from unsuccessful adopters of new initiatives (Brinkerhoff, 2003). The method has two components: The first component involves an evaluator identifying training participants who were the most successful and the least successful in applying their learning on the job, selecting a random sample of each and conducting deep-dive interviews to determine the exact nature of and reasons for the (non)success. The second component involves evaluator documentation of the interviews, turning the interviews into brief but compelling stories to serve as the basis for lessons learned in decision-making.

The model has been criticized for being applicable only in the most ideal cases where the employer and the training organizers are closely related, where an evaluation design has already been built during the training process, or where there are no competing deadlines or reduced budgets (Holton & Naquin, 2005). Nevertheless, there has been some empirical research in which the Brinkerhoff model has been applied to evaluate programs in the non-profit sector (Coryn, Schroter, & Hanssen, 2009), in health education (Olson, Shershneva, & Brownstein, 2011), and in library science (Kim, 2006). Still unclear is the extent to which the Brinkerhoff model has been adopted by practitioners to measure the business impact of employee learning, both formal and informal.

Other examples include the Kraiger, Ford, and Salas (1993) model based on three categories of learning outcomes (cognitive, skill-based, and affective) and the evaluation measures appropriate for each of these categories, and the Kaufman and Keller (1994) five levels of Enabling and Reaction, Acquisition, Application, Organizational Outputs and Societal Outcomes. Table 11.1 summarizes the measurement and evaluation models that focus on L&D practitioners.

Models for Decision-Makers

Evaluation models targeting decision-makers seek to determine the contribution of learning to an organization's bottom line using finance-based indicators such as Return on Investment (ROI). Jack Phillips' ROI model was among the earliest of these finance-based models. The Phillips's model defines business impact in terms of an organization's economic profitability and focuses on ROI as one measure of an organization's financial outcomes. The model monetizes the results of a specific training program by asking the participants or their supervisors to assign dollar values to those results and provide a confidence level ranging from 0 to 100 percent to the

Table 11.1 Summary of Measurement and Evaluation Models Targeting Learning and Development Practitioners

Authors	Key Model Concepts	Working Definitions
Kirkpatrick (1959, 1996, 2010)	• Reaction-Learning-Behavior-Results • Return on Expectations (ROE) added to four levels • Focus on training program/intervention and its results	• Learning through training; potentially applicable to other employee development activities • Impact = business results derived from learning interventions as measured by (a) on-the-job performance/Level 3 and (b) quantifiable business results (e.g., reduced costs, increased production)/Level 4
Kraiger, Ford and Salas (1993)	• Cognitive, skill-based, affective learning outcomes • Each type of learning outcome includes particular categories and foci of measurement	• Learning through training • Impact = positive attitudinal changes toward learning and ability to perform skills without conscious monitoring
Kaufman and Keller (1994)	• Enabling and Reaction-Acquisition-Application-Organizational Outputs-Societal Outcomes • Planning and results based on identity of clients and beneficiaries of the deliverables	• Learning through training; potentially applicable to other employee development activities • Impact = benefits, performance improvements, cost-benefit/cost consequences analysis, such as timely outputs

Holton (1996)	• Influence of mediating variables (motivation, perceptions of training, transfer climate) • Relationships between learning, individual performance, organizational performance	• Learning through training • Impact = transfer to on-the-job performance
Kraiger (2002)	• Assesses the training program, changes in the learner and changes in the organization • Focus on intended purpose for evaluation (decision-making, marketing, feedback to participants, instructors, instructional designers)	• Learning through training; potentially applicable to other employee development activities • Impact = outcomes at the intervention, learner and organizational level as measured by trainee reactions
Brinkerhoff (2003)	• Success Case Method focusing on systems • Evidence- and story-based • Focus is the performance management system and the role that learning played in it to achieve results • Contextual reasons for training transfer/successful vs. unsuccessful cases	• Learning through training and the interaction of training with performance management factors • Impact = business results derived from learning interventions and employee performance as measured by ROI and statements of benefits derived from actual cases, verifiable records, and direct evidence of business value in specific cases of training usage

dollar values (Phillips, 1997a,b). The Phillips model involves six steps for operationalization: (a) collect data regarding the costs and benefits of the intervention; (b) isolate the effects of training using quantitative and qualitative data from pre- and post-training evaluations; (c) convert quantitative data and, if possible, qualitative data to monetary values; (d) calculate monetary benefits and summarize (in narrative form) non-monetary benefits; (e) calculate monetary costs of the training; and (f) calculate ROI using the accounting formula (total benefit-total costs)/total cost × 100 percent.

Phillips's ROI model has been lauded for enhancing awareness of the importance of evaluation and ROI measurement among decision-makers and scholars alike (Alexander & Christoffersen, 2006; Wang, Dou, & Li, 2002). Furthermore, there have been a number of empirical studies using Phillips's ROI to evaluate the impact of training and of other performance improvement interventions in a variety of industries and countries (Aksu & Yildiz, 2011; Czeropski & Le, 2010; Laing & Andrews, 2011; Percival, Cozzarin, & Formaneck, 2013).

Nevertheless, the ROI model has been criticized for excluding indicators that do not lend themselves to monetization, for being backward-looking and, thus, unhelpful for forecasting purposes, for subjectivity in relying on perceived monetary value, and for excluding non-monetary returns – customer satisfaction, employee job satisfaction, etc. – that have an economic impact on business results (Cairns, 2012; Ford, 2004; Giangreco, Carugati, & Sebastiano, 2010; Patel, 2010; Wang, Dou, & Li, 2002; Wang & Wang, 2005). Moreover, there is limited evidence of widespread adoption of the model in either the public or the private sector. Other finance-based models include Robinson and Robinson's (1989) training cost-benefit model, Kaufman and Watkins's (1996) Organizational Elements Model (OEM) training cost-consequences analysis, and Wang, Dou, and Li's (2002) systems approach to measuring the monetary and non-monetary ROI of learning and development investments.

The Learning Effectiveness Measurement (LEM) model purports to tie employee learning – defined as training – directly to business results. It involves an iterative process of creating a causal chain analysis to trace the impact of learning through a chain of causes and effects – from skills, knowledge, and attitudes to behavior to individual and team performance to organization performance – culminating with financial business results. Originally developed at IBM, LEM encompasses the following phases (Spitzer, 2005): (a) predictive measurement via causal chain analysis, performed before an intervention is selected or designed to help make the best learning investments, target the highest performance improvement opportunities, and provide data to increase the effectiveness of the intervention; (b) baseline measurement, done any time before the intervention is implemented; (c) formative measurement during design, to ensure that predictive measurement data are implemented in the design and implementation plan so that maximum effectiveness can be realized; (d) in-process measurement during implementation to track intervention effectiveness during deployment and enable corrective actions in a timely manner; and (e) retrospective measurement, performed after the intervention is fully implemented to collect post-intervention data and provide input for final evaluative decision-making.

Although the LEM model has received some recognition for its conceptual contributions to learning impact measurement (Aguinis & Kraiger, 2009; Griffin, 2012), there has been little empirical research validating the model. Moreover, there is little evidence of the extent to which adoption of LEM has advanced beyond IBM.

The Bersin & Associates Impact Measurement Framework (Bersin, 2008) takes a more holistic approach to training evaluation by offering an implementation-ready approach to capturing training's impact on the business. Using the four phases of training – problem definition, training solution, trainee performance improvement, and organizational performance improvement – the model helps determine what to measure across all four phases, including sustaining alignment with business goals, efficiency of training development processes, and the programmatic, environmental, and organizational elements that influence impact. The nine measurement areas cover quantitative and qualitative key performance indicators of satisfaction and learning, as well as direct impact measures of individual and organizational performance.

In 2011, the Bersin model was updated to include three new indicators to measure the impact of informal learning: Contribution, defined as the frequency with which employees contribute content to the organization's knowledge-sharing system as well as the percentage of all employees who contribute; Feedback, defined as the mechanism for identifying the popularity and success of a content item (think of the Facebook "Like" function); and Activity, or volume of traffic to the organization's informal learning-knowledge-sharing systems (Bersin, 2011).

The Bersin Impact Measurement Framework seems to resonate with practitioners. In addition to the many case studies published by Bersin & Associates, organizational adaptations and variations on the model have been applied to case studies of game-based training (Austin, 2013), and the model has been integrated into the learning and talent management measurement technology offerings of one of the world's largest human capital analytics vendors (KnowledgeAdvisors, 2009). With the 2013 acquisition of Bersin & Associates by Deloitte's Human Capital Consulting practice, there is the potential for widespread adoption of the model among Deloitte's 5,000+ clients worldwide. Table 11.2 summarizes the measurement and evaluation models that focus on decision-makers.

Table 11.2 Summary of Measurement and Evaluation Models Targeting Decision-Makers

Authors	Key Model Concepts	Working Definitions
Robinson and Robinson (1989)	• Focus on five categories of expenses: direct costs, indirect costs, development costs, overhead costs, compensation for participants • ROI = Operational results/ Training costs	• Learning through training • Impact = ROI
Kaufman and Watkins (1996)	• Two-tiered matrix of elements: outcomes, outputs, products, processes and inputs by what should/could be and what is • Data collected for each element compared to costs for each program as a whole and for all participants	• Learning through training; potentially applicable to any development intervention • Impact = modified ROI
Phillips (1994, 1997)	• Extends Kirkpatrick to five levels including ROI • Ten techniques to isolate the effects of training vs. other sources of business improvement	• Learning through training; potentially applicable to other employee development activities • Impact = economic profitability, specifically accounting-based ROI via perceived monetary values
Wang, Dou, & Li (2002)	• Equation-based model using input, process, output of an intervention	• Learning via any type of intervention • Impact = net effect of intervention that contributes to overall business outcomes
Spitzer (2005)	• Predictive-Baseline-Formative-In-Process-Retrospective LEM model • Alignment with learning design and development phases	• Learning through training • Impact = business results (financial and behavioral based on perceptual ratings) derived from priorities of organization's leaders
Bersin (2008)	• Nine-component model that centers around satisfaction, learning adoption, utility, efficiency, alignment, attainment, individual performance • Contribution-Feedback-Activity to measure the contribution of informal learning	• Learning through training; informal learning through structured activities (e.g., postings to enterprise-supported collaboration sites) • Impact = causal chain of quantitative and qualitative indicators

Summary

The practitioner-focused models and the models targeting decision-makers share some similarities in that they all seek to provide a roadmap to selecting and tracking the key indicators linking employee learning to organizational performance. They are also consistent in acknowledging that different organizations have different perspectives on what constitutes "performance." Nevertheless, there are challenges associated with these models, including (a) focus on the training dimension of learning, with little emphasis on other forms of formal learning or informal learning; (b) wide variation in the meaning of "impact," with working definitions ranging from accounting-based indicators to perceptual measures of value; and (c) limited empirical evidence validating the models or the extent to which they have been adopted.

With all this definitional turbulence, it remains unclear as to what organizations are actually doing to measure the business impact of employee learning. Anecdotal evidence suggests that practitioners use a variety of measures of reductions in cost – reduced employee turnover, decline in the number of sick days taken, etc. – as indicators of the contribution of employee learning to business performance (Bingham & Galagan, 2012). Moreover, there appears to be considerable variation by industry sector.

At this point, you may be thinking, *I'll just focus on measuring learning outcomes and leave the business issues to my boss for now.* Think again! Even if you are an early-career designer, understanding the linkages between business and learning is critical to your success. Dr. Catherine Lombardozzi, industry thought leader and Founder of Learning 4 Learning Professionals, offers her take on the importance of measuring the business impact of learning in *E-Suite Views:*

SvR: Let's talk about business impact measurement. Does that have any relevance for instructional designers, having to measure the business impact of learning? And that includes informal as well as formal learning. What are your thoughts on that?

CL: Of course, measurement is important and business impact is important. The funny thing is, in my experience, business leaders are not all that interested in investing in what it takes to actually measure the things that some learning leaders are saying we have to measure. They're not interested in the deep dives and these scientific comparison studies that show that learning occurred. They're simply interested in the performance outcomes and the business outcomes – and those are already being measured. They don't have to do anything extra, they should already be measuring outcomes. What we need to look at is if there are relationships between the work that we're doing and people's ability to perform. Now, to actually get that variable measured without being confounded by 100,000 other variables is very difficult. I personally am in favor of really good survey design that gets self-reporting from the learners as well as from their management team and validates whether the learning efforts are making people feel like they are more capable doing what it is they are being asked to do.

SvR: How would you respond to critics who say that self-assessments are way too subjective, that people lie or say what is expected? What would you say to that?

CL: I think you need to couple it with a manager's survey. You get reports from the learners themselves but then you couple that with the management survey – I would have to look it up but I'm pretty sure there are also studies that say that self-assessments are not as bad as people think they are. I believe that there's also research that shows that people are pretty good at assessing their own comfort level and some of their own capabilities. You have to use really good survey design, you have to get multiple points of input, triangulate. The effort it takes to do that is still much less than the effort it would take to try to isolate learning as a variable. That is so hard to do; even if you do, you're going to run up against business leaders who are savvy enough to say, "Yes, but I still don't have the performance or you're making assumptions that I don't agree with."

SvR: Speaking of those "yes, but" type of business leaders, there are some business leaders who say of Learning and Development, particularly something that requires resources such as technology or funding or any kind of resource, "I need to know the cost-benefit of my Learning and Development investments and the only thing I understand are dollars and cents," which means monetizing learning outcomes. What would you say to those folks?

CL: You know, I think those kinds of calculations are relatively easy to do on the back of a napkin and if you're satisfied with a back-of-a-napkin calculation, I think that works. I remember in an organization I used to work with, our senior business leader said, "We want an ROI for Learning and Development." So, I said, "Let's talk about how ROI is calculated." I did a lot of research and looked at all the leading thinkers in terms of how that's done and it's based on a set of assumptions that are very arguable. If you can get everybody to agree on the assumptions, then you can do a nice back-of-the-napkin calculation. But cost-benefit doesn't necessarily mean a monetary benefit. There are other benefits. So, you can say, we're going to invest $100,000 in people, time and effort, but what we're going to get out of that is a mentoring program that's going to help improve our bench strength overall and these are the components of the mentoring program we're proposing; this is why we think it's going to work based on research, based on what we know, and based on your own assessments of what you think you'll get out of the mentoring program. You're showing them the benefits in terms of more intangibles rather than saying every one of your mentored employees is going to save the company $100 million or some number.

SvR: Now, suppose you have a client who says, "Okay, you're proposing program X as the solution to my problem. I want to know how you're going to measure the business impact of *that.*" *What would you say to that person?*

CL: They are measuring the business impact. They're coming to you with a learning need because they have business goals that they're trying to achieve. They're already measuring the business impact. To try to isolate the learning impact on the business impact is another issue. So, let's say we're doing a learning program to increase sales. We can try to isolate the people who took the program, and what the difference in their sales numbers was. But sales are also going to be impacted by the economy, what our competitors are doing, by all these other things. So, the sales program may have achieved what we wanted it to achieve but we still can't get the business outcome we want, not because the capability isn't there, but because there are other factors interfering with the number. That's why you need business skills. If you can't make that case, you're up a creek. You've got to really understand how that fits together so that you can articulate it to your business leaders. You need to know what's already being measured that they're trying to impact with the learning effort. It may not even be a business outcome like sales. It could be bench strength, promotability, customer satisfaction scores. There are lots of things they could be measuring that they're looking to impact through the Learning and Development program.

As Dr. Lombardozzi notes, much of the data needed to demonstrate business impact are already being collected. It is up to the L&D team to find out where those data are and how to "translate" those data into actionable recommendations articulated in a language that makes sense to the business leadership. To do this requires tapping into your existing evaluation toolkit.

Tapping into Your Instructional Designer's Evaluation Toolkit

The Starting Point

Before you end up reinventing the wheel, it is important to determine what your organization's current approach is to evaluation. In addition to the L&D professionals in the organization, functional and operational area managers can provide insights into what measurement data are available and where those data are stored. Here is a list of questions to help you conduct a quick audit of your organization's current evaluation approach so that you can better plan and conduct an evaluation of your L&D efforts:

1　Do we evaluate individual initiatives and if so, how and when?
2　Do we take a programmatic view and evaluate all or specific subsets of L&D initiatives and if so, how and when?
3　Who are the people involved in the evaluation process?
4　Were the metrics, measurements, and models that are currently being used constructed with the collaboration and buy-in of our key stakeholders, particularly those with authority over the L&D budget?
5　How does our evaluation approach compare with other companies in our industry sector?
6　Do we evaluate an initiative/program to confirm that it is being carried out as designed and if so, how do we do that?
7　Do we evaluate an initiative/program to determine the extent to which it achieved the intended results?
8　Do we evaluate the extent to which the costs of an initiative/program are justified by the results achieved?
9　What are the business performance indicators against which we evaluate our L&D initiatives?
10　Are the results of our evaluations shared with top management and if so, how?
11　What does management do with the results of our evaluations?

Asking these questions will get others in your organization to start thinking about how mature the organization's measurement approach is (or is not). It will also help you to determine the extent to which the L&D function contributes to your organization's strategic priorities.

Evaluation Planning, How and When

Part of building and sustaining alignment of L&D efforts with business goals is involving the functional and operational stakeholders in reaching agreement on an evaluation plan for each intervention you select. The purpose of an evaluation affects the identification of stakeholders for the evaluation, the selection of specific evaluation approaches, methods and tools, and the timing of evaluation activities. As discussed in Chapter 4, the time to start thinking about evaluation is during the front-end analysis phase, when you are conducting your performance analysis, and cause analysis, when you and your stakeholders are examining the various alternatives for solving a performance problem. Partnering with functional and operational stakeholders will provide a clear definition of performance expectations which you, the learning professional, can "translate" into a set of skills or competencies. You can then make an informed decision about what type of intervention is needed so that the solution is aligned with business needs.

Using the stakeholder identification process discussed in Chapter 6, evaluation planning begins with identifying those who can directly benefit from and use the evaluation results. Depending on the size and scope of the intervention, you want to identify an evaluation stakeholder workgroup of six to ten members who you can engage throughout the plan development process as well as during the implementation of the evaluation. The process of developing your evaluation plan collaboratively with your stakeholders will foster a shared understanding of what it is you are building, why you are building it, and how you will know that the intervention is achieving its intended result. Your evaluation plan also serves as an advocacy tool for evaluation resources based on negotiated priorities and agreed upon stakeholder information needs. Table 11.3 provides an example of a basic worksheet for a leadership development program that you can use to work with your stakeholders to draft an evaluation plan.

As with traditional instructional design, you and your stakeholders may want evaluation to take place iteratively, to encompass the processes and outcomes for each stage of the intervention. Formative evaluation may be used to ensure that the intervention being developed is tested and revised

Table 11.3 Evaluation Purpose Worksheet: Leadership Development Example

Group Interested in an Evaluation	What Is to Be Evaluated	How Will the Results Be Used	Evaluation Purpose
Executive Team	• High-performer readiness for promotion	• Promotion rate of participants over next three years	• Formative • Summative • Confirmative
Business Unit Directors	• Accuracy of identification of high performers qualifying for leadership development program	• Number of candidates completing the program successfully	• Summative • Confirmative

to meet agreed-upon goals. It is particularly useful in the early stages, so that you can make adjustments before making costly investments. The traditional methods used for formative evaluation of instruction – expert review, one-to-one, small group, field test (Morrison, Ross, Kalman, & Kemp, 2013; Tessmer, 1994) – can be used for any intervention aimed at improving performance. However, the pressures of time and resources may require alternative methods. Technology-based tools allow the learning professional to collect and analyze data quickly with limited resources. Social media (wikis, blogs, professional networks such as LinkedIn), focus groups conducted via web conferencing, and online survey tools are some examples of alternative methods.

Once your intervention has been implemented, you want to determine the immediate effectiveness, efficiency, impact, and value of that intervention. Summative evaluation enables you to examine the immediate results of an intervention and make recommendations to decision-makers about the next steps. Typical summative evaluation question areas include:

- What were the immediate changes in knowledge, skills, or attitudes?
- What changes in performance are taking place?
- What are the attitudes toward the intervention itself?
- Does the intervention meet the needs of the organization?

The same tools that you use for formative evaluation can also be used for summative evaluation. However, some organizations may use statistical analyses to identify significant differences in the data, so that there is both a quantitative and a qualitative basis for decision-making. With a basic knowledge of statistics, a learning professional can capitalize on statistical software packages to collect, analyze, and generate reports from summative evaluations.

Organizations also want to determine the impact of an intervention on performance over time, particularly in terms of knowledge and/or skill retention. This is the role of confirmative evaluation. Think of confirmative evaluation as a continuation of summative evaluation, the former immediately after the intervention, the latter after some time has passed. Confirmative evaluation measures the business impact of an intervention from an individual perspective – the change in behavior – and from an organizational perspective – the impact of that change on the business. It also examines the integrity of the intervention over time and identifies any changes in the field, the market, the industry, the organization, that would reduce the sustainability of the content and structure of the intervention.

Your initial audit of your organization's current approach to evaluation will determine which evaluation approach to select from your toolkit and which stakeholders you need to engage to ensure that the evaluation methods, metrics, and measures you select are consistent with organization goals and are feasible given available time and resources. Just as you

Table 11.4 Evaluation Methods Worksheet: Leadership Development Example

Evaluation Question	Indicator/Performance Measure	Method	Data Source	Frequency	Responsibility	Cost Considerations
Does the leadership program meet the needs of the organization?	• Participant vs. non-participant promotion rates after three years	• Quantitative	• HRM System	• Annual check	• John Smith	• None
Do the participants use the leadership skills covered in the program?	• Participant feedback on skills (not) used (and why) • Business unit director feedback on new skills observed in use	• Qualitative • Qualitative	• Interviews • Interviews	• Quarterly • Quarterly	• Liz Slaney • Sandra Niles	• None • None

Table 11.5 Communications Plan Worksheet: Leadership Development Example

Target Audience (Priority)	Goals	Tools	Timetable
Executive Team	• Keep informed of key milestones	• RSS Feed to Executive Dashboard • Email	• Monthly
Business Unit Directors	• Engage in end-to-end design, development, implementation of program	• Status Meeting Reports • 30-second "Highlights" Voicemail	• Bi-monthly • Weekly

do with learning outcomes, your performance indicators/outcomes should be SMART (specific, measurable, achievable, relevant, time-bound). Table 11.4 contains a worksheet using the leadership development program example to help you align your evaluation questions with indicators/performance measures and data sources.

The last but certainly not the least consideration in evaluation is planning for the sharing of lessons learned, communication, and dissemination of the evaluation results. When you discuss with your stakeholders how the evaluation results will be used, you should also determine who should learn about the findings and how they should receive that information. This includes the timing, style, tone, medium, and format of the evaluation reporting. Using the leadership development program as an example, Table 11.5 provides a worksheet for preparing the communications component of your evaluation plan.

Developing your evaluation plan simultaneously with the intervention allows you and your stakeholders to think through the process and resources required for the evaluation. It facilitates the links between intervention design and development and evaluation and creates a feedback loop of information for intervention improvement and decision-making.

Lessons Learned for the Successful Use of Evaluation

Dilbert© often wonders why his engineering projects are not related to his company's priorities. That's a dilemma that you as a learning designer want to avoid at all cost, and the successful use of evaluation is one way to reduce the risk of a disconnect between L&D and organizational goals. The successful use of evaluation can help you to (a) support senior management in developing the organization's overall evaluation strategy, (e.g., identification of the skills/competencies needed to develop current and future talent; (b) work with middle management and supervisory staff to design an evaluation strategy at the program level (e.g., a leadership development program to support the organization's succession planning goals); and (c) plan and implement the evaluation of a specific learning and development initiative (e.g., a series of e-learning modules to introduce a new office software system).

Evaluation Self-Check

You are in the process of conducting a performance analysis to address the problem of customer complaints about long response times to resolve billing issues. Working with your stakeholders, you have identified three to four potential interventions. At what point should you start thinking about evaluation?

a) During the intervention selection process;
b) When designing and developing the selected intervention;
c) When implementing and monitoring the intervention; or
d) Back during the performance analysis phase.

Of the four options, (d) is the optimal choice. As you collaborate with key stakeholders to select the most effective and feasible intervention to solve the problem of customer wait times, you are already integrating evaluation questions into the selection process as you compare each of the alternative interventions in terms of alignment with the performance improvement objectives, human and financial resource requirements, and short- and long-term impact. This enables you to sustain stakeholder buy-in throughout the intervention life cycle.

Food for Thought

1 Your organization has consistently used Kirkpatrick's Levels 1 and 2 for training but never conducted any systematic evaluation of its other performance improvement initiatives. What can you as a learning designer do to help build a culture of evaluation in your organization?

2 Every year, the Association for Talent Development gives its BEST awards to recognize organizations that demonstrate enterprise-wide success in using the learning and development function strategically to achieve business results. Winners are drawn from a variety of industry sectors and governance structures. Go to the ATD website and select a winner in the same industry sector as your own organization. What is that winner doing that **your** organization is also doing?

3 Now, what is that winning organization doing that your organization is **not** doing?

Up Next

In this chapter, we have (a) examined the current landscape of evaluation models, metrics, and measures that tend to dominate the scholarly and practitioner literatures; (b) described some tips for taking the same evaluation tools and techniques that instructional designers use and applying them to a variety of learning and performance improvement opportunities; and (c) summarized some key lessons learned for the effective use of evaluation that reduce the likelihood of a Dilbert©-like disconnect between our L&D initiatives and our organization's priorities. We now move from demonstrating the value of learning design and technologies to trends and opportunities, which is the last section of this book.

References

Aguinis, H., & Kraiger, K. (2009). Benefits of training and development for individuals and teams, organizations and society. *Annual Review of Psychology*, 60, 451–74.

Aksu, A., & Yildiz, S. (2011). Measuring results of training with ROI method: An application in a 5-star hotel in Antalya region of Turkey. *Toursimos: An International Multidisciplinary Journal of Tourism*, 6(1), 193–212.

Alexander, M., & Christoffersen, J. (2006). The total evaluation process: Shifting the mental model. *Performance Improvement*, 45(7), 23–7.

Alliger, G., & Janak, E. (1989). Kirkpatrick's levels of training criteria: Thirty years later. *Personnel Psychology*, 42(2), 331–42.

Aragon-Sanchez, A., Barba-Aragon, I., & Sanz-Valle, R. (2003). Effects of training on business results. *International Journal of Human Resource Management*, 14(6), 956–80.

Austin, B. (2013, March 11). Game-based e-learning: Learning transfer and ROI vs. traditional learning. *Training Magazine Network*. Retrieved from www.trainingmag.com/digital-archives.

Barnett, K., & Mattoxx II, J. (2010). Measuring success and ROI in corporate training. *Journal of Asynchronous Learning Networks*, 14(2), 28–44.

Bartel, A. (2000). Measuring the employer's return on investments in training: Evidence from the literature. *Industrial Relations*, 33(3), 502–24.

Beech, B. (2008). Aggression prevention training for student nurses: Differential responses to training and the interaction between theory and practice. *Nurse Education in Practice*, 8(2), 94–102.

Bersin, J. (2008). *The Training Measurement Book: Best Practices, Proven Methodologies and Practical Approaches*. San Francisco, CA: John Wiley & Sons.

Bersin, J. (2011). *The Impact Measurement Framework: An Update for the Measurement of Informal Learning*. Retrieved from www.hrosummits .com/hrosummiteu/wp-content/uploads/2011/11/Measurement-Framework-Update.pdf

Bingham, T., & Galagan, P. (2012). Service masters. *T + D Magazine*, 66, 36–41.

Brinkerhoff, R. (2003). *The Success Case Method: Find Out Quickly What's Working and What's Not*. San Francisco, CA: Berrett-Koehler Publishers.

Brinkerhoff, R., & Apking, A. (2001). *High Impact Learning: Strategies for Leveraging Business Results from Training*. Cambridge, MA: Perseus Books.

Cairns, T. (2012). Overcoming the challenges to developing an ROI for training and development. *Employment Relations Today*, 39(3), 23–7.

Coryn, C., Schroter, D., & Hanssen, C. (2009). Adding a time-series design element to the success case method to improve methodological rigor. *American Journal of Evaluation*, 30(1), 80–92.

Craig, R. (1996). *The ASTD Training and Development Handbook*. New York, NY: McGraw Hill.

Czeropski, S., & Le, D. (2010). Validation ROI: An HPT case study from the medical device industry. *Performance Improvement*, 49(2), 8–15.

Ford, D. (2004). Evaluating performance improvement. *Performance Improvement*, 43(1), 36–41.

Giangreco, A., Carugati, A., & Sebastiano, A. (2010). Are we doing the right thing? Food for thought on training evaluation and its context. *Personnel Review*, 39(2), 162–77.

Griffin, R. (2012). A practitioner friendly and scientifically robust training evaluation approach. *Journal of Workplace Learning*, 24(6), 393–402.

HCM Advisor Group. (2012). *Transforming Learning into a Strategic Business Enabler*. Chicago, IL: Human Capital Media.

Ho, M. 2016 *State of the Industry*. Alexandria, VA: Association for Talent Development (ATD).

Hodges, T. (2002). *Linking Learning and Performance*. Woburn, MA: Butterworth-Heinemann.

Holton, E. (1996). The flawed four level evaluation model. *Human Resource Development Quarterly*, 71(1), 5–22.

Holton, E., & Naquin, S. (2005). A critical analysis of HRD evaluation models from a decision-making perspective. *Human Resource Development Quarterly*, 16(2), 257–80.

Kauffeld, S., & Lehmann-Willenbrock, N. (2010). Sales training: Effects of spaced practice on training transfer. *Journal of European Industrial Training*, 34(1), 23–37.

Kaufman, R., & Keller, J. (1994). Levels of evaluation: Beyond Kirkpatrick. *Human Resource Development Quarterly*, 5(4), 371–80.

Kaufman, R., & Watkins, R. (1996). Cost-consequences analysis. *Human Resources Development Quarterly*, 7(1), 87–100.

Kim, J. (2006). Measuring the impact of knowledge management. *IJLA Journal*, 32(4), 362–7.

Kirkpatrick, D. (1959). Techniques for evaluating training programs. *Journal of American Society of Training Directors*, 13(3), 21–6.

Kirkpatrick, D. (1996). Measuring the results of training. In R. Craig (Ed.), *The ASTD Training and Development Handbook* (pp. 313–41). New York, NY: McGraw-Hill.

Kirkpatrick, J., & Kirkpatrick, W. (2010). *Training on Trial*. New York, NY: American Management Association.

KnowledgeAdvisors. (2009). KnowledgeAdvisors adds Bersin & Associates measurement framework to the metrics that matter offering and adds industry analyst Josh Bersin to its distinguished advisory board. Retrieved from www .businesswire.com/news/home/20090223005249/en/KnowledgeAdvisors-Adds-Bersin-Associates-Measurement-Framework-Metrics#.VA3pzZV0y00.

Kraiger, K. (2002). Decision-based evaluation. In K. Kraiger (Ed.), *Creating, Implementing, and Managing Effective Training and Development* (pp. 331–76). San Francisco, CA: Jossey-Bass.

Kraiger, K., Ford, J., & Salas, E. (1993). Application of cognitive, skill-based, and affective theories of learning outcomes to methods of training. *Journal of Applied Psychology*, 78(2), 311–28.

Laing, G., & Andrews, P. (2011). Empirical validation of outcomes from training programs: A case study. *International Journal of Human Resource Studies*, 1(1), 111–18.

Long, L., DuBois, C., & Faley, R. (2008). Online training: The value of capturing trainee reactions. *Journal of Workplace Learning*, 20(1), 21–37.

Morrison, G. R., Ross, S. M., Kalman, H. K., & Kemp, J. E. (2013). *Designing Effective Instruction* (7th ed.). Hoboken, NJ: John Wiley & Sons.

Nadler, L. (1984). *The Handbook of Human Resource Development*. New York, NY: John Wiley & Sons.

O'Leonard, K. (2013). *The Corporate Learning Factbook 2013*. Oakland, CA: Bersin by Deloitte.

Olson, C., Shershneva, M., & Brownstein, M. (2011). Peering inside the clock: Using success case method to determine how and why practice-based educational interventions succeed. *Journal of Continuing Education*, 31(S1), S50–9.

Patel, L. (2010). Overcoming barriers and valuing evaluation. *Training and Development*, 64(2), 62–3.

Percival, J., Cozzarin, B., & Formaneck, S. (2013). Return on investment for workplace training: The Canadian experience. *International Journal of Training and Development*, 17(1), 20–32.

Peterson, D., & Kraiger, K. (2003). A practical guide to evaluating coaching: Translating state-of-the-art techniques to the real world. In J. Edwards, J. Scott, & N. Raju (eds.), *The Human Resources Program Evaluation Handbook* (pp. 262–82). Newbury Park, CA: Sage.

Phillips, J. (1994). *In Action: Measuring Return on Investment*. Alexandria, VA: American Society of Training and Development (ASTD).

Phillips, J. (1997a). *Handbook of Training Evaluation and Measurement Methods* (3rd ed.). Houston, TX: Gulf.

Phillips, J. (1997b). *Return on Investment in Training and Performance Programs*. Houston, TX: Gulf.

Robinson, D., & Robinson, J. (1989). *Training for Impact: How to Link Training to Business Needs and Measure the Results*. San Francisco, CA: Jossey-Bass.

Scriven, M. (1996). Types of evaluation and types of evaluator. *American Journal of Evaluation, 17*(2), 151–61.

Short, T., & Harris, R. (2010). Challenges in aligning workplace learning with business goals: A perspective from HRD professionals in New Zealand. *Australian Journal of Adult Learning, 50*(2), 358–86.

Spitzer, D. (2005). Learning effectiveness measurement: A new approach for measuring and managing learning to achieve business results. *Advances in Developing Human Resources, 7*(1), 55–70.

Tessmer, M. (1994). Formative evaluation alternatives. *Performance Improvement Quarterly, 71*(1), 3–18.

Wang, D., Dou, Z., & Li, N. (2002). A systems approach to measuring return on investment for HRD interventions. *Human Resource Development Quarterly, 13*(2), 203–24.

Wang, G., & Spitzer, D. (2005). Human resource development measurement and evaluation: looking back and moving forward. *Advances in Developing Human Resources, 7*(5), 5–15.

Wang, G., & Wang, J. (2005). Human resource development: Emerging markets, barriers, and theory building. *Advances in Developing Human Resources, 7*(1), 22–36.

Wick, C., Pollock, R., & Jefferson, A. (2010). *The six disciplines of breakthrough learning: How to turn training and development into business results.* 2nd ed. San Francisco, CA: Pfeiffer.

Wick, C., Pollock, R., Jefferson, A., & Flanagan, R. (2006). *The six disciplines of breakthrough learning.* San Francisco, CA: Pfeiffer.

Zwick, T. (2006). The impact of training intensity on establishment productivity. *Industrial Relations, 45*(1), 26–46.

Part IV

Issues, Trends, and Opportunities

12 Analytics

Tapping into the Enterprise Infrastructure

In Part III, we focused on demonstrating the value of the Learning and Development (L&D) function, with an emphasis on successfully implementing instructional and non-instructional interventions that enhance learning and are aligned with the needs of the business. Now it's time to round out our discussion by focusing on the issues, trends, and opportunities for advancing your career as a learning design and technologies professional.

Part of the process of becoming a trusted learning advisor includes familiarizing yourself with the tools and technologies that are in use across the entire organization and identifying how those tools/technologies can support the L&D function. Much of the data that the designer requires to assess needs and diagnose performance problems can be found in an organization's existing databases and information systems. The enterprise software systems essential to the operation of just about any business include the Finance, Human Resources (HR), and Customer Relationship Management (CRM) systems, with many organizations also having a Learning Management System (LMS). Capitalizing on the large amount of data in these systems requires knowing what data are available, where the data are stored, who is responsible for that data, and what is required to synthesize and analyze the data. In other words, the learning design and technologies professional needs to be familiar with data analytics and how to apply the tools and techniques of analytics to support learning.

Analytics is one of those terms that tends to set heads spinning. Visions of complex algorithms, statistics, equations, and all manner of numerical contortionism may immediately spring to mind. Part of the angst associated with analytics comes from the variety of contexts in which the term is used and, thus, how it is defined. In the education sector, the term is *learning analytics*, with one definition describing learning analytics as "the measurement, collection, analysis and reporting of data about learners and their contexts, for purposes of understanding and optimizing learning and the environments in which it occurs" (Siemens, 2012, p. 4). An alternative definition looks at analytics-as-process, namely, "the process of developing actionable insights through problem definition and the application of statistical models and analysis against existing and/or simulated future data" (Cooper, 2012, p. 3), with an emphasis on the groups of individuals in education who use those insights: teachers and learners, to support educational aims and objectives; researchers, to support the development of research proposals and achieve impact; and management and support services, to support operational and strategic activity. In business, analytics is defined more broadly:

> Analytics often involves studying past historical data to research potential trends, to analyze the effects of certain decisions or events, or to evaluate the performance of a given tool or scenario. The goal of analytics is to improve the business by gaining knowledge which can be used to make improvements or changes. (Analytics, n.d.)

When applied to learning in non-academic settings, Mattox, Martin, and Van Buren (2016, pp. 13–14) offer this definition:

> Learning analytics is the science and art of gathering, processing, interpreting and reporting data related to the efficiency, effectiveness and business impact of development programmes designed to improve individual and organizational performance and inform stakeholders.

Just about every operational area in an organization can benefit from the insights produced by analytics to make fact-based decisions, and the term *analytics* is often prefixed with the particular area of application. For example, Web analytics profiles website traffic; marketing analytics provides insights into current and potential buyers of a product/service, etc. In short, analytics is a tool that helps organizations engage in data-based decision-making.

At this point, you may be thinking, I *just need to know about learning analytics. All that other stuff is above my pay grade.* Dilbert© might view analytics as just another bit of jargon that negatively affects his work productivity but as learning professionals, we cannot and should not take that view. Analytics allows the L&D professional to demonstrate how employees are trained, developed, and motivated to deliver business results. Analytics also provides employees with a clear picture of how they contribute to the organization's success and how their individual performance will be measured. Although not specifically listed among the IBSTPI competencies, analytics enables the learning designer to apply the business skill of data-driven decision-making to managing the design function, one of IBSTPI's managerial competency areas. Analytics helps to determine which learning methodologies are most effective, which vendors and suppliers provide the best value, where costs can be reduced without hurting quality, which human resources enterprise-wide need additional learning and development opportunities, and whether the L&D function is aligned with business goals. The L&D leader matches learning data with other employee data to identify where and how learning contributes to organizational performance indicators, such as sales, employee retention, career growth, and leadership development.

Nevertheless, most organizations are still novices when it comes to the field of analytics. This is particularly true of organizations that lack strong evaluation practices, such as those outlined in the previous chapter. However, even organizations with a firm command of evaluation strategies may still lag when it comes to analytics. Much of the problem is due to the fact that organizations use a variety of stand-alone software systems to manage the business, resulting in duplication of efforts, lack of critical data, and inconsistent processes. Unless you work for IBM or an organization of similar size that can take advantage of cloud-based technologies that enable integration of enterprise-wide software systems, it is likely that your organization's software systems are not integrated. In this chapter, we will:

- Explore the current state of analytics as a field of study;
- Discuss the various ways in which the use of learning analytics in non-academic workplace settings (business, government, non-profit organizations) differs from its use in academic workplace settings (higher education);
- Identify ways in which learning analytics can support learning designers; and
- Examine the various ways in which the learning designer can determine an organization's learning analytics capability.

State of the Field

The Big Picture

The L&D function is part of an interconnected, complex environment. Consequently, any discussion of learning analytics should begin with a high-level view of how organizations use data. At the 50,000-foot level, organizations seek to take large amounts of data and turn that data into information that can be used to sustain and grow the business. Generally, organizations focus on using a consistent set of metrics (e.g., amount of revenue generated from sales, number of clients acquired over a given period, cost of production) to measure past performance and inform business planning by querying, reporting, and analyzing multiple databases to answer questions like "what happened," "how often," "how many." This set of activities is known as business intelligence, "a framework that consists of a set of theories, methodologies, architectures, systems, and technologies that support business decision-making with valuable data, information, knowledge, and wisdom" (Sun, Sun, & Strang, 2016, p. 3).

Take those same databases and apply sophisticated modeling techniques to predict future performance or discover patterns that cannot otherwise be detected – "why is this happening," "what will happen next," "what is the best/worst that can happen" – then you are engaged in business analytics. Most organizations have some business intelligence capability in that they are able to query and report on their data in order to react to what the data says about past performance. Less pervasive is the ability to optimize and correlate data and predict the next best action or the most likely action for proactive decision-making, which is the strength of analytics.

Like project management, analytics began as a work-related approach rather than as a research-based body of knowledge. Unlike project management, however, research and scholarship on analytics are still in its infancy. The emergence of analytics as a field of study is inexorably tied to the evolution of computing power and the speed of data processing, beginning in the 1950s with the commercial introduction of the IBM mainframe computer that could produce and capture a large quantity of information and discern patterns in it far more quickly than humans. For the first time, organizations could record, aggregate, and analyze data about sales, production processes, and customer interactions. Vendors developed and sold software applications to create enterprise data warehouses or repositories that captured and stored data, along with business intelligence applications to query and report the data. The occupation of data analyst emerged, although the data analyst spent more time preparing data for analysis and reporting than in actual analyses. Moreover, the data captured concerned performance after-the-fact, telling decision-makers what happened in the past (e.g., revenue generated, production costs, wages, and salaries) but not why things happened.

The next big boost in computing power came in the early 2000s with the Internet, high-speed networks, and Silicon Valley firms that introduced new kinds of data. Public distribution of audio and video files and text-based content from social networking sites were among the many data sources that were external to any one organization, increasing the volume of available data as well as the speed at which these disparate forms of data were being generated. New technologies for faster data processing, new databases able to handle the mix of unstructured data types, and machine-learning methods that partially automated the development and testing of models from the fast-moving data, along with innovative reporting tools that enhanced or replaced standard text-based reports with colorful graphics-based displays all emerged in this period. The occupation of data scientist emerged, and these quantitative analysts possessed computational as well as analytical skills. Companies like Google and Amazon built up traffic to their websites through better search algorithms, recommendations from friends and colleagues of site visitors, suggestions for products to buy, and highly targeted ads, all driven by analytics rooted in enormous amounts of data.

As the twenty-first century advances, organizations in nearly every industry sector are coming to realize the power of analytics to advance their business. Citing three 100-plus-year-old multinational firms who have "seen the light" and begun optimizing their business decisions through analytics, one industry analyst noted:

> The common thread in these examples is the resolve by a company's management to compete on analytics not only in the traditional sense (by improving internal business decisions) but also by creating more-valuable products and services. This is the essence of Analytics 3.0. (Davenport, 2013, p. 68)

Clarification of Terms

Analytics as defined in the previous section of this chapter began to gain scholarly interest in parallel with its technology underpinnings. Consequently, it is not surprising that the fields of Engineering and Computer Science were the first contributors to research on data analytics. The research addressed issues such as algorithms, database structures, and other "back-end" technical issues associated with the large amounts of data to be captured, archived, extracted, and processed for analysis. As L&D professionals, our focus is on the non-technical "front-end" of data analytics, the transition from raw data to information that allows us to answer the who-what-where-when questions, then proceed to knowledge or the application of data and information to answer the "why" questions, followed by understanding and wisdom that can then inform decision-making (for more information about the relationship between data, information, knowledge and wisdom, see Ackoff, 1989).

A stream of research that focuses on the non-technical "front-end" of data analytics for business decision-making seeks to clarify many of the concepts associated with developing an analytics capability in organizations. One such concept is *big data*. First introduced by Laney (2001), the term *big data* attributes three characteristics to the data to which analytics is being applied:

- *Volume*: Now measured in petabytes (one quadrillion bytes or the equivalent of 20 million filing cabinets worth of text), big data is not only the purview of online companies like Google or social networking sites like LinkedIn, but is collected by organizations in a variety of sectors, such as healthcare, manufacturing, and retail. For example, Walmart collects 2.5 petabytes of data every hour from its customer transactions (McAfee & Brynjolfsson, 2012).
- *Velocity*: The speed of data creation is real-time or nearly real-time, compared with end-of-day batch collection typical of the 1980s and 1990s. Organizations can now forecast performance based on

incoming activity rather than extrapolating from past performance. For example, a mall retailer can look at parking garage data to predict the day's sales.

- *Variety*: The types of data range from multimedia to text and include data from social networks, GPS signals from cell phones and other relatively new sources, as well as traditional databases, such as Finance, HR, and CRM systems.

The Volume-Velocity-Variety descriptors now form a relatively common framework for describing big data (see, for example, Chen, Chiang, & Storey, 2012; Kwon, Lee, & Shin., 2014).

Gandomi and Haider (2015) identified three additional characteristics of big data. The first of these is veracity, which represents the unreliability inherent in some sources of data (e.g., customer sentiments posted to social media) but which may contain valuable information that an organization can use to target the marketing of its products/services. The veracity of big data has generated its own stream of research, including theoretical models for assessing veracity (Lukoianova & Rubin, 2014), the life-and-death implications of veracity in healthcare (Raghupathi & Raghupathi, 2014), and computational methods for improving data veracity (Kepner et al., 2014). The second additional characteristic draws on velocity and variability to create a characteristic called variability/complexity. A term popularized by Brian Hopkins, industry analyst at Forrester Research, variability refers to the variation in the data flow rates, while complexity refers to the fact that big data are generated through a myriad of sources. This imposes the challenge of connecting, matching, cleaning, and transforming data received from different sources. The third characteristic is value and refers to the low value density of big data, meaning the data received in the original form usually have a low value relative to its volume. However, a high value can be obtained by analyzing large volumes of data. Bottom line: Big data is a constant flow of enormous amounts of data coming in at high speed with no immediately discernible structure or pattern. Analytics turns that data onslaught into usable information for decision-making.

Another stream of research that is focused on concept clarification is the stream centered on the taxonomy of data analytics (Bedeley, Ghosal, Iyer, & Bhadury, 2016; Chandler, 2015; Delen & Demirkan, 2013; Watson, 2013). This research stream defines four categories of analytics:

- *Descriptive analytics*: *What happened?* Commonly known as standard business reporting, this category refers to the use of data to identify business problems and opportunities based on what is currently happening in the business or what has happened in the recent past. Descriptive analytics uses data mining and data extraction techniques to summarize large amounts of raw data. Most basic statistics fall into this category, such as average dollars spent per new employee hire, or total number of courses on the organization's LMS. Organizations use descriptive analytics to summarize and describe different aspects of the business.

- **Diagnostic analytics**: *Why did it happen?* This category of analytics seeks to examine the reasons behind the summary information resulting from descriptive analytics using inferential statistics, such as regression or applying text analysis tools to extract themes from large amounts of text-based data.
- **Predictive analytics**: *What could happen?* Using statistical models and forecasting techniques, predictive analytics combines the historical data in an organization's multiple enterprise software systems to identify patterns in the data and capture relationships between various data sets. Predictive analytics can be used throughout the organization, from forecasting customer behavior and purchasing patterns to identifying trends in sales activities.
- **Prescriptive analytics**: *What should be done?* This category of analytics provides the decision-maker with a number of different possible actions and guides the decision-maker toward a solution. Prescriptive analytics attempt to quantify the effects of future decisions in order to advise on possible outcomes before the decisions are actually made, similar to what-if scenarios. Using a combination of techniques and tools, such as business rules, algorithms, machine learning, and computational modelling procedures applied against input from many different data sets, prescriptive analytics can help decision-makers deliver the right products and services at the right time to the right target audience, maximizing both the customer experience and the organization's bottom line. Prescriptive analytics are complex and, thus, have not been adopted on a large scale.

A third stream of research focused on concept clarification concerns how best to present the results of data analytics in a form that makes sense to decision-makers and to other non-technical users seeking to find patterns in the data. The most common approach to communicating the results of analytics is through data visualization, the presentation of data in a pictorial or graphical format (Berinato, 2016; Krum, 2013; Nussbaumer Knaflic, 2015). When you conduct research and present your findings in graphs and charts, including scatterplots, maps, bar charts, infographics and the like, you are using data visualization to help your audience spot trends, outliers, and issues quickly and in an engaging manner. Given the large quantities of data involved in analytics, manual data visualization like creating PowerPoint charts is out of the question. Instead, software programs that can create displays with or without interactive features are available from commercial vendors, such as SAS and IBM. In addition, government-sponsored data visualization projects are underway in several universities to explore and develop ways to apply data visualization to the analysis needs of various government agencies (for a review of data visualization research trends, see Few & PERCEPTUAL EDGE, 2007).

The Promise

There is ample evidence from industry research to indicate a growing interest in the field of data analytics in non-academic settings. For example, IBM surveyed more than 1,200 information technology professionals and business decision-makers in 13 countries and 16 industries (developer-Works & IBM Center for Applied Insights, 2012) and found that nearly one-third (30 percent) of those surveyed report significant deployment of business analytics, with plans to increase their investment in business analytics by 10 percent or more in the next two years. Key findings of a survey of some 3,000 executive managers worldwide, along with in-depth interviews with leading researchers (LaValle et al., 2011), indicated that (a) top-performing companies view analytics as a competitive differentiator; (b) the top two barriers to implementing data analytics are lack of understanding of how to use analytics to improve the business, and lack of management bandwidth; and (c) executives are focusing on supplementing standard historical reporting data with emerging approaches that convert information into scenarios and simulations that make insights easier to understand and act on. There has also been theoretical/conceptual research that views data analytics as having the potential to transform economies and increase organizational productivity (Manyika et al., 2011) as well as to increase an organization's competitive position (Kiron et al., 2011).

However, challenges also exist. McAfee and Brynjolfsson (2012) identify five challenge areas that have to be addressed in order to capitalize on the affordances of data analytics:

- Leadership. The C-suite has to set clear goals, define what success looks like, and ask the right questions to ground decision-making.
- Talent management. The knowledge, skills, and abilities required to implement data analytics reside in multiple functions/occupations. The organization must invest in the people (e.g., data scientists) who have the skills in cleaning and organizing large data sets and who are comfortable speaking the language of business and helping leaders reformulate their business issues in ways that big data can tackle.
- Technology. The back-end infrastructure is a must-have for data analytics, including investments in the tools to handle the volume, velocity, and variety of big data.
- Decision-making. Leaders across the organization need to maximize cross-functional cooperation to bring together the right people with the right problem-solving techniques with the right data.
- Company culture. Data analytics requires an organizational mindset that backs away from the "HiPPO (the highest-paid person's opinion)

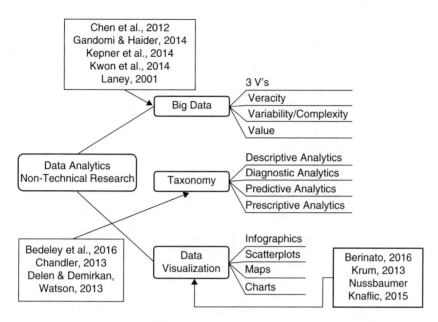

Figure 12.1 Non-Technical Data Analytics Research Streams.

approach" and toward collaborative thinking grounded in hard evidence.

Other challenges include data security, the ethical use of the data, and viewing data analytics implementation as a one-off project rather than a continuous cycle of optimization.

The extent to which organizations have addressed these challenging areas has served to inform models describing an organization's analytics capability maturity (see, for example, Cosic, Shanks & Maynard, 2012; LaValle et al., 2011; Santiago & Shanks, 2015). However, there has been little or no testing and validation of these models, and commercial consulting firms have sometimes been the go-to default option for organizations seeking to get started with data analytics. Figure 12.1 provides a graphical representation of the main themes characterizing the field of data analytics from the non-technical "front-end" perspective.

Learning Analytics in Academic vs. Non-Academic Workplace Settings

Academic Settings

When thinking about learning analytics in academic settings, what probably springs to mind is the number of hits on a university LMS. Although that may be the most well-known application of learning analytics (Arnold,

2010; Denley, 2012; Fritz, 2010), the use of learning analytics in academic settings, most particularly in higher education, is broader in scope. Buckingham Shum (2012) identified higher education analytics as existing at various levels of the institution. Micro-level analytics focuses on tracking individual students and includes activities such as click-by-click online activity, library loans, and social networks. The purpose of micro-level analytics is to identify and explore factors related to student success. Meso-level analytics focuses on institutional level data to explore the efficiency of the institution's business processes, workflows, student retention, and the like. Macro-level analytics focuses on cross-institutional analyses, such as state-wide access to standardized assessment data over students' lifetimes. In a special issue of the journal *American Behavioral Scientist*, research on learning analytics included studies on the relationship between student academic performance and social ties (Gašević, Zouaq, & Janzen, 2013), dashboard applications for learning (Verbert, Duval, Klerkx, Govaerts, & Santos, 2013), and data visualization to inform the design of learning environments (Thompson et al., 2013). However, much of the research in academic settings has focused on establishing leading indicators of academic performance and retention, leading to calls for more attention to using learning analytics for effective instructional practice (Gašević, Dawson, & Siemens, 2015).

In a systematic mapping study of the literature on learning analytics in academic contexts from 2011 to 2014, Moissa, Gasparini, and Kemczinski (2015) sought to classify 116 studies in terms of goals, data types, techniques, stakeholders, and interventions. The results of that mapping study indicated that different types of data and techniques are being used to achieve research goals but that there has been little attention paid to interventions grounded in the results of learning analytics. The authors found similar results in a separate review on the application of learning analytics to MOOCs. Those findings echo Gašević, Dawson, and Siemens's (2015) point about the need for using learning analytics to improve instruction. Ferreira and Andrade (2016) sought to differentiate between the various types of analytics used in higher education based on a review of the literature. Basically, they differentiated between (a) academic analytics or the use of data to support the management of the activity of an institution (financial, educational, marketing, etc.) and focusing on monitoring issues related to the academic success of individual students (e.g., identification of at-risk students, enrollment patterns by demographic characteristics); (b) learning analytics focusing on the use of modeling techniques and learning outcomes assessments to target instruction, curricula, and support; and (c) predictive analytics or what-if scenarios at the student, department, and university level to make decisions. Noting the challenges that institutions face in acquiring the technological systems and processes required to implement a consistent and broad-based analytics capability, the authors created a conceptual prototype of a database that integrates records from a learning content management system (LCMS), academic management services, and a quality management service at a Brazilian institution. Although still in progress, the authors' work highlights the complexities of implementing a comprehensive approach to analytics in higher education.

In assessing the state of learning analytics in higher education, one analyst from Gartner, a leading firm in the analysis of information technology in the higher education sector, noted that institutions tend to view learning analytics and institutional analytics as part of one whole but are more likely to invest in tools for institutional analytics – the use of institutional data to improve administrative processes – than in tools for learning analytics, the use of data about learners and their environments to improve student learning outcomes (Morgan, 2016). Gartner attributes this lag in investment in learning analytics capability to (a) the relative lack of maturity of learning analytics tools and solutions (i.e., LMS tools, emerging tools such as beacons and sensors on campus and in classrooms) vs. those for institutional analytics; (b) potential conflicts with faculty autonomy and control over curriculum and teaching; and (c) the time and effort required to build stakeholder relationships across the institution to devise action, intervention, and governance plans required for decision-making based on insights from learning analytics.

Examples of other issues that the literature on learning analytics in academic settings addresses include issues of privacy and the ethical use of data (Slade & Prinsloo, 2013), patterns of usage in MOOCs (Klobas, 2014), as well as the current state of theory and practice (Daniel, 2017). Still evolving is a body of empirical research on the use of learning analytics to improve teaching and learning. The Society for Learning Analytics Research (SoLAR), an interdisciplinary network of international researchers, is dedicated to exploring the role and impact of analytics on teaching, learning, training, and development. However, the bulk of the Society's efforts focuses on academic workplace settings.

Non-Academic Settings

Unlike academic settings in which learning analytics is about learning, learning analytics in non-academic settings is about performance and the extent to which all forms of learning – formal training events, informal learning via social networks, etc. – contribute to employee performance. In academic settings, "researchers seek to understand [sic] LA from multiple perspectives: learners, institutions, and effectiveness. Corporations do not share this obligation. Context influences the nature and type of analytics" (Siemens, 2012, p. 5). Consequently, it is not surprising that much of the published work on learning analytics in non-academic workplace settings consists of individual company case studies, market research studies focused on the extent to which organizations have implemented or plan to implement a learning analytics capability or opinion pieces and primers from analytics software vendors and consultants (Dearborn, 2014; Masie, 2013; Mattox, Martin, & Van Buren, 2016).

To expand and grow, organizations need to know how to invest in facilities, technology, and people, the latter sometimes referred to as the organization's human capital. With the cost of human capital ranging from two to six times the cost of financial capital (Fitz-Enz, 2009), organizations are increasingly turning to analytics to assess the contribution of workforce performance to company performance:

> Workforce analytics is a set of integrated capabilities (technologies, metrics, data, and processes) to measure and improve workforce performance. The goal is simple: put the right people with the right skills in the right work, provide them with the necessary training and development opportunities, and engage and empower them to perform at their highest possible level. (Harvard Business Review Analytical Services, 2013)

In other words, workforce analytics combines organizational performance data such as business key performance indicators (KPIs), individual performance data, HR data such as hiring and retention, with learning data such as LMS data, to analyze current performance, identify and analyze performance gaps and the root causes of those gaps, and identify opportunities for performance improvement interventions. Learning analytics is a subset of workforce analytics.

Learning Analytics for the Learning Designer

Earlier in this book, we discussed needs assessments and ways to identify performance gaps that are due to gaps in knowledge, skills, and abilities (KSAs). Just as comprehensive methods of evaluation help you to determine whether an intervention has addressed the targeted KSA, learning analytics helps you determine whether the newly acquired KSA is being applied on the job over time. This provides decision-makers with evidence of the value of L&D in closing gaps between the organization's strategic goals and its workforce capabilities. If your organization's enterprise-wide software applications include systems for HR, an LMS, a central location for storing and managing learning content, and tracks some basic business metrics (e.g., KPIs), then you, the learning designer, can request some basic reports that combine data from various sources within the organization to provide insights into L&D program effectiveness.

Table 12.1 provides some examples of the types of effectiveness questions that learning analytics techniques can answer, and the actions you can take based on those answers. Let's say you've created a training module on leadership skills for non-managers. The purpose of the module is

Table 12.1 Evidence of L&D Effectiveness through Learning Analytics: Leadership Skills Example

Desired Evidence	Data Sources	Statistical Techniques	Decisions
Relationship between employee training outcomes and occupational rank	• LMS • HR system	• Descriptive statistics • Correlation analysis	• Revise the training program to reduce outcome differences across participant groups • Document training pre-requisites to encourage enrollment by those most likely to succeed
Forecast employee outcomes in a training event based on the number of embedded links that employee clicks	• LMS • LCMS/CMS	• Descriptive statistics • Regression analysis	• Incorporate content from the most frequently accessed links into the training event
Desired Evidence	*Data Sources*	*Statistical Techniques*	*Decisions*
Relationship between employee participation in a training program and job performance ratings	• LMS • HR system	• Descriptive statistics • Correlation analysis	• Promote program benefits within the organization • Assist managers in customizing individual development plans
Relationship between employee participation in training programs and business metrics/KPIs	• LMS • HR system • CRM system • Finance system	• Descriptive statistics • Multiple correlation analysis • Structural equation modeling (SEM)	• Prioritize investments in training on those programs with the greatest impact on business performance
Relationship between employee training performance, engagement with content, and employee retention	• LMS • LCMS/CMS • HR system	• Descriptive statistics • Multiple correlation analysis • Multiple regression analysis SEM	• Predict at-risk attrition based on training performance • Incorporate training performance and engagement metrics with career planning

to teach employees of any occupational rank how to lead others without actually holding the title of supervisor or manager. Your documented learning outcomes are: (a) define the attributes common to leaders; (b) explain the importance of influence, how to earn it, and how/when to use it; (c) describe the ways to build a professional network; (d) explain what motivates others; and (e) develop a plan for leading. You have assessments, measures, and metrics for each of those outcomes, as well as pre- and post-training self-assessments of leadership capabilities. All of the data associated with the training is located in your organization's LMS, and all information about the participants' current roles and rank within the organization is located in the HR system. In addition to the descriptive statistics that you would generate from the LMS (number of participants by department, number of participants by rank, performance on each of the assessments), you could see if there is a relationship via correlation analysis between high/low performance on each of the learning outcomes and participant rank or department. If there are significant performance differences by rank on one or more of the outcomes, you could then revise the training to provide more scaffolding in the content areas related to those outcomes and reduce the gaps between the participant ranks. Use this same example to work your way through the rest of Table 12.1. By asking yourself *how* you want to demonstrate the value of your initiatives, you are better able to select *which* data sources offer that evidence, *what kind* of analytical techniques you need to apply to get that evidence, and *what decisions* you can make based on that evidence.

The best way to illustrate how learning designers use learning analytics is to get the practitioner's perspective. Let's see what Siobhan Curran, Director of Learning Technology and Analytics at DTCC Learning, has to say about learning analytics in *E-Suite Views*:

SvR: One of the hottest buzzwords in the field today, of course, is analytics. However, because instructional designers come from a variety of backgrounds including education, you have a lot of career changers from K–12 who want to get into the learning and development field. They often find it confusing to differentiate between learning analytics and business analytics and many of the other contexts in which the word analytics is used. What would you recommend that these folks need to know about analytics in order to build their competencies in the learning profession?

SC: I agree with that. I would recommend instructional designers start by gathering all of the data that are currently available to them via their LMS, project management software, Google Analytics, hosting services like YouTube and Vimeo, etc., and then breaking it out into three buckets. Number one, Standard Learning Analytics, the typical data we get from an LMS –

registration, attendance vs. registration, evaluation feedback, time to completion, etc. Number two, Operational Efficiency, analytics that show the resources it takes to complete an initiative, including vendor expenses, technology costs, and revenue data. Number three, Learner Engagement and Content Governance, analytics that show the number of hits to your online offerings, how long users are staying on a content page, etc.

These days, getting data is the easy part. The challenge is synthesizing it, making it relevant and actionable. Once you have gathered your data, list key metrics and establish why they are important to you and your stakeholder audience. See if you can identify any trends and then, establish benchmarks for improvement.

This is all easier said than done. Implementing a thoughtful and impactful analytics program takes time and commitment. The single most important thing you can do is commit to making analytics part of your process and your everyday conversation when talking about learning. When defining a project, scope out what analytics you will need to prove ROI, learner uptake, and success, and embed it in the project plan and project meetings as part of the conversation.

SvR: Now, those kinds of analytics, as well as sales data, of course, are very important to the business partners but the question that I get from learning professionals is, "Well, I'm a learning designer or instructional designer. Why do I need to know that? I only want to know what I need to know." How would you respond to that?

SC: As lifelong learners, we should all be curious about what the data tell us! If you have a problem or a challenge, is there data that can help you? Maybe you released a 10-minute learning module and the analytics tells you learners are only spending an average of two minutes in your content. Should you retool your efforts and develop two-minute modules, chunk the information differently so that the learner has a more consumable piece of learning as opposed to one huge gargantuan e-learning that they will never make it through? You can look deeper into your learner assessment results and see if a particular question is frequently answered incorrectly, thus enabling you to determine if there is a problem with the question or the content.

SvR: So, those examples are excellent examples of how to use the analytics in what instructional designers call summative evaluation: how your instruction was put together, did it work, did it not work, and where did things go wrong. What about when trying to figure out what kind of intervention to put together in the first place? Can analytics be of help there?

SC: So, yes. I don't know if you're talking about doing needs assessment through quantitative and qualitative analytics or ....

SvR: Absolutely, absolutely.

SC: As I mentioned previously, make analytics part of your daily conversation about learning solutions. When defining learning needs, it is important to use both quantitative and qualitative data. You may not always have the time or resources to do both but here is a simple method that can be implemented easily. First, conduct some interviews. Simply talk with your target audience about their needs. Ask lots of open-ended questions and look for trends in their answers. Second, conduct a survey. Use trends from your qualitative study and form questions to validate these points. Additionally, create questions that will help clarify feedback that was confusing. And three, once you have gathered all the feedback, synthesize the quantitative and qualitative data, and then socialize it with your team and business partners as a final check. This is a simple and balanced analytics strategy that is not difficult to execute and will yield accurate needs.

SvR: Can you share a story about how using analytics either helped or hindered you in your work as a learning professional and what your key takeaways were from those lessons learned?

SC: Your analytics must be relevant to the business to be credible and productive. One of the most successful analytics I presented was also one of the most simple and easy to derive. We had a certification process and exam that new help desk employees had to pass to take phone calls from clients. The certification process included mastery on several products and the time to completion could stretch out to months. This delayed speed to competency meant that seasoned help desk staff who could be handling more difficult issues were spending time solving simple issues that could be handled by these junior level new employees.

We analyzed the program and determined that new employees could master a portion of the easier issues within two weeks, thus getting them on the phone with clients in a fraction of the time and freeing up the seasoned staff to deal with more complex issues.

The very simple metric that shows huge value:

Current Speed to Competency = 6–12 weeks

New Speed to Competency = 2 weeks

SvR: Last thing or next to last thing, one of the scary things about analytics for those with a traditional instructional design background is the fact that there may or may not be a data analyst in house to do the back-end piece. How does the designer

SC: go about, first of all, finding out if there is indeed an analytics capability in the organization? And second, communicating with those back-end folks about the kind of data that they need to do their jobs?

SC: Yeah, that's really difficult. One of the many challenges of that is even if your organization has a Business Information or Analytics team, learning that is not tied to revenue may not be their priority. This is what I have found in my own organization; sales analytics takes precedence over all.

SvR: Right, yeah.

SC: Many organizations have a Business Data office or an IT function that handles data automation, but many don't. This has been one of the biggest challenges of my career in analytics. A few tips:

- Do an analysis of what it takes you to manually compile your data, and then, compare the resources you spend with the cost of an automated solution. If your cost is less with an automated solution, pitch the solution to your analytics team.
- Don't be afraid of data! Anyone who works with data, loves to talk about it. Find that person and engage him/her. Use him/her to help you brainstorm your solutions or what you need to move forward.

SvR: That's a good approach.

SC: I didn't get it, though.

SvR: Well, business cases aren't always successful. We know that.

SC: No, no, I learned a lot from it but I didn't get it.

Learning Analytics Capability and How to Recognize It

Now that you know what learning analytics can do for you, the question is: *Does my organization have the wherewithal for learning analytics?* A good starting point is what the International Institute for Analytics calls "the nine signs your company is analytical" (Nevala, 2015). Specifically, your organization may possess the right mindset for a true analytics capability if it:

1 Views metrics as signposts, not strategy. The focus is not just on the numbers but what the numbers represent.
2 Solves for results, not innovation. Learning designers often solve potential problems as well as existing problems, but always do so with a purpose. Analytics should also be purposeful at all times.
3 Practices what it preaches. Executives and managers are open to questions and consider data when making decisions, even if the data are contrary to their expectations.
4 Includes failing. A mindset of continuous improvement means learning from failures rather than punishing those whose initiatives fail.

5 Hyper-focuses on enabling behaviors. The critical behaviors and processes required to drive change are recognized and supported to become a data-driven organization.

6 Teams up. IT specialists learn the ways of business, business professionals learn about data, cross-functional collaboration is essential to increasing analytic competency and literacy.

7 Tells stories. Communicating what analytics is all about should be grounded in the art of storytelling rather than simply a dry report of the nuts and bolts of activities and initiatives.

8 Infuses analytics from top to bottom. Advances in data presentation, such as data visualization, means that analytics can be embedded into every aspect of the organization's operations.

9 Establishes analytics as a core competency. Investments in analytic skills, process, tools, along with a point person (e.g., a Chief Analytics or Data Officer), show a commitment to analytics as a core business competency in its own right.

Grossman and Siegel (2014) stressed the importance of building a critical mass of in-house analytics expertise, ensuring that the analytics staff are deployed in a way that supports business processes, and having an analytics governance structure to ensure that analytics processes are supported by the organization as a whole. They offered four simple questions about analytics in general that can help you determine the extent of your organization's learning analytics capability:

1 Do **senior leaders** in the organization recognize the importance of analytics?

2 Is there a critical mass of **data scientists** who understand the organization and does the breadth of their expertise span not just building analytic models but also deploying them?

3 Do the data scientists in the organization understand the various **processes** required for selecting the right models to build, how to build them correctly, and deploy them into operational systems and processes so that value is generated?

4 Is there a **governance structure** in place to support analytics and to integrate analytics and big data into the organization's overall strategy?

At a minimum, the answer to the first question should be *yes*. If the organization's leadership is either unaware of or not committed to data-driven decision-making and the role that analytics plays in providing that data, then it is unlikely that the organization is ready to undertake the analytics journey. Although L&D can analyze data from the organization's LMS, using that data strategically, as we saw with Table 12.1, requires an ability to analyze data from multiple data sources with the right people, tools/technologies, and processes. Absent leadership commitment, those requirements will either be non-existent or hidden in occupational silos throughout the organization. The answer to the first question also indicates the extent to which the organization's culture would be receptive to analytics for data-driven decision-making.

But what if the answers to questions two through four are *no* or generate blank looks from your supervisor or colleagues, leaving you with that Dilbert©-like feeling? A simpler way of identifying the presence or absence of analytical ability in the organization is to ask who has the statistical and mathematical skills to build and work with data sets and models. The obvious go-to areas to ask this question are your Finance department and your IT department. Finance is most likely to have data analysts accustomed to finding patterns and identifying trends in the organization's financial data, particularly in terms of the organization's key performance indicators (KPIs). IT is more likely than any other department to have people experienced with database query, extraction, and reporting tools that allow managers to view the status of the organization's KPIs on a regular basis. Sometimes an HR business analyst is statistically inclined and has experience with packages such as SPSS or SAS statistical tools that can help perform the analyses. In any event, start with your L&D colleagues and your supervisor, then move to your internal contacts to identify those hidden pockets of analytics talent. Finally, in the absence of a robust analytics capability, you should consider reviewing with your team what you currently can do with the data you have, then discuss the kinds of questions you would like answered to demonstrate the contribution of L&D to organizational performance. Do I sense a business case opportunity?

Learning Analytics Self-Check

Your supervisor tells you that management is thinking about starting an analytics initiative but is not sure whether to include L&D in that initiative. Your supervisor recognizes the importance of your group being a part of the initiative right from the start but is worried about the time required to participate and is unclear about how to make a case for including L&D but needs to respond to senior management in a few days. Which of the following would you do?

a) Agree with your supervisor and suggest that you wait until the organization has an analytics solution up and running before getting L&D involved.

b) Work with your supervisor to quickly identify where in the organization employees with analytical capabilities work and seek their advice.

c) Identify one or two questions, the answers to which would demonstrate the value of L&D (e.g., what percentage of employees who complete currently available in-house training opportunities get promoted within 6 months of training completion?).

d) Develop an infographic illustrating the amount of participant activity in your LMS.

The best choice is (c) because it allows you to quickly demonstrate the alignment of L&D initiatives and activities with one of the organization's strategic goals (providing a career path to improve retention). Your LMS contains the data about who has completed what training; the HR database contains information about promotions within 6 months of the end of a particular training initiative. Downloading the relevant variables and fields from the two databases into a spreadsheet, then performing a simple cross-tabulation would yield an answer to the question about promotion. This will yield a quick win that your supervisor can use immediately in building her case for involvement. Option (b) should be undertaken but requires more time than the few days your supervisor needs to respond. Neither options (a) nor (d) support L&D as a strategic partner.

Food for Thought

1 Explore the Advance Distributed Learning (ADL) website information on xAPI, an e-learning software specification that allows organizations to capture data about human performance, along with associated instructional content. Think of various ways that your organization could take advantage of xAPI to demonstrate L&D's impact on organizational performance.

2 Register for one of the free MOOC analytics courses on edX.org. Are your analytical skills at the level you expected?

Up Next

In this chapter, we have reviewed the current state of analytics as a field of study and examined the ways in which the use of learning analytics differs in non-academic workplace settings vs. academic workplace settings. We have also identified ways in which learning analytics can support the learning designer's work, as well as explore how the learning designer can determine an organization's learning analytics capability. We now turn our attention to a challenge that affects not only the use of data and analytics but also the entire ecosystem in which the learning designer operates, namely, issues of ethics.

References

Ackoff, R. L. (1989). From data to wisdom. *Journal of Applied Systems Analysis*, *16*, 3–9.

Analytics. (n.d.). *BusinessDictionary.com*. Retrieved from www.businessdictionary .com/definition/analytics.html.

Arnold, K. (2010). Signals: applying academic analytics. *EDUCAUSE Review*. Retrieved from http://er.educause.edu/articles/2010/3/signals-applying-academic-analytics.

Bedeley, R. T., Ghoshal, T., Iyer, L. S., & Bhadury, J. (2016). Business analytics and organizational value chains: A relational mapping. *Journal of Computer Information Systems*, 1–11.

Berinato, S. (2016). *Good Charts: The HBR Guide to Making More Persuasive Data Visualizations*. Boston, MA: Harvard Business Review Press.

Buckingham Shum, S. (2012). *Learning analytics*. (UNESCO Policy Brief). Retrieved from http://iite.unesco.org/pics/publications/en/files/3214711.pdf.

Chandler, N. (2015). *Agenda Overview for Analytics, Business Intelligence, and Performance Management 2015*. Stamford, CT: Gartner, Inc.

Chen, H., Chiang, R. H. L., & Storey, V. C. (2012). Business intelligence and analytics: From big data to big impact. *MIS Quarterly*, *36*(4), 1165–88.

Cooper, A. (2012). What is analytics? Definition and essential characteristics. In *CETIS Analytics Series* (Vol. *1*, pp. 3–9).

Cosic, R., Shanks, G., & Maynard, S. (2012). *Towards a business analytics capability maturity model*. Paper presented at the Australasian Conference on Information Systems, Geelong, Victoria, Australia.

Daniel, B. K. (Ed.). (2017). *Big Data and Learning Analytics in Higher Education: Current Theory and Practice*. Cham, Switzerland: Springer International Publishing.

Davenport, T. H. (2013). Analytics 3.0. *Harvard Business Review*, *91*(12), 64–72.

Dearborn, J. (2014). Big data: A quick-start guide for learning practitioners. *TD Magazine*. Retrieved from www.td.org/Publications/Magazines/TD/TD-Archive/2014/05/Big-Data-a-Quick-Start-Guide.

Delen, D., & Demirkan, H. (2013). Data, information and analytics as services. *Decision Support Systems*, *55*(1), 359–63.

Denley, T. (2012). Austin Peay State University: degree compass. *EDUCAUSE Review*. Retrieved from http://er.educause.edu/articles/2012/9/austin-peay-state-university-degree-compass.

developerWorks, & IBM Center for Applied Insights. (2012). *2012 IBM TechTrends Report*. Retrieved from www.coeforict.org/wp-content/uploads/2013/04/IBM-Skills-Gap-Report-PDF.pdf

Ferreira, S. A., & Andrade, A. (2016). Academic analytics: anatomy of an exploratory essay. *Education and Information Technologies*, *21*(1), 229–43.

Few, S., & PERCEPTUAL EDGE. (2007). *Data visualization: Past, present and future*. Retrieved from www.perceptualedge.com/articles/Whitepapers/Data_Visualization.pdf.

Fitz-Enz, J. (2009). Predicting people: From metrics to analytics. *Employment Relations Today*, *36*(3), 1–11.

Fritz, J. (2010). Video demo of UMBC's "Check My Activity" tool for students. *EDUCAUSE Review*. Retrieved from http://er.educause.edu/articles/2010/12/video-demo-of-umbcs-check-my-activity-tool-for-students.

Gandomi, A., & Haider, M. (2015). Beyond the hype: Big data concepts, methods, and analytics. *International Journal of Information Management*, *35*(2), 137–44.

Gašević, D., Dawson, S., & Siemens, G. (2015). Let's not forget: learning analytics are about learning. *TechTrends*, *59*(1), 64–71.

Gašević, D., Zouaq, A., & Janzen, R. (2013). "Choose your classmates, your GPA is at stake!" The association of cross-class social ties and academic performance. *American Behavioral Scientist*, *57*(10), 1460–79.

Grossman, R. L., & Siegel, K. P. (2014). Organizational models for big data and analytics. *Journal of Organization Design*, *3*(1), 20–5.

Harvard Business Review Analytical Services. (2013). *Connecting workforce analytics to better business results.* Retrieved from https://hbr.org/resources/pdfs/comm/sumtotal/hbr-sumtotal-report-aug.pdf.

Kepner, J., Gadepally, V., Michaleas, P., Schear, N., Varia, M., Yerukhimovich, A., & Cunningham, R. K. (2014). *Computing on masked data: A high performance method for improving big data veracity.* Paper presented at the High Performance Extreme Computing Conference (HPEC), Waltham, MA.

Kiron, D., Shockley, R., Kruschwitz, N., Finch, G., & Haydock, M. (2011). Analytics: the widening divide. *MIT Sloan Management Review.* Retrieved from http://sloanreview.mit.edu/reports/analytics-advantage/.

Klobas, J. (2014). Measuring the success of scaleable open online courses. *Performance Measurement and Metrics, 15*(3), 145–62.

Krum, R. (2013). *Cool Infographics: Effective Communication with Data Visualization and Design.* Indianapolis, IN: John Wiley & Sons.

Kwon, O., Lee, N., & Shin, B. (2014). Data quality management, data usage experience and acquisition intention of big data analytics. *International Journal of Information Management, 34*(3), 387–94.

Laney, D. (2001). 3D Data management: Controlling data volume, velocity, and variety. Retrieved from http://blogs.gartner.com/doug-laney/files/2012/01/ad949-3D-Data-Management-Controlling-Data-Volume-Velocity-and-Variety.pdf.

LaValle, S., Lesser, E., Shockley, R., Hopkins, M. S., & Kruschwitz. (2011). Big data, analytics and the path from insights to value. *MIT Sloan Management Review, 52*(2), 20–31.

Lukoianova, T., & Rubin, V. L. (2014). Veracity roadmap: is big data objective, truthful and credible? *Advances in Classification Research Online, 24*(1), 4–15.

Manyika, J., Chui, M., Brown, B., Bughin, J., Dobbs, R., Roxburgh, C., & Byers, A. H. (2011). *Big data: the next frontier for innovation, competition, and productivity.* Retrieved from www.mckinsey.com/business-functions/digital-mckinsey/our-insights/big-data-the-next-frontier-for-innovation.

Masie, E. (2013). The uncharted territory of big learning data. *TD Magazine.* Retrieved from www.td.org/Publications/Magazines/TD/TD-Archive/2013/12/The-Uncharted-Territory-of-Big-Learning-Data.

Mattox II, J. R., Martin, J., & Van Buren, M. (2016). *Learning Analytics: Measurement Innovations to Support Employee Learning.* Philadelphia, PA: Kogan Page Limited.

McAfee, A., & Brynjolfsson, E. (2012). Big data: The Management Revolution. *Harvard Business Review, 90*(10), 59–68.

Moissa, B., Gasparini, I., & Kemczinski, A. (2015). A systematic mapping on the learning analytics field and its analysis in the massive open online courses context. *International Journal of Distance Education Technologies, 13*(3), 1–24.

Morgan, G. (2016). *Assessing the State of Learning Analytics in Higher Education.* Stamford, CT: Gartner.

Nevala, K. (2015). *Nine signs your company is analytical.* Retrieved from http://iianalytics.com/research/nine-signs-your-company-is-analytical.

Nussbaumer Knaflic, C. (2015). *Storytelling with Data: A Data Visualization Guide for Business Professionals.* Hoboken, NJ: John Wiley & Sons.

Raghupathi, W., & Raghupathi, V. (2014). Big data analytics in healthcare: Promise and potential. *Health Information Science and Systems, 2*(3), 1–10.

Santiago, R. D., & Shanks, G. (2015). A dashboard to support management of business analytic capabilities. *Journal of Decision Systems, 24*(1), 73–86.

Siemens, G. (2012). *Learning analytics: envisioning a research discipline and a domain of practice.* Paper presented at the LAK 2012 Second International Conference on Learning Analytic and Knowledge, Vancouver, BC, Canada.

Slade, S., & Prinsloo, P. (2013). Learning analytics: Ethical issues and dilemmas. *American Behavioral Scientist*, 57(10), 1510–29.

Sun, Z., Sun, L., & Strang, K. (2016). Big data analytics services for enhancing business intelligence. *Journal of Computer Information Systems*, 56(1), 1–8.

Thompson, K., Ashe, D., Carvalho, L., Goodyear, P., Kelly, N., & Parisio, M. (2013). Processing and visualizing data in complex learning environments. *American Behavioral Scientist*, 57(10), 1401–1420.

Verbert, K., Duval, E., Klerkx, J., Govaerts, S., & Santos, J. L. (2013). Learning analytics dashboard applications. *American Behavioral Scientist*, 57(10), 1500–9.

Watson, H. J. (2013). All about analytics. *International Journal of Business Intelligence Research*, 4(1), 13–28.

13 Professional Ethics
It May Not Be Illegal but ...

Consider this. The director of the Technical Support department has submitted a request for training to your Learning and Development (L&D) group because of poor scores given to her department on the customer satisfaction survey. You are doing some upfront analysis to make sure that training is, indeed, the optimal solution. In the process, you have learned from employee survey data that one of the barriers to closing a very important skills gap is the perception that the director of Technical Support is only interested in advancing department employees that she – the director – believes to have management potential, while leaving other department employees – even those who are good workers – to their own devices. You share this information with the director and recommend getting to the causes of this perception, so that concrete actions can be taken to remedy the situation. You explain that employee perceptions will affect both how the training is received and how what is learned in the training is used. The director asks you to identify the employees who said negative things about her so that she can address them herself, which would allow you to focus your attention on designing the training. If you comply with her request, are you violating the ethics of your profession?

If you said, yes, you would be absolutely right. Employee survey data is almost always collected anonymously, with the clear understanding that the results are to be reported only in the aggregate, and that the responses of individual employees will remain confidential. Respondent confidentiality is part of the ethical handling of data for any professional in any industry (Kaiser, 2009, 2012; Singer, 2008). Even though the director in this scenario may have good intentions – namely, saving you time and effort – complying with her request would still be a violation of professional ethics. Your organization ensures your customers of the confidentiality of their data; the same applies to employee data.

Now, consider this. You are working with your L&D group to prepare a proposal for a management development program for a new, external client. Your organization has worked long and hard to get this client's business; so, there is widespread concern about proposing a package of solutions that will deliver a quality program at the lowest price possible.

A few days after your organization submits its proposal, the client responds and says he will accept your proposal if you remove the needs assessment work, along with its associated costs and timing. If your L&D group agrees to remove the needs assessment from the proposal, is that a violation of professional ethics?

We get requests like that all of the time, you may be thinking. Requests to reduce the price of professional services are certainly a normal part of the competitive landscape in which L&D professionals must work. Whether we are acquiring a new client or setting the stage for repeat business, we should always be mindful of the triple constraints of quality, time, and cost. Nevertheless, in this particular scenario, the request was not merely to cut the price of the proposed solution package but to do so at the expense of one particular – and critical – component of the design process, namely, the collection and analysis of evidence to support your recommended package of solutions. In other words, your L&D group is being asked to make a less-than-informed recommendation. Earlier in this book, we examined the criticality of evidence-based decision-making to the success of L&D solutions and the consequences of short-cutting the data gathering and analysis process. To comply with the request in this scenario not only carries the risk of proposing a solution that will fail to address the root causes of the client's problem but also forces your L&D group to consider the extent to which it is (not) adhering to one of the essential IBSTPI standards and performance competencies, namely, "identify and respond to ethical, legal, and political implications of design in the workplace" (IBSTPI, 2014).

The good news is that ethics violations of the same scale and notoriety as an Enron or a Wells Fargo have not occurred in the field of L&D. However, this is not to say that L&D professionals always behave ethically or that ethics violations in our field are less damaging than in finance, medicine, or other fields where the bad apples capture the headlines. In fact, the conditions that lead to unethical behaviors in our field are not always as obvious as in the first scenario presented above. In fact, as designers, we may sometimes be unaware of where good business practices end and ethical challenges begin. In a profession that relies heavily on referrals, clarity about what is (not) a challenge to the ethics of our profession is essential. Furthermore, professional ethics, both as practice and as theory, is part of the larger field of business ethics and ethical decision-making. Consequently, in this chapter, we will

- Review the highlights of the business ethics literature, including definitions, models, and main themes related to ethical decision-making;
- Examine the codes of conduct for ethical behaviors among L&D professionals, including learning design and technologies professionals; and
- Identify some of the ethical pitfalls (and how to avoid them) in a rapidly changing landscape.

Business Ethics: Not an Oxymoron

When David Mayer, Associate Professor of Management and Organizations at the University of Michigan's Ross School of Business, asked the question, "Is business ethics an oxymoron?" (Mayer, 2015), he was sharing the thinking of both scholars and the general public about the overemphasis in business on economic gain at the expense of ethical behavior. The money vs. morality dichotomy is not just a function of highly publicized scandals or stories of CEO compensation packages larger than the GDP of some countries. Scholars in a variety of disciplines have published studies demonstrating that greed is often baked into the university business curriculum and, thus, transfers to leadership behaviors in organizations (Takacs Haynes, Josefy, & Hitt, 2015; Wang, Malhotra, & Murnighan, 2011). Others have argued that it is part of the belief in American culture that money correlates with moral and ethical deficiency (Kouchaki, Smith-Crowe, Brief, & Sousa, 2013; Martin, Cote, & Woodruff, 2016). Money vs. morality is only one of many streams in a very robust and active area of business ethics research.

Business ethics as a field of study is large, with roots going back to Aristotle. Contributors to business ethics research come from a variety of disciplines, such as philosophy, economics, law, and public policy, among others, A comprehensive review of the business ethics literature is far beyond the scope of this book (for a high-level introduction, see Moriarity, 2016). Instead, we will focus on those aspects of the literature that relate to ethical decision-making, including factors that influence how L&D professionals make decisions about designing and developing interventions to solve business problems.

Definitions

By now, it should come as no surprise that there is rarely a universally accepted definition of anything that relates to human behavior. This certainly holds true when seeking a definition of business ethics. Lewis (1985) attempted to synthesize the hundreds of definitions he found in the literature by defining business ethics as "rules, standards, codes, or principles which provide guidelines for morally right behavior and truthfulness in specific situations" (p. 381). However, the relatively abstract nature of his synthesized definition and the dearth of research on how managers actually apply those moral rules, standards, codes, and principles in their personal and professional lives led Lewis to conclude that defining business ethics was "like nailing Jello to a wall."

Nevertheless, attempts to formulate definitions continue. Some scholars have sought to identify those characteristics that distinguish business ethics from ethics as defined in other disciplines. For example, Dean (1993) offered a four-tiered definition of ethics, morals, values, and business ethics as follows:

1   Ethics consists of the rules or standards that govern the conduct of the members of a group.
2   Morals are the personal judgments, standards, and rules of conduct based on fundamental duties of promoting human welfare, acknowledging human equality or justice, and honoring individual freedom or respect of persons.
3   Values refer to the core beliefs or desires that guide or motivate the individual's attitudes and actions, such as honesty, integrity, and fairness.
4   Business ethics are the moral principles or standards that guide behavior in the world of business.

Using this four-tiered definition, Dean focused on normative ethics or the practical task of establishing moral standards and acceptable behaviors, including the way in which professionals articulate their duties and view the consequences of their actions. Normative ethics is the foundation for decisions but first require an awareness and understanding of that foundation in order to engage in ethical decision-making:

> To make professionally sound and ethical decisions and contributions, we must be aware of the factors that influence our work. Increasing our awareness of ethical and professional standards and adhering to them, will increase the likelihood of adding value to our clients, our organization, our field, ourselves, and the communities we affect through our work. (Dean, 1993, p. 1043)

Shaw (1996) sought to describe the features of business ethics as an academic field of study and pedagogical topic in North America. Based on a review of the extant literature, Shaw identified three models of business ethics: (a) the standard model or individual moral decision model that focuses on the individual and the moral choices, dilemmas, and decisions that individuals face in an organizational context; (b) the politics model that focuses on the business system as a whole, its overall morality, its institutional norms, organizational structures, and priorities; and (c) the virtue model that focuses on moral sensitivity, practical wisdom, a commitment to certain core human values, a tolerance for moral ambiguity, and an appreciation of the moral complexity of our lives. Shaw called for the integration of all three models into one academic paradigm but acknowledged that business ethics may be too rich a field for any one form of intellectual inquiry to capture. Frisque, Lin, and Kolb (2004) used the broad definition of ethics as principles, norms, and standards of conduct governing an individual or group as the basis for teaching and training ethics in corporations and universities. Their rationale for ethics teaching/training revolved around the centrality of individual responsibility to ethical behavior in the workplace, and the resurgence of ethics programs, conferences, and professional codes of conduct.

Guerra (2006) offered a slightly different perspective, defining ethics as focusing on values and what is right and wrong in a moral context. Only then can one establish principles of right behavior to guide the actions of individuals and groups. Ethics "examines issues beyond the adherence to social convention; it explores rational existence" (pp. 1025–6). Guerra further noted that ethics differs from religion in that it seeks to justify its principles based on logic rather than supremacy. Svensson and Wood (2008) constructed a business ethics framework consisting of three principal components (expectations, perceptions, and evaluations) interconnected by five sub-components (societal expectations, organizational values, norms and beliefs, outcomes, societal evaluation, and reconnection). However, there is no evidence that the framework has ever been tested or operationalized in a real-world context.

Other definitions of business ethics include:

- The study and examination of moral and social responsibility in relation to business practices and decision-making in business (Business ethics, n.d. a);
- The study of proper business policies and practices regarding potentially controversial issues, such as corporate governance, insider trading, bribery, discrimination, corporate social responsibility, and fiduciary responsibilities (Business ethics, n.d. b);
- Awareness of organizational values, guidelines and codes, and behaving within those boundaries when faced with dilemmas in business or professional work (SHRM, 2017); and
- The application of a moral code of conduct to the strategic and operational management of a business (Applied Corporate Governance, n.d.).

All of these definitions share some common terms, such as "moral," "values," and "conduct." However, universal agreement as to the meaning of these terms and how to operationalize them remains elusive. The challenge associated with defining business ethics is similar to the challenges associated with ethics as a field of study as well as practice in that "ethics requires trust, and trust is built on a foundation of moral and cultural norms. A significant issue facing ethicists and writers on the subject is that there is no common global culture" (Hill, 2006, p. 1048).

Models and Themes

An alternative approach to defining business ethics has been to describe what constitutes ethical decision-making in business. In his seminal work on individual decision-making and behavior, Rest (1986) constructed a four-step model: (a) recognize the moral issue; (b) make a moral judgment; (c) resolve to place moral concerns ahead of other concerns; and (d) act on the moral concerns. In other words, the core of the Rest model is moral awareness, which he defined as the ability to interpret a situation as being moral, and moral judgement as the ability of a decision-maker to decide which course of action is morally correct. Moral intent is the ability to prioritize moral values over other values, and moral behavior is the application of moral intent to the situation.

Building on Rest's four-step model, Jones (1991) developed the concept of moral intensity. Moral intensity is the extent to which an individual views an issue as a moral one, and that perception is influenced by (a) the magnitude of the consequences or the sum of harm and benefits of an issue to those involved; (b) social consensus or the degree of social agreement that a proposed act is good or bad; (c) probability of effect or the probability that the act will actually take place and will harm or benefit those involved; (d) temporal immediacy or the length of time between the present and the act; (e) proximity or the feeling of immediacy to those involved; and (f) concentration of effect or the strength of consequences for those involved.

Gatewood and Carroll (1991) sought to develop a framework to assess the ethical performance of members of an organization. They began with a review of the literature on ethics measurement and used the following principles of measurement to build their conceptual framework:

1 The measurement system should be linked to the philosophy, culture, strategy, and goals of the organization.
2 Measurement should be applied to all levels of employees in the organization.
3 Multiple measures should be used within jobs and across levels.
4 Different measurement systems may be appropriate for different organizational units.
5 Measurement may be applied to an individual or a group of workers, depending on the characteristics of the work.
6 Measurement should address both long- and short-term aspects of performance.
7 Measurement should address both behaviors and results.
8 Whatever is being assessed should be under the control of the individual(s) being evaluated.

By separating individual from group performance, behavior from results, and actions taken that are discretionary from actions that are in response to mandates of law, Gatewood and Carroll sought to make operationalizing the framework more feasible by enabling organizations to be specific in the standards of expected ethical behavior or results, and then incorporate those standards into existing performance measurement systems. However, there is little evidence that organizations have adopted the Gatewood and Carroll framework.

Part of the money vs. morality stream of research discussed earlier, Cohen's research (1993) explored the role of the work environment and the extent to which organizational norms and values create an ethical climate. Using the terms "ethical" and "moral" interchangeably, Cohen defined ethical conduct as intentionally responsible action that seeks to prevent, avoid, or rectify harm to organizational constituents. Unethical conduct would be the evasion of responsibility, violation of social contracts, and in most cases, producing harm to organizational constituents. She deemed ethical climate to be a product of organizational culture and defined it as the way in which an organization typically handles issues such as responsibility, accountability, communication, regulation, equity, trust, and the welfare of constituents. Using Robert Merton's (Merton, 1968) theory of social structure and anomie – a condition of normlessness and social disequilibrium resulting from a discrepancy between means and ends – Cohen discussed the process by which organizational anomie produces work climates discouraging ethical conduct among employees. Specifically, when organizational culture creates anomie, this is not conducive to an ethical climate. Unethical conduct emerges when management places excessively strong emphasis on goal attainment without a corresponding focus on observing legitimate procedures to accomplish those goals. Only when management takes steps to reduce anomie by modeling exemplary behaviors, policies, and decision-making can an ethical work climate be created.

In their review of the business ethics literature, O'Fallon and Butterfield (2005) sought to find common themes in the studies of descriptive ethics, which is concerned with explaining and predicting an individual's actual behavior. They observed that the most consistent predictors appear in the studies that test for the direct effects of gender, ethical philosophies (idealism, relativism), cognitive moral development, locus of control, the use of cunning and duplicity by management, and religions. Mixed findings were most common in studies focusing on education level, work experience, nationality, and age. The variables examined most often were codes of ethics, ethical climate and culture, industry type, organizational size, and rewards and sanctions. O'Fallon and Butterfield noted that codes of ethics and ethical climate/culture dominate the organizational research field of ethical decision-making, with the most common research questions relating to how an organization's code of ethics impacted or influenced the ethical behavior of employees and management. While noting advances, they critiqued the lack of solid theoretical grounding, problems in the operationalization and measurement of ethical/unethical behavior, and the lack of consideration of interaction effects.

Appelbaum, Iaconi, and Matousek's (2007) review of the literature examined the impact of deviant workplace behaviors on organizations. They examined positive deviant behaviors – intentional behaviors that depart from group norms in honorable ways, are praiseworthy, and have honorable intentions regardless of the outcomes – as well as negative deviant behaviors – those that violate norms, policies, and internal rules. The authors argued that toxic organizations depend on employees who are dishonest and deceitful in order to be successful but that psychological empowerment is likely to be a key enabler of positive deviance. The survival of an organization in the face of negative deviant employees was possible with a remodeling of organizational norms, attitudes, and social values centered on the organization's core values.

Table 13.1 summarizes the main themes from the conceptual studies of ethical decision-making. Efforts to describe the components and process of ethical decision-making and how to measure ethical behaviors were the dominant themes in the literature. In an update to O'Fallon and Butterfield's review, Craft (2013) added that despite the addition of new variables being studied, Rest's 1986 four-step model remains the foundation of research on ethical decision-making. Rest's model can be found at the heart of more recent literature reviews on topics such as corporate social responsibility (Malik, 2015; Scherer & Palazzo, 2011), ethics, and organizational performance (Carter & Greer, 2013; Chun, Shin, Choi, & Kim, 2013), as well as discipline-specific literature reviews, such as social work (Gough & Spencer, 2014) and small business/entrepreneurship (Welsh & Birch, 2015).

Some of the themes just reviewed have been studied empirically. For example, there have been empirical studies of the relationship between moral intensity and ethical decision-making (see, for example, Barnett, 2001; Sweeney & Costello, 2009), with social consensus found to be the dominant influence. However, some studies were conducted using student samples and most relied on self-assessments of moral intensity, key problems identified in the research methods literature (Fuchs & Sarstedt, 2009; Podsakoff & Organ, 1986).

In contrast, Trevino, Weaver, Gibson, and Toffler (1999) sought to investigate ethical attitudes and behaviors as they actually occur in the workplace. To do this, they mailed a survey questionnaire to the homes of 10,000 randomly selected employees at all levels in six large US companies in a variety of industries. They found that consistency between policies and actions as well as dimensions of an organization's culture, such as ethical leadership, fair treatment of employees, and open discussion of ethics in the organization, have a greater impact on employee attitudes and behaviors regardless of whether or not the organization has a formal ethics or

Table 13.1 Highlights of Conceptual Studies of Ethical Decision-Making

Focus	Authors	Themes

Description of ethical decision-making	Rest (1986)	• Four-step model:
		  • Recognize moral issues
		  • Make moral judgments
		  • Resolve to place moral concerns ahead of other concerns
		  • Act on moral concerns
		• Moral awareness and intent as core constructs
		• Moral behavior as application of moral intent

Influences on decision-making	Jones (1991)	• Moral intensity influencers:
		  • Magnitude of consequences
		  • Social consensus
		  • Probability of effect
		  • Temporal immediacy
		  • Proximity
		  • Concentration of effect

Ethical performance measurement	Gatewood and Carroll (1991)	• Eight principles of measurement:
		  • Linked to organizational philosophy, culture, strategy, goals
		  • Applied to all levels of employees
		  • Multiple measures within jobs, across levels
		  • Specific measurement systems for specific business units
		  • Individuals and groups measured separately
		  • Long- and short-term performance measurement
		  • Behavior and results measured separately
		  • Assess what is controllable by those being assessed

Ethical climate	Cohen (1993)	• Focus on goal attainment without emphasis on legitimate procedures to accomplish goals yields anomie • Anomie in work environment contributes to unethical conduct • Anomie reduced when management models ethical conduct in behaviors, policies, and decision-making
Exploration of common themes in the literature	O'Fallon and Butterfield (2005)	• Codes of ethics and ethical climate/culture dominate ethical decision-making research • Most common research questions relate to impact of organizational codes of ethics on employee and management behavior • Critique of "soft" theoretical grounding in current models and measures of ethical behavior
Deviant workplace behaviors	Appelbaum, Iaconi, and Matousek (2007)	• Positive deviance departs from group norms in honorable ways • Negative deviance violates, norms, policies, internal rules • Psychological empowerment of employees enables positive deviance • Remodeling of organizational norms, attitudes, social values to deter negative deviance

compliance program. Conversely, what hurts most is an ethical culture that emphasizes self-interest and unquestioning obedience to authority, and the perception that the ethics or compliance program exists only to protect top management from blame. Weaver (2004) continued the theme of consistency between policy and action when he stated, "When employees are convinced that their company is committed to fixing its ethical problems, they are more likely to blow the whistle internally, in constructive ways, when they observe a problem" (p. 121). A perceived lack of ethics would not only discourage whistle-blowing but would also be a barrier to information sharing needed for organizational success due the lack of trust and high degree of cautiousness.

Empirical research on the effects of ethical climate has focused on employee job satisfaction (Deshpande, 1996), on scope and quality of medical care for dying patients (Hamric & Blackhall, 2007), on the likelihood of deviant behaviors (e.g., theft and sexual harassment) (Peterson, 2002), and on customer service performance (Yin Lau et al., 2017). However, there was wide variation in the structure and content of the instruments used to measure ethical climate. The relationship between codes of conduct and ethical attitudes and behaviors has also been explored in the field of accounting and finance. For example, in a study of 613 US management accountants, Somers (2001) found that corporate codes are associated with less perceived wrongdoing in an organization but not with an increased propensity to report observed unethical behavior. Furthermore, Somers found that organizations adopting formal codes of ethics exhibited value orientations that went beyond financial performance to include responsibility to the community at large. In contrast to corporate codes of ethics, professional codes of ethical conduct had no influence on perceived wrongdoing in organizations nor did those codes affect the propensity to report observed unethical activities. However, there are studies whose findings are just the opposite of Somers, which suggests that the nature of the accounting profession, if not the finance industry as a whole, may act as hidden variables affecting ethical behavior.

Summary

The literature on ethical decision-making attributes both individual and organizational factors to ethical workplace behaviors. For the individual, awareness of what is (not) ethical behavior helps to determine the extent to which that individual perceives an issue as (a) posing an ethical challenge and (b) requiring a response. The organizational environment, particularly the culture and tone set by management, helps to determine the extent to which the individual feels empowered to address ethical challenges. Organizations often rely on their own ethical codes of conduct to mitigate the disconnect between what the organization deems to be (un)ethical behavior and what the employee perceives as the organization's commitment to ethical behavior. Public and private sector organizations may also offer ethics training to help employees respond appropriately when questionable issues cross their paths. However, the components of ethics training may vary based on industry sector and on whether training is offered as part of a suite of compliance training, as is often the case in the public sector, or on the extent to which an organization's leadership deems ethics to be strategic to organizational sustainability and growth.

Ethics in the Field of L&D

Although ethics tends to be a less visible topic in publications, conferences and events, or other outlets by which we engage with others in our profession, professional ethics has a clear and prominent place in the field of L&D. The scholarly and practitioner literature, as well as the professional codes of conduct published by the various associations for L&D professionals, illustrate the importance of ethics to our field.

L&D Professional Ethics in the Literature

As the L&D profession expanded to include not only instructional designers but also performance improvement specialists, specialists in Human Resource Development, Human Capital, and other areas of workforce development, the topic of professional ethics also gained more visibility in professional publications. As part of a research-based series aimed at helping Human Resource Development (HRD) practitioners better understand their field and improve their performance, McLagan (1989) identified thirteen ethical issues that may arise for professionals working in the HRD domain, including L&D professionals:

1 Keeping an appropriate level of confidentiality.
2 Answering in the negative to improper or unsuitable requests.
3 Showing respect for copyrights and for all sources of intellectual property in general.
4 Taking care that statements, data, and recommendations are truthful.
5 Balancing the needs and interests of individuals with those of the organization.
6 Assuring clients and consumers of one's involvement, participation, and a sense of co-ownership.
7 Avoiding conflicting interests.
8 Controlling and counterbalancing personal prejudices and preferences.
9 Showing respect for and interest in (and also standing up against discrimination) differences between persons and peoples.
10 Doing justice to clients' and consumers' interests.

11 Showing understanding for direct and indirect effects of interventions and taking initiatives against negative consequences.
12 Fixing reasonable cost prices and standard prices for products and services.
13 Making an appropriate use of power and influence.

McLagan reduced these issues to four main dilemmas:

1 Professional integrity (issues 1–4, 12), which consists of strictly applying professional standards, rules, and criteria for the profession, and adapting these rules and standards in order to safeguard the interests of or favor the persons concerned. McLagan offered an example of the professional integrity dilemma that is not unlike one of the scenarios offered at the beginning of this chapter, namely, the omission of a needs analysis due to budgetary or time constraints, even though needs analysis is a necessary process for the precise setting of aims and final responsibilities.
2 Detached involvement (issues 6–8, 10), which concerns the designer-client relationship in which intense involvement is balanced with objectivity. McLagan's example of detached involvement was the client who makes extensive use of course material found on his own but does not want to hear anything about other possible solutions, while still demanding full effort and dedication from L&D for a solution that he found himself. This is similar to the department head returning from a conference and demanding that his L&D group adopt the latest-and-greatest what-not exhibited at the conference, regardless of whether or not that what-not solves a current or potential problem.
3 Ambivalent manipulation (issues 5, 9, 13), which refers to the aim of content and training in relation to participants. The example provided is a situation in which a training package is offered to employees as a career development opportunity when, in fact, it is actually a means of selection in order to fire a proportion of the employee base. The dilemma is whether all the aims of training – including those formulated at the organizational level – should be made known to employees, considering the risk that nobody might want to take the training being offered.
4 Accepted responsibility (issue 11), which concerns client and L&D expectations about responsibility over the training design and development. McLagan offered an example of the L&D professional who thinks that the client with wishes that are at variance with ethical practices would change his mind during the development process, whereas the client thinks that L&D will eventually comply with his wishes.

McLagan concluded that it is the responsibility of the L&D professional to recognize and address ethical dilemmas through (a) orientation sessions to help anticipate and identify ethical dilemmas at an early stage, and

(b) analysis of and intervention planning for ethical dilemmas. What McLagan did not offer was a concrete plan of action for implementing either of these two methods. Bergenhenegouwen (1996) advocated the adoption of McLagan's orientation sessions and analysis of/planning for ethical dilemmas in The Netherlands and the UK. Bergenhenegouwen was responding to the lack of an ethical professional code for industrial trainers in those countries at that point in time but, like McLagan, offered no concrete plan of action for implementation.

The rise of the Internet and its role in L&D stimulated research on the relationship between ethics and technology. Lin (2006) explored the environmental factors in which technology operates in all occupational areas of HRD – instructional design, performance improvement, etc. – using a PEST (political, economic, socio-cultural, technological) analysis to examine trends that affect the ethical issues related to the use of technology. Political trends included new laws and regulations, established by federal agencies, and increased political cooperation among countries to establish 21st century ethical perspectives in a global environment. Economic trends included globalization and ethical business conduct, while socio-cultural trends focused on issues of diversity and multiculturalism. Technological trends centered around privacy, intellectual property, violent content on the Internet, and digital literacy. In a review of the literature focused on learning technologies, Lin identified the following potential ethical breaches:

- HRD professionals may lie about their technological credentials to potential customers in order to sell technology-related products.
- HRD professionals may choose to disclose insufficient and inaccurate information in order to win business.
- Technology serves as a replacement for all existing solution alternatives, thus overshadowing the customer's learning needs.
- Instructional interventions are not appropriate to the customer's or the user's needs because performance analysis of the use of technology is not conducted.
- Some organizations may reuse or reorganize learning content without paying for digital rights in order to lower the cost of design, development, and delivery of such material.
- Personal data, such as training records, are disclosed to unintended audiences.
- Employees' online activities and personal information are tracked and categorized within the organization without the acknowledgment of the employees.
- Equal access to training and other technology-based, career-enhancing activities are denied to those who have no power or resources.
- The interpretation of the ethical use of technology, such as intellectual property, is divergent and culture-specific.

Lin noted that to overcome potential ethical minefields, HRD professionals need to analyze the effects of technology applications on learning, adding that HRD professionals should conduct appropriate performance analysis to justify that technology applications are the best fit and can supplement the intervention.

Although the HRD literature addressed professional ethics issues fairly early on, Moore and Ellsworth (2014) conducted a review of the literature specific to instructional design and technology and concluded that there was little research focused on ethical concerns. They also highlighted the lack of explicit educational preparation in university instructional design and technology programs to manage ethical issues, particularly when compared to ethical awareness and scaffolding in other domains. Not long after the publication of Moore and Ellsworth's critique, the journal *Educational Technology Research & Development (ETR&D)* devoted an entire issue to explore the relationship of ethics and privacy in learning analytics and design. As part of that special journal issue, Gray and Boling (2016) noted that despite the existence of codes of ethics in the L&D professions, ethics is not part of the daily vocabulary of instructional design and technology practitioners. Drawing on the work of ethics scholars from other disciplines as a foundation, Gray and Boling defined ethics as a systematic expression of rules or normative commitments often associated with professions or communities. As such, professional ethics differ from values, defined as more personal in nature, determining the extent to which ethics on a professional level or morality on a social level are applied in everyday decision-making.

To illustrate how ethical decision-making permeates daily instructional design practice, Gray and Boling conducted a content analysis of eight journal articles that documented how specific design artifacts came into being, identifying design decisions or aspects that exemplified the selection of or reliance on an ethical framework. Their findings identified six ethical and value-related themes: (a) prioritization of constraints; (b) maintenance and buy-in of stakeholders; (c) cultural or site-specific adaptation; (d) inclusion and equality of access; (e) agency of the learner; and (f) design philosophy. The themes illustrated how ethics and values are intertwined with the instructional designer's character and are inscribed in the designs they create. They concluded by calling for a heightened understanding of the ethical and value-related concerns in the training and practice of instructional design, along with greater sharing of documentation around design artifacts to enrich the literature on ethical decision-making in instructional design.

Another article in the special issue of *ETR&D* focused on normative ethics in educational technology (Spector, 2016) and proposed an educational technology ethics framework consisting of three interacting dimensions: (a) values, comprised of constructs such as lifelong learning, inquiry, respect, knowledge, and diversity; (b) principles, such as providing clear and specific goals and expectations, fairness and openness in assessing and evaluating progress, and recognizing the contributions of all those involved; and (c) people, including the designer, developer, instructor, and the student. This framework, along with all of the other articles in the journal's special issue, was focused on academic settings rather than workplace settings. Nevertheless, the various influencers of ethical decision-making (values, beliefs, organizational culture, etc.) apply to both academic and non-academic settings.

Professional Codes of Conduct

The professional associations identified in the first chapter of this book have also published professional codes of ethics for their members. As shown in Table 13.2, the ethics statements are framed in the context of the respective target audiences of each association but contain many of the same basic principles.

First documented in 1974, then updated in 2007, The AECT Code of Ethics (AECT, 2007) is targeted toward educators and practitioners employed in academic settings. The Code consists of three core components, with each component containing a number of focus statements. For example, the first component, Commitment to the Individual, consists of nine focus statements concerning the designer as well as the learner. Elements such as the right of access to materials of varying points of view, the protection of privacy and personal integrity, the promotion of current and sound professional practices in the use of technology in education, and the avoidance of content that reinforces or promotes gender, racial, or religious stereotypes are included in the focus statements aimed at commitment to the individual. The second component, Commitment to Society, contains six focus statements concerning fair and equitable practices, clear, distinct, and honest representation of personal and organizational views, and nonacceptance of gratuities, gifts or favors, among other elements. The third and final component, Commitment to the Profession, contains ten focus statements concerning, among other things, professionally accepted guidelines and procedures for conducting research, and the reporting of illegal or unethical conduct of fellow members of the profession to the AECT Professional Ethics Committee.

The Academy of Human Resource Development established its Standards on Ethics and Integrity in 1999. Aimed at HRD educators and practitioners in all workplace settings, the AHRD code of ethics (Academy of Human Resource Development, 1999) reflects the interdisciplinary nature of HRD as a profession and the multiple functional roles and occupations within that profession. To that end, AHRD begins with a set of six general principles – competency, integrity, professional responsibility, respect for people's rights and dignity, concern for other's welfare, and social responsibility – that are similar in content to the AECT core commitments. AHRD adds seven categories of standards that reflect potential

Table 13.2 Professional Codes of Conduct for L&D Professionals

	AECT	AHRD	ATD	ISPI	IBSTPI
Target Audience	• Educators • Practitioners employed in educational settings	• Academics • Practitioners in all workplace settings	• Practitioners in non-academic settings	• Performance improvement practitioners in industry, government, private consulting, and academia	• Practitioners in L&D-related occupations
Code of Ethics	• Commitment to the individual (e.g., right of access to materials, opportunity for program participation)	• General principles (competence, integrity, professional responsibility, respect for people's rights and dignity, concern for other's welfare, social responsibility)	• Recognize individual rights and dignities • Develop human potential	• Add value • Validated practice • Collaboration • Continuous improvement • Integrity • Uphold confidentiality	• Identify ethical, legal, political dimensions of ID practice and instructional products (advanced)
	• Commitment to society (e.g., honest representation of the institution or organization with which the person is affiliated, no acceptance of gifts, gratuities or favors that might impair professional judgment)	• General standards (e.g., boundaries of competence, third party requests for services, records, and data)	• Provide highest level quality education, training and development • Comply with copyright laws and the laws and regulations governing work position • Keep informed of pertinent knowledge and competence in the field	• Plan for, respond to ethical, legal, political consequences of design decisions (advanced)	

(continued)

Table 13.2 Professional Codes of Conduct for L&D Professionals (*continued*)

AECT	AHRD	ATD	ISPI	IBSTPI
• Commitment to the profession (e.g., no use of coercive means of promises of special treatment to influence colleagues, avoid commercial exploitation of Association membership)	• Research and evaluation standards (e.g., data collection, informed consent, deception in research)	• Maintain confidentiality and integrity • Support peers and avoid contact that impedes their practice	• Recognize, respect intellectual property rights of others (essential)	
• Publication of work (e.g., publication credit, ownership of intellectual property)	• Advertising and other public statements (e.g., media presentations, avoidance of false or deceptive statements)	• Improve public understanding of workplace learning and talent development	• Adhere to regulatory guidelines and organizational policies	
• Privacy and confidentiality (e.g., maintenance and ownership of records, disclosures)	• Represent professional credentials, qualifications, experience, and ability fairly and accurately	• Comply with organizational and professional codes of ethics (essential)		
• Teaching and facilitating (e.g., limitation on training and instruction, assessment of performance)	• Contribute to continuing growth of the profession			
• Resolution of ethical issues and violations (e.g., cooperation with ethics committees, improper complaints)				

ethical challenges associated with each of the HRD occupational functions. For example, there are ethical standards for research and evaluation, a function undertaken by nearly all HRD professionals; standards for publication of work, a function undertaken primarily by HRD scholars; and standards for teaching and facilitating, a function undertaken by educators and trainers. In 2011, AHRD supplemented the Standards document with a formal Whistleblower Policy document that spells out the processes and procedures for handling complaints under the Resolution of Ethical Issues standard. AHRD reviews and updates the Standards as needed.

The Association for Talent Development (ATD) takes a broader approach to professional ethics. As part of its vision and mission (Association for Talent Development, 2017), ATD lists eleven statements that serve as a "public declaration" of talent development professionals' obligations to themselves, their profession, and society. The statements are intended to serve as guidance so that professionals can self-manage their ethical behavior. Consequently, the statements are a blend of generic commitments to ethical behaviors and some of the basic professional skill/competency statements discussed in the first chapter of this book.

The International Society for Performance Improvement (ISPI) code of ethics is grounded in six principles that reflect the fact that its members primarily tend to be performance improvement consultants working with external clients. The principles go beyond ethical behaviors and include statements about the quality of work delivered to clients (International Society for Performance Improvement, 2016). For instance, the Add Value Principle focuses on delivering results; the Validated Practice Principle emphasizes use and promotion of strategies and standards in performance technology; the Collaboration principle stresses the importance of being a trusted strategic partner; the Continuous Improvement principle focuses on the professional's own skills and abilities; the Integrity Principle stresses honest and truthful representations; and the Uphold Confidentiality Principle focuses on conflict of interest as well as confidentiality. To receive ISPI (re)certification, professionals must sign a statement saying that they agree to adhere to the six principles.

The International Board of Standards for Training, Performance and Instruction (IBSTPI) has typically embedded codes of ethics into the competencies and performance statements of each of the functional occupations for which it has defined standards (evaluators, instructional designers, instructors, online learners, training managers). The IBSTPI ethical standards for instructional designers address many of the same ethical issues and behaviors described in the other association standards just discussed. Where IBSTPI differs is in the classification of each ethical standard into those competencies most appropriate for new instructional designers (essential) and those for experienced instructional designers (advanced). Moreover, IBSTPI places a particularly strong emphasis on copyright and intellectual property:

Given current-day conditions, one of the many ibstpi standards that deserves special attention is that which indicates the importance of respecting the copyright and intellectual property rights of others. In an era where the Internet is regularly used to display and share a wide variety of types of intellectual property, and where tools for copying and editing such properties are abundant, copying and using the intellectual property of others, without first seeking and receiving their permission, has become an all-too-common activity. Those involved in the instructional design profession need to be acutely aware of the ethical and legal issues involved in undertaking this inappropriate activity and must avoid engaging in it. (Koszalka et al., 2013, p. 38)

Summary

By now, it should be clear what is meant by ethical behavior and what is expected of L&D professionals in the workplace. Of the many issues addressed in the various codes of ethics just reviewed, copyright and intellectual property are the issues that are both legal issues and ethical issues. Legal issues are issues governed by laws and regulations about what people can (not) do, with specific penalties and consequences associated with violations. Ethical issues are issues grounded in moral standards that govern what people should (not) do, but have no fines or associated penalties when people fail to abide by those moral standards. An action may be legal but that doesn't make it ethical. Dr. Chris MacDonald, director of the Jim Pattison Ethical Leadership Education & Research program at Toronto's Ryerson University, offered the following examples to illustrate the difference between legal and ethical behavior:

Most kinds of lying are perfectly legal, but lying is generally recognized as being unethical; breaking promises is generally legal, but is widely thought of as unethical; cheating on your husband or wife or boyfriend or girlfriend is legal, but unethical, though the rule against it is perhaps more honoured in the breach. (MacDonald, 2011)

Identifying Ethical Pitfalls

Despite consistency across the various professional codes of ethics and the importance of ethical behavior discussed in the scholarly and practitioner literature, L&D professionals may still find themselves facing a potential ethical dilemma when asked to make trade-offs as part of the design decision-making process. Let's see what Paul Roitman Bardack, Attorney and Senior Solutions Architect at SAIC, has to say about ethical behavior and learning professionals in the last of our *E-Suite Views*:

SvR: As part of their academic studies, aspiring professionals, either in instructional design or human performance technology, are told about the importance of ethical behaviors. If you look at some of the industry standards, whether it be from IBSTPI or whether it be from ISPI, they all have very clear statements about ethical standards and behaviors but there's little insight as to what constitutes ethical behavior, ethics, or how that differs from issues like copyright and intellectual property. What is it that Learning and Development professionals need to know or at least be aware of, when it comes to ethics?

PRB: Yes, don't oversell beyond what the client needs. That's my most immediate response and where I believe I understand the question, that you're not asking me about following the law of copyright or intellectual property. That's not what you're talking about. You're talking about the standards that govern the ordinary day-to-day behavior of the person who's doing instructional systems design or otherwise engaged in the learning or training fields. I believe that's what you're asking.

SvR: That's correct.

PRB: Yes. So, what I see is the biggest ... Okay, let me take a step back. In my last answer, I talked about greater segmentation within the field. So, if there's greater segmentation, then each person who has a more refined, more specialized base of knowledge, a more refined target audience for her or his needs, there's greater pressure on them to sell their services. There's a lot of competition out there. They've got to sell their services. How do you sell these services? You market. You constantly try to sell and selling could be in the private sector. For example, where I currently work, selling could be in the university sector, it could be in the NGO sector, could be in government, but you're always trying to sell your services to validate why you should continue to be employed. I think the economic pressure, day to day pressures, keep selling, keep selling, keep selling and, therefore, the ethical question is: At what point do you ... have you crossed the line where you're selling something that you're not so sure the client really needs, and you're taking advantage because the client, by almost any definition, doesn't know what they need? That's why they're seeking to hire someone else because they don't know how to proceed in this.

         For example, I have seen ... go back to the ADDIE process. I have seen other professionals in this field, who, even though the client really needed help only, say, with just design, but in selling the prior analysis or follow-on development and implementation services, argue that it's a package and it's iterative and you can't have one without the other. So, the client is thinking,

"Geez, I just want somebody to design something. I thought it was a relatively manageable project but I now hear that to do it right, I've got to buy all these other services and they're making a compelling case that I need all these services but I didn't budget for that. I wasn't thinking that I needed that but maybe I do." That, I think is the ethical, from my vantage point, the biggest ethical dilemma that I see in the learning, training field. All this economic pressure to push you to the line and maybe, even sometimes over the line of selling what the client may not necessarily need.

SvR: It's interesting you should bring up that particular type of example because one of the challenges, particularly for the entry level or early career designer, is knowing the difference between overselling, like the example you just gave, and just sound instructional design best practice. For example, the client who says, "Go design me something and don't include evaluation." "Well, how do you know it worked?" type of thing is the classic example. So, how do they recognize best practice vs. over the line?

PRB: Every case is different and I know in my own professional life, I was trained as a lawyer. I think I told you that.

SvR: Right.

PRB: So, what I like to do, the way lawyers work, you just ask lots and lots and lots and lots of questions even though others would say, "Oh, that's a dumb question," but you keep probing, keep probing and in doing it, what I'll find is that, no, I really don't have to ethically, before you get to ethics, substantively, I really don't have to sell all aspects of the ADDIE process because they don't have to evaluate to the extent that others evaluate. Maybe in another year, maybe in another three or five years. They may need a more formal evaluative mechanism later but for now, just starting from ground zero and, you know, good enough may be good enough. So, you ask a lot of questions about the client's needs and where are they coming from, where was the client before, what are they hoping to do, why are they hoping to do it, what are the options they previously considered, what are the budgetary constraints, what are the logistical constraints, what are the small "p" political constraints upon them. If you really get a full picture of the context in which the client is operating, well, if you do it right, it'll become pretty apparent to you and to the client, more or less simultaneously, what's needed and what's overselling. That's the way substantively to shape an engagement with the client and to do so in a way that is substantively comfortable to everybody and therefore you have avoided the potential ethical conflict. You're not

	overselling because you and the client are trying to figure out the need and you both see the same thing at the same time.
SvR:	That makes sense if you're the consultant who's selling or even if you're a business analyst for the company. What if you're just another instructional designer sitting in the Learning and Development department of an organization and somebody else sells the business. Does that mean you don't have to really be … you don't get confronted with ethical issues or do they pop up in some other way?
PRB:	So, in my example, you're right. In my example, I was thinking to say about me or one of my colleagues in the consulting firm in which I currently work but in your example, let's say, you're working for the … make it something over 1,000-member XYZ Corporation. You're working in the Learning and Development department and your deputy chief financial officer comes by and says, "You know, we really need a course to train people in, you know, accounting and bookkeeping and whatever. Could you help us create that course?" I think that's the example that you have in mind with this question. Was I right?
SvR:	Yes, that kind of situation exactly.
PRB:	I don't think it's any different if I may push back a little bit from your question. I would say it's no different, that just because you're in the same company, you have different cost centers. In my example, the chief financial officer, they're going to have a budget for the overall operation of that organization for the next fiscal year or maybe they'll even have it so well sub-divided that there's a training sub-budget within the overall operation budget. Either way, there's a finite amount of dollars, there's a finite amount of hours that the employees can spend on this. I don't think it's any different. You're basically, in your example for this question, a consultant to others within your own organization. You're still a consultant to them and it's still the same, to me, the same processes should be followed, the same ethical considerations should be followed.
SvR:	Can you share a story from your own experience about how ethics came into play during a Learning and Development engagement or initiative? It could be positive or negative or both.
PRB:	Okay, I can come up with one that's both positive and negative. It was before I came to work for my current firm. I was working for another large consulting firm and we had a huge online education-related contract with one of the military service organizations, I mean it's huge, couple of hundred million dollars. Very, very big and we consulted on everything from instructional systems design and in-classroom teaching to train-the-trainers to the hardware and software aspects of networking. It was very

easy within such a big budget where being $50,000 off is just an accounting error. It was very easy constantly to be saying, "Hey, to do design right, to do this right, to do that right, we really need another day or two, or another week or two to really…" because here all the questions that you really want answered, and in a world without limits, without budgets, can't argue that, because ideally it's a pretty broad term. You could go on for another day or two, or a week or two and ask lots of questions. So, we do that and the client initially said yes, but after a while the client kind of caught on and I was a member of the firm, I was also the principal point of contact with the client and I found after a while, I had to tell the client, "No, you don't need this." So, I called a meeting of my bosses, my peers, and my client and I just laid it on the line, "This is what I'm seeing. I have to be honest, I have to call it like I see it. I would love for the outcome of this meeting to be … I tried to act ethically but I misunderstood, but here's what I'm seeing and you guys need to talk." It turned out that the client was livid. My firm apologized. The client was on the verge of firing our firm, it was a huge project, and the client only kept us because I was honest. True story.

SvR: Wow. On the one hand, you feel good that you saved the day. On the other hand, that had to be a painful situation.

PRB: And the proof of it is that it got me back in another way, by not promoting me when I was ready for a promotion. That's the firm.

SvR: Bottom line is: Sometimes you have to make some hard choices.

PRB: Yes. Ethics isn't for sissies.

SvR: I like that line, definitely keeping it.

PRB: Yes, I'd never thought about it before this moment but it's really true. Going back to, I guess was my answer to your first question, that there's an economic imperative, there are a lot of people doing this work. There's an economic imperative to constantly justify why the clients should hire your company, why they should hire you. How much income are you bringing into our training organization's budgets, that sort of thing. It's this constant pressure over the last several years. I think the pressure has grown significantly and so, it's the kind of situation that I describe of what we're selling, whether it's a private consulting firm seeking external clients or even internally within the company or the office of, say, the chief learning officer, trying to sell to the office of the chief financial officer or the office of general counselor, the office of the sales or whomever. At some point, if there's an ethical clash, don't be surprised if you feel the wrath of all those around you because they're being judged on selling. You're calling their judgment into question. Don't be surprised if that wrath lands upon you. Don't be surprised.

There is a certain irony to Mr. Bardack's story about "overselling" the client. On the one hand, the story illustrates the highly competitive nature of the L&D industry, and the ease with which L&D professionals can use aspects of the design process – the performance analysis, in Mr. Bardack's story – to "upsell" to clients. On the other hand, the very questions that Mr. Bardack recommended that we ask clients are the same questions we use in performance analysis, but the client is not being charged separately for the information but the answers are used to create the end product. This may explain why some learning providers embed performance analysis into their proposals rather than show performance analysis as a separate line item with separate costs. That way, the client cannot ask to skip performance analysis to save money. Nevertheless, Mr. Bardack is correct in noting that a full-blown performance analysis may not be essential in all cases, so that the L&D professional needs to walk that fine line between what makes good business sense and what constitutes an ethical pitfall.

Dilbert's© Guide to Avoiding Ethical Pitfalls

If you were to ask Dilbert© about how he would characterize ethical behaviors in his organization, he might respond with words like "management ignorance" or "management denial." Although management does set the tone for ethical behavior in the workplace, we can only control our own individual behaviors. Nevertheless, not all ethical dilemmas are predictable or avoidable, nor are the consequences of available alternatives for solving an ethical dilemma clear, as we have just seen in Mr. Bardack's story. Here are some ideas for avoiding potential pitfalls when faced with issues that may potentially involve professional ethics:

- **Ethics vs. anger:** You first need to determine if the issue is, indeed, one relevant to the ethics of your profession. Sometimes a claim of "that's unethical" really means "I'm so upset with your proposal that it must be unethical!" If the issue in question cannot be linked to a specific element of the ethics code to which your work group subscribes or the ethics code of your organization, then you're facing an issue of anger, not ethics.
- **Just the facts, please:** Like every other aspect of decision-making, deciding how to address ethical issues requires complete and accurate information. Taking the time to get to the root of an ethical issue allows you to consider all of the factors that might influence ethical decision-making (e.g., previous experiences with the client, outcomes of a similar ethical dilemma with another client, the terms and conditions of the contract or Statement of Work).
- **Seek out the ethics gurus:** Addressing ethical issues can involve a complicated process that is influenced by our own values, perceptions, and experiences. Seeking out those in your organization who have a strong

commitment to the L&D profession and are keenly sensitive to ethical challenges can provide valuable insights.

- **Do those what-ifs:** Just as you consider alternative solutions to performance problems, consider alternative courses of action to address the ethical issue. Armed with your organization's policies, procedures and guidelines, and the ethics code from your professional association or your organization (or both), step through the consequences of your solution alternative with your ethics gurus as well as with your L&D team.

- **Start off on the right foot:** A fundamental means of avoiding ethical pitfalls is to clearly set guidelines and expectations with all parties concerned right at the beginning. Solid communication and documentation help ensure that all parties know what has (not) been discussed and agreed.

- **Practice, practice, practice:** Cultivating ethical behaviors is an active process continuing throughout our careers. Just as we need to keep up with the latest developments in strategy, tools, and technologies, we need to seek new information, think critically, and keep current with trends and issues related to professional ethics. Developing our sensitivity to ethical issues requires the same kind of effort as in the old joke about how to get to New York City's Carnegie Hall: practice, practice, practice.

Professional Ethics Self-Check

You are working on a training module designed to provide new supervisors in your organization with basic managerial skills. The module will be deployed via your organization's internal LMS and is available only to employees inside your organization. Because the module is for internal use only, you provide links to several YouTube videos that deal with supervisor training. You also scan several articles from *Harvard Business Review* to include in the module, along with a PowerPoint presentation from a skills webinar you attended that was given by the Society of Human Resource Management (SHRM). Finally, you print out and then scan a copy of an employee's performance review to use as a case study example, making sure to black out the employee's name to protect confidentiality. Have any of these actions been violations of professional ethics?

a) No, because it's all for internal use only and not subject to any ethical legal guidelines or legal mandates.
b) Not if you cited the sources of your materials.
c) No, because steps were taken to protect confidentiality and to give proper attribution to sources.
d) Yes, there are both legal and ethical violations.

We can immediately eliminate option (a) because ethical guidelines apply to both internal and external contexts; the same applies to ethical mandates unless the mandate(s) state specifically that only a specific context is included. Option (b) is also a non-starter. Citing your sources in and of itself is insufficient. How much of the source material you are using determines whether or not permission is required of the source owner. For example, those who post YouTube videos can submit a copyright infringement notification requesting removal of an unauthorized use of their creative work. *Harvard Business Review*, along with most journal publications, have very specific terms and conditions for use of their content, as do associations like SHRM. In short, attribution alone may still be a legal violation of copyright and intellectual property. Option (c) also falls short because you did not take sufficient steps to protect employee confidentiality in this scenario. Performance review documents contain information such as department name, supervisor, rank, etc., all of which could make the employee identifiable despite having blacked out his/her name. Bottom line: Option (d) is the correct response.

Food for Thought

1   The American Society of Association Executives (ASAE) is an advocate for ethical behaviors in not-for-profit organizations. Review the Standards of Conduct posted on its website. What similarities do you see between the ASAE codes of ethics and the professional codes of ethics of the various L&D-related associations? Are there any differences?
2   Does your current place of work have a formal, documented code of ethics? If it does, what are the similarities to/differences from the L&D professional codes of ethics?
3   There are several online ethical self-assessments available for free. Take one or two of those self-assessments. Are the results as you expected? Why (not)?
4   Now, take one or more of the online workplace ethics quizzes intended to identify how ethical you perceive your workplace to be. Are the results as you expected? Why (not)?
5   Share the results of your workplace ethics quizzes with a trusted colleague. Are the results what he/she expected? Why (not)?

Up Next

In this chapter, we have (a) reviewed the highlights of the business ethics literature; (b) examined the codes of conduct for ethical behaviors for L&D professionals; and (c) identified some of the ethical pitfalls and ways to avoid those pitfalls in a rapidly changing landscape. We will now take a step back and reflect on all of our workplace behaviors and gauge our progress toward becoming a trusted learning advisor.

References

Academy of Human Resource Development. (1999). Standards on ethics and integrity. Retrieved from http://c.ymcdn.com/sites/www.ahrd.org/resource/resmgr/imported/ethics_standards.pdf.

AECT. (2007). Code of professional ethics. Retrieved from http://aect.site-ym.com/members/group_content_view.asp?group=91131&id=309963.

Appelbaum, S. H., Iaconi, G. D., & Matousek, A. (2007). Positive and negative deviant workplace behaviors: Causes, impacts, and solutions. *Corporate Governance: The international journal of business in society*, 7(5), 586–98.

Applied Corporate Governance. (n.d.). Define business ethics: Discussion and debate. Retrieved from www.applied-corporate-governance.com/define-business-ethics.html.

Association for Talent Development. (2017). Mission and vision. Retrieved from www.td.org/About/Mission-and-Vision.

Barnett, T. (2001). Dimensions of moral intensity and ethical decision-making: An empirical study. *Journal of Applied Social Psychology*, 31(5), 1038–57.

Bergenhenegouwen, G. J. (1996). Professional code and ethics for training professionals. *Journal of European Industrial Training*, 20(4), 23–9.

Business ethics. (n.d.a). Dictionary.com's 21st Century Lexicon. Retrieved from www.dictionary.com/browse/business-ethics.

Business ethics. (n.d.b). Investopedia. Retrieved from www.investopedia.com/terms/b/business-ethics.asp.

Carter, S. M., & Greer, C. R. (2013). Strategic leadership: Values, styles, and organizational performance. *Journal of Leadership & Organizational Studies*, 20(4), 375–93.

Chun, J. S., Shin, Y., Choi, J. N., & Kim, M. S. (2013). How does corporate ethics contribute to firm financial performance? The mediating role of collective organizational commitment and organizational citizenship behavior. *Journal of Management*, 39(4), 853–77.

Cohen, D. V. (1993). Creating and maintaining ethical work climates: Anomie in the workplace and implications for managing change. *Business Ethics Quarterly*, 3(4), 343–58.

Craft, J. L. (2013). A review of the empirical ethical decision-making literature: 2004–2011. *Journal of Business Ethics*, 117(2), 221–59.

Dean, P. (1993). A selected review of the underpinnings of ethics from human performance technology professionals – Part one: Key ethical theories and research. *Performance Improvement Quarterly*, 6(4), 6–32.

Deshpande, S. P. (1996). The impact of ethical climate types of facets of job satisfaction: An empirical investigation. *Journal of Business Ethics*, 15(6), 655–60.

Frisque, D. A., Lin, H., & Kolb, J. A. (2004). Preparing professionals to face ethical challenges in today's workplace: review of the literature, implications for PI, and a proposed research agenda. *Performance Improvement Quarterly*, 17(2), 28–45.

Fuchs, S., & Sarstedt, M. (2009). Is there a tacit acceptance of student samples in marketing and management research? *International Journal of Data Analysis Techniques and Strategies*, 2(1), 62–72.

Gatewood, R. D., & Carroll, A. B. (1991). Assessment of ethical performance of organization members: A conceptual framework. *Academy of Management Review*, 16(4), 667–90.

Gough, J., & Spencer, E. (2014). Ethics in action: An exploratory survey of social worker's ethical decision making and value conflicts. *Journal of Social Work Values and Ethics*, 11(2), 23–40.

Gray, C. M., & Boling, E. (2016). Inscribing ethics and values in designs for learning: A problematic. *Educational Technology Research & Development*, 64(5), 969–1001.

Guerra, I. J. (2006). Standards and ethics in human performance technology. In J. A. Pershing (Ed.), *Handbook of human performance technology* (3rd ed., pp. 1024–46). San Francisco, CA: Pfeiffer.

Hamric, A. B., & Blackhall, L. J. (2007). Nurse-physician perspectives on the care of dying patients in intensive care units: Collaboration, moral distress, and ethical climate. *Critical Care Medicine*, 35(2), 422–9.

Hill, J. (2006). Professional ethics: A matter of duty. In J. A. Pershing (Ed.), *Handbook of performance improvement* (3rd ed., pp. 1047–66). San Francisco, CA: John Wiley & Sons.

IBSTPI. (2014). *Instructional Designer Competencies – Welcome to ibstpi*. Retrieved from http://ibstpi.org/instructional-design-competencies/.

International Society for Performance Improvement. (2016). ISPI code of ethics. Retrieved from www.ispi.org/ISPI/Credentials/ISPI_Code_of_Ethics.aspx? WebsiteKey=8b8db682-5734-4be7-b952-33fdabafb78d.

Jones, T. M. (1991). Ethical decision-making by individuals in organizations: an issue-contingent model. *Academy of Management Review*, 16(2), 366–95.

Kaiser, K. (2009). Protecting respondent confidentiality in qualitative research. *Qualitative Health Research*, 19(11), 1632–41.

Kaiser, K. (2012). Protecting confidentiality. In J. F. Gubrium, J. A. Holstein, A. B. Marvasti, & K. D. McKinney (Eds.), *The SAGE Handbook of Interview Research: The Complexity of the Craft* (2nd ed., pp. 457–64). Thousand Oaks, CA: SAGE Publications, Inc.

Koszalka, T. A., Grabowski, B. L. H., Wallington, C. J., Senior, F. A., Russ-Eft, D. F., & Reiser, R. A. (2013). *Instructional Designer Competencies: The Standards* (4th ed.). Charlotte, North Carolina: Information Age Publishing.

Kouchaki, M., Smith-Crowe, K., Brief, A. P., & Sousa, C. (2013). Seeing green: Mere exposure to money triggers a business decision frame and unethical outcomes. *Organizational Behavior and Human Decision Processes*, 121(1), 53–61.

Lewis, P. V. (1985). Defining business ethics: Like nailing Jello to a wall. *Journal of Business Ethics*, 4, 377–83.

Lin, H. (2006). Ethical applications of technology in HRD. *Performance Improvement Quarterly*, 19(4), 91–105.

MacDonald, C. (2011). What's legal isn't always ethical. Retrieved from https://businessethicsblog.com/2011/12/22/whats-legal-isnt-always-ethical/.

Malik, M. (2015). Value-enhancing capabilities of CSR: Avbrief review of contemporary literature. *Journal of Business Ethics*, 127(2), 419–38.

Martin, S. R., Cote, S., & Woodruff, T. (2016). Echoes of our upbringing: How growing up wealthy or poor relates to narcissism, leader behavior, and leader effectiveness. *Academy of Management Journal*, 59(6), 2157–77.

Mayer, D. (2015). Is "business ethics" an oxymoron? Fast Company. Retrieved from www.fastcompany.com/3053836/the-future-of-work/is-business-ethics-an-oxymoron.

McLagan, P. (1989). *Models for HRD Practice: The Practitioner's Guide*. Alexandria, VA: American Society for Training and Development.

Merton, R. K. (1968). *Social Theory and Social Structure* (4th ed.). New York, NY: The Free Press.

Moore, S. L., & Ellsworth, J. B. (2014). Ethics of educational technology. In J. M. Spector, M. D. Merrill, J. Elen, & M. J. Bishop (Eds.), *Handbook of Research on Educational Communications and Technology* (pp. 113–27). New York, NY: Springer.

Moriarty, J. (2016). Business ethics. *The Stanford Encyclopedia of Philosophy.* Winter 2016. Retrieved from https://plato.stanford.edu/entries/ethics-business/

O'Fallon, M. J., & Butterfield, K. D. (2005). A review of the empirical ethical decision-making literature: 1996–2003. *Journal of Business Ethics, 59*(4), 375–413.

Peterson, D. K. (2002). Deviant workplace behavior and the organization's ethical climate. *Journal of Business and Psychology, 17*(1), 47–61.

Podsakoff, P. M., & Organ, D. W. (1986). Self-reports in organizational research: Problems and prospects. *Journal of Management, 12*(4), 531–44.

Rest, J. R. (1986). *Moral Development: Advances in Research and Theory.* New York, NY: Praeger.

Scherer, A. G., & Palazzo, G. (2011). The new political role of business in a globalized world: a review of a new perspective on CSR and its implications for the firm, governance, and democracy. *Journal of Management Studies, 48*(4), 899–931.

Shaw, W. H. (1996). Business ethics today: A survey. *Journal of Business Ethics, 15*(5), 489–500.

SHRM. (2017, 2/17/2016). Introduction to the Human Resources Discipline of Ethics and Corporate Social Responsibility and Sustainability. Retrieved from www.shrm.org/resourcesandtools/tools-and-samples/toolkits/pages/introfethicsandsustainability.aspx.

Singer, E. (2008). Ethical issues in surveys. In E. D. de Leeuw, J. J. Hox, & D. A. Dillman (Eds.), International handbook of survey methodology (pp. 78–96). New York, NY: Psychology Press Taylor & Francis Group.

Somers, M. J. (2001). Ethical codes of conduct and organizational context: A study of the relationship between codes of conduct, employee behavior and organizational values. *Journal of Business Ethics, 30*(2), 185–95.

Spector, J. M. (2016). Ethics in educational technology: Towards a framework for ethical decision-making in and for the discipline. *Educational Technology Research & Development, 64*(5), 1003–11.

Svensson, G., & Wood, G. (2008). A model of business ethics. *Journal of Business Ethics, 77*(3), 303–22.

Sweeney, B., & Costello, F. (2009). Moral intensity and ethical decision-making: An empirical examination of undergraduate accounting and business students. *Accounting Education, 18*(1), 75–97.

Takacs Haynes, K., Josefy, M., & Hitt, M. A. (2015). Tipping point: Managers' self-interest, greed, and altruism. *Journal of Leadership & Organizational Studies, 22*(3), 265–79.

Trevino, L. K., Weaver, G. R., Gibson, D. G., & Toffler, B. L. (1999). Managing ethics and legal compliance: What works and what hurts. *California Management Review, 41*(2), 131–51.

Wang, L., Malhotra, D., & Murnighan, K. (2011). Economics education and greed. *Academy of Management Learning & Education, 10*(4), 643–60.

Weaver, G. R. (2004). Ethics and employees: Making the connection. *Academy of Management Perspectives, 18*(2), 121–5.

Welsh, D. H., & Birch, N. J. (2015). The ethical orientation of US small business decision makers: A preliminary study. *Journal of Small Business Strategy, 8*(2), 41–52.

Yin Lau, P., Terpstra Tong, J. L. Y., Lien, B. Y., Hsu, Y. C., & Chong, C. L. (2017). Ethical work climate, employee commitment and proactive customer service performance: Test of the mediating effects of organizational politics. *Journal of Retailing and Consumer Services, 35,* 20–6.

14 Ten-Point Sanity Check
Avoiding Self-Inflicted Wounds

By now it should be abundantly clear that as a Learning and Development (L&D) professional, you have much more to think about than just creating opportunities for learning. The scope of your current position along with your goals for advancement require a firm understanding of what you do, how you do it, and what others think about your work. In other words, you need to constantly reflect on your current behaviors so that you can draw lessons learned to capture and retain the confidence of those around you – managers, peers, entry-level colleagues – that you are, indeed, a trusted learning advisor.

If you completed a university-based program in a learning-related field (instructional design/technology, human resource development, learning science, etc.) at some point in your career, you probably recall having to document your reflections on what you learned in the various courses or programs. The documentation may have taken the form of reflection papers, blog postings, journal entries, digital portfolios, or some other vehicles for recording and sharing your thoughts about both the process and the content of what you learned. Grounded in adult learning theory and the learning sciences literature, the goal was to use reflection to improve learning and practice because reflection enables students to learn from experience, develop skills in self-assessment, transfer tacit self-knowledge into explicit plans for improvement, and develop a new and different frame of reference to carry forward into continual personal and professional development (Gibbs, 1988; Kolb, 2014; Moon, 2002; Quinton & Smallbone, 2010; Sadler, 1989; Smith & Pilling, 2007). Reflection as a concept is related to double loop learning (Argyris, 1976), a theory of personal change that is oriented to professional education, particularly in terms of management development. Double loop learning focuses on solving complex, ill-structured problems based on a "theory of action" (Argyris & Schon, 1974) that examines reality from the perspective of individuals as actors. It focuses on closing the gap between espoused views and hypotheses and actual behaviors. The end result of double loop learning should be more effective decision-making and better acceptance of failures and mistakes.

I'm working now and don't have time for all that writing, you may be thinking, and you would be right in terms of the content that may have been required for your reflective writing when you were a student. For those who have never engaged in formal reflective writing, the term "reflection" may conjure up visions of cross-legged gurus poised on a cloud with eyes closed while deep in contemplation. *Nothing like that happens in the real world of work*, you may think. However, reflective practice in the workplace is an integral part of career growth and development in a variety of professions, from healthcare (Bulman & Schutz, 2013; Caldwell, 2013; Ghaye & Lillyman, 2014) to social work (Ruch, 2005; Thompson & Pascal, 2012), to engineering design (Bucciarelli, 1988; Rotimi & Ramanayaka, 2015), to teacher education (Duckworth, Wood, Dickinson, & Bostock, 2010). Established in 2000, the journal *Reflective Practice* focuses on the different kinds of reflective practice and the purposes they serve, reflection and the generation of knowledge in particular professions, the ways by which reflection is taught and learned most meaningfully, and the links between reflective learning and the quality of workplace action.

Reflective practice encompasses not only the technical skills and competencies of your profession but also the social and business skills required by employers. Furthermore, reflective practice enables you to turn professional challenges and mistakes into learning opportunities to help advance your career. In this chapter, we will:

- Explore the definitions and models of reflective practice in the workplace that are provided in the literature;
- Identify some of the most common (but correctable) mistakes L&D professionals make as they engage in reflective practice in the workplace; and
- Share some tips to jump-start and sustain effective reflective practices.

Reflective Practice: More than Just "Think Before You Act"

A common-sense approach to how an L&D professional reflects on his/her work might go something like this:

- I have just completed this L&D project.
- These are the things that worked/did not work for me during that project.
- If I could do it again, here are the things I would do differently.
- Here are the lessons learned that I will apply to the next L&D project.

At first glance, these four bullets from a post-project debriefing represent how I, the practitioner, might have operationalized the following definitions of reflective practice:

> In reflective practice, practitioners engage in a continuous cycle of self-observation and self-evaluation in order to understand their own actions and the reactions they prompt in themselves and in learners. The goal is not necessarily to address a specific problem or question defined at the outset, as in practitioner research, but to observe and refine practice in general on an ongoing basis. (Florez, 2001)

> Reflective practice involves thinking about and critically analyzing one's actions with the goal of improving one's professional practice. Engaging in reflective practice requires individuals to assume the perspective of an external observer in order to identify the assumptions and feelings underlying their practice and then to speculate about how these assumptions and feelings affect practice. (Imel, 1992)

Although the four bullet points indicate that I'm taking what I learned in the past and translating it into a plan of action for future use, it's only part of the story. Reflective practice is a shared, collaborative activity that includes learning from others. It is a continual learning process rather than a one-off at the end of a project.

There have been multiple streams of research in a variety of disciplines (e.g., philosophy, psychology, and learning sciences) contributing to the reflective practice body of knowledge (for a comprehensive review of these contributions, see Lyons, 2010; Lawrence-Wilkes & Ashmore, 2014; Lawrence-Wilkes & Chapman, 2014–2015). For our purposes, we will explore only a small segment of the reflective practice literature, extracting key components that can guide us in avoiding self-inflicted wounds at work.

Definitions and Models in the Literature

Schon (1983) introduced the concept of the reflective practitioner as someone who uses reflection as a tool for revisiting experience, both to learn from it and for framing the complex problems of professional practice. Schon argued that the conventional technical-rational view of professional practice is not the only way professionals go about solving problems. Professionals also use a form of tacit knowledge that is linked to specific activities (called "knowing-in-action"), and develop "repertoires" of solutions, then learn how to "reframe" difficult problems into those they can deal with more readily. As a result, Schon deemed the crucial competence for all professionals to be reflection, both during an activity ("reflection-in-action") and after an activity ("reflection-about-action"). Applied to the learning designer, for example, this means that design models and processes are only part of the designer's problem-solving toolkit. Lessons learned during and after a design project or other professional activities also help the designer to solve problems.

Reflective practice is similar to the concepts of reflective learning and self-regulated learning in that all three involve the processing of learning in a variety of ways. Reflective learners explore their understanding of their actions and experience, and the impact of those actions and experiences on themselves and others. A reflective practice model enables learners and entry-level practitioners to compare their own practices with those of experienced practitioners, thus helping them to develop a greater sense of self-awareness about the nature and impact of their performance, which in turn creates opportunities for professional growth and development (Osterman & Kottkamp, 1993). Zimmerman (1998) attributed the ability to self-reflect as a characteristic of the self-regulated learner, with self-regulation consisting of (a) self-evaluation, where learners evaluate how well they are doing by comparing their performance to others when no formal standards are available; (b) attributions about the causal meaning of the results, such as whether a poor performance is due to limited ability or insufficient effort; and (c) adaptation, where learners adapt their performance until they find the strategy that works for them.

Boud, Keogh, and Walker (1985) took a more broad-brush approach to defining reflective practice, labeling it "a generic term for those intellectual and affective activities in which individuals engage to explore their experiences in order to lead to a new understanding and appreciation" (p. 19). Bright (1993) described reflective practice as an active, dynamic, action-based and ethical set of skills, placed in real time and dealing with real, complex and difficult situations, while Thompson (1996) described it as "cutting the cloth to suit the specific circumstances, rather than looking for ready-made solutions" (p. 222). Bulman (2008) defined it as reviewing experience from practice in order to describe, analyze, evaluate, and then inform and change future practice, while Oelofsen (2012) succinctly described it as "a process of making sense of events, situations, and actions that occur in the workplace" (p. 22).

Other scholars have focused on reflection as the core component of reflective practice. For instance, Dewey (1933) was probably the first to focus on the depth and quality of reflective thinking by identifying the criteria for reflection as (a) a meaning-making process that moves a learner from one experience to the next with deeper understanding of its relationships with other experiences; (b) a systematic, rigorous, and disciplined way of thinking with roots in scientific inquiry; (c) occurring in interaction with others; and (d) requiring attitudes that value the personal and intellectual growth of oneself and of others. Atkins and Murphy (1993) identified the most important skills for reflection as being (a) self-awareness, the ability to analyze feelings and how a situation affects an individual and how an individual affects a situation; (b) description, the ability to articulate feelings and experiences verbally and in writing; (c) critical analysis, which involves examining the components of a situation, identifying existing knowledge, challenging assumptions, and exploring alternatives; (d) synthesis, the integration of new knowledge with previous knowledge, to develop new perspectives; and (e) evaluation, the process of making judgments about the value of something using criteria and standards.

Moon (1999) defined reflection as a process of thinking about what we have done, learned, and experienced, while Kennison and Misselwitz (2002, p. 239) defined reflection as "the purposeful contemplation of thoughts, feelings, and happenings that pertain to recent experiences" to challenge one's initial thinking and feelings, then create and clarify the personal meaning of the lived experience." Pavlovich (2007) summarized reflection as a method that consists of (a) describing; (b) analyzing; (c) developing new meaning/understanding; and (d) acting. Mann, Gordon, and MacLeod (2009) added that reflection involves a number of skills, such as observation, self-awareness, critical thinking, self-evaluation, and taking others' perspectives, and has the outcome of integrating this understanding into future planning and goal setting.

Another approach to defining reflective practice was to place it in the context of professional education. For example, Pollard and Tann (1993) returned to Schon's concept of the reflective practitioner and argued that the reflective teaching practitioner displays the following characteristics:

- An active concern with aims and consequences, as well as means and technical efficiency;
- Competence in methods of classroom inquiry (gathering data, analysis, evaluation) to support the development of teaching competence;
- Attitudes of open-mindedness, responsibility, and wholeheartedness;
- Teacher judgment informed partly by self-reflection and partly by insights from educational disciplines; and
- Collaboration and dialogue with colleagues.

In a review of the literature on reflective practice in teacher education, Loughran (2002, p. 42) affirmed the importance of context to how reflective practice is defined and, thus, how it is used:

> Effective reflective practice is drawn from the ability to frame and reframe the practice setting, to develop and respond to this framing through action so that the practitioner's wisdom-inaction is enhanced and, as a particular outcome, articulation of professional knowledge is encouraged. What is learned as a result of reflection is, to me, at least equally as valuable as reflection itself. It is through the development of knowledge and understanding of the practice setting and the ability to recognize and respond to such knowledge that the reflective practitioner becomes truly responsive to the needs, issues, and concerns that are so important in shaping practice.

In her guide to reflective practice in the healthcare professions, Taylor (2010) emphasized the importance of reflective practice to ensuring quality care of patients, particularly given the economic, historical, political, social, and personal constraints within which the modern healthcare professional must operate. Taylor described reflection as a lifelong process in which reflective practitioners must stay alert to practice, share their reflections, and create daily habits to sustain reflective practice. Mann, Gordon, and MacLeod (2009) reviewed 29 studies published in the medical education literature and noted that most models of reflective practice depict reflection as triggered by awareness of a need or disruption in usual practice. The common premise was that of returning to an experience to examine it, deliberately intending that what is learned may serve as a guide in future situations, and incorporating it into existing knowledge. They characterized two dimensions to the models of reflection in the literature:

- An iterative dimension, whereby the process of reflection is sparked by experience, which then produces a new understanding, and the potential or intention to act differently in response to future experience. Among the models deemed to conceptualize reflection as an iterative process were Boud, Keogh, and Walker (1985) and Schon (1983).
- A vertical dimension, which includes different levels of reflection on experience, with surface levels being more descriptive and less analytical than the deeper levels. Dewey (1933) and Moon (1999) were cited among the models focusing on depth and quality of reflective thinking.

The instructional design literature has largely focused on tools and processes to promote reflection rather than definitions or models of reflective practice. For example, after observing challenges students were experiencing in discussing their design ideas in a group setting, Luppicini (2003) constructed a three-component typology of reflective design "what" and "how" questions (Reflective Action Instructional Design/RAID):

1 Actor referenced reflective practices

   a Reflections-on-others: What is the role of others involved?
   b Reflections-from-others: What do they think?
   c Reflections-on-self: What do I think of myself and my role in practice?

2 Action referenced reflective practices

   a Reflection-to-action: What led to this action?
   b Reflection-in-action: What is happening now?
   c Reflection-on-action: What happened so far?
   d Reflection-from-action: What could happen?

3 Situation referenced reflective practices

    a Reflections-to-situation: What expectations do I have about the setting?

    b Reflections-on-situation: What do I think about the setting?

    c Reflections-from-situation: How would I change the setting?

In their discussion of the differences between formulaic approaches – relying on tools/technologies alone (called Technology I) or instructional design methods and processes alone (called Technology II) and a reflective approach – the use of tools, technologies, methods, and processes based on the characteristics and goals of the particular situation (called Technology III) – to solving learning problems, McDonald & Gibbons (2009) offered three reasons why instructional design practitioners are drawn away from reflective practices into more reductive approaches, a phenomenon they described as "technological gravity":

1 Distracted focus or the rejection of reflective practice for the pursuit of other rewards (e.g., financial rewards).
2 Status quo adherence, or searching for practices that are legitimate, professional, respectable, or traditional. Indicators include unsettling change or organizational stress, lack of urgency for change, and feelings of threat to personal identity.
3 Oversimplification or loss of reflective practice in the pursuit of routinization, with unpredictability and overreaction to problems as indicators.

Avoiding technological gravity can occur by continually aligning technology use with goals for practice through legitimate evaluation; adopting guiding principles about one's practice to help practitioners make decisions, view constraints in creative ways, and solve problems without abandoning goals; and cultivating opinion leaders who can help alter the culture of the field, leading reflective practice to becoming a more accepted alternative. Other studies have advocated the use of Schon's reflection-in-action to structure instructional design student activities (Tracey & Baaki, 2014), the writing and sharing of instructional designers' design stories (Honebein & Goldsworthy, 2009), along with guidelines for scaffolding reflective practice (Hong & Choi, 2011), to help instructional designers improve practices.

    Among practitioners working in non-academic settings, there is also a firm belief in the value of reflective practice. For instance, Gail Heidenhain, Board Chair of the International Association of Accelerated Learning Practitioners (IAALP), includes reflective practice among the pillars of Accelerated Learning Design:

    If learning is about change and transforming how people think and their ability to act by building skills and applying them in the real world, then reflective practice plays a key role. Research on transformative learning highlights three things that are needed for transformation to happen: the right experiences, reflection on those experiences, and dialogue about what they have experienced and discovered. In AL programs, you will find reflection before, during, and after activities, and you will find different types of reflective activities in support of deeper learning and transformation. (Heidenhain, 2014)

Cheetham and Chivers (1998, 2001) interviewed 80 practitioners from 20 different professions in the UK, followed by a survey of 372 practitioners in the fields of dentistry, accounting, Civil Service, surveying, the Anglican Church, and training. The primary purpose of the interviews was to collect information about the factors that contribute to the acquisition of professional competence. The interviews supported the importance of reflection with approximately 96 percent of interview participants being aware of reflection and 81 percent claiming to reflect regularly about their professional work. However, the depth, quality, mode (before, during, or after) and the object (or topic) of reflection varied considerably. The object of reflection tended to fall mainly under the following broad headings: (a) performance (own or of others); (b) procedures (the way things are done); (c) problems; and (d) philosophy (of what is done). The authors concluded that reflection is a meta-competence in and of itself, as described below:

> There is no doubt it qualifies as such because it enables people to go beyond their other competencies, to analyse, modify and develop them. At the same time, reflection has a particularly unique position, acting as a sort of "gate-keeper" to certain kinds of development. For this reason, we give it the sub-title "super-meta." (p. 274)

The surveys, however, painted a slightly different picture. When asked to rate the importance (using a 5-point scale) of various types of informal learning in helping them to become fully competent, the responding practitioners gave a relatively modest average rating of 3.58 to "self-analysis or reflection":

> This could cast doubt on the wisdom of placing too much emphasis on reflection within initial development programmes. It may be that reflection does not become fully effective until practitioners have built up sufficient experience against which to reflect. (Cheetham & Chivers, 2001, p. 270)

To date, there remains little research-based evidence of the extent to which L&D practitioners in non-academic workplace settings in the U.S. use reflection to enhance their professional competence.

Summary

Figure 14.1 offers a graphic representation of the various definitions and models of reflective practice in the workplace in the literature. Common to all three approaches – concept definition, skill set definition, and professional education context – is the importance of continuous, interactive,

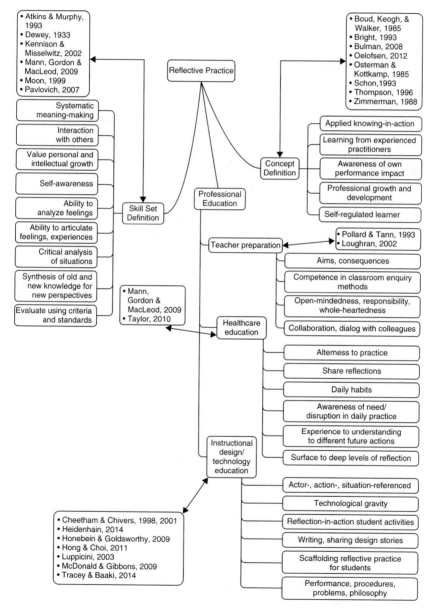

Figure 14.1 Highlights of the Reflective Practice Knowledge Base.

and systematic reflective practices as an integral part of the professional's day-to-day work. Moreover, both scholars and practitioners emphasize the importance of reflective practice. However, even though L&D professionals may think they are engaging in reflective practice, they are more likely to focus on tools, techniques and processes, and their own perspectives and behaviors. As a result, they end up making some career-limiting mistakes that have nothing to do with their design and learning technology competences.

Self-Inflicted Wounds

During the more than two decades I spent in the corporate world, I read and heard quite a few opinions and perspectives about L&D professionals, some very positive, others not so much. Most of the unfavorable views were not about the professionals' technical skills but focused instead on how L&D professionals perceive their role and themselves as professionals. Similar comments can be found on L&D-related discussion boards on LinkedIn, on the myriad blog postings by freelance L&D consultants, as well as by those employed in various organizations and industry sectors. The comments include those of L&D professionals themselves reflecting on their own lessons learned, as well as comments from those outside of our profession offering their insights into what value-add L&D professionals do (not) provide to their respective organizations.

It goes without saying that each professional is an individual and that what characterizes one professional may not be characteristic of another. Nevertheless, here are some (correctable) annoyances that I've seen and heard, ranked in order of frequency of mention (from least to most frequently mentioned) by those in and outside of the L&D field, along with suggestions for avoiding these annoyances:

10 **Over-sharing:** Everyone should be passionate about what they do and should convey that passion while doing it, no question. Nonetheless, as with all things, context is key. When responding to a request for training, do you start your initial conversations with *We always conduct an upfront analysis to make sure training is the right solution and if so, which pedagogies and constructivist principles ....*? Our clients (internal or external) need to know that we are going to identify and solve their problems and rarely want to know chapter-and-verse about how we are going to do it. After all, if someone asks us for the time, we don't tell them how to make a watch.

9 **SME ≠ idiot:** When designing learning opportunities, we've all experienced challenges with subject matter experts (SMEs) at some point in our career. In addition to the normal challenges associated with working with others outside of our immediate workgroup, some SMEs may not have a clear picture of exactly what it is that a learning designer

does and why the subject matter needs to be "designed" before it can be delivered to the target audience. Considering the discussions that still occur in our community about definitions and scope of the profession, the lack of clarity among those outside of our profession as to who we are and what we do cannot be attributed solely to ignorance. Although it may be frustrating to have to explain the design expertise vs. content expertise roles when working with a SME for the first time, our nonverbal communication (body language, facial expressions, etc.) sometimes betrays that frustration.

8 **Hero-martyr syndrome:** As problem-solvers, we get tremendous satisfaction when our solutions work. For situations that were particularly messy, we may feel like we've saved the day and want to share that heroic feeling with others. After all, tooting our own horn helps build recognition for the value of what it is that we do. The challenge is not to play the hero card for too long and at every available opportunity. To others, we've just done our jobs, not invented a cure for cancer. Conversely, when things go wrong, as they sometimes do, we strive to examine and correct our errors but sometimes tackle what we deem to be the errors of others. With no control over the latter, it is tempting to fall into the designer-as-victim mindset.

7 **Do it right or do the right thing:** Our L&D toolkit is filled with methods, models, and processes that have served us well over the years, but as we saw in the first chapter of this book, the world of work and learning has changed. We need to be quick as well as be systematic and thorough. Importantly, we need to do what works for each individual client. If the solution solves the client's problem, the fact that it does not exactly match a particular model or is not perfect in its elegance, so what? As a former boss once said to me when faced with a deliverable deadline, *I'd rather have progressive improvement than postponed perfection.* Sometimes, good is indeed good enough.

6 **From educator to sales person:** In recent years, educators, particularly those in public education, have been faced with having to "sell" the value of what they offer and how it is being offered to a broader set of audiences with diverging and sometimes conflicting points of view. L&D professionals have always had to sell, to persuade people to change their behavior through participation in instructional and non-instructional learning opportunities aimed at modifying those behaviors. There are national mandates for compulsory education and state standards for particular school grades and subjects. L&D professionals have only the business needs and performance/skills gaps with which to work; so, we have to "sell" the value of our learning products in terms of the benefits to learners. Learning for the greater good *sans* evidence is losing its potency as a reason-for-being in education; it never was a credible argument in non-academic workplaces.

5   **Organizational technology as constraint:** Although technology budgets in the private sector may be larger than those in the educational sector, they are neither unlimited nor all-encompassing. For all the buzz around technology-based solutions for learning, not to mention our own fondness for particular courseware development tools and delivery platforms, the annoying truth is that many organizations are still grappling with their own information technology and data security issues. These issues are magnified when L&D has to create technology-based solutions for global organizations. Listening to stakeholders about the scope and depth of technology constraints and brainstorming with them to consider alternatives and workarounds is frequently cited as a shortcoming of L&D professionals.

4   **Designer as desk jockey:** As dedicated professionals, we are committed to giving our full attention to the tasks at hand, especially when calling upon our creativity as well as technical knowledge to build learning opportunities. This often leads to a heads-down approach to our work, where we call on others only when we need specific information or action. Just as we seek a work-life balance, we also need to seek a work-workplace environment balance by getting out of our chairs and getting to know others inside the organization. Even if we haven't been asked to create learning opportunities for a particular department or workgroup, we should visit that department/workgroup to learn what it is that they do and how their work contributes to the organization. This will not only help us to learn more about the organization but help the organization to learn more about us.

3   **Technocrat vs. strategic thinker:** Even when we are recognized as experts in the design and development of learning opportunities for individuals, we are often overlooked as strategic thinkers who can see the big picture when it comes to an organization's talent strategy. How can we proactively create opportunities to support the organization's long-term talent strategy? Are we helping the organization to develop current employees to meet organizational goals five years from now, or are we only focused on a current performance gap and a current skill set?

2   **Resistance to business thinking (the "ick" factor):** There's nothing wrong with wanting to spend your entire career designing formal instruction, but as time goes by and you want to advance as a designer, you need to be able to efficiently and effectively address the business issues associated with your craft. Can you provide an accurate accounting of the total costs of a learning opportunity? If you work for an organization that sells learning solutions to others, do you know how to price those solutions competitively and profitably for your organization? Every occupation has a business component, so we need to get over any notion that helping others to learn has nothing to do with money and business.

1   **My credential is bigger than yours:** You invested time and money to formalize your L&D knowledge, whether through a university-based degree program or an association certification. Great! But neither the degree nor the certification comes with a guarantee of omniscience. The Internet is full of discussions – some dating back to the mid-2000s – about whether or not a degree is necessary to be an L&D professional, particularly when it comes to instructional design. That's the wrong question. Whether or not you subscribe to theories about differences in learning styles, there is little debate about differences in learning preferences. Ours is a field that does not prescribe a single path to entry as does medicine or accounting or law. This allows those who love to help others learn to join through a variety of entry points. Whether we formalize our learning with a degree, a certificate, or through our own efforts depends on where we want to practice our profession. Yes, a degree is a strong ticket to entry, and yes, your certification shows that you and others can attest to your skills and abilities. To advocate for one credential over the other not only causes unnecessary friction within the L&D profession but also reinforces negative perceptions among those outside of L&D.

The Un-Dilbert© Guide to Sustaining Reflective Practices

In Dilbert's© world, reflective practice often means finding ways to look like you are accomplishing more while really doing less. Fortunately, L&D professionals tend not to be so cynical. Now that you know what it means to be a reflective practitioner and are familiar with the many tools and techniques for reflection, here are some additional thoughts to help you sustain your reflective practices in the workplace:

- **Reflection is not a solitary process but it is a goal-focused process.** Are you reflecting on a particular event (past, present, or future)? Are you reflecting on how well you manage stakeholders? Knowing why you want to reflect helps you to select the time, place, and tools you will use for reflection.
- **Work doesn't get in the way of reflection; it's an integral part of reflection.** Only you know when you are feeling prepared enough to spend quality time thinking about your practice. Good time management is essential to your overall professional survival, so it is essential that you build reflection time into your schedule.
- **Keep that professional portfolio current.** Whether you're a freelancer or an employee in an organization, you should be keeping a portfolio with examples of your work products. The portfolio is not only a marketing tool but a "living" record of your reflective practice in action.
- **Try reverse mentoring.** Traditional mentoring involves pairing a more experienced employee with a less experienced employee to help the

latter advance his/her knowledge in a particular area. Reverse mentoring emerged as a means for younger employees to help older employees familiarize themselves with the latest workplace trends, particularly in the area of technology. The same principle would apply to reverse mentoring in L&D, enabling the more senior professionals to gain insights into the twenty-first-century workplace that can inform practice. The rapid growth of reverse mentoring programs across a variety of organizations attests to the value of those one-on-one relationships as providing opportunities for reflective practice.

Becoming a reflective practitioner requires practice and commitment to the development and organization of the reflection process. It is a highly individualized process and you should find the structure, method, and tools that work best for you.

Reflective Practice Self-Check

Which of the following offer opportunities for L&D reflective practice?

a)   External conferences and events;
b)   Internal meetings;
c)   Performance reviews; or
d)   Any time and venue I choose.

If, as we have seen, reflective practice is a highly individualized process for which you select the methods, tools, and structures that fit your own goals for reflection, then (d) is the obvious choice. Any activity or event can serve as a learning opportunity if it aligns with your specific goals for reflection. After all, haven't you been using the Self-Check and Food for Thought sections at the end of each chapter of this book to reflect on your practice?

Food for Thought

1   Select one or two of the reflective practice self-assessment quizzes available on the Internet. Were your scores as you expected? Why (not)?
2   Select an L&D colleague and share your thoughts on reflective practice? Are they similar? Different?
3   How supportive of reflective practice is your department? Your organization? What are the indicators of (non-)support?

Up Next

In this chapter, we have (a) explored the definitions and models of reflective practice in the workplace that are provided in the literature; (b) identified some of the most common (but correctable) mistakes L&D professionals make as they engage in reflective practice in the workplace; and (c) shared some tips to jump-start and sustain effective reflective practices. The next and final chapter offers some suggestions for advancing your career in and beyond the L&D function.

References

Argyris, C. (1976). *Increasing Leadership Effectiveness*. New York, NY: Wiley.

Argyris, C., & Schon, D. (1974). *Theory in Practice*. San Francisco, CA: Jossey-Bass.

Atkins, F., & Murphy, K. (1993). Reflections: a review of the literature. *Journal of Advanced Nursing, 18*(8), 1188–92.

Boud, D., Keogh, R., & Walker, D. (1985). Promoting reflection in learning: a model. In D. Boud, R. Keogh, & D. Walker (Eds.), *Reflection: Turning Experience into Learning* (pp. 18–40). New York, NY: Nichols.

Bright, B. (1993). What is reflective practice? *Curriculum, 16*, 69–81.

Bucciarelli, L. L. (1988). An ethnographic perspective on engineering design. *Design Studies, 9*(3), 159–68.

Bulman, C. (2008). An introduction to reflection. In C. Bulman & S. Schutz (Eds.), *Reflective Practice in Nursing* (pp. 1–24). Chitchester, UK: John Wiley & Sons Ltd.

Bulman, C., & Schutz, S. (Eds.). (2013). *Reflective Practice in Nursing* (5th ed.). Hoboken, NJ: John Wiley & Sons.

Caldwell, L. (2013). The importance of reflective practice in nursing. *International Journal of Caring Sciences, 6*(3), 319–26.

Cheetham, G., & Chivers, G. (1998). The reflective (and competent) practitioner: a model of professional competence which seeks to harmonise the reflective practitioner and competence-based approaches. *Journal of European Industrial Training, 22*(7), 267–76.

Cheetham, G., & Chivers, G. (2001). Part II — How professionals learn — the practice! What the empirical research found. *Journal of European Industrial Training, 25*(5), 248–92.

Dewey, J. (1933). *How We Think* (2nd ed.). Buffalo, NY: Prometheus Books.

Duckworth, V., Wood, J., Dickinson, J., & Bostock, J. (2010). *Successful Teaching Practice in the Lifelong Learning Sector*. Exeter, UK: Learning Matters.

Florez, M. C. (2001). Reflective teaching in adult ESL settings. Available online at https://eric.ed.gov/?id=ED451733.

Ghaye, T., & Lillyman, S. (2014). *Reflection: Principles and Practices for Healthcare Professionals* (2nd ed., Vol. 1). London, UK: Andrews UK Limited.

Gibbs, G. (1988). *Learning by Doing: A Guide*. Birmingham, UK: SCED.

Heidenhain, G. (2014, April 15). The pillars of accelerated learning. Available online at www.td.org/Publications/Blogs/L-and-D-Blog/2014/04/The-Pillars-of-Accelerated-Learning-Design.

Honebein, P. C., & Goldsworthy, R. C. (2009). Is your design story limiting you? Purposefully perturbing our practices through instructional design "mashups." *Educational Technology, 49*(4), 27–33.

Hong, Y. C., & Choi, I. (2011). Three dimensions of reflective thinking in solving design problems: a conceptual model. *Educational Technology Research and Development, 59*(5), 687–710.

Imel, S. (1992). Reflective practice in adult education. Available online at www.ericdigests.org/1992-3/adult.htm.

Kennison, M., & Misselwitz, S. (2002). Evaluating reflective writing for appropriateness, fairness and consistency. *Nursing Education Perspectives, 23*(5), 238–42.

Kolb, D. (2014). *Experiential Learning as the Science of Learning and Development* (2nd ed.). Indianapolis, IN: Pearson FT Press.

Lawrence-Wilkes, L., & Ashmore, L. (2014). *The Reflective Practitioner in Professional Education*. Basingstoke, UK: Palgrave Macmillan.

Lawrence-Wilkes, L., & Chapman, A. (2014–2015). Reflective practice. Available online at www.businessballs.com/reflective-practice.htm.

Loughran, J. J. (2002). Effective reflective practice: in search of meaning in learning about teaching. *Journal of Teacher Education, 53*(1), 33–43.

Luppicini, R. (2003). Reflective action instructional design (RAID): a designer's aid. *International Journal of Technology and Design Education, 13*(1), 75–82.

Lyons, N. (2010). Reflection and reflective inquiry: Critical issues, evolving conceptualizations, contemporary claims and future possibilities. In N. Lyons (Ed.), *Handbook of Reflection and Reflective Inquiry: Mapping a Way of Knowing for Professional Reflective Inquiry* (pp. 3–24). New York, NY: Springer.

Mann, K., Gordon, J., & MacLeod, A. (2009). Reflection and reflective practice in health professions education: a systematic review. Advances in Health Sciences Education, *14*(4), 595–621.

McDonald, J. K., & Gibbons, A. S. (2009). Technology I, II, and III: criteria for understanding and improving the practice of instructional technology. *Educational Technology Research and Development, 57*(3), 377–92.

Moon, J. (1999). *Reflection in Learning and Professional Development: Theory and Practice*. London, UK: Kogan Page.

Moon, J. A. (2002). *Learning Journals: A Handbook for Academics, Students and Professional Development*. London, UK: Kogan Page.

Oelofsen, N. (2012). *Developing Reflective Practice: A Guide for Health and Social Care Students and Practitioners*. Banbury, UK: Lantern Publishing.

Osterman, K. F., & Kottkamp, R. B. (1993). *Reflective Practice for Educators: Improving Schooling Through Professional Development*. Thousand Oaks, CA: Corwin.

Pavlovich, K. (2007). The development of reflective practice through student journals. *Higher Education Research & Development, 26*(3), 281–95.

Pollard, A., & Tann, S. (1993). *Reflective Teaching in the Primary School* (2nd ed.). London, UK: Cassell.

Quinton, S., & Smallbone, T. (2010). Feeding forward: using feedback to promote student reflection and learning—a teaching model. *Innovations in Education and Teaching International, 47*(1), 125–35.

Rotimi, J. O. B., & Ramanayaka, C. D. (2015). Reflective practice and technical rationality in construction project planning. *Civil Engineering and Environmental Systems, 32*(4), 301–15.

Ruch, G. (2005). Relationship-based practice and reflective practice: holistic approaches to contemporary child care social work. *Child & Family Social Work, 10*(2), 111–23.

Sadler, J. R. (1989). Formative assessment and the design of instructional systems. *Instructional Science, 18*(2), 119–44.

Schon, D. (1983). *The Reflective Practitioner*. San Francisco, CA: Jossey-Bass.

Smith, R., & Pilling, S. (2007). Allied health graduate program: supporting the transition from student to professional in an interdisciplinary program. *Journal of Interprofessional Care, 21*(3), 265–76.

Taylor, B. (2010). *Reflective Practice for Healthcare Professionals: A Practical Guide*. Berkshire, UK: Open University Press.

Thompson, N. (1996). *People Skills*. Basingstoke, UK: Macmillan Press Ltd.

Thompson, N., & Pascal, J. (2012). Developing critically reflective practice. *Reflective Practice, 13*(2), 311–25.

Tracey, M. W., & Baaki, J. (2014). Design thinking, design process and the design studio design, designers, and reflection-in-action. In B. Hokanson & A. Gibbons (Eds.), *Design in Educational Technology* (pp. 1–14). New York, NY: Springer.

Zimmerman, B. J. (1998). Developing self-fulfilling cycle of academic regulation: an analysis of exemplary instructional models. In D. H. Schunk & B. J. Zimmerman (Eds.), *Self-Regulated Learning: From Teaching to Self-Reflective Practice* (pp. 1–19). New York, NY: The Guilford Press.

15 Beyond Learning Design
Taking Your Career to the Next Level

In the previous chapter, we examined the importance of reflecting on our current behaviors to avoid making mistakes that could threaten our credibility as trusted learning advisors. Now it's time to reflect on all of the topics covered in this book to determine how they can serve us in managing the progress of our individual careers.

If you are interested in moving into Learning and Development (L&D) management, the outlook is good. The US Bureau of Labor Statistics (Bureau of Labor Statistics, 2017) labels the L&D field as "Training and Development" and projects the employment of training and development managers to grow by 7 percent from 2014 to 2024, which is about the same growth rate as the average for all occupations. The median annual salary – the salary at which half those employed in an occupation earn more than that amount and half earn less – for training and development managers was $102,640 (USD) in May 2015, with the highest salaries earned in the industry sectors of (a) professional, scientific, and technical services; (b) management of companies and enterprises; (c) finance and insurance; (d) healthcare and social assistance; and (e) educational services (state, local, and private). Evidence of the health of L&D management occupations is also easily found in the large number of postings on electronic job boards such as SimplyHired.com and Indeed.com, as well as in the job advertisements on sites like LinkedIn and Facebook.

I like doing what I'm doing and I'm not sure if I want to be a manager, you may be thinking. If you have already found your bliss, excellent! However, as we saw at the beginning of this book, the nature of work and the workforce are constantly in flux. What satisfies you now may be altered by circumstances beyond your control. In addition, people experience changes in their personal lives that can affect how they view their professional lives. As Dilbert© and his colleagues often remark, it's always good to have a Plan B. Moreover, your Plan B should be revisited and updated on a regular basis. In this chapter, we will

- Examine the reasons why you should take charge of your own career planning and development;

- Identify ways in which you can assess where you are in your career vs. where you expected to be when you entered the L&D field;
- Explore opportunities for advancement in and beyond learning design and technology; and
- Share some final thoughts about the business of learning design and technology.

From Organizational Career Paths to DIY

What It Means to Have a Career

When you first entered the workforce, you probably wrestled with whether you wanted to commit yourself to a particular occupation or just get a job until you figured out what kind of career you wanted to have. The *Job Seeker's Guide*, an online resource funded by the US Department of Labor, offers the following definitions:

> A job is a specific position or work for which you get paid. An occupation is a type of job with the same job duties. People who work in an occupation do similar tasks and need similar training. A career is a journey that lasts your whole life. Your career includes education, training, work experience, and community involvement. It also includes unpaid work and hobbies. (Is a job the same as a career? n.d., para. 2)

For better or worse, however, the lines between these three perspectives on labor market participation are not as clear as they used to be. We often hear the stories of retirees who spent their entire careers at a single organization, or who spent their entire working lives in a single occupation but were employed by multiple organizations. Those currently active in the labor force are unlikely to experience lifetime employment with a single organization or even lifetime commitment to a single occupation.

Some university career counseling services have tried to update the definitions to more accurately reflect the realities of the 21st century. For example, the Minnesota State College system (MyMnCareers, 2017) compares having a job with having a career by stating that "if life were a video game, a job would be just one level. Having a career means that you are committed to playing the game to get better over time and advance to higher levels" (para. 4). Further complicating the picture has been the rise of what has been called the "gig economy," where individuals take on a series of short-term, on-demand jobs, whether as a self-employment option (e.g., freelancers, independent consultants) or as contingent workers seeking flexibility and variety in applying their skill sets in a variety of workplace contexts (Dishman, 2017; Torpey & Hogan, 2016). The multifaceted and personal nature of careers and career paths requires a new approach to defining a career. In their review of the literature on careers, theories, and practices, Sullivan and Baruch (2009) offer a comprehensive and, I believe, true-to-life definition of a career:

> We define a career as an individual's work-related and other relevant experiences, both inside and outside of organizations, that form a unique pattern over the individual's life span. This definition recognizes both physical movements, such as between levels, jobs, employers, occupations, and industries, as well as the interpretation of the individual, including his or her perceptions of career events (e.g., viewing job loss as failure vs. as an opportunity for a new beginning), career alternatives (e.g., viewing limited vs. unlimited options), and outcomes (e.g., how one defines career success). Moreover, careers do not occur in a vacuum. An individual's career is influenced by many contextual factors, such as national culture, the economy, and the political environment, as well as by personal factors, such as relationships with others (e.g., dual-career marriages). (p. 1543)

It should be clear that a career is a very personal choice grounded in a variety of individual and contextual factors that have rendered previous perspectives and definitions somewhat obsolete. Consequently, it makes sense for us as individuals to map out our own careers, as opposed to waiting for someone else to point us in the right direction. In fact, organizations now expect employees to take charge of their own careers, then request support or assistance in executing their individual career plans.

Career Self-Management

The do-it-yourself (DIY) approach to career planning and development is grounded in the literature on career planning and self-management. Career self-management refers to all efforts and activities by employees to be pro-active in managing their careers. It includes efforts to define and realize personal career objectives, which may (not) correspond with the organization's objectives (King, 2004; Kossek, Roberts, Fisher, & Demarr, 1998; Orpen, 1994). Career self-management includes the insights that individuals develop about their own career aspirations, as well as the behaviors they initiate in order to manage their careers. In her review of 200 articles on career development issues published in 1995 alone, Stolz-Loike (1996) found that the demise of lifetime employment with a single organization began with the downsizing during the 1980s, when organizations began trimming their workforces to compete more effectively in a shifting economy. Older workers (those above 45 years of age) were the most visible casualties, particularly those who had not achieved management positions or had been in the same management position for several years. Employers began to expect all of their employees to engage in career self-management. To remain employable, "employees must continually develop new, cutting-edge skills that are valued within the marketplace. Additionally, they must be well informed about global trends that affect the success of any business endeavors" (Stolz-Loike, 1996, p. 131). The growth in continuing professional education participation, whether in the form of post-secondary degrees, certifications, or informal, topic-specific activities (e.g., conference workshops) throughout the 1990s is an example of the move toward career self-management (Grzyb, Graham, & Donaldson, 1998). In short, *just doing my job* has not been sufficient for a very long time:

> To be successful, workers need (a) broader skills; (b) educational credentials, which represent the beginning of a lifelong learning process; (c) flexibility; (d) adaptability; and (e) problem-solving skills. Employees also need to be career strategists who actively plan their career paths so they can build new skills through on-the-job training and develop effective business networks. (Feller, 1995, p. 158)

The need for a Plan B has become increasingly important, particularly since the dynamics of the labor market make it impossible to foresee and plan for all challenges. Lent (2013) advocated for two types of pro-activity for career self-management, namely, routine career renewal and preparing to cope with particular events. Routine career renewal focuses on keeping yourself marketable by updating your skills and expanding your interests, enriching or redesigning your current job, negotiating with your manager to take on more responsibilities, and engaging in prosocial and generative activities, such as mentoring more junior colleagues. Coping focuses on "emergency preparedness" activities, such as maintaining a balance of social support and job contact networks, periodically monitoring the job boards to see what is available, what is required, and detect any changes in employer expectations, as well as engaging in worst-case scenario exercises in which you strategize about next steps in case of job loss in the short- and long-term.

Career self-management aligns with another research stream, namely, the stream of research focused on subjective career success. This stream of research is grounded in the belief that career evaluation can only be correctly conducted through self-assessment because there are no absolute criteria in the modern business world. Consequently, career evaluation must be based on the individual's own particular criteria (Hall, 2002). Nonetheless, career self-management does not mean that employers should sit back and let employees fend for themselves. This research stream also advocates for employer responsibility for providing continuous learning opportunities and the resources needed by employees to manage their own careers (Hall, 2002; Hall & Moss, 1998). Furthermore, results of an organizational case study (Lips-Wiersma & Hall, 2007) suggested that employer responsibility for supporting employee career management is integrated into five core management practices: (a) developing capacity and employability; (b) strategic and structural integration; (c) cultural integration; (d) diversity management; and (e) communication. In other words, to engage successfully in these five management practices requires supporting employee career development. Moreover, studies have shown that employer support of employee career self-management is closely associated with productivity and job satisfaction (see, for example, Sturges, Conway, Guest, & Liefooghe, 2005; Tschopp, Grote, & Gerber, 2014).

Summary

Figure 15.1 provides a graphic representation of the literature focused on career self-management. The selection of publications focused on defining and managing a career highlights the broad but very personal

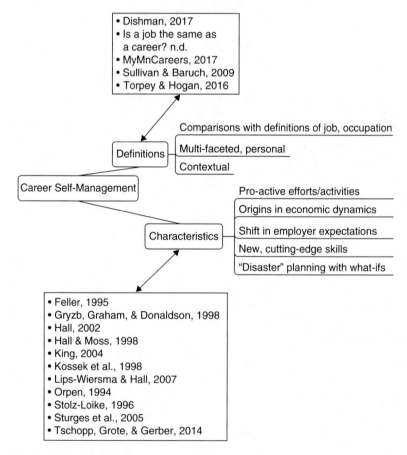

Figure 15.1 Highlights of the Career Self-Management Literature.

nature of what it means to have a career in the twenty-first century, so that do-it-yourself (DIY) is essential for remaining employable in an ever-changing labor market. The research focused on describing the characteristics and attributes of the process of career self-management emphasizes the need to continuously self-assess, update skills and abilities, and go above and beyond what may (not) be written in your current job description. Fortunately, career self-management is not as daunting as it may appear.

Know Before You Go: Your Career Thus Far

Getting the Lay of the Land

If you are like me and depend on your GPS to help plan a road trip, you know that you must key in your current location in order for the GPS software to generate the best route. The same principle applies in career self-management. Although some schools of thought in the career counseling literature would begin by asking you to identify your future career goals, then direct you to figure out what you need to get there, I subscribe to the view of Prof. Arthur Markman, cognitive scientist at the University of Texas Austin, that past experience shapes how you think about, and thus, plan for the future.

We use our ability to envision the future to help us make plans. Our beliefs about what might happen in the future help us to plan for obstacles that will confront us. A lot of good research on planning suggests that those people who prepare for failure are the ones best equipped to handle problems when they come up. By setting your predictions for the future in a familiar landscape, you allow yourself to use your memories of the past to help you predict what might go wrong in the future. If you are only able to think abstractly about the future, then you are much less likely to find specific problems that may arise (Markman, 2011, para. 6–7).

Taking stock of where you are now is the first step in managing your career. You may have a preference for specific tools and techniques (flowcharts, mind maps, etc.), but you can start with a simple list of questions to assess your current situation, as illustrated in Figure 15.2:

- **Reflect on the L&D field:** Whether you entered the field accidentally or purposefully, think back to the reasons why you became an L&D professional. Was there a particular occupation (e.g., design, training others) that attracted you? Did you pursue a formal program of study for that occupation? What were your expectations before your first L&D job? When you left that first job, had your initial expectations been met? Why (not)? How many L&D jobs have you had since that first job? To what extent did those subsequent jobs (not) meet your expectations? Before accepting your current job, what factors contributed to your decision to remain in the L&D field? As a mid-career

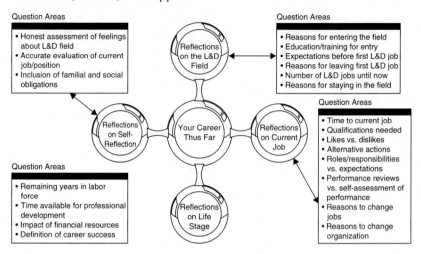

Figure 15.2 Assessing the Current State of Your Career.

professional, knowing why you have persisted in the field through the inevitable ups-and-downs will help you determine whether L&D was and still is your "passion" or a means to some other (yet to be determined) end.

- **Reflect on your current job:** If you have remained with the same organization throughout your L&D life or have worked at multiple organizations, think about the path you took from your first job/position to your current job/position. How long did it take? What did you have to do to get there? What could/would you have done differently? What do you like (dislike) about your current job? How does your current role and responsibilities match up to your expectations? How do your performance reviews compare with your own views of your performance? What are some of the factors that could motivate you to change jobs? Would that change take place inside or outside of your current organization?

- **Reflect on your life stage:** Although definitions vary by field of study, the term "life stage" generally refers to a specific phase of human life, such as being single, independent and working, being a parent of young children, being an "empty nester" (those whose children have recently left home), or being a "baby boomer" those born after World War II, from circa 1946 to 1964). How you define your life stage and where you are vs. where you expected to be at this time will color your assessment of what you want to do going forward. How many more years do you want to remain in the labor market? How much time do you have to undertake professional development activities? What role do financial resources play in your personal and professional decisions? What do you consider to be a successful career?

- **Reflect on your reflections:** In her bestselling book *The Money Class*, finance guru Suze Orman (2012) counseled us to "stand in our truth" to achieve our vision for the future. In other words, we need to be honest with ourselves when examining our current situation in order to plan for a future that is realistic and achievable. The same applies to career self-management. Have you honestly assessed your feelings about the L&D field? Is your assessment of your current employment situation accurate or what you would like it to be? Have you considered familial and social obligations in your assessment of your current life stage? If you are totally honest with yourself when reflecting on your experiences in the field, your current job, and your life stage, the next steps in planning out your career are more likely to build upon who you are, what you have accomplished to date, and whether or not you really want to advance in or move beyond learning design and technology.

Getting to Plan B

Once you have a solid understanding of where you are, you can now think about where you want to go. Still not quite sure? No worries. Not everyone can describe their ultimate career goal. Instead of asking yourself, *Where do I want to be five years from now?*, start by asking, *How can I make sure that my organization sees me as more valuable at the end of this year than it did at the beginning of the year?* In other words, start planning ways to improve your performance at work beyond what is spelled out in your current job description:

- **Close current performance gaps:** If your organization has a formal performance review process, whether it is the traditional annual review between you and your immediate supervisor, or the more timely and comprehensive 360-degree feedback process that includes evaluations from your peers and other key contacts as well as your supervisor, the review should indicate any gaps in performance that you may have. Are the gaps due to knowledge, skills, or experience? Is there some element of your job or the field with which you need to become more familiar? Are there particular trends about which you would like to learn more? Are there new technologies on the horizon that you would like to explore? The performance analyses and intervention selection processes discussed in Chapters 3 and 4 apply not only to closing the performance gaps of others, but can also be applied to closing your own performance gaps. To close your own performance gaps, your list of potential interventions may include learning opportunities, such as pursuing formal instruction, doing independent reading, attending webinars, or attending the local chapter event of one of the professional associations. How you prioritize your list of opportunities will depend on the severity and impact of the performance gaps you are trying to close. In other words, you are taking your role as learning advisor and applying it to your own professional development.

- **Re-visit the stakeholder identification process:** In Chapter 6, we defined a process for identifying the relevant individuals impacted by particular performance problems and assessing their degree of influence on our ability to develop solutions. The same process applies to improving your own performance and advancing your career. Aside from your immediate supervisor, who else has influence over advancement? To whom does your supervisor listen most closely? Who are the players involved in making promotion decisions? Who can serve as your advocate when you want to work on a high-profile project or assignment? Chances are that many of these stakeholders belong to the same professional associations to which you belong. Contact them about an upcoming association event and suggest meeting there to talk about ways to apply lessons learned from the event in your organization. Think about other ways to build a stronger professional relationship with these stakeholders to help raise your profile. Of course, building relationships takes time, so you will want to start with the high-value (to you) stakeholders first, just as you do when working with project stakeholders. At the same time, do not forget to keep working on your external network connections via your online communities.
- **Publish without perishing:** Think about the last professional conference you attended. Who were the session presenters? How did they come to be session presenters? Whether the presentations were good, bad, or indifferent, the presenters gained exposure to an audience they may not ordinarily have reached. Professional conferences offer practitioners a variety of session types (roundtables, poster sessions, etc.) in which to share their knowledge. Professional associations also solicit blog contributions or practitioner stories about lessons learned in the field. Tweet about your favorite talk or webinar. You will not be hailed as a thought leader overnight, but a consistent flow of posts, comments, or tweets will help build your reputation over time.
- **Document your value-add impact:** So, you have participated in some learning opportunities, engaged with stakeholders you deem helpful to your professional development, and published a couple of blog postings and a few tweets. Now it is time to connect the dots and show how these activities have contributed to closing your performance gaps and demonstrating your value-add to the organization. In other words, note not just what you did during the course of the year but what benefits to you personally and to the organization as a whole resulted from these activities. Capturing your value-add in stories about how you used what you learned to help clients or colleagues is

a common way of demonstrating your value. Even if you have not as yet had an opportunity to apply all that you have learned, document some potential uses that would benefit the organization.

Establishing and implementing your own annual plan for professional development can help you identify and flesh out some long-term goals that you previously may not have considered. If you've already committed to a specific long-term goal, your annual plan can serve as a way of reaching that goal incrementally.

Defining and Implementing Plan B

There are hundreds of books, blogs, and opinion pieces published by scholars, career coaches, and consultants, each offering a roadmap to building the ideal career. Some recommend that you take a leaf from the strategic planning book of corporations and identify your own personal mission and vision statement, with the former being what you are going to do and how you are going to do it, and the latter being a description of what your future looks like after you achieve your mission (McClure, 2003; Migan, Rauen, & Srsic-Stoehr, 2009). Others emphasize the need to consider the influence of negative workplace behaviors and experiences (failure, job insecurity, unfair treatment, harassment, and incivility, etc.) on how individuals define their career goals (Baruch & Vardi, 2016; Kuron, Schweitzer, Lyons, & Ng, 2016). All of these are suggestions for you to adopt (or not), depending on what would work best for you. However, there is some consensus as to what constitutes key components in the career planning process. Table 15.1 provides a sample worksheet of how you would organize your career plan using those components.

- **Goal decomposition:** In instructional design, goals are decomposed into sub-goals, which, in turn, can be translated into learning objectives and outcomes. The same applies to career planning. What level do you want to reach in your career? What are some of the job titles that you may hold when you are at the top of your game? These are questions for the long-term, which, for the mid-career professional, spans the next three to five years. The example in Table 15.1 illustrates what that goal decomposition might look like if your long-term career goal is to be a member of an organization's leadership team and be responsible for the strategic planning and management of the organization's talent pool. Job titles associated with this level include Chief Talent Officer, Chief Learning Officer, and Vice President of Human Resources, among others. Based on your research, you have discovered that selected managers and directors are the ones promoted to the top level; so, you set promotion to be one of those selected levels as your short-term goal.

Table 15.1 Career Planning Worksheet Example

PART A	
Goals	
Long-term (3–5 years)	• Member of the C-Suite in a Fortune 1000 organization in the professional services sector responsible for developing and implementing talent strategies that contribute to the achievement of organizational strategic goals • Job titles: Chief Talent Officer, Chief Learning Officer, VP of HR
Short-term (1–2 years)	• Promotion to managerial position responsible for talent management • Job titles: Director of Talent Management, Training and Development Manager, Director of HR
Rationale	
Professional benefits	• Move beyond L&D into "full people management"
Personal benefits	• Opportunity for greater interaction, strategic thinking
Barriers to Goal Achievement	
Personal	• Committed to current geographic region • Somewhat uncomfortable talking with business people
Skills, knowledge, competencies	• Limited knowledge of accounting, finance • Unfamiliar with business units other than L&D

Options for Barrier Removal/Reduction

Personal

- Brainstorm with family
- Establish more/stronger network ties with professionals already in the C-suite

Skills, knowledge, competencies

- Job shadow
- Receive cross-training
- Find a mentor, role model

PART B

Steps Required to Achieve Goals	Target Date	Completion Date
Long-term		
1. Receive promotion to L&D department head	18 months	
2.		
3.		
Short-term		
1. Mentor two new L&D hires	6 months	
2.		
3.		

- **Rationale:** This is where you again stand in your truth. Why do you want to achieve that long-term goal? What professional and personal benefits do you think you will achieve? In our example, the opportunity to go beyond L&D to the proactive and strategic planning of the organization's talent pool, as well as increased opportunities for interaction in and outside the organization, are the reasons for selecting the Chief Talent Officer goal.

- **Barriers to goal advancement:** The barriers over which we have direct control are those rooted in our personal circumstances and in our own knowledge, skills, and competencies. In our example, commitment to residing in a particular geographic region would be a barrier to seeking out opportunities in other locations. Existing comfort levels with people or processes (you're standing in your truth again) may also be a barrier to goal achievement. In crafting your annual plan for professional development, you have already identified gaps in your current knowledge and carry the same gap analysis through to identify what is needed to advance your career goals.

- **Options for barrier removal and reduction:** Sometimes the personal barriers we think exist are not as firm as we had initially thought. Have you shared your goals with family members or with others to whom you have personal obligations? What ideas and suggestions do they have to offer? What kind of outreach activities will help you increase your comfort level with people in other occupations or positions? As we saw in Chapter 1, research indicates that most learning in the workplace occurs outside of formal instructional events; so, resist the temptation to fill your knowledge/skill gaps with online or classroom training events. What opportunities are available to learn from others? In our example, you could job shadow your supervisor, observing his/her day-to-day work. Ask to receive cross-training in sales, so you could learn how your organization targets and sells its products or services. Seek out a mentor or role model to discuss and enhance your work-related knowledge and broaden your perspective.

- **Steps required to achieve goals:** This is your action plan where you identify steps that are SMART (specific, measurable, achievable, realistic, and time-bound) and map back to your short- and long-term goals. In our example, one step in achieving your long-term goal is to receive a promotion to L&D department head, and to receive that promotion in 18 months. A step on the way to that promotion is to mentor two newly hired L&D employees in six months, which would serve as hard evidence of your leadership capabilities.

Some Final Thoughts

In an interview published in the *Journal of Leadership Studies*, Dr. David Vance, former president of Caterpillar's corporate university and now president of the Center for Talent Reporting, explained why people in the Learning and Development (L&D) and Human Resources (HR) fields do not possess the management skills needed to reach leadership positions.

Part of the explanation lies in the background of those in L&D and HR. When asked, many say they were attracted to these functions, especially L&D, because they are "people" persons. They like working directly with people and helping them. Many have told me that if they wanted to work with numbers, they would have gone into accounting. In other words, they opted into these fields precisely because they believed they would not have to deal with numbers. There appears to be a self-selection process at work where many currently in the L&D and HR fields do not embrace numbers or analysis. While that may not pose a problem for individual contributors (depending on their job responsibilities), it most definitely is a problem if the leaders are selected from this pool (Vance & Moss Breen, 2016, p. 35).

Dr. Vance's point about L&D professionals deeming themselves to be "people persons" would generate little argument. His notion that numbers are, by choice, outside of the scope of interest of the L&D professional could certainly be debated. However, his perception of the L&D professional is not unique, as we saw in Chapter 14. Despite the fact that numbers and analysis are part of the processes that learning design and technologies professionals use regularly, such use focuses on learning rather than performance in support of business goals. Advancement in and beyond the field requires making sure that you are not pigeon-holed into that stereotype of the L&D professional.

Throughout this book, you have read the comments of the thought leaders in our field shared in *E-Suite Views*. Here are a few more of their comments focused on planning your future:

> You know, I love professional development, personal development. I knew years ago that this was the space I was supposed to play in. We need more mid-career and young professionals, and when I say young, I mean anywhere from eight to 80. We need more of us to push that envelope: that innovation, that creativity to create training sessions or enhance or modify sessions that are already in place, we need to develop them, share them, create e-books, create books. Anything that's going to strengthen this arm of the profession.
> –Chris Daniel, PMP®, Founder and Principal,
> Re-group Consulting

I think the big thing in Learning and Development right now is that we have to be more cognizant of the broader arena in which we play. We should not be aspiring to be only classroom designers. We should be aspiring to be people who support Learning and Development and that means really expanding our knowledge about adult learning and all of its iterations – social learning, experiential learning, whatever – we have to understand all of those things. We have to really get a handle on how that can be applied to how people learn in a business context. We have to understand a much broader picture.

–Catherine Lombardozzi, EdD, Founder,
Learning 4 Learning Professionals

You need to be the lifelong learner that you're trying to get other people to be. When you see that new shiny thing, take a second to read up on it. I attend probably two to three webinars a week and I've been in the field for 25 years. I know that not everybody finds the time or considers that a good use of their time but I have a need to understand the new shiny so I can figure out where it fits and whether it's something that I need to spend more time on. There's so much information out there so for me, the free webinars are my main go-to. The other thing is to participate. If you're interested in that new thing, take one. If you're interested in gamification, find a webinar on gamification. You have to find it, it's not going to come to your door.

–Dawn Adams Miller, Director, Learning Strategy, MetLife

Do a lot of reading outside of instructional design in fields that are tangential to us, like behavioral psychology. I do a lot of reading in positive psychology and find a lot of great stuff there. I read about interface design, especially with e-learning, there's a lot to be learned. Everything we do in e-learning is an interface but we learn so little about that. In fact, in many of our programs, we learn nothing about interface design. The other thing is to get involved in practitioner research and actually do it and learn by doing it yourself. Definitely get involved with social media. I can't even explain to people how much the people I've met internationally and the connections I've made on social media have influenced and changed my life. That itself is an ongoing "conference" and I'm amazed about how people in our field are involved in social connection. And find really good conferences. You'll find different things at different conferences; don't stay in one place. People tend to stay in one place and you only see the same faces. You can find out the best conferences for you by being on Twitter because you're going to hear from all kinds of people on Twitter.

–Patti Shank, PhD, CPT, President, Learning Peaks, LLC

Taking charge of your career by capitalizing on each and every opportunity to learn how the L&D function can contribute to organizational performance is key to advancement. Ours is an exciting field that values analytical as well as creative talent. Importantly, it allows the individual professional to define and build his/her own career path based on self-defined goals. Is it an easy profession? Certainly not. But then we're not cubicle workers stuck in the same job for years but still unable to see how their efforts make a difference. Maybe Dilbert© would like to enter the world of Learning Design and Technology.

References

Baruch, Y., & Vardi, Y. (2016). A fresh look at the dark side of contemporary careers: Toward a realistic discourse. *British Journal of Management*, 27(2), 355–72.

Bureau of Labor Statistics, U.S. Department of Labor. (2017). *Occupational Outlook Handbook, 2016–17 Edition*. Retrieved from www.bls.gov/ooh/management/training-and-development-managers.htm.

Dishman, L. (2017, January 5). How the gig economy will change in 2017. *Fast Company*. Retrieved from www.fastcompany.com/3066905/the-future-of-work/how-the-gig-economy-will-change-in-2017.

Feller, R. W. (1995). Action planning for personal competitiveness in the "broken workplace." *Journal of Employment Counseling*, 32, 154–63.

Grzyb, S. W., Graham, S. W., & Donaldson, J. F. (1998). The influence of organizational and demographic variables on participation in continuing professional education. *The Journal of Continuing Higher Education*, 46(1), 2–15.

Hall, D.T. (2002). *Careers In and Out of Organizations*. Thousand Oaks, CA: Sage.

Hall, D.T., & Moss, J.E. (1998). The new protean career contract: Helping organizations and employees adapt. *Organizational Dynamics*, 26(3), 22–37.

Is a job the same as a career? (n.d.). Retrieved from http://il.jobseekersguide.org/node/12

King, Z. (2004). Career self-management: Its nature, causes and consequences. *Journal of Vocational Behavior*, 65, 112–33.

Kossek, E. E., Roberts, S., Fisher, S., & Demarr, B. (1998). Career self-management: A quasi-experimental assessment of the effects of a training intervention. *Personnel Psychology*, 51, 935–62.

Kuron, L. K., Schweitzer, L., Lyons, S., & Ng, E. S. W. (2016). Career profiles in the "new career": Evidence of their prevalence and correlates. *Career Development International*, 21(4), 355–77.

Lent, R. W. (2013). Career-life preparedness: Revisiting career planning and adjustment in the new workplace. *The Career Development Quarterly*, 61(1), 2–14.

Lips-Wiersma, M., & Hall, D. T. (2007). Organizational career development is not dead: A case study on managing the new career during organizational change. *Journal of Organizational Behavior*, 28(6), 771–92.

Markman, A. (2011, August 12). Your view of the future is shaped by the past. *Psychology Today*. Retrieved from www.psychologytoday.com/blog/ulterior-motives/201108/your-view-the-future-is-shaped-the-past.

McClure, J. (2003). *How to Find Your Dream Job and Make It a Reality: Solutions for a Meaningful and Rewarding Career*. Victoria, Canada: Trafford Publishing.

Migan, K. C., Rauen, C. A., & Srsic-Stoehr, K. (2009). Strategies for success: Orienting to the role of a clinical nurse specialist in critical care. *AACN advanced critical care*, 20(1), 47–54.

MyMnCareers (2017). Is a job the same as a career? Retrieved from www .careerwise.mnscu.edu/mymncareers/finish-school/job-vs-career.html/

Orman, S. (2012). *The Money Class: How to Stand in Your Truth and Create the Future You Deserve*. New York, NY: Random House.

Orpen, C. (1994). The effects of organizational and individual career management on career success. *International Journal of Manpower*, 15(1), 27–37.

Stolz-Loike, M. (1996). Annual review: Practice and research in career development and counseling – 1995. *Career Development Quarterly*, 45(2), 99–140.

Sturges, J., Conway, N., Guest, D., & Liefooghe, A. (2005). Managing the career deal: The psychological contract as a framework for understanding career management, organizational commitment and work behavior. *Journal of Organizational Behavior*, 26(7), 821–38.

Sullivan, S. E., & Baruch, Y. (2009). Advances in career theory and research: A critical review and agenda. *Journal of Management*, 35(6), 1542–71.

Torpey, E., & Hogan, A. (2016, May). Working in a gig economy. *Career Outlook*. Retrieved from www.bls.gov/careeroutlook/2016/article/what-is-the-gig-economy.htm.

Tschopp, C., Grote, G., & Gerber, M. (2014). How career orientation shapes the job satisfaction–turnover intention link. *Journal of Organizational Behavior*, 35(2), 151–71.

Vance, D., & Moss Breen, J. (2016). The challenge of human capital leadership. *Journal of Leadership Studies*, 10(2), 34–8.

Glossary

360-degree Feedback   A method that provides an employee with performance feedback from his/her supervisor plus 4–8 peers, direct reports, co-workers and clients. People providing the feedback are individuals with whom the employee interacts on a regular basis and are normally selected by mutual agreement.

ADDIE   The generic label attached to a model of instructional design that includes analysis, design, development, implementation, and evaluation. With origins in military inter-service training, the idea was to proceed through each step in a linear fashion and complete each phase before moving to the next. Contemporary practitioners have revised the model and use it in a more iterative fashion.

Bottom-Up Budget Derivation   This approach to budgeting requires gathering a detailed cost estimate for all activities and deliverables associated with the L&D project, then adding them up to arrive at the total project cost.

Break-Even Analysis (BEA)   The point (in time and/or currency amount) at which the cash outflow for an initiative equals the related cash inflow.

Cause Analysis   Also called Root Cause Analysis (RCA) and refers to the process of identifying the underlying factors contributing to a problem or performance gap, as part of an overall assessment process.

Chief Learning Officer (CLO)   The highest ranking corporate officer (C-suite level) responsible for an organization's Learning and Development function. Reports to either the Chief Executive Officer (CEO) of the Head of HR or the Chief Talent Officer.

Coaching   A Learning and Development method in which an individual supports an individual or group in achieving a specific professional goal by providing, training, advice and guidance.

Cost Avoidance   Describes how much money will be saved with a proposed initiative versus maintaining the status quo.

Cost-Benefit Analysis (CBA)   Involves adding up the benefits (tangible and intangible) of a course of action and comparing those benefits with the costs associated with that course of action, all of which must be monetized.

Data Extraction A process in which unstructured data sources in different data formats are retrieved, loaded into a staging area of a database, and queried using application programming interfaces. It is normally the first step in data mining.

Data Mining The process of analyzing hidden patterns of data for categorization into useful information for decision-making using computer-generated algorithms.

Direct Costs Costs that are easily attributable to a specific project and charged on an item-by-item basis, such as the cost of a new software product purchased specifically for the project.

Educational Technology A field of research and theory that focuses on the material tools and theoretical foundations for supporting teaching and learning. It is normally associated with the affordances of technology to support teaching and learning in formal institutional settings (K-12, higher education).

Electronic Performance Support Systems (EPSS) Online resource systems containing digital versions of job aids such as checklists, decision tables, worksheets, etc.

Fixed Costs One-time costs that are unaffected by any changes in project activity; designer salary is a fixed cost.

Gap Analysis Aimed at performance improvement, compares the actual performance with the desired performance to identify what specifically needs to be improved.

Human Computer Interaction (HCI) A field of study focused on how people interaction with computers and to what extent computers are (not) developed for successful interaction with human beings. Includes the impact of factors such as cognitive styles, advances in interface technology, and user preferences.

Human Performance Technology (HPT) A field of study focused on improving performance in the workplace grounded in rigorous analysis at the individual, group, and organizational levels to identify performance gaps, provide appropriate interventions, and evaluate results against requirements. The field is also known as Human Performance Improvement (HPI).

Human Resource Development (HRD) A sub-field of Human Resources that focuses on helping employees develop personal and organizational skills, knowledge and abilities, with the intent of developing the organization's workforce to a level that enables the organization and individual employees to accomplish their work goals in service to organizational goals.

Indirect Costs Costs for items that benefit multiple projects, such as telephone charges and office equipment.

Instructional Design A process and a discipline focused on the systematic creation of learning interventions grounded in research and theory.

Instructional Systems Design (ISD) Now synonymous with instructional design, the term was focused on models encompassing analysis, design, development, implementation, and evaluation.

Instructional Technology A field focused on the theory and practice of design, development, utilization, management and evaluation of processes and resources for learning and is closely aligned with the research and theory around instructional design.

Learning and Development (L&D) A subset of Human Resource Development (HRD) that focuses on improving individual and group performance through increasing knowledge, skills, and abilities. This sphere of activity is part of an organization's talent management strategy and seeks to align group and individual goals and performance with those of the organization as a whole.

Learning Culture The artifacts, espoused beliefs and values, and basic underlying assumptions that encourage continuous, shared learning to increase knowledge, competence, and performance of individuals, business units, and the organization as a whole.

Life Stages Originally analyzed in the social sciences, a concept focused on the changing definition, demarcation, and social experience of the phases of human development.

Mentoring A type of performance intervention in which a more experienced or knowledgeable individual guides a less experienced/knowledgeable individual in a one-on-one partnership.

Monetization Assigning a numerical financial value to a non-monetary element, such as assigning value to a website based on the amount of advertising space sold.

Needs Assessment The collection and analysis of qualitative and quantitative data to identify gaps between current performance and desired performance, identify factors impacting performance, prioritize performance gaps against business goals, and recommend corrective actions.

Performance Intervention A set of sequenced, planned actions designed to help an individual, group or organization improve one or more aspects of performance.

Request for Proposal (RFP) Normally used in a competitive bidding process, the RFP describes the statement and scope of work to be done, the specification of issues and target audience to be addressed, schedules to which the vendor must adhere, type of contract, specific product/service requirements, and other technical requirements, terms and conditions.

Shadowing A type of performance intervention whereby an employee acquiring skills/knowledge follows another employee through the work day to observe those skills/knowledge in action.

Subject Matter Expert (SME)   An individual recognized as an authority in a particular domain or field.

Talent Management   A strategy designed to ensure that the organization is able to meet current and future workforce needs to achieve its vision and goals.

Top-Down Budget Derivation   Senior management provides the project team with a pre-determined amount of money and the team must determine how to complete the project within that fixed amount.

Training and Development   Used by the U.S. Department of Labor and by some organizations to describe the Learning and Development domain.

Transformational Change   A change in the underlying strategies and processes of an organization that results in a gradual, enterprise-wide shift in the business culture.

User Experience (UX)   The totality of all aspects of an end-user's interaction with a company, its products and services.

Variable Costs   Costs that change with activity levels, such as the cost of gift certificates to volunteers who complete usability testing of a learning module prior to its finalization and release.

List of E-Suite Views Contributors

Paul Roitman Bardack, J.D. Attorney and Senior Solutions Architect SAIC http://www.saic.com/	Following a successful career in law and government relations, Mr. Bardack has dedicated more than 20 years to the growth of the eLearning industry, specializing in the planning, development, and management of online education and job training enterprises.
Claudia Barnett, Ph.D. Performance Improvement Consultant & CEO CGB Associates, LLC https://www.linkedin. com/in/claudia-barnett- phd-0064953/	Dr. Barnett is a training and performance improvement consultant specializing in the healthcare sector. Since establishing CGB Associates in 1995, she has worked with a variety of healthcare facilities in the U.S., and her consulting services have included Change Management Analyst, Instructional Designer, Curriculum Developer, Application Analyst and an At the Elbow support individual for Physicians and Nurses.
Mike Beitler, Ph.D. President Beitler and Associates http://mikebeitler.com/	Following a long and successful career in the banking industry, including a 10-year stint as a Chief Financial Officer, Dr. Beitler's consulting expertise is sought by industry and government, and he is often called upon to teach courses in domestic and international business schools.
Stuart Belle, Ed.D Director of Knowledge Management and Learning Strategy PACT http://www.pactworld.org/	Dr. Belle is a well-known thought leader in knowledge management and organizational learning, with more than 15 years of experience in over 20 countries, and a passion for translating research into practice.
Siobhan Curran Director, Learning Technologies and Analytics Depository Trust & Clearing Corporation (DTCC) http://www.dtcc.com/	With more than 15 years of experience as a learning professional, Ms. Curran specializes in the implementation of comprehensive analytics programs for data-driven decision-making, with a focus on the financial industry sector.

Harold Cypress Human Resources Training and Development Manager Planned Systems International http://www.plan-sys.com/	Mr. Cypress has nearly three decades of experience in business and the Human Capital profession, including Chief Learning Officer experience at Deloitte and Global Learning Director at Booz and Company, and specializes in teaming with organizational leaders to align learning, development, and talent management with business objectives.
Chris Daniel, PMP© Founder and Principal Re-group Consulting http://www.onechrisdaniel.com/	Known in the industry as "the consultant in jeans," Mr. Daniel has more than 15 years of experience in project management and learning and development, providing certification training to organizations such as The Boeing Company, Anne Arundel Workforce Development Corporation, and Honda.
Gerry Lang VP, Learning Services Marketing Conduent https://www.conduent.com/	Mr. Lang has more than 20 years of experience in the business of learning and talent management. He has worked in management positions at major corporations such as Xerox, Korn/Ferry, and Microsoft, and holds a Master's degree in Educational Technology from San Diego State University.
Catherine Lombardozzi, Ed.D. Founder Learning 4 Learning Professionals http://l4lp.com/	Dr. Lombardozzi has more than 30 years of experience in the Learning and Development industry, specializing in professional development services to learning practitioners and decision-makers.
Dawn Adams Miller Director, Learning Strategy MetLife https://www.metlife.com/	A veteran in the L&D field, Ms. Miller has applied her ability to align learning initiatives with business needs in a variety of industry sectors and organizations, including Oracle, Cisco, TIAA-CREF and Microsoft, and her instructional products have received awards from the Brandon Hall Group and *Chief Learning Officer* Magazine.
Russ Powell Principal, Training and Development Consultant Peregrine Performance Group http://peregrine.us.com/	A workforce performance improvement consultant for more than 20 years, Mr. Powell has managed award-winning training and performance improvement projects with organizations such as Sun Microsystems and the U.S. Coast Guard, and is also a Senior Judge for the Brandon Hall Research Excellence in Learning Awards.

Patti Shank, Ph.D., CPT President, Learning Peaks LLC https://www.pattishank.com/	A recognized thought leader, Dr. Shank has 20+ years of experience with performance and learning analysis, instructional design, the science of learning, and working with individual and organizational problems. She has worked as director of research for The eLearning Guild and served as the head of health education and training for a healthcare system.
Barbara Wilson-Tarver, Ed.D Director of Training and Outreach U.S. Department of Defense http://defense.gov	Dr. Wilson-Tarver has more than 10 years of experience in leading training initiatives, including work for the Armed Forces Services Corporation and Booz Allen Hamilton, and specializes in government sector projects.

Index